DARK TRADE

Nothing Personal: The Business of Sex

DARK TRADE

LOST IN BOXING

Donald McRae

MAINSTREAM
PUBLISHING

EDINBURGH AND LONDON

For Alison

First published in 1996 by
MAINSTREAM PUBLISHING COMPANY (EDINBURGH) LTD
7 Albany Street
Edinburgh EH1 3UG

ISBN 1 85158 874 4

Reprinted 1996

A catalogue record for this book is available from the British Library

'24 Hours to Tulsa'
Words and music by Burt Bacharach and Hal David
© Copyright 1963 Intersong Music
Used by permission of Windswept Pacific Music Ltd and MCA Music Ltd

'Something's Gotten Hold of My Heart'
Words and music by Roger Cook and Roger Greenaway
© Copyright 1967 Maribus Music Ltd
Dick James Music Ltd, 47 British Grove, London W4
Used by permission of Music Sales Ltd

Typeset in Garamond

Printed and bound in Great Britain by Butler & Tanner Ltd

CONTENTS

ACKNOWLEDGEMENTS

THIS BOOK COULD NEVER HAVE BEEN WRITTEN WITHOUT the thoughtful and consistently entertaining company of its featured fighters. The best moments, inevitably, belong to them – to James Toney, Mike Tyson, Oscar De La Hoya, Roy Jones, Michael Watson, Naseem Hamed and Chris Eubank. Each of them provided extraordinary insight into boxing and their own lives.

Sherry Toney became a good friend and I will always cherish the telephone calls and faxes and the tasty memories of all her 'Speciality Cakes & Pies' packages.

Even though they understood that I would side with the fighters before themselves, the biggest promoters in boxing were unfailingly approachable. Bob Arum, Don King and, especially, Frank Warren were as interesting as they were affable.

There were hundreds of other boxing characters who were also kind enough to broaden my understanding of the ring round which they worked. Specific thanks are owed to the following for the time and help they gave me: Muhammad Ali, Roberto Alcazar, Andy Ayling, Nigel Benn, Frank Black, Riddick Bowe, Jay Bright, Frank Bruno, Bill Cayton, Julio Cesar Chavez, Dena DuBoef, Joel De La Hoya, Mickey Duff, Lou Duva, Jesse Ferguson, Bob Foster, Eddie Futch, John Horne, Tom Johnson, Brendan Ingle, Jackie Kallen, Hank Kaplan, Sugar Ray Leonard, Stanley Levin, Butch Lewis, Lennox Lewis, Tim Littles, Frank Maloney, Everett Martin, Bronco McKart, Eugene McKart, Bill Miller, Robert Mittleman, Eddie Mustafa Muhammad, Steve Nelson, Rock Newman, Pat Putnam, Chris Peters, Steve Robinson, Alfie Smith, Dingaan Thobele, Jimmy Tibbs, Johnny Tocco and Jeremy Williams.

My agent Bill Hamilton never wavered in his support of this book. His backing was much appreciated as the months turned into years.

Bill Campbell and Peter MacKenzie at Mainstream were as great to work with as ever. They, too, were unstinting in their encouragement even when it must have seemed to them that I was writing an almost biblical epic. I owe them a lot – as well as a few more drinks.

Judy Diamond at Mainstream put up with my endless changes and rewrites with extraordinary good humour and patience. I also would like to thank her for suggesting the cover images.

Sandor Szenassy's understanding of the great heavyweights was instructive and, as I neared the end, I took much heart from his own superior work. I would like to thank him, Frank Warren and Lucy Thorburn for the use of his two paintings.

There were many great boxing writers and editors who assisted me throughout this book. When I began I went to see the two best boxing newspapermen in this country. I remember visiting Ken Jones at his home in early 1991 – he was both informative and supportive. I was lucky enough to get to know Hugh McIlvanney even better and I have never forgotten the times we spent together in Las Vegas or London. He was inspirational and witty whether talking about books or boxing.

Henry Mullan, another great boxing doyen, was always friendly and helpful – and he and Claude Abrams at *Boxing News* were good enough to run a number of my rambling articles over the years. My respect for them, and for all the staff at *Boxing News* and *Boxing Monthly*, is boundless. I will still be buying their magazines long after this book is forgotten. Glyn Leach at *Boxing Monthly* was always willing to pass on a telephone number or contact name and I still remember fondly the few beers we had together one freezing week in Tulsa.

Apart from salvaging some of my more wayward articles, Tim Hulse at *Esquire* gave me the opportunity to write about Toney, De La Hoya, Hamed and Jones relatively early on in their careers.

In this book's own formative stages, Kath Meadows was the first person with whom I discussed my writing about boxing. I valued her enthusiasm and interest as well as her suggestions that I should begin with Muhammad Ali and South Africa. Luke Alfred and Rob Nixon both offered invaluable advice as I struggled with the earliest outline.

When it came to the actual writing the following people were irreplaceable:

Ronnie Sull, Fulham's answer to Don King, knew exactly when to open my door and shout 'Showtime, Baby!' or some less printable boxing words, to gee me up when I was feeling bored.

Ainslie Clarke was one of the first to read the opening chapters and she helped me with numerous suggestions as well as instigating a rethink of the title.

I greatly appreciated Mike Fisher's scrupulous sharpening of my sloppier ravings.

Tim Musgrave, despite having to put up with descriptions of his sister's exotic dance routines in a book about boxing, was never less than generous or incisive. He was also instrumental in my reworking the introduction and in dating distinct sections.

Erika Wood, my unofficial but inspirational American 'editor', knows she's got that dubious position for life – if she can stand it. She was always bang on target, whether dealing with structural complexities or words like 'babe'.

I listened particularly closely to Jay Savage's perceptive comments for he understood better than anyone the kind of book I hoped to write. His telephone calls from Johannesburg also made me laugh through some of the longest days.

Hilton Tanchum's crucial supply of memories and boxing tapes from Johannesburg were as reliable as his wit and interest. I don't call him my boxing guru for nothing.

In the end, the fact that I could have a sweet chinwag with toughies like Toney and Tyson was due most of all to my parents. They know all that they have done for me but I would like to thank them again – and also to warn bookshop owners to watch out for a five-foot-tall woman who might re-arrange their shelves so that this book looks just a little more eye-catching.

My sister, Heather Simpson, spent more time than anyone else in reading and re-reading 350-odd pages. When this book does work it's most often down to her. I might not have converted her to boxing but she has made me believe even more strongly in her intelligence and diligence. I owe her at least a warehouse full of expensive wine but, for now, I'll just have to thank her again.

Lastly, there's Alison. This, truly, is her book as much as it is mine. She shared everything with me and even allowed me to write about her in the following pages. Although we had a lot of fun and laughter along the way she was even more important when I moaned and groaned and wondered if I would ever reach the last page. Her sudden and explosive renditions of 'Let's Git Ready To Rrrrruuummmbbbllle!' electrified those darker moments. She was there to the very end – always my best friend and first reader, my drinking pal and dancing partner, my boxing confidante and my wife. Thanks go, most of all, to her.

INTRODUCTION

I CAN STILL REMEMBER HOW IT STARTED. ON A COLD EVENING in June, in the South African winter of 1967, the sun disappeared behind our high garden wall. The darkness came and covered everything. It even swallowed up the white roses and the green metal swing at the far end of the lawn. I thought we might never see the sun again. I pulled the heavy blankets over my head. It didn't help. I was scared of the dark. I was frightened of all it hid, of the sounds it suddenly made.

The giant trees scraped against an upstairs window, clawing and tapping against the glass as if calling out to me. 'Let us in,' their leaves sighed, 'let us in . . .'

But, in the distance, there was another noise. It was like nothing I had ever heard before.

'*Tsa-huuuuunh! Tsa-huuuuunh!*'

It stopped; and then began again. I slid out of bed. It was worse not knowing. Holding my thumbs for luck, I slunk towards the window. I peeped through the zebra-patterned curtains.

Lines of black men trudged along either side of the road below. Under the yellow street-lights their balaclavas made me shiver. Tiny mists of breath slipped from their mouths as they walked. We called them 'natives'. I was never sure why, for it was just a name everyone used. The natives were not the same as us. They were black. They stayed in the shadows.

Some of them stopped to watch another circle of black men. They threw dice in a pool of light which fell from the corner shop opposite our new house. Whenever one of the natives picked up the small cubes he would blow on his hands. Then he would flick the dice, and groan.

'*Tsa-huuuuunh! Tsa-huuuuunh!*'

It was supposed to feel like we had reached home. Earlier that day we had moved back to the town where I had been born six years before. Germiston, 'the largest railway junction in the Southern Hemisphere'. Ten miles east of

9

Johannesburg, it was meant to be a step up from the place we had just left. But we had never heard the moaning of natives in Witbank, which was Afrikaans for 'White Bank'. I didn't know what 'Germiston' meant. I just knew that it was different. Its natives sounded ghostly. They sounded angry.

I closed my eyes again. I tried to listen for the trains beyond the gamblers.

The night passed and I woke to a quieter sound. Grey doves cooed in the sunshine. The shop across the street looked like any other Greek-owned store you could see in Witbank. By mid-morning even the dice-men looked ordinary. They were just natives, shuffling together for another game.

I was a slow kid. I was strictly small-town then. It took me weeks to work out that their gambling was also a cover for the business they ran from the drains adjoining our garden. Whenever someone wanted 'a nip', he would take up a spot in the band and cry: '*Tsa-huuuuunh!*' That was a sign for 'The Godfather', a fat black man called Samson, to wonder over to the drain, lift up the lid, reach down and bring out the brown bottles of beer. If the lookout spotted a blue police van, the lurching groans grew louder. It was better to be caught running a dice-game than a shebeen.

As the months passed, I grew used to them. I liked the natives in our neighbourhood. They made me laugh. More importantly, whenever my football flew over the brick wall one of the betting-boys would wheel away to gather it in full stride.

My favourite retriever was a wiry man the others called Cassius. It all began with Cassius. He was the one who hooked me. He juggled the ball like a black-faced clown, shifting it from a knee to a shoulder before letting it settle magically on his thigh. He pulled mad faces at me. One day, as he did his tricks with the ball, he sang a strange song: 'Ali, Ali, float like a butterfly, sting like a bee, Ali, Ali, Muhammad Ali.'

He flipped the ball back and dropped into a hunched pose. 'Put your dukes up, *baasie* [little boss]!' he whispered. 'C'mon, float wit' me, sting wit' me!' Cassius flicked rangy left hands into the winter sunshine as his huge feet danced. He wore a pair of battered brown sandals which had split at the seams. They fluttered over the tar while the soles flapped up and down in a jitterbug of their own. Cassius's fists flashed in the air. Breath snagged at the back of his throat and his voice became husky with effort.

'*Jy is die baas . . . jy is die baas!* [You are the master . . . you are the master!]' he said as he boxed against his shadow, dipping and weaving against the wall on top of which I had scrambled. His words chugged in a way which made me think he was going away like one of our trains. But the rumble soon turned into a lullaby.

'Ali is the master . . . Ali is the master!' he half-hummed, half-sang.

When he tired of hitting the thin Highveld air, he clasped his hands behind his back and swayed sweetly, sighing, 'Butterfly, butterfly,' as if serenading me.

The shebeen drinkers dissolved into fizzing laughter. 'Don't worry, *baasie*,' one of them called out to me, 'Cassius's just crazy!'

'Who's Ali?' I eventually asked the insane joker.

'The *baasie* don't know?' Cassius said sternly.

I must have shook my head dumbly for he spoke more gently again.

'Ali is a boxer, *baasie*, the best boxer in the whole world. The heavyweight champion of the world!'

I felt a thrill rise through me. With glistening eyes he told me how he himself was nicknamed after Ali – how Ali had been born Cassius Clay. I struggled to understand how one man could have two names. Cassius stumbled before drifting on to say that the extraordinary boxer was a black American. He was a dancer and a puncher, a fighter and a poet – the man who owned those happy bee and butterfly lines. And then, with a shimmy and a wave of his fist, Cassius was on his way back to the gambling corner.

Samson ambled over to the drains while Cassius scooped up the dice. After he had blown on his hands, he echoed, 'Float . . . float . . . float!' He threw the numbers. Their final roll was greeted by a roar. Cassius had won. He flashed a thumbs-up. 'Sting, my *baasie*, sting!' He used his teeth to lift the top from the new bottle of beer. Cassius tilted it towards the sky. The thick beer bubbled and frothed through the glass neck and down into his gulping throat.

One Saturday afternoon his sweating and bloated face swam into mind again. A dozen of us were jammed together near the front of the Rialto Cinema in downtown Germiston. All the boys, including me, were dressed in brown shoes, long socks, shorts, checked shirts and Brylcreem-greased short-back-and-sides. The girls wore sandals, party dresses and Alice-bands in their long hair. It had become the fashion to pack us off to the movies whenever another birthday arrived. While we weren't keen on the mothers' choice of *The Sound of Music* or *Annie Get Your Gun*, we loved the pre-film entertainment. I was big on *The Lone Ranger* and those zany serials which always ended with a woman tied to the track as a train raced towards her. The picture then faded into a 'To Be Continued Next Week . . .' promise. We howled in dismay.

Each short was accompanied by fifteen minutes of 'World News From Movietone'. We did not have television in South Africa, and so even old news at the movies meant everything to us. We loved the pictures of the Rolling Stones taking America by storm and seeing the goals from the previous year's FA Cup final. But they were nothing compared to the mixing of Cassius and Muhammad on our Saturday screen. I was stunned by what I saw.

Almost twenty-five years later I managed to track down a copy of that footage and, watching it in London again in 1992, I at last understood the enormity of what a boxer had done to me in a darkened Transvaal cinema. I could finally give words to the feelings of exhilaration and shock which gripped me that hot afternoon.

The 'Cassius' jolted me the most, hearing the name of a native booming through the Rialto. 'This is Cassius Marcellus Clay,' the Movietone broadcaster intoned grandly, 'the young Negro who could have become the greatest fighter the world has ever seen . . .' I was surprised not to see my gambling boy but a much leaner and more beautiful face. I was even more astonished by the rush of words screaming out of his open mouth: 'I am the greatest! I shook up the world! I'm the greatest thing that ever lived! I don't have a mark on my face and I upset Sonny Liston and I just turned twenty-two years old. I must be the greatest! I showed the world, I talk to God every day. I'm the king of the world! I'm pretty! I'm a bad man! I shook up the world! I shook up the world! You must listen to me. I am the greatest! I can't be beat! I am the greatest! It was no match. I want the world to know I'm so great that Sonny Liston was not even a match. I don't have a mark on my face. In the fifth round I couldn't see a thing. My face was burning and I whupped him. He couldn't hurt me. I'm the prettiest thing that ever lived. I shook up the world. I want justice . . .'

I had never seen a black man on the Rialto screen before – nor anyone as charismatic or supposedly deranged. I pulled my shirt-sleeve angrily away from the clutching hand of the little girl sitting next to me. Like the rest of us, her mouth hung open as she tried to understand what was happening. 'Who's that naughty native?' she asked anxiously.

I thought of Cassius and the simple words he used. 'He's a boxer.'

'The best boxer in the whole world!' Cassius had said. A quarter of a century later, when I recognised more of what I watched, I saw what he meant. The newsreel showed Ali destroying Cleveland Williams with a speed which made the savagery look lustrous on monochrome film. He knocked down his opponent four times in the opening round as easily as if he was tipping over a skittling series of empty beer bottles. Cassius Clay, as the newscaster called him, was as slick as a seal purling through clear water. There were also more sombre moments when he planted his feet in the middle of the ring. He then appeared deadlier than a club beating down on a pup, his blows spraying blood from a cut he had already opened. But I was struck more by the ease and grace of his movements than the sheer violence. He popped off heavy punches like he was casually stripping a whirl of petals; and, all the while, he skimmed across the ring with dazzling dance steps.

'But Clay has an ugly side to his otherwise enterprising personality,' our chum with the handlebar-moustache warned. The action switched to his next, and last, fight against Ernie Tyrell.

Ali brought his face right up against Tyrell's. Their noses touched. In a moment of surreal intensity, the talkative Ali said just three words: 'What's my name?'

Tyrell responded with the wrong two: 'Cassius Clay.'

'He used my slave name,' Ali wailed, 'this makes it personal . . . here's what I'll say: "Don't you fall, Ernie!" Wham! "What's my name, Ernie?" Wham! "What's my name?" Wham! I'll just keep doing that until he calls me Muhammad Ali. I want to torture him. A clean knockout is too good for him.'

Our birthday gang found every 'wham!' to be thigh-slappingly hilarious. But the man on the microphone called the fight 'cruel'. Ali fractured Tyrell's cheekbone and left the retina of his left eye swollen and torn. By the eighth round Tyrell was helpless as Ali taunted him. He yelled, 'What's my name, Uncle Tom, what's my name!'

I had no clue who the hell Uncle Tom was; but those fight snippets were more dramatic than anything I'd ever seen in *The Lone Ranger* or *Spider-man*. After two minutes on film, boxing became a shadowed world with its own secret codes.

It certainly appeared more exciting than pictures of the Vietnam War, Richard Nixon, banner-wielding hippies and Ali in a suit and tie facing the cameras. I think I understood that Ali was in some kind of trouble. But words like 'black nationalist', 'ban', 'prison' and 'exile' must have swirled above my head – even though they would become such deeply South African terms in later years.

But I held on to the simple fact that Ali refused to go into the army. In South Africa all white boys ended up in the army. We knew our turn was coming. My eldest cousin had already been called up. We thought he might end up fighting in South-West Africa or even Angola. A cloud had formed on my otherwise blank horizon. In the end the army would always be waiting – for me and for Ali.

I sat on the garden wall the following morning, yearning to tell Cassius of Ali sparkling at the Rialto. As much as I wanted to share with him the wonder of seeing Ali move and shout, I also looked forward to Cassius relying on my report – for natives were not allowed to enter the cinema.

I saw him at last after lunch that Sunday. Samson sauntered over to a truck which carried six white men. There were four of them in the back and two up front. They wore an assortment of safari suits and string vests. Their greased hair was bristly but they stashed steel combs in their socks which they pulled up from the boots to the knees. They were 'hillbillies' to my mother and 'rockspiders' to me. The truck revved impatiently while they bartered with Samson. They wanted drink from the drains. Samson often did business with whites on the Sabbath. Except for the churches, everything else was shut on a Sunday. Our sewer was the one place in Germiston where a white man could buy a drink.

Cassius, who had just arrived, was sent to deliver the order once Samson had dragged up the booty – half-jacks of brandy and quarts of Black Label. From the top of my perch I watched Cassius float across the road like he still thought he was Ali. No one laughed. The men in the truck were not to be teased. But they had seen his shake of the hips. Cassius kept quiet for he knew he had gone too far. I watched him silently hand over the liquor with a curious bow of his head. He rubbed his hands nervously as if he was trying to wash them. I saw him squeeze his fingers together in prayer as he waited for the money.

He shook his head and said '*Aikona!* (No Way!)'

'*Voetsak kaffir!* (Fuck off kaffir!)' the beefiest man bawled in reply. Samson shrugged tiredly before stepping towards the truck. But it was already too late.

Cassius, leaning down into the car, was hit full face in the face by the driver's head. As blood arced out of Cassius's nose, I shook soundlessly. The beating slowed time to a dragging tick. Something terrible happened every second. The truck doors opened and the men jumped out. A knee sank into Cassius's face, splitting his top lip. He fell down. They kicked him. They punched him again. He looked crumpled and dead. I slipped from the wall and ran inside. We called the police. They were already on their way.

The hillbillies chuckled and drank as if the thought of jail could never scare them. Black people milled silently around, at a distance, watching Cassius lift his head. He had left a flat pillow of blood on the street.

When the police came, it was to Cassius they turned, dumping him into the back of their van. They chatted for a while longer with the white men before picking out Samson. He was forced into the same caged hold as Cassius.

It was weeks before Cassius returned to our corner. I found it hard to face him. While he would sometimes wave weakly to me he never again said, 'Put your dukes up,' or tried to perfect his Muhammad Ali impersonation. Like his hero he had been forced into a kind of exile. Slowly, Cassius faded from the imaginary ring he had danced in above our drains.

I did not see any link between boxing and such random violence. I preferred to dream of the day I'd be discovered as a South African sporting genius. My friends and I practised our skills, sometimes having to dodge the sprinklers on the grass while hitting and kicking a ball. Even Muhammad Ali, banned from the ring, was forgotten.

It took an Afrikaans teacher, our moustached and muscled Meneer (Mister) Naude, to remind me. Five years on from my first meeting Cassius, Ali was back; and Naude was an even more ardent disciple than my lost boy on the corner. He had the power, too, to fix our concentration on the ring.

We called Naude 'The Crocodile'. He was big, scaly and dangerous. He was also slimy, oiling his hair down with Vitalis. He wore checked suits, yellow shirts and hush-puppies. We hated him but, like any crocodile, we feared him. We wanted him to like us, rather than hurt us.

Although we never admitted it, we were also fascinated by him. Naude was a compulsive liar. His stories of fighting in the army, walking thirty miles to work whenever his car broke down and drinking with Transvaal rugby players were fantastic. Naude knew more about sport than even we did. But he seemed on the verge of tears whenever he spoke about the great Afrikaners who had played in the Springboks' green and gold. His face reddened when he told us that the rest of the world no longer wanted to play against us. They were cowards.

Boxing was not far behind rugby on Naude's list. He said that fighters were gladiators. And the fighter he loved most was Muhammad Ali. Sometimes, Naude made me think of the white men who'd attacked Cassius. But his bloodshot eyes glittered whenever he spoke about Ali, a black boxer who touched him more than any other man.

Naude explained that 'This man is not like our natives, he is from another place . . .' In 1972, Ali had won over the world. He had Cassius, he had me and he even had Mister Naude.

There were rumours that negotiations had begun for Ali to fight in Johannesburg. I never really believed them. But the gossip hardened into facts. Ali signed to fight Al Jones, another black American, in Johannesburg on 18 November 1972. The fight was to be promoted by Bob Arum, a Jewish lawyer from Brooklyn, and a South African consortium called Reliable N.E. Promotions. Ali would be paid $250,000 while a clause in his contract stressed that: 'Promoter acknowledges that Ali's party and Jones's party will be multiracial. Promoter agrees that hotel or residential accommodations to be provided by the Promoter for Ali and his party will not require any segregation whatsoever on the basis of race. Promoter also agrees that the audience at the bout will be multiracial. Seating at the bout will either be on an integrated basis, without regard to race, or on a segregated basis which will provide separate but equal seating for whites and non-whites.'

I imagined Cassius and I, and my best friend Hilton, travelling to the fight together. Ali could help the broken gambling man. Boxing would bring back the old Cassius. He and Ali would make us laugh again with their butterfly and bee impressions.

Yet the promotion, and my dream, collapsed. Unable to match the promise of their name, Reliable N.E. Promotions failed to find enough money to pay both boxers.

But, even without Ali, Naude was determined. He would take us deeper into boxing. We were supposed to be studying woodwork while the girls were stuck in another classroom learning to sew. Meneer Naude, instead, tapped two sets of black boxing gloves against each other. He spoke quietly. '*Ja, nou sal ons sien. Wie is die manne hier?* [Yes, now we will see. Who are the men here?]'

Even now I can feel the sinking of my heart. I was certain that Naude would choose me. He chortled to himself. It pleased him to watch us tremble. Thirty pairs of eleven-year-old eyes ducked away from his gaze. It flashed like lightning round the thunder of his riddle.

'*Wie is die groot vegters vandag, wie?* [Who are the big fighters today, who?]'

Meneer Naude walked up and down the narrow corridors of wooden desks. He swung a couple of gloves in each huge hand. 'C'mon, let's see,' he finally said, leading us outside.

We formed a circle on the scorched playground. He told us that we were going to box. A fight would not be over until at least one boy was bloodied or crying. Naude then picked out the two largest boys in the class. They were our heavyweights. The first was built like a miniature tank, with slabs of muscle and chunky forearms. He'd told us that he had once had sex with a sheep. We believed him. He was that tough. The other boy was just fat and frightened. The slugger knocked him out with one punch – an overarm smash.

Our fat friend crashed to the hard ground, banging his head as he went down. Naude knelt over his victim. 'Hell, man, what a punch! What a punch you took, Fattie!' he muttered, spraying water over the unconscious boy. 'Wake up now, man, wake up!' The boy opened his eyes with a whimper. Naude was happy again. 'You're okay now, Fattie, you're gonna be as right as rain!'

We were in the middle of another drought. The boy's pale cheeks wobbled as Naude helped him up. 'Fattie' was packed off to the sick bay while we got on with the business of boxing.

Fight followed fight. Naude pointed out his victims: '*Jou . . . en, ja, jou!* (You . . . and, yes, you!)'

While the first four pairs of opponents were identified I tried to hide from Naude's piercing eyes. Whenever I thought they were nearing me I would pull my right eyelid down as if trying to remove some dust. I hoped he would not pick on a half-blind fighter. I was lucky. Naude ignored me. Each time it felt as if I had been lifted from a metal hook. I sighed with relief and watched two others move to the centre of our ring.

There had always been fights in the playground. The 'Fight! Fight! Fight!' chant dragged kids across the schoolyard. No one, it seemed, could stop themselves. Yet, usually, nothing happened. The *brekers* (bruisers) just pushed each other around nervously.

But Naude gave us no choice. We had to box. Our stomachs turned and our mouths dried. While most of the boys shouted encouragement to those in the middle, I couldn't make a sound. I was terrified.

When Naude's jabbing finger next settled on one of my best friends, a pale and thin English boy whose family had left London for Germiston only a few years before, I saw my chance. As the meneer hunted for another fighter, asking, 'Who wants the cockney, who wants the limey?' I stuck my hand into the air. I knew why I had not done the same thing when a similar question had been asked of a much stronger immigrant boy from Scotland. I would have battled against the big Scot. But I knew I could dominate my kinder friend.

A boxing promoter building up his fighter in the early stages of his career would have seen my offer as sensible and creative matchmaking. Only a fool, surely, would take on a more formidable foe when easier pickings were on offer? A boxer's first objective was to ensure that if harm had to be done then his rival, rather than himself, should be on the receiving end. Even then I understood boxing.

An evil grin split open Naude's sun-beaten face. He pulled me out of the crush at the front. '*Ja, ja, ja!*' he sniggered. 'I see you want the limey bad, hey?'

I looked away from Mark, my pal, and stared at the ground instead.

'What's this then?' Naude asked suspiciously, twisting my ear painfully. 'Don't you want to fight your *moffie* [queer] friend?'

I felt a teary tang beneath the surface of my eyes.

'Are you going chicken on me?' Naude sneered.

'No,' I said abruptly, blinking once, twice, three times in rapid succession. My eyes suddenly felt cool and clear. 'I'll fight him.'

'Of course you'll fight him. Get those *blerrie* [bloody] mitts on now . . .'

As the gloves were tied on I felt ill. I looked at Mark, my sickly mate from Tottenham who had ended up six thousand miles from home. I saw his fear and knew that I had the fight won. I moved quickly towards him. I punched my friend hard in the face. A jolt shot up the length of my arm. Mark's top lip started to bruise and a loud '*oooohhhh!*' from the other boys reeled through my head. I stepped away but he came back at me, hitting out furiously. His anger startled me. He threw three or four quick punches. I was surprised how I felt more numbed than hurt. It was as if his fists were hitting someone else.

Strangest of all, I found that I still had time to think as we fought. Should I go down? It was a way out. But, even as temptation tugged, I knew I could not allow him to beat me. I would never hear the end of it. I went after him, hitting him with wild lefts and rights. I was fighting and I liked it. The pump of adrenalin, rushing and coursing through me, was addictive. I felt curiously alive. Everything around me looked bright and sharp. I could see the faces and hear the cries of the others driving me forward.

Mark's face was streaked with thin lines of blood. There were tears in his brown eyes. I hit him again and Naude shouted, '*Ja, ja!*'

I hesitated before punching him one last time. As he wiped his eyes my arm was raised. I felt small and mean.

The rest is lost in a haze, leaving swirling memories of Mark and I making our peace, sensing that we had grown closer despite my willingness to hurt him. Mark was good to me. He knew why I had done it. 'You didn't mean it,' he said quietly.

The days drifted by. We were happy, only worrying sometimes that the world outside hated us. We blamed the Boers. The English cricket team had not even been allowed to enter the country because they had selected a 'coloured' player – the Cape Town-born Basil D'Olivera. South Africa had become the skunk of international sport. Cricket and rugby tours by our white teams were cancelled by the British, Australian, French and New Zealand governments. It had been nineteen years since we had last been allowed to compete in the Olympic Games.

In our own country blacks and whites were not allowed to run or jump against one another. We were not allowed to dribble a ball past each other or even to watch sport together. The idea of two men of opposite colour actually fighting was staggering. But the following year, in 1973, it was announced that white South Africa's favourite's boxer, Pierre Fourie, would challenge the dreaded Bob Foster – a black man. Foster would defend his world light-heavyweight title against Fourie in the American's home town of Albuquerque, New Mexico. A white boxer had not faced a black rival in the South African ring since 1923.

Pierre Fourie was also more interesting than most other white South African sportsmen. For a start, he came from our town. He used to live in Jewel Street, on the Germiston-Johannesburg border. He had been stabbed more than ten times by an assortment of weapons including knives, broken bottles and even a sharpened bicycle spoke.

Like Cassius he had also been attacked by a white gang – in his case by hammer-wielding bikers. Fourie was from the other side of the Germiston tracks and yet he had risen to a position of prominence in white society. He politely rejected his street-fighting days. He favoured a scientific boxing style which saw him move almost as fluidly as Muhammad Ali.

Yet in some of our newspapers it was pointed out that, if it had not been for apartheid, the fighter's life would have been grim. The government protected working-class whites like Fourie. They were given a chance to make something of themselves, despite being so outnumbered by 'the blacks'.

Pierre Fourie himself was silent on such issues, preferring instead to examine more personal matters. One Saturday afternoon he said softly on radio that he would never forget that he had killed a man, a black boxer called Winston Nkwanyana. They used to spar together, a fact which shocked the segregationists. 'Whenever we fought,' Fourie said, 'it was like a conversation. We used few words but when we swapped punches we came to know each other as well as most men can . . .' They had a boxing bond despite their being sequestered by colour, language and everything else embedded into South African life. When they parted Fourie would drive home to the suburbs while Nkwanyana waited in line for a bus back to the townships.

After one gruelling session Nkwanyana shook hands with Fourie. He promised to work with him again a few days later. He looked tired as he pulled on his street clothes. Within an hour of saying goodbye to Fourie, Winston Nkwanyana collapsed into a coma. He'd become so dehydrated while fighting that his brain had emptied of fluid, swelling with the steady blows. Fourie rattled Nkwanyana's brain as if it were rolling around an empty box. With each shake of his box, Winston absorbed more damage. He might have felt it if he had been an ordinary man; he was a fighter. His courage would not allow him to back down. He fought hard against Fourie, eager to earn his keep as a sparring partner. His own hunger for recognition, as much as Fourie's crisp jabbing, ruined him. Winston Nkwanyana died before his family managed to get him to the township hospital.

I was haunted by Fourie's story, by his claim that the tragedy had hardened him to boxing. He wanted to give the game up but it was his family's future; and so he fought out of need rather than pleasure. He did not sound like our Afrikaans master. It appeared incredible that a fighter should prove to be a gentler and better man than a teacher.

Bob Foster's life was not as well documented in South Africa. He was most famous for being the first man to have cut Ali in a fight. Despite being sent repeatedly to the canvas, Foster hurt Ali. Foster's jab was the best in boxing and only the rare combination of Ali's speed and forty-pound advantage eventually caught up with him. He was quoted as saying that while he had an immense liking for Ali he had relished 'busting him up'. As Ali was stitched up on a long dressing-room table, he laughed when Foster said, with a wince, 'Well, you beat me all right, but you're not so pretty now, are you, champ?' Apart from these snippets, we only knew that Foster was one of boxing's greatest-ever light-heavyweights and that he still worked in the local police force in Albuquerque.

I went to bed the night before the fight with a twitching energy. I checked every twenty minutes that the clock was still ticking and set for the 5 a.m. alarm. I half-dreamed a vision of what Albuquerque might be like. It was a name with which I had become obsessed. 'Albuquerque' sounded like the sort of town where Clint Eastwood would ride in on a silvery stallion and where everything forbidden to us surely existed. At 4.58 I decided I was rooting for the Sheriff, even if he was the guy dressed in black.

I switched on the little radio that early South African summer morning, just before dawn, and heard sounds singing down the wire, all the way from Albuquerque, New Mexico, America. Boxing had transported me from Germiston, it had brought me into the more exotic world which existed beyond our suburbs.

But it did not allow me to linger long in fantasy. I learned again that boxing was rooted in harsh realities. It made me understand why I would never want to be a fighter. The ring was a bleak place in which to dream. My heart turned over as they came together, the black American and the white South African.

In the opening round Foster systematically beat up Fourie with a series of clubbing jabs and overhead rights. It was as if he had begun a mission to rid the planet of Fourie, as if one Afrikaner symbolised apartheid. I knew that Foster had heard about the death of Winston Nkwanyana. I suddenly feared his deadly form of revenge. There was also bad blood between the two for, at the weigh-in earlier that day, Fourie had said that 'Tonight's the night, Bob!' But his flat accent mangled the 'Bob' so Foster heard it as 'boy'.

I could hear the echo of the crowd deepening with every punch thrown by Foster. As I clutched the radio tightly it no longer mattered who won the fight as long as Fourie was not killed. Through the static and across the seas I finally heard the bell. I was as relieved as Pierre Fourie.

The minute's rest settled the South African. He began to evade some of Foster's swings. The ringside voices quietened a little. But the next fourteen rounds unfolded painfully for Fourie. He remained on the short end of the freakishly tall Sheriff's extended stick. The ease of the victory must have turned the birds' chirruping outside into a hollow lament for Meneer Naude. I knew that his elephant ears, red and burning, would be pasted to his own radio as confirmation rolled in of Bob Foster's walloping win. 'Next time,' he said later, 'we'll bloody well get that Foster next time . . .'

Naturally, this being boxing, a rematch was already being planned. The South Africans had the money and Bob Foster was prepared to listen, knowing as he did that boxing was about hard cash more than anything else. He said that a crisp $250,000 would entice him to Johannesburg. John Vorster's government had still to be convinced. They clamped down on any activity which had the potential of favouring a black over a white man. Yet their grip on the country was loosening. No one wanted to play with us anymore. The sports boycott had bitten and our hearts were bleeding. Why did everyone despise us? What had we done that was so bad?

When I was on my way to school or off to watch a game or a movie I kept seeing the same sign: 'Whites Only'. When we rode our bikes over a railway bridge near our home we had to negotiate the partition in the middle which divided it into two sections: 'Whites Only' and 'Non-Whites'. We pedalled over the bridge on the one side, yelling and laughing, while on the other side of the four-foot-high metal barrier, older black men and women walked alongside us in silence. Sometimes they were so quiet they seemed invisible.

But a white man fighting a black man was different. The struggle was coming.

But boxing also gave me hope. I thought of the photographs I'd seen of Fourie and Foster together in an Albuquerque dressing-room, holding each other in respect and admiration. Where else would I see such a sight? Foster and Fourie even liked each other.

In a gesture towards the hostile outside world as well as its own isolated community, the South African government declared that Foster would be welcomed to Johannesburg as 'an honorary white'. The concept confused me as much as Bob Foster. He hardly left the confines of the new and prestigious Carlton Hotel in downtown Johannesburg. He was not taking any chances. He had no desire to test the limits of his honorary status. He kept to himself, encouraging our newspapers to depict him as 'brooding' and 'sullen'.

On the night of the fight an emotional commentator's description of Foster's 'dark, hooded presence on the long walk to the ring' disturbed me. Boxing was brutal and scary. But it was also electrifying.

The second bout was much closer. Fourie boxed cleverly for the first twelve rounds, keeping pace with Foster and matching him point for point. It was only in the last nine minutes that the American edged ahead. His grinning delight at retaining the title was obvious when he flung his arms around Fourie and hugged him close.

Even though the townships were overjoyed, the suburbs and farmlands found consolation in the spirited display of their idol. Fourie had come close to joining Ali, Joe Frazier and Ernie Tyrell as the only men to have defeated Foster. His achievement was acclaimed all the more for he was fifty pounds lighter than the heavyweights.

Despite those white heroics, honorary or otherwise, the biggest black men still dominated our imagination. Muhammad Ali most of all. But Meneer Naude and Cassius – the two men who'd framed my knowledge of Ali – were both gone. I left Naude and my old school behind while Cassius took a slow bus from the Transvaal to his tribal home in the more verdant valleys of Zululand. One day he was in Germiston, skulking on the corner, *suiping* (sipping) from a pint of kaffir-beer, and the next he had vanished. It was months before Samson heard from him again. I was moved by the message that he had 'said a special goodbye to the *baasie*'. My sadness perhaps had more to do with the fact that I felt compelled to feign indifference, as if I was just too damn cool to care either way. I wondered why, at thirteen, I had to try to look so fucking hard, why I could not have just shed a tear as 'The Godfather' did when rubbing his rheumy eyes.

'You know, *baasie*,' Samson said, 'he was never the same after that one time, the time they *donnered* [clobbered] him and then locked him away.'

'I know,' I replied, trying to shrug again as if I had already passed through Cassius's pain.

Samson just smiled and said, 'Maybe Ali will do it one last time for Cassius?'

I raised my hands and shoulders in dismay. 'How can he?' I asked.

In 1974 there was no heavyweight bigger or more threatening than George Foreman, who had become world champion when he razed Frazier in three rounds. He rained down bludgeoning punches, bringing sorrow to every fighter he faced. Only a thirty-two-year-old Ali remained.

'Foreman by knockout – early and very sad!' I predicted mournfully.

'The Rumble in the Jungle' was promoted by Don King. The dice-man underlined his ingenuity. He hit upon the innovative scheme of taking the Foreman-Ali fight 'back to Africa', to Zaire, whose President, Mobutu Sese Seko, agreed to pay the boxers an unprecedented ten million dollars each.

Although 'Africa' felt as far removed from the suburbs of Germiston as it must have done in Hertfordshire or New Hampshire, King brought the continent into our classrooms. Teachers less frantic than Naude confessed their fondness for Ali. They favoured him over the more imposing Foreman. Ali was also hailed by the black cleaners and gardeners who serviced the school. And our gambling corner – from the Greek shop owner to the biggest drinkers – still belonged to Muhammad. Only Ali could forge such an unholy alliance.

Maybe it was because I feared so much for Ali that I'd made my forecast to Samson. A quick knockout was the only way I could see him escaping permanent damage. Only Mr Bennie da Silva, my Portuguese friend's father and our latest boxing expert, tipped an Ali victory. He was a small, stocky man who would delight us by throwing vegetables and fruit in the air so that he could punch them as they fell while he carried out his own bizarre impersonation of Ali. 'Muhammad is the master,' he said seriously in his kitchen. 'He's the supreme dancer. He'll dance the night away until Foreman is dizzy and can take no more. He'll rumba through the rumble and then,' Mr da Silva yodelled as he threw up the last few oranges and hit them on the jab, 'it'll be pop, pop, pop! Ali puts big bad George away! The king, then, will be crowned in Africa . . .'

As if out of the Good Book itself, it came to pass. The only difference from the Bennie da Silva version being that Ali did not do the rumba. Huddled over our BBC World Service radios we quivered to hear that Ali simply refused to dance. He not only stood still but, in an act of supposed madness, he leaned against the ropes and allowed Foreman to hit him, to punch himself out. Ali took every ruinous blow Foreman could throw and still he stood, waving his man in and then doing the 'Rope-A-Dope' trick we tried to copy the next morning.

And then, truly, as if he was as exultant as Bennie da Silva jabbing at fruit in a Germiston kitchen, Ali began to pick off Foreman. Through the hum and buzz of the radio link it sounded like Ali was weaving his magic round Foreman's big head as if it was nothing more than a bad black orange that needed to be peeled and flipped in the bin.

Abruptly, near the end of the eighth round, it was all over. A cry reverberated from our tiny speakers. It was as penetrating as any factory siren: 'Foreman is down! Foreman is down!' I tumbled in disbelief, wondering if there could be as much bliss in the hearts of Cassius and Meneer Naude, wherever they were that memorable daybreak. Ali, just as Mr da Silva had said, was the king of the world again and we felt strangely proud that it had happened near our home – in Africa from where, at last, we knew we came.

I left South Africa in 1984, having spent my last years working in Soweto. Like Meneer Naude I was a teacher. I was not an especially good teacher, especially during those moments when I had to impart the intricacies of Victorian literature while army vehicles strayed past our dust-ridden classrooms. I learnt much more than I ever taught. And I unearthed further answers in boxing.

It was a curious situation in which I found myself. After twenty-one years of suburban pleasure, Soweto was an ominous place on my first morning. The township was covered in thick smog and my face appeared alien in the midst of a million darker skins. At least I was a novelty for the others. Within an hour of my arrival, not long after nine on a Monday morning, a couple of men whisked me away for a welcoming nip. The shebeen was not below the drains in the style of Cassius and Samson. Instead, it was a small brick house run by an old man called Dutch. On the brown wall of the shebeen's main drinking area I saw a photograph of Muhammad Ali. In the adjoining passageway there was a shot of Bob Foster with his arms raised. I nodded at them as if saying, 'hi, I'm back,' to old friends.

'I can already tell,' my new pal Shortie grinned, 'you're gonna do fine here.'

I had two of the very best years of my life in Soweto. During the writing of this book, memories of that time have continually returned. I remember the poems which were written for me about Muhammad Ali and, after I had left, how Mike Tyson became such an iconic figure to some of my brightest students.

But this is not a book about South Africa – even though I've often thought that while you do not have to be a South African to understand boxing, it certainly helps. All the violence and absurdity, the beauty and pathos of boxing were found in Germiston and Soweto life.

This is not even a book about Muhammad Ali or Bob Foster, although I met both men after I flew from Johannesburg to London. When I saw Ali there were so many things I wanted to tell him – mainly about Cassius and how I too had not gone into the army – that I ended up saying virtually nothing.

In contrast, I told Bob Foster almost everything. I was so overwhelmed by having breakfast in Albuquerque with big Bob – who was as fit and garrulous as Ali was quiet and slow – that I kept cajoling him to eat more and more. I'm still not quite sure why but I developed a quasi-American accent as I instructed the smiling sheriff: 'You take those ham an' eggs, Bob,' I kept murmuring, 'you get 'em down you, baby!' He could not have been sweeter to me or to my wife, Alison, who now only has to see the words 'ham' or 'egg' to break down in helpless laughter.

We do not laugh as much when we remember Muhammad Ali. But I love him no less. I was just hopeless when I met him. He smiled at me and I shook his hand. Whenever I tried to say something, I thought of him screaming on screen in the Rialto Cinema in downtown Germiston: 'I'm the prettiest thing that ever lived! I'm the king of the world! I'm a bad man! I shook up the world! I am the greatest!' But, together at last, twenty-five years later, I was almost as silent as him. He didn't mind. He did not need me to tell him anything more. He knew.

So this, in the end, is a book about some of the fighters who have followed him. I, in turn, have trailed them for the last five years. They are all men who have dreamed that they might one day be as great as him, as Muhammad Ali. It is an impossible task but, still, they try, uncovering fame and heartache along the way. Cassius, I am sure, would find something to like in each of them.

I

THE BADDEST MAN

WHILE THE SUN BURNED HIGH IN A BLUE DESERT SKY I
waited for him. The heat had emptied the streets, turning Vegas
ghostly in the early afternoon sunshine. I'd reached the bare edge of town,
miles beyond the Strip, far from the clank and reek of money churning in
the casinos and topless bars along Glitter Gulch.

'Watch yourself round these parts, bub, watch yourself . . .' Maxie, my
morose pal from the Yellow Checker Star Cab Company, had muttered
when he left me standing on that stretch of wasteland – empty but for a
blue and yellow tin building someone once had the wit to dub 'The Golden
Gloves'.

But I felt strangely serene as I rocked back on a step outside the gym. I
knew he was near but also that there would be time enough to fret, to think
of him as 'The Baddest Man on the Planet'. Those were his words; and he
loved the sound of them.

The fight surroundings were as grimy as his hotel, The Mirage, was
ornate with its deluxe suites, Lanai-bungalows, white-tiger enclosure and
exploding fountains of fire. There was no such grand style here as the sun
grilled down, slowly melting the cheesy tar beneath my feet.

Mike Tyson was an hour late; but who would expect punctuality from a
man tagged 'the biggest thug in America'?

Another ten minutes passed. I felt a prickle of uncertainty. It was still
three weeks before the rape; and yet all year the papers had predicted that
he was slipping out of control. Only the week before, in the very gym
outside which I sat, Tyson had demolished the $20,000 lens of an ABC
television camera. The surviving footage showed the fighter stalking the
cameraman, perspiration gliding down his face in a glistening parody of
tears. A gold tooth shone as he snarled, 'Get outta my face, you fuck.' He
swung a short right cross which smashed the camera in half. Its picture
exploded into blackness. While the network threatened a lawsuit for assault,

Tyson faced more pressing charges from two women who accused him of groping them in a New York club and an Atlantic City carpark.

Something terrible had unravelled inside Tyson.

A different TV clip, hyping his imminent bout against Donovan 'Razor' Ruddock, carried a similar message. Wearing thick Raybans and speaking in his incongruously high-pitched and lisping voice, Tyson slurred at Ruddock: 'I can't wait for June 28. I can't wait to kiss those great big lips of yours. I'm gonna make you my girlfriend. Don't you know that you're really a transvestite?'

The 'girlfriend' jibe was cheap jailhouse slang; and Tyson's sneering was interspersed with him repeating, 'It doesn't count if he isn't dead, it doesn't count if he isn't dead . . .' He then turned to Ruddock and said, 'You're dead, you pretty thing, you . . .'

Tyson had long been known for his malicious remarks. I first met him in 1986 when he was nineteen years old. Then, after fighting Jesse Ferguson, he claimed that 'I was trying to push the bone in his nose back into his brain.' He laughed as he spoke. A sly chortle licked round his words as if he wanted us to applaud their brutal clarity. A few months later Tyson confessed that 'I aimed for his ear, I wanted to bust his eardrum. Every punch had bad intentions . . .' He had just become the youngest-ever world heavyweight champion after hitting Trevor Berbick with such force that the Jamaican reeled across the ring, fell, got up, toppled over, staggered to his feet and lurched into the opposite corner where he collapsed again, all in the space of a crammed ten seconds.

Four years down the Tyson track, there was a grisly hue to the taunts he aimed at Ruddock. We were less than a week away from their fight – a rematch of a bout stopped prematurely three months earlier. The referee had intervened just as Ruddock began to crumble. I knew how much Tyson resented that denial of his certain knockout. He wanted to hurt Ruddock. Sometimes he wanted to hurt everyone.

Even as I rose unsteadily to my feet, I could hear the crunch of gravel. A black Lamborghini-Diablo wheel-spun its way into the dirt entrance. I saw Tyson and three of his homeboys. The fighter was bareheaded while the others wore regulation 'Team Tyson' baseball caps.

Tyson slid from the car and stretched. I was surprised again at how short he was in person. Five foot ten inches. But what he lacked in height he made up for in width. His chest was fifty inches broad, his neck nineteen-and-a-half inches thick. For all the talk of decay, there was not an inch of wasted flesh on his squat body. As he rolled his shoulders, stretching his arms in front of him, he flexed that neck with juddering twists and turns. He stared at me, his small eyes dark and clouded.

Suddenly, Mike Tyson moved towards me, reminding me of a giant hammerhead swerving in for the kill. Public Enemy's 'Don't Believe the Hype' rolled in behind him, crashing down in great waves from the car.

Then, with the whine of rap driving him on, Tyson was alongside me, within touching distance, inside punching range.

'Hello, Mike . . .' I said.

'Yeah,' he answered as he tapped me on the shoulder with a bunched fist. It didn't even hurt. 'We talkin'?'

I nodded. Tyson grunted and swept past me into the gym. The door slammed behind him and his entourage. I was alone again; and it felt like I had, somehow, survived round one.

Darkness settled over the ring as they began to fight. The two boxers came together in the old routine, throwing punches at each other, slipping in and out of pain. In the broiling gym they moved slap bang into an unchanging pattern where the famous fighter dished out damage to the older journeyman. I had travelled five thousand miles to see that first boxer, 'The Baddest Man', this American bogeyman. Yet I could not lift my eyes from the other fighter, a bravely affecting if shambling brawler who called himself 'The Boogie Man'.

I could have reached through the sagging ropes and touched him, I was that close to the Boogie Man, but there is something discouraging in the sound of a big man being hurt. The little groans and snuffles he let slip made it seem as if Jesse Ferguson could feel the coming of a bad head-cold. I took a step back as if the virus might be catching. The wheezing sob at the back of his throat grew louder. Mike Tyson was all over him, piling in heavy jabs to the face which left me shivery with sympathy for Ferguson – the man whose nose Tyson had wanted to drive into his brain.

The gregarious Jesse, not being one to take such things personally, tried to keep up morale. He clutched at Tyson in a mournful samba. He would have preferred to slow-dance all afternoon if Tyson had not ripped left hooks to his midriff and long right crosses to the jaw with serious intent. The power of those punches sprayed the air with sweat and water as if Tyson had hit a small geyser hidden inside his sparring-partner's skull. Feeling some of that sticky wetness on my own face I retreated to a safer distance.

For someone on the brink of catastrophe, Tyson seemed unusually composed. No matter what they shouted at him from outside the ropes – whether it was 'Keep working downstairs, baby!' or 'Stick that jab in his face, Mike, stick it!' – Tyson went about his business remorselessly. He might have been the boss arriving an hour before anyone else to ensure that the office was running in good order. He snapped Jesse's head back and forth as if opening and shutting the creaking drawers of an old filing cabinet. Then Tyson sank combinations into the body like he was feeding consecutive sheets of paper into a fax machine.

Apart from a Spartan headguard, he wore a faded T-shirt, white tracksuit bottoms and black gym shoes which squeaked in tandem with Ferguson.

Tyson was oblivious to everyone but the human punchbag sloping in front of him. He controlled the ring in a style he no longer found possible in his life outside boxing. Fighting was the easy part for him, the way of life he understood best. It was everything else trailing behind which threatened to uncork his psychosis.

Norman Mailer claimed that 'the closer a heavyweight comes to the championship, the more natural it is for him to be a little more insane, secretly insane, for the heavyweight champion of the world is either the toughest man in the world or he is not, but there is a real possibility that he is. It is like being the big toe of God . . .' For poor Jesse and me there was little doubt. If Tyson not only matched Mailer's 'toughest man in the world' proviso, he also carried a wildness in him which resembled the devil's raised fist.

Mailer had written further that 'when the heavyweights become champions they begin to have inner lives like Hemingway or Dostoevsky, Tolstoy or Faulkner, Joyce or Melville or Conrad or Lawrence or Proust'. I could not imagine any Proustian sigh echoing softly through Tyson as he battered the Boogie Man. A muffled hissing rose from Jesse's mouth.

The buzzer suddenly sounded. Tyson swivelled his head so that his eyes locked with mine between the middle and top ropes of the ring. He stared at me for a moment before letting loose a grin that glinted at the end of my short-sighted gaze. His expression changed again and, trying to fathom his mood, I squinted slightly – hoping that it did not look like I was winking coyly at the world's most ferocious fighter. It made no difference. Through the haze of the gym and my own myopia I could only be sure that some kind of smile had parted his lips.

When you're confronted by an angry black boxer, it's not the simplest thing in the world to admit being one of those white South Africans who'd lived with apartheid for twenty-three years. But, with my accent, I offered up the fact early on in my exchanges with black American fighters. It tended to shatter the ice of our professional relationship. I stopped being just another white guy asking damn-fool questions and became the damn fool himself: 'South Africannnnnnnnn!' the bug-eyed boxer would yelp before shaking his head with incredulous laughter. 'You crazy!!!?'

In my efforts to shrug off liberal guilt and, at least in my own head, get down with the homeboys, I'd learnt not to blink at their surprise. Instead I told some hopefully gritty anecdote about teaching English in Soweto. As the only white guy in the township's meanest neighbourhood, I'd talked long and hard about boxing. The ring had been our common ground, I warbled, our tunnelling through apartheid. That snappy link would allow me a brief justification of my suburban past; of how, subsumed as a boy in a country like South Africa, I supposedly had an understanding of racism strangely analogous to their own. It was mostly blather but it helped us talk more easily.

But who could guess what Iron Mike might think?

I looked over at the Boogie Man for consolation. Blood trickled from his nose. He used an arm to brush it away, spreading the red streak into a moustache. It made him look more forlorn than dapper. Tyson, in the opposite corner, drank from a slender bottle of water which one of his posse tilted gradually with each swallow. The plastic container bent and crackled as air rushed in to replace the liquid pouring into Tyson's mouth and down his chest.

Squashed into protective headgear, his rough-hewn features were flattened. I wondered how different he must have looked in those barely conceivable days when they teased him for being effeminate. As he returned to the centre of the ring I saw him in a more surreal light. The headguard was not dissimilar to a poor baby's bonnet, worn and trampled over the ears and tied in a big bow around his chin. His face popped out behind the cap's high sides, with puffed-up cheeks and sunken eyes. Mike Tyson as a bonneted baby.

The more I stared at Tyson the easier it became to reconcile his thumping of the Boogie Man with the vulnerability he'd felt on the streets of New York. They had hit him then because he was short and fat and spoke with a lisp which reduced him in everyone else's eyes to a 'Little Fairy Boy'. He was six years old and lived in a brownstone in Bedford-Stuyvesant, the most desperate quarter of Brooklyn, where he had been born on 30 June 1966. The fact that we were only days away from his twenty-fifth birthday helped merge Vegas's Mighty Mike and Brooklyn's Little Fairy Boy. It was a cruel name for someone like Tyson to have been lumbered with, a jibe which emasculated him when he was still a boy.

Yet Tyson never had much of a childhood. When he was born his father was forty-two years old. Jimmy Kirkpatrick was a black construction worker who weighed over two hundred pounds – more than enough to have passed the heavyweight limit. But Jimmy was not a boxer. He had no plan in life, no routine, no prospects. Although he had fathered another boy, Rodney, and a girl, Denise, with Lorna Tyson before Mike's birth, Jimmy Kirkpatrick was more dedicated to drinking and roaming than sustaining a family. Less than a year later, Mike's father disappeared.

Living on welfare, Lorna and the three kids drifted through New York's ghettoland. From Bed-Stuy they weaved down to Brownsville. There, on Amboy Street, they existed on a diet of husked-out loaves of bread and saw a few more men stumble through Lorna's life. The gangs in Brownsville, the dead-end boys of America, soon noticed Mike. He was a hulking wreck, the boy they designated to be 'Dirty Mike' or 'Big Head Mike'. But they used more than just punchlines against him. When he was not whipped by Rodney, who weighed 280 pounds by the time he was twelve, Mike was being clobbered at school or on the tenement corners.

It sounded like a story of Dickensian misery, except that in *Hard Times* and *Bleak House* the worst neighbourhoods weren't infested with gun-running gangs or on the verge of discovering crack. But, as in Dickens, there was a sentimental refuge for Mike. He had his birds, the pigeons he cared for on the roof of an abandoned building across the street.

When we'd met five years before, when his distance from Brownsville was reflected less through a star-shaped prism than the freshness of teenage memory, Tyson said, 'I loved those birds. They'd fly in the sky, up and away from Brownsville, above all that dirt and shit. And they always came back to me – they never left me for long. I loved that.'

Then, one day, everything changed. A bigger boy climbed the emergency steel stairway where Mike kept his pigeons. He scooped up a bird and, laughing, made the Fairy Boy beg for mercy. 'The bird was fluttering with fear,' Tyson said, 'and I was ready to cry. The boy didn't care about nothin' but hurt. He twisted his hands and broke the bird's neck. I heard the crunch. I went mad . . . crying and screaming and kicking and punching . . . first time I ever fought. I fucked him up so bad. I was so angry, like I can still taste the feeling. After that I got off on the violence. I saw its power.'

Just as I responded to the fighter's mazy emotion, Tyson equated that moment with an earlier moment of destruction. A swell of delight, 'like an orgasm', had surged through him when he snapped the head off one of his sister's dolls at the age of five or six. He had shown her what it was like to feel suffering.

Tyson eventually bullied anyone he wanted, hooking up with a teenage gang called the Jolly Stompers. He used his fists to get a reputation; but in Brownsville you needed something more metallic to impress the big boys. Just before his twelfth birthday Tyson bought himself a gun and started serious thieving, in tow with his sombre homeboys. He ended up in juvenile jails like Spofford and Tryon outside New York. It was then that he began to box.

The air was rancid when Tyson swaggered back to his corner. His chest rose and fell. Sweat trickled down the bridge of his nose and splashed on to the wooden floor like a leaking tap. The silence was broken by the booming thump of the gym's sound-system. It kicked in with a heavy beat. Sparring was over. Tyson looked tired as they cut the gloves from his hands.

'Give me another minute,' he murmured as he drifted past me to tackle the speed-ball next. He walloped the small pear-shaped bag with a velocity which made it sing on its steel spring. As he worked he sighed with rhythmic severity, as if he could feel the shadows at sail within him.

His whole life had been chiselled from themes of loss and deceit. While still a child he had lost both his parents – his father almost instantly and then his mother – to drink and neglect and then death. Ever since then he had been searching for a new family. First there had been the seventy-two-year-old Cus D'Amato, looking like Marlon Brando in *Apocalypse Now* with his bulbous bald head, small round eyes which were half-blind, pot-belly and jabbering mouth which wove a spell of myth around both Tyson and boxing. D'Amato, the legendary Italian-American trainer, had rescued Tyson from Brownsville and the detention centres. The fourteen-year-old Mike embodied a last chance to fulfil his arcane fight philosophies. For the next four and a half years, until Cus died when Tyson was nineteen, they lived together in a house full of young white boxers in the Catskills in New York State.

Cus was determined to mould him into the greatest boxer of all time. He believed that nothing should deter Tyson from becoming the perfect fighter, combining speed and power, technique and resolution. But to achieve that blend, Tyson had to give up his life for boxing. The human cost emerged later, beginning with Cus's death from pneumonia on 4 November 1985. Tyson lost the person he had loved more than any other; but the inadequacies of his relationship with Cus were such that he was also left helpless against the rest. He was lied to by Cus's managerial backers, Jim Jacobs and Bill Cayton, who, beyond marketing him brilliantly, hid from Tyson the extent of their control. But Tyson loved and trusted Jacobs. He was easily fooled. When Jacobs died in 1988 it emerged that he had suffered from leukemia for years and had not revealed even a hint of his illness to Tyson – who, only weeks before, unwittingly signed away almost half of his lifelong fortune to the Caytons and Jacobs' wife. Tyson took Jacobs' death badly. He was more embittered when he learned that he'd been duped by his second mentor.

Yet they were veritable angels in comparison to Robin Givens whom he married and divorced in the year of Jacobs' death. Their union was damned despite Tyson's hapless adoration. Givens and her mother treated him like an idiot child while transferring $10,000,000 from his account to their own. But the boxer's anger towards women ran much deeper. Its source lay within his distorted past.

D'Amato had understood that the shaping of an extraordinary champion required an abnormal breeding. So when the sixteen-year-old Tyson confided to him that he believed he was repulsive to girls, Cus turned an emotional schism into a boxing motivation. Instead of offering comfort, D'Amato listened to Tyson's confession with derision. After a long silence he walked out of the room and returned only when he had found a baseball bat. 'Here,' he said, 'keep this bat. You'll need it when you're heavyweight champion of the world to fight off all the women who'll be chasin' after you.'

After such an upbringing, Tyson did not consider it odd to believe that violence and desire were inextricably linked. What restraints would he ever be able to place upon himself, especially in a world as studded with greed and disorder as Don King's version of boxing? For, on 'Showtime', King's favourite pay-per-view television network, Tyson's rage was stoked and hawked as if it was nothing more than a minted delight.

He smashed the speed-ball against the head-board with an intensity which sent a tremor through the apparatus. As it squealed on its hinges he began to shadow-box, letting out staccato grunts which sounded familiar with hurt. He made lonesome *'Tsa-huh! Tsa-huh!'* noises as he slipped away into that dream-state the best boxers reach for when the night of a fight closes in on them.

Tyson was ready for Razor – and for me.

'You're dead, you pretty thing, you . . .'

I stood up shakily, unusually conscious of my own potential prettiness. It was not a burden I was used to shouldering but, as with those who look most beautiful just before death, who could say with certainty that I would not appear suddenly lovely to Mike Tyson? Remembering the crooning promises he'd uttered to Ruddock I watched him walk towards me. My head felt fit for bursting. I had sat still so long, in the sun and in the gym, that it felt like I was the one turning slowly mad.

He perched in front of me, on the fringe of a blue canvas ring. His lips pursed as he anticipated my opening question. I fumbled with a tiny tape-recorder, trying to escape the words skipping across my brain.

'It doesn't count if he isn't dead, it doesn't count if he isn't dead . . .'

The memory of his smashed, whispery voice framed our silence. I watched the cassette's thin loop of tape begin its run from left to right through the plastic container. Tyson breathed softly above its whirring hiss. I could think only of his breakneck sayings.

'You're dead, you pretty thing, you . . .'

Tyson dislodged something acrid from the back of his throat. I wondered if he was about to whistle up a thick globule as a reminder that it was time for me to speak. As a concession I cleared my own throat, thinking how odd it was to swap phlegm-ridden noises with such a broad-chested fighter.

'So . . .' I finally asked in a gesture of surrender, 'how're things?'

Tyson looked down at his hands. He opened and closed his right fist as if deciding whether to imitate a flower or a punch. I was slipping beneath my own ineptitude, deserving a punch. 'Okay,' he said with a little sigh, 'things are okay . . .' His hand opened again, like a flower I thought. Tyson had fielded a lot of dumb ones over the years.

'You still flying the birds?' I stuttered, transfixed by my own idiocy. As soon as the words left my mouth I swallowed hard, as if I could somehow drag them back. All afternoon I had steeled myself to ask the penetrating rather than the obvious. At least my first question had just been banal; 'You still flying the birds?' sounded like some pathetic attempt at ghetto-jive or a dated allusion to the fighter's preoccupation with women.

Tyson wiped his face with a white towel. 'You one of those who always asks me about the pigeons?' he brooded.

'No,' I answered quickly.

'Hey, I don't mind. It's better than asking me if I'm goin' nuts!'

'Bang goes the second question . . .'

Tyson stared impassively back at me.

I spoke hurriedly again. 'Do people really ask you that? Whether it feels like you're going crazy?'

'Nah – they're too frightened. But I know that's what some of them think.'

'Why would they think that?'

''Cos of all the stories running round right now.'

'What kind of stories?'

'I don't want to talk about them.'

Our earlier quiet returned. Tyson's fist closed tightly round itself in the shape of a right hook. Hesitantly, I attempted to trash all those who wanted to trawl through his private life while pointing out that, if he ever felt in need of confession, I could cup my ear with sensitivity.

'What do you mean – exactly?' Tyson asked suspiciously.

'Well, I've heard that sometimes it's easiest to find you in a topless bar after midnight . . .'

'Shit, man,' Tyson said with a cold laugh, 'they talk fuckin' crap!'

'You're dead right, Mighty Mike,' I said with a gulp. Mighty Mike! How low would I go?

Tyson smiled again and said, 'It doesn't matter, y'know, they can say what they like about me. I know the truth.'

His lopsided grin encouraged me, making me warm to him again. I wanted him to like me. For the short time we were face to face, it seemed to matter that our exchange became more humane.

Tyson breathed sadly. 'Look, people are always gonna believe the worst things about me . . .' He had a misted look in his eyes. 'There's so much garbage floating around me now that I can't help but think how it all started. All I wanted to do was fight, to get into the ring as a way of improving myself. I still do. I'm a fighter. That's what I am.'

'But still,' I asked, taking my chance, 'do you feel you're being pushed towards a crisis?'

'No . . .' He stopped again; and then decided to say it: 'But, you know, I feel I'm alone.'

'When were you the loneliest?'

'When Cus died. Before then I always hoped it'd change. After Cus I had to see the truth – I always lose the people I love . . .' Tyson punched the open face of his left palm, quietly but repeatedly, as if each blow might daze his words.

'Do you still think of Cus?'

'I miss him as much as ever. It's no easier now than when he died. I'm still coverin' up the hole he left in me. Cus was everything to me – he was like a father. My friend. He was my mentor, my trainer. I lost all that.'

'Do you think much about your real father?'

33

'Not if I can help it.'

I felt I should move the subject forward, away from his most private history. 'It's like the story that was told to me by Chris Eubank, the British boxer –' I started to say.

'I know who he is,' Tyson butted in, reminding me of his position as not only a boxing archivist but also as a contemporary expert.

'What do you think of him?' I asked Tyson in surprise before bestowing a lick of flattery. 'I know how much he admires you . . .'

'He's kinda strange.'

I agreed and pressed on. 'Eubank spoke about the time he spent in the South Bronx – how those years scarred him, how hard he found that life –'

'Yeah! You talk about South Africa but, man, in Brownsville and the South Bronx there's the same oppression. Those are black places. Places white America just don't understand.'

'And when you compare Brownsville with Vegas?'

'Oh, man,' Tyson chuckled, with a sound as doleful as it was amused.

'And when you're staying somewhere like The Mirage and you think back to your earliest days in Amboy Street –'

'I ask the same thing: "Can this be the same life?" From there to here, from the ghetto to the casino. It can fuck your head in . . .'

I was haunted by a story told by Camille Ewald, the old Italian woman who lived with Cus and his boys in the Catskills house. On the day they met Tyson, Cus told her that 'This is the one I've been waiting for all my life – my third champion, the best one of all!' But Camille was compelled more by the memory of Mike running up the long drive from the bottom of Cus's garden. He ran to her, his face full of shy hope, and asked if she'd mind if he picked some flowers and took them back to Tryon. 'Of course,' she murmured when she learned that he had never seen roses before. She helped him choose as many flowers as he wanted and only heard later that they withered and died before he'd even returned to the reformatory.

'But I was just trying to get by,' Tyson said, undermining any attempt to see his life as a protracted metaphor. 'I was thinking only of survival – and boxing offered something more than that. If it hadn't been for boxing I'd have wound up a long time ago in jail or even dead – one o' the two. I found a new identity in the ring, I discovered a reason to believe that there were good things in life for me too . . . otherwise, you know, a cell or a coffin were waiting.'

'Do you still see boxing as your salvation?' I wondered.

Tyson resumed his steady but upsetting punching of one hand against the other. Cell or coffin, cell or coffin, each thud seemed to say. 'Not now,' he said.

'Why not?'

'When you look at the scumbugs around boxing, you think there must be something hollow at the centre. They're eating into the heart and soul of the fighters. Fighters are warriors, they're gladiators – but they get treated like shit. You wonder if you wanna go down this crazy slope . . .'

'What's the worst thing about boxing?'

'Everybody's in it for themselves. But they lie, they try to tell you different. Maybe I'm not meant to live this insane life for too much longer – who knows?' Tyson smiled mysteriously, encouraging me to venture further into choppy waters.

'The excesses of boxing – the fame, the media, the deceit – must anger you.'

'Maybe . . .' Tyson said blankly.

'What about the incident last week when you smashed the camera in half?'

'I was mad at the time. It felt like they were showing me no respect, giving me no space to move. I snapped. It was wrong. I've said sorry, y'know . . .'

'What about the women who've brought charges against you for lewd behaviour –'

'What about them? What about the women?'

'There always seems to be trouble with women . . .' I mumbled.

'I meet lots of women, some good, some bad – maybe more bad than good, just like everyone.'

Tyson's attitude towards women was anchored in a kind of despair which led him to say: 'All these women who sleep with me, they don't want me. They want the cash. Hey, I look in the mirror every day and I know that I'm not Clark Gable. I wish I could find a girl who knew me when I was broke and thought I was a nice guy . . .' While Tyson could put on that sweet little boy voice at will, and evoke sympathy for such a rich guy's plight, he spoiled his persona as a sensitive soul snared in an ogre's body by hunting down women. For all his declarations of boxing's depravity he was not averse to using wealth as a bait for his more predatory instincts.

'There's so much money in boxing – can it lead to anything but heartache?' I asked. 'There's talk now that you'll meet Evander Holyfield for the title in boxing's first $100,000,000 fight –'

'I don't care about the money!' Tyson said sharply. 'One hundred million is just a figure to me. The money just goes – it has no meaning.'

'Whereas the title?'

'Well, now, the title!' Tyson exclaimed with a smack of his lips. 'The title's different! That's all I want back – my title as undisputed heavyweight champion of the world. Not the money, not the women, not any of those things. I'd fight Holyfield for nothing – everyone knows that's true. Fuck the money and the rest of it – I want the title! That's all that really matters to me now.'

'Why is it so important?'

'Because it's my destiny,' Tyson said gently, as if his words had opened a fragile gift from someone he'd once loved. 'Cus always told me that – "The title's your destiny," he'd say, "you should keep it for a very long time. You have the ability to hold onto it as long as you want" . . .'

'So why do you think you lost it last year?'

'Maybe I lost sight of what the title meant. When I first won the championship I was so aware of who I was following – Jack Johnson, Jack Dempsey, Gene Tunney, Joe Louis, Rocky Marciano, Sonny Liston, Muhammad Ali! Man, all those great fighters! It sent shivers down me when people said my name in the same breath. But then I got sloppy, I began to think I was invincible. And that, of course, just ain't true. If nothing else, boxing teaches you that you're – uh, what's the word – fallible? Yeah, I was fallible . . . I lost a fight I should've won. I lost my fear of losing. Y'know, I once just refused to consider the possibility of losing. But most of the great fighters lose at some time or another – and then they come back . . .'

The gym was almost deserted. There was only the faint echo of feet skipping across the floorboards as an unknown fighter jumped rope with a light but complex jigsaw of steps. Tyson looked across the empty space at the other boxer.

'Are you worried about this next fight?' I asked.

'No.'

'But isn't this the hardest time of all – with only a few days left – when doubt creeps in?'

'Look, I know I'm gonna win this fight on Friday night. I beat Ruddock only a few months ago. The referee stopped the fight too soon. This time I'm gonna knock him out.'

'What do you feel towards Ruddock?'

'I respect his power. He'll come to fight.'

'But you called him a transvestite, you said you were going to make him your "girlfriend", that it would only count if he was dead at the end.'

'Hey, hey,' Tyson said quietly, 'you know what happens at those press conferences. I get bored. I say things I don't really mean. I was just stirring things up. Everyone looks so fucking smug eating their little cakes and looking up at the niggers talking about fighting. Those words get jumped on and blown up. They're ghetto words, they're not meant to be analysed by all those white reporters.'

'But they had such a sad ring . . .'

'Maybe I was feeling a little sad when I said them . . . I dunno . . . All I can say is that Ruddock and I are gonna face each other in the ring on Friday night. When the bell goes it's just me and him. In the front rows there're gonna be all the movie stars. They get off on it. An' they know that, with Ruddock an' me, it's not gonna be pretty. We're gonna be dropping bombs in there. It'll be me and Ruddock – one on one. An' you know what? I like the sound o' that . . .'

Tyson spoke with such acerbic lucidity that I felt a sense of foreboding. He locked his hands and stretched them in front of him. One of his fingers clicked, making me wince. Tyson looked away, words falling from him seamlessly.

'That's the only thing that's certain in my life. Fighting Razor Ruddock. Who knows what else is coming? I don't . . . an' sometimes, you know, I don't even care. Sometimes I get a real bad feeling in my stomach, that it's gonna come crashing down an' I'll be back where I started.

'It's always been that way. Look what happens to fighters – even the best of them. Joe Louis ended up a doorman at Caesars Palace. He was in a wheelchair at the end. Sonny Liston died in this town, a drunk and a junkie with no money. Even Ali, look at Ali. I love Ali but when they introduce him at my fights I look away. Sure, they cheer him, but where's his beauty now, his speed, his talent? It's gone, it's gone.

'You ask any boxer, whether he's Muhammad Ali or me, whether he's from Brooklyn or Britain. In the ring you're in the hurt business. Getting hurt, giving hurt – like always, dreaming of getting out to a better place, but you know you're never gonna stay there long.

'So I got no illusions about boxing – none. This is a brutal business. It's the hurt business. But I'm a fighter – that's all I can do. It's my destiny.'

The sky outside was a dark and steady blue. The two fighters were ready to walk. It was just past eight and the sun had slid from sight to allow The Mirage to ascend again in blinking neon. Yet there was enough of a reddish glow to ensure that the first stars to be seen were those being hailed from the centre of the ring.

Jack Nicholson! Clint Eastwood! Whitney Houston! Bruce Willis! Sylvester Stallone! Michael Jordan! Tommy Hearns! Sugar Ray Leonard! The names breezed by in a froth of adulation, dragging celebrities from their seats so they could turn and wave to twelve thousand fans with smiles as wide as their wallets were deep. They were called forth in glory by a suave announcer called Jimmy Lennon Jnr – a tuxedo-clad joker who revelled in his 'Yes, folks, it's showtime!' catch-phrase. It excited me less than that raving 'Let's Get Ready To Rumble!' stomach-churner.

A pale slice of moon shone down over The Mirage. There were howls of expectation from the cheaper seats at the top of the steep banks of scaffolding assembled in the hotel carpark. Don King circled the ring like an electrocuted shark booming out his own favourite aphorism – 'Only in America! Only in America!'. He slapped his thickly jewelled fins together in delight. It was like watching a party through a sinking, glass-bottomed boat, as though I was trying to stay above the sea of hysteria.

Tyson had completed our interview graciously, talking eloquently of past fighters. Yet I left the gym that day full of disquiet. It had been impossible to miss the ache in much of what he said about boxing and his own life. Tyson said, more than once, 'I'm past caring'; but he did so in a way that made me feel as if the opposite was more likely to be true.

But I also realised that I'd been fortunate to have met him on a day when his mood was unusually pliable. There were too many previous examples of malevolence in his character to allow me to shut my eyes to danger. Some of those incidents were caused by his own weakness but others were beyond his control – fate having instilled such an assortment of disadvantages and warped characters into his life. If that was what it took to create the world's most famous fighter then my heart went out to him instead of just beating faster in the expectation of seeing him fight.

While Razor Ruddock marched to the ring in a white gown and Bob Marley's 'Get Up, Stand Up' reminded him of his Jamaican birthplace, I thought how Tyson had been the first fighter to have renewed my interest in boxing after Muhammad Ali's conclusive decline in 1980. I had thrilled to the dramatic spectacle of Tyson cutting a swathe to the title in 1986. For the next three and a half years I had been no less persuaded by the pall of dread he extended over the heavyweight division – nowhere more effectively than on the night he dumped the previously outstanding Michael Spinks in Atlantic City with a display of fury and skill which, for the ninety-one seconds it lasted, captured the magnetism of boxing at its most epic. Tyson in turmoil was another proposition.

I became more interested in him as a man, no matter how distracted, than as a fighter. And how could that be anything but a good thing as the promise of violence hung heavily in Vegas's balmy evening air?

The fan behind me – a swarthy gambler wearing crocodile-skin shoes, white slacks, a floral shirt and a crimson Panama hat – sounded like he was hyperventilating with anticipation. 'Just you wait, babe, just you wait!' he gasped to the sweet-faced young woman next to him. She was dressed in a black evening dress whose elegance accentuated the splashiness of his outfit. 'This is the big one!' he shouted. He realigned the contents of his under-wear. 'Big Boy Tyson! Mighty Mike Ty-sonnnn! Can you feel it, babe, can you feel the electricity!' 'Babe' smiled demurely at me, as if in agreement that the electrical charge should be attached through the flowery shirt and onto his taut nipples. Big Boy's hoopla was picked up by a gang further back. I was sure Tyson could hear us from his dressing-room.

Beneath the cruel exterior Tyson presented, as Public Enemy's 'Welcome to the Terrordome' cranked out across The Mirage, he was still subject to fear. He had shown signs of a tenuous 'inner life' as a fifteen-year-old boy in 1982, when he defended the National Junior Olympics belt he'd won the year before with an awesome exhibition of punching power. After he had knocked out his first four opponents, Tyson suffered an emotional collapse. It was an hour before the final. Against a backdrop of blue Colorado mountains he began to sob. He couldn't fight anymore. He was too scared to enter the ring. His trainer Teddy Atlas wrapped an arm around Tyson's shoulders, telling him how well he had done to reach that point. 'Come a long way,' Tyson snivelled, 'it's all right now . . . I'm Mike Tyson . . . everybody likes me, yes, everybody likes me . . . I've come a long way, I'm a fighter now, I'm Mike Tyson . . .'

His words were swallowed up by tears. Tyson was afraid of losing. If his boxing career went off-track he would be of no use to Cus D'Amato. For all his immaturity, Tyson recognised that D'Amato had need of him as a fighter rather than as a person. He had to keep winning or else he'd be on a bus back to Brownsville. The fact that he went on to win the tournament on a technical knockout confirmed Atlas's inspiration and his own determination; but that memory had always struck me more as a pointer to the hurt inside him.

As he strode towards the ring, rap billowed around him. Tyson wore his usual uniform. Black shoes and trunks and a white towel, out of which a ragged hole had been cut so that it could be placed over his head to make a crude gown. There were no satiny robes or designer accoutrements for Tyson. With his 'strictly business' look he harked back to early-twentieth-century fighters like the two Jacks – Johnson and Dempsey. Tyson wanted to club his opponent into submission. His style of boxing was about battering coercion rather than showbusiness.

But when he walked past me Tyson appeared lethargic. There was none of his typical neck-flexing or head-rolling. He looked robotic even though Big Boy hollered in his ear, 'Go, Mike, Go! Let's take him out, man, let's take him out!' as if they were soul-mates bent on vengeance against the murderer of their twin-wives. Even Babe clapped her hands in rapture as the Tyson entourage swept by, wearing 'Team Tyson – It's A Family Affair' and 'Kick Ass' T-shirts and baseball caps.

And then, at last, the ropes separated. Tyson ducked into the ring to a shudder of noise. He and Ruddock looked away from each other as Jimmy Lennon Jnr ripped through the introductions. The two fighters were both cheered while Don King grinned through the boos cascading down on the announcement of his own name. 'Showtime!' he mouthed again; and then, inevitably, 'Only in America!'

Mills Lane, the referee, was a small terrier of a man – a county judge from Reno who prided himself on his expansive collection of guns and on administering law and order both in and out the ring. Mills, plainly, was in no mood for chit-chat as he brought the fighters and their trainers together. His bark resounded through Jimmy Lennon's microphone. 'Okay! You've heard my instructions in the dressing-room! Any questions in this corner?' he yelped, turning towards a motionless Tyson. 'Any questions in this corner?' he asked Ruddock. Razor glared at Tyson. 'All right!' growled the excitable ref as he moved towards the epiphany of his own trademark saying. He took in a deep breath, smashing his fist against the touching gloves of Ruddock and Tyson. Mills let the words go: 'Let's get it on!'

Babe had dissolved into incomprehensible laughter. She made a gargling sound over which she had no hold, as if she had abandoned herself to the night. 'All right! Now you're gettin' it, babe!' said Big Boy as he stepped back from his maddened partner.

Tyson was the first to land a significant blow, a right hand which brushed the Razor jaw. But instead of following up with a combination, Tyson teed off another uppercut. It missed, as did Ruddock's left hook which he called 'The Smash'.

They slugged at each other in the centre of the ring, neither showing much skill. It was strange, although not unexpected, to see nothing of the bobbing and weaving, the lateral movement of Tyson in his prime. He simply planted his feet and threw one punch at a time.

'Way to go, Mike, you're the man!' marvelled the ever-moving mouth below the Panama hat. Richie Giachetti, the paunchy trainer in Tyson's corner, was less impressed: 'What's this one-punch stuff? Combinations, Michael, combinations!' he instructed with an odd air of formality.

Mills Lane was even stricter as he stopped the fighting midway through the second round. He warned both boxers to keep their punches up. Tyson took the directive to heart for, as Lane gestured them back into action, he threw a looping overhand right. It knocked Ruddock down onto the blue canvas splattered with Don King's crown logo. But Ruddock bounced off his back, a rueful grin indicating that he had only been stunned.

The crowd's delirium intensified when, early in the fourth round, Tyson followed up his first advance with a right cross which landed on the button of Razor's jaw. As if connected by wire to that bone, Ruddock's eyes flew wide open, intent on blocking any dimming of the lights when he landed squarely on the seat of his pants. It was as if he had been dropped from on high by a large winch with his legs stretched out in front of him. I couldn't help myself – I jumped with Big Boy and 12,000 others. But, again, Razor was up before the referee could get past the count of three. His swelling jaw split open in another gumshield-flashing smile.

'Weird sense of humour, Razor . . .' the reporter next to me muttered.

'It's all over, babe, it's all over now!' Big Boy moaned huskily as he slammed the back of my chair.

But at the end of the round, as at the conclusion of the fifth and the sixth, Ruddock was not only still standing but punching back. At the sound of every bell he cupped Tyson lightly round the head, aware that he was fighting someone mortal rather than the monster of old. Tyson looked tired whenever he sat down on his stool. He no longer believed he was sharing the ring with a transvestite.

'Wake up, Michael, wake up!' Giachetti yelled. He covered Tyson with a white towel. The fighter looked like a small boy sitting unhappily in a barber's chair.

As often as he hit Ruddock, Tyson left himself open for the counter-punch. His once-wily defence wilted during their ponderous slugfest. It seemed as if he was willing Ruddock to hit him so that he could prove his chin's resemblance to a rock. Like two men failing to drown each other in a swamp, they jarred each other relentlessly without ever rising from the mud.

Tyson was ahead comfortably on points; but his publicity machine insisted that he was never meant to be less than lethal. That myth, however, had been wrecked. The disorder of his personal life seeped through every facet of his performance. At the end of the eleventh round Tyson returned to his corner to find that his 'Team', his new family of helpers, had forgotten to bring out his stool. Tyson trudged away to a neutral corner as he waited for his entourage to earn their daily $5,000-per-man salary by lifting the wooden chair back into the ring.

Ruddock's face was grotesquely puffed. His jaw had been broken in the fourth. He and Tyson banged their way through the last three minutes. When the final bell rang, they exchanged a private glance of relief and respect. Tyson shovelled the gleaming white gum-guard out of his mouth and held it stiffly in his right glove. He shook his head in admiration for Ruddock. Razor smiled in response. It was an unusual grimace full of ironic humour. He lifted his head to a blackened sky as if to give thanks that it was over. The fighters embraced and spoke soft words to each other as the trainers poured water over their steaming heads.

'Warriors, babe! Warriors!' Big Boy exclaimed while Jimmy Lennon Jnr prepared to announce the wide and unanimous points victory for Tyson. When he heard that he had won Tyson was full of savage grace for his opponent – 'Man, did he hurt! He hits like a mule! God!' Trying to prolong the intimacy of their ending he went to cradle Razor's lowered head again, as if he could hold back the time when they had to leave the ring and return to life. But, too soon, Don King came between them, breaking their clinch and bringing them back to reality, where Ruddock would be whisked away to hospital with his fractured jaw and Tyson taken to the waiting hordes of reporters for yet another of those press conferences he loathed. Showtime, for Mike Tyson, was zigzagging to a close.

I left Las Vegas on 30 June, the day Mike Tyson turned twenty-five, hounded by gloomy forecasts that he was destined for the crossroads. Yet no one could have known then that Showtime really was over, that we had seen the last of Tyson in the ring for another four years. Not even the most strident boxing cynic could have predicted that, two months after fighting Ruddock, Tyson would be charged with various sexual felony counts and end up in jail for raping eighteen-year-old Desiree Washington. How could we have guessed that this crazed story would continue with him, as Prisoner 922335, staring down the barrel of a six-year sentence in an Indiana prison?

But, in the early morning hours of 18 July 1991, Tyson had whispered to Desiree Washington: 'Don't fight me! Don't fight me, mommy!'

Desiree Washington was a bright girl from a good home in Coventry, Rhode Island. She had pleased many people in her short life, winning numerous academic prizes and local beauty contests. The year before she'd been awarded a leadership scholarship to visit Moscow – which she received from Vice-President Dan Quayle, Indiana's favourite Potato-man. She wanted to become a medical team worker in Africa or perhaps a diplomat. Desiree even had a fantasy that one day she might be America's first black woman president. In her spare time, she was a senior Sunday-school teacher at the Ebenezer Baptist church where she also sang in the choir.

At the Miss Black America final, Desiree was a high-school amateur compared to the worldly lovelies who worked the pageant circuit. The organisers, meanwhile, had asked Tyson to feature in their promotional video. Would he dance with the girls, they encouraged, would he get close to them while the film was being shot?

'Yeah, I'll do that! I like that part!' Tyson responded.

The eventual film captured Tyson stroking the women as he shuffled and crooned, 'You're beautiful, you're the girl of my dreams, I'd love to get together with you . . .' in his restless rap. He wore a silk T-shirt and long baggy shorts, with a thick gold pendant of a big cat swinging down to his belly. On his chest, there was a prominent 'Together In Christ' badge.

Tyson moved along the line of aspiring women, panting his approval. He stopped in front of Desiree Washington and sang to her: 'Ooooh, I'm in a dream, Day after day, Beautiful women – such an array, What can I say?'

She giggled and covered her face as if she couldn't believe she had come close to a celebrity as large as Mike Tyson. She began to laugh, almost hysterically, as Tyson stepped even closer. Then they hugged each other.

Afterwards, Tyson propositioned most of the girls, picking up a few telephone numbers along the way. But he was different with Desiree. Perhaps realising that she epitomised everything he was not, Tyson spoke gently. He bowed his head, telling her she was 'a nice Christian girl'.

When her parents arrived the next morning, on 20 July, in Indianapolis, Desiree broke down. Her father, Donald, recalled that: 'She told me that she went out on a date with Mike Tyson and, before she could say anything else, she knew I was a Mike Tyson boxing fan. The man could do no wrong in the ring – knockouts in one round, two rounds. He was great – in the ring. I idolised him, I idolised him. My father was a boxer when he was young – so we come from a family that follows boxing. So I said, "Oh great, how did it go? Did you get a picture?" And she says, "Dad, it wasn't so great. I've got some bad news for you. He's a rotten man, a dirty man. He's no good . . ." And my heart fell down. I thought maybe he used profanity all night long, you know, maybe he didn't have any morals, maybe he slapped her – that was the worst I wanted to think. And then she hit me right between the eyes: "Dad, he raped me".'

I had interviewed Tyson in Las Vegas only three weeks before. For all his despair I had never expected he would plummet so far. I had seen another side, the 'real' inside of him, I thought. Yet I suspected Tyson's guilt the moment I heard news that he had been charged.

I had always liked him when we met. But his charm towards me was countered by more salient truths. There had been too many outbreaks of rage towards women to respond otherwise. Who could forget him once saying, 'I like to hurt women when I make love to them. I like to hear them scream.' There were also all the lawsuits lodged against him for oppressive sexual conduct. While a percentage of those claims were intended to fleece him of his fortune, there were too many instances which he could not deny. With hindsight, the catalogue of abuse in his relationships had been part of a long chain – leading to the rusted last link of rape.

I trawled back over that anecdote of Cus D'Amato offering Tyson a baseball bat 'to fight off all the women' when he eventually became heavyweight champion of the world. D'Amato had fulfilled the epitaph engraved on his tombstone: 'A boy comes to me with a spark of interest, I feed the spark and it becomes a flame, I feed the flame and it becomes a fire, I fuel the fire and it becomes a roaring blaze . . .'

That 'roaring blaze' had eventually hit Indianapolis; and it seemed as if a prison cell might be the saving of Mike Tyson, from himself and all those he had once loved and trusted.

2

THE FORCE

I HAD TYSON IN MIND EVEN BEFORE I STEPPED OUT ONTO THE street in King's Cross and saw the man. On a sultry September afternoon he moaned as if the fires of hell already coursed through him. His smooth black face glowed with the effort of wailing above the slow din of traffic. A couple of junkies lounged against the window at WH Smith, with clothes and hair as matted as the coat of their scrawny Alsatian. They stared at the pink and open mouth of the howler with a look of dusk in their eyes, as if his cries made no sound through the crack and the smack.

'Hear me, hear me!' he implored. 'Jesus knows, the baby Jesus knows! If there's to be redemption then there must be truth. Mike Tyson is innocent, Mike Tyson is innocent! Jesus knows, Jesus saves!'

And yet two days before, on Monday the ninth, Tyson had been indicted in Indiana on four counts of rape, criminal devious conduct and confinement. The previous month, on 7 August, a former Miss Black America, Rosie Jones, had filed a $100,000,000 lawsuit against Tyson, alleging that he had 'assaulted, battered and humiliated' her by grabbing her buttocks at the previous year's Indiana Black Expo. While Tyson and Don King knew that they would be able to pay off a glamorous chancer like Jones in an out-of-court settlement, Desiree Washington sought a conviction. Tyson's trial by jury was set for January 1992 and, considering his victim's resolve, it was plain even then that he was on his way down.

But, across the seas and through the blurring mists of his mind, this gleaming billboard of a man would not believe it. He walked in circles as he chanted, slamming a fist against the home-made placard slung over his shoulders. The words on it shook whenever his strangled vocal hit the name of his hero: 'Tyson! Tyson! Tyson!' On the front of his board, in a boyish scrawl, he had written 'INNOCENT MAN!' below a photograph torn from *The Sun* of Tyson bulging out of a black Armani suit. The back of his banner featured a lurid blue and silver impression of a polka-dot haloed Jesus.

I was disturbed less by the babbler's crossing of Christ and Mighty Mike than by the coincidence of his appearance on the very day I resumed my acquaintance with the ring. As menacing as he could be, Tyson still had that sporadic capacity to turn up as the good guy. I was drawn to boxing for that precise reason, that even in such a soiled and greedy world you find men who are bright and fine.

Tyson had sustained that hope for a while and yet, unlike the man with his foghorn voice and Old Testament delivery, my faith in the fighter had been badly rocked. But the black wise-blood refused to be deterred. He banged on for a few minutes more, repeating the same set of words over and over again, his voice rising in exultation when he realised that my presence had swelled his congregation by another quarter – or a third if you discounted the mangy mutt. 'Hear me, hear me' was the only signal that a new loop had begun for, otherwise, the 'Jesus knows' and 'Jesus saves!' blurred into every new protestation that 'Mike Tyson is innocent, Mike Tyson is innocent!'.

By the time our sermon on the King's Cross mount was over, another apparently pious image filled my head. I blinked and saw again Tyson's 'Together In Christ' badge heaving on his immense chest as he locked in on Desiree. I could imagine his expression, confiding and complimentary, telling her that she was 'such a nice Christian girl'.

'Mike Tyson is innocent!' the Pope of St Pancras suddenly yelped again. We jumped in surprise. There were sufficient flecks of foam at each corner of his mouth to convince me and the weary dog that the brimstone boy was as close to barking as it is possible to get. He pointed at me and sputtered, 'Behold, the son of God hath spoken. Beam me up, brother Solomon, beam me up from Babylon . . .'

'Oi, mate,' the first junkie whispered from his slouch, 'listen, before you go . . .'

'Aaah, a snowy white lamb speaks,' the preacher purred.

'You got any change?'

'We all need change, my son,' the holy one intoned with a bow, 'we all need change . . .' He set off across the Pentonville Road, humming tunelessly as he slapped his long fingers hard into the open palm of each hand. His board of faith clattered noisily while Jesus bobbed and weaved on his back.

'Religious boxing nuts, y'know, are always the worst,' the second addict sighed. He had the bearing of an expert who had studied a rare breed too long. His red and twitching eye fell upon me. He shook his head as if he could somehow glean that I was on my way to meet yet another fighter who pledged himself to Jesus; a boxer who called himself 'The Force', after Christ.

'Know what I mean, pal?' the junkie breathed.

I shrugged and hurried away towards the syringe- and condom-strewn alleyway which led to a gym at the back of the railway station. Mike Tyson would have recognised boxing's street origins in that setting. But I pushed on, hoping that I might find a happier detour in a different story.

I can still remember his voice. He spoke quietly, his words sounding more grave than savage while we sat together in the old St Pancras gym.

'Ten more days . . .' he murmured, 'ten more days till I break his heart . . .'

His eyes glittered for a moment, and then he smiled. Michael Watson was 'The Force'. I believed in his power. But the grin faded as quickly as it had come, for he was a serious and perceptive man. He knew there would be trouble ahead.

Even then Chris Eubank shadowed him. His gaunt face tightened every time he thought of his opponent, that dangerous dandy, a strutting thesaurus of contradiction, that gloved peacock who yearned to be a celebrity rather than a mere fighter.

'I want Chris Eubank,' Watson said huskily, as if stricken by the harshest desire. 'He's all I can think of now – on my mind it's just Eubank, Eubank, Eubank . . .' Watson's jawbone jutted whenever he bit down on that name, cutting it to pieces: 'Eu-bank'. His head ducked towards mine and I pictured the few times in my life I'd wanted to hit another man while reeling with anger or drink. But that feeling always faded. Nothing bad ever happened.

This is different. Something dark picked up speed.

I had travelled to St Pancras in anticipation of drama. After Tyson, I was not drawn merely to the pristine qualities of Michael Watson's character. I knew that neither he nor Eubank could claim the artistry I revered in my videos of Ali, the two Sugar Rays, Robinson and Leonard, and lighter Mexican fighters like Salvador Sanchez and Julio Cesar Chavez.

But with Iron Mike on his way out, the contrast of Eubank and Watson sustained my fascination with boxing. The thrilling symmetry in their abilities made them even more interesting.

Both fighters had secured their reputations in the ring by defeating Nigel Benn, a courageous puncher who savoured his image as boxing's 'Dark Destroyer'. Yet, where Watson's victory had done little to diminish his obscurity outside fight circles, Eubank had built upon his success over Benn to discover fame and wealth.

The difference was one of image. Eubank tagged himself as 'Simply the Best' – that lousy Tina Turner ditty sharing with him a dearth of subtlety. Jesus was The Force in Watson's corner, a metaphor which won favour on *Songs of Praise* but fared less well during Saturday night's peak-time viewing on ITV's *Big Fight Live*. In boxing you need more than a belief in Jesus and a solid set of fighting attributes to top the ratings. But Watson was just a black boxer from a respectable working-class home in Islington. The Force was dependable but ordinary.

Eubank realised that 'there's a nasty taste to this business. If you have nothing of significance to say, if you don't make any statements, you're just a good fighter. And it's not enough. You have to have more. So the reason I earn the most money is that I have a little bit of everything. I can box, I can fight, I can dance, I can strut, I can show off, I can behave arrogantly, I can charm, I can communicate with people who have PhDs in philosophy and make them feel intimidated. I can dabble anywhere and everywhere. Michael Watson cannot. In accordance with this I am not seen today as a boxer – I'm seen as a presence. Michael Watson can only box so he has none of my presence or my money . . . it's that simple.'

I said some of those words to Watson and felt the bitterness rise inside him. His resentment towards Eubank went deeper than hype. 'Chris Eubank has no respect for anyone,' Watson muttered. 'I'm a better fighter than him – but I've not been given respect from Eubank or the money I deserve.' He wore a white Joe Bloggs T-shirt and black training pants and boots – every wiry inch of his six-foot frame primed for retribution. 'The problem,' he said eventually, 'is that Eubank has no respect for boxers or boxing. None! But he's a boxer himself. Where's the logic?'

I stayed silent for he did not expect any reply. The other boxers in the gym knew better than me the feelings tumbling through him. Even though the patterns of skipping and sparring lent an ominous rhythm to his words, Watson ignored their methodical training. He was there to talk rather than to work.

'There's something seriously wrong with Chris Eubank's brain, with his way of thinking. Why should he attack boxing – the very thing that makes him a very good living, that has lifted him out of nowhere? Why should he describe boxing as "barbaric"? Ah, I dunno man, it makes no sense . . .'

'But Mike,' I interrupted, 'boxing is barbaric. Why do people go to fights? They go to see one man hurt another, they're there for the knock-outs, not your defensive skills . . .'

'I know, man, I know. But would you call me barbaric?'

'No.'

'Then why does Chris Eubank?' Michael Watson seemed so gentle then, as he shook his head, that I lent over and patted him on the shoulder. Watson smiled again. 'Hey man, it's okay. He's the crazy one.'

'Why do you think he dismisses other boxers?' I asked.

Watson sucked at his sunken cheeks, a babyish gurgle calming him. His nostrils twitched as he smelt the intimate stench of the world he loved. The layers of stale sweat were sweetened by disinfectant and liniment oil. All around us young black men, and a few white fighters too, beat out an insistent clamour of punching and grunting. Watson's face softened as his head dipped slowly round the gym.

'Eubank's not like these guys,' he replied. 'He would like to come from Eton but he comes from Peckham. He would like to be a white model but he's a black boxer. I think Chris Eubank is ashamed of his roots. Why else would he put so much pressure on himself, pretending he was born with a silver spoon in his mouth?'

Dry flecks of spittle lined the corners of Watson's own mouth. He looked thirsty. Without an ounce of fat on him it appeared as if it had been weeks since he had last tasted a decent spoonful – silver or otherwise – of anything. He had battled often to make the middleweight mark of 160 pounds; and so it was a kind of freedom that he would next meet Eubank at the super-middleweight mark which meant that he could relish the retention of another eight pounds. It was impossible to see how his painfully taut body had managed to shed such weight. If you had taken a pair of tweezers to his skin you would not have readily found any flesh to pinch. But Watson was more concerned with the flab of Eubank's language.

'The way he speaks,' Watson said as his tongue darted across thin and cracked lips, 'the words he uses, that's not the way Chris Eubank speaks to his own mother. It's sad but I have to say that I've never seen another black man try so hard to look and sound white. I don't understand it – I just think he's a very weird and confused guy.'

Watson had hit upon one of boxing's most recurring themes. Even a marquee-name like Eubank was unable to reconcile his formative impoverishment with his present wealth. There was a tragic undertow to the fact that fighters' increased status depended on their continued violence. It was as if, in wanting to improve their lives, they had to hark back constantly to the destructive memories they longed to escape. The one life fed the other, as unerringly as a dirty river does the sea.

Watson and Eubank were also enveloped by more delicate questions of identity. Apart from their uneasy parity amongst the world's best middleweights, they symbolised opposite extremes within the ring. If Watson represented the fleeting purity of fight tradition, Eubank personified the bombast which transformed boxing into 'Showtime' – or violence as entertainment. Each fighter dismissed the other as a caricature, as either a loser or a fraud.

Eubank was rightly regarded as a 'personality'. He was as much an absurd chatshow celebrity as a fighter, as infamous for wearing outfits consisting of monocle, tweed jacket, jodhpurs and riding boots as for his lisping denunciations of boxing as a 'grotesque blood-sport'. Watson, meanwhile, was consigned to the sidelines as the fight-game's consummate 'professional'.

From Watson's perspective there was an even rawer edge to their enmity. I saw his anger when it was pointed out that Eubank's income was double his own, despite the fact that they were at identical stages of their respective careers. Where Eubank drew in both the crowds and the headline-writers, Watson's appeal was evident only to the cognoscenti. When Eubank and Benn fought each other for six-figure purses in 1990, Watson received only £15,000 for featuring in a bout on their undercard – even though, the year before, he had been the first fighter to dent Benn's unbeaten record. Watson had repelled the Dark Destroyer with authority before coolly knocking him out in the sixth. Eubank, in contrast, relied upon the iron in both his chin and his ambition to stop Benn in a bout which resembled a street-fight for the nine rounds it lasted.

Watson's failure to cash in on a more skilful achievement began with his refusal to either launch a verbal assault against Benn before the bout or, moments after he had won, propose to his girlfriend on national television. Chris Eubank, of course, completed both tasks – and so catapulted himself into a position of booming notoriety.

They had already met between the ropes. The day before I left for America to meet Tyson, on Saturday, 22 June 1991, at Earl's Court 2 in West London, Watson and Eubank fought each other for the first time. Few British bouts had so divided other boxers, trainers, promoters, writers and fans. Unbeaten in twenty-seven fights, Eubank had a more impressive record than Watson who had lost twice before and drawn once during the twenty-nine times he had fought professionally. And yet Watson, the twenty-six-year-old challenger who had fought some superior opponents, had as many experts picking him to win as did Eubank, the 'world' champion, who was two years younger. The boxers were so closely matched that, in casual fight-game terminology, they cancelled each other out in a WBO (World Boxing Organisation) middleweight title fight. I was almost disappointed that there were no overwhelming attacks or knockdowns – just thirty-six minutes of moderate British boxing offset by some sloppy misses and clumsy footwork which would have been punished by an American champion like James Toney, holder of the IBF (International Boxing Federation) equivalent of Eubank's title.

While I'd felt relief that neither fighter was hurt, I still wanted more than they'd given. I wanted to see them match each other blow for blow. Back and forth, up and down, two wills balancing on a see-saw of determination and bravery missing from my own routine life.

The build-up to that bout had simmered with intensity. Yet Eubank and Watson fought fitfully, as if they knew there would have to be more than one act to their drama, that an ambiguous opening sometimes unfolds into a gripping narrative. As Eubank said later, 'we tried our hearts out' – but neither was left broken. Watson's heart, however, suffered another chip when his rival lifted a fiercely disputed points decision to retain the WBO belt. Eubank's dubious victory elicited furious booing, his return to the dressing-room being accompanied by a bronzed hail of beer-cans and coins.

Hugh McIlvanney, writing later that night in *The Observer*, led the complaints of Watson's more eloquent supporters by describing his performance as a 'triumph for honest orthodoxy over imaginative bombast . . . Eubank had always appeared capable of hitting more powerfully but his worthwhile assaults had been separated by so much posing and strutting, so many wasteful movements and irrational lulls, that the scorecards came as a shock.'

But, depending on which side of the ring you were seated, an argument could be made for either fighter. It was left to that beaming promoter, Barry Hearn, to promise instead that we had only seen the first in a possible series of Eubank-Watson bouts. 'There's little option,' he enthused as the pound signs twitched his eyebrows in oily unison, 'but to get these two to fight again in a few months' time. It's what the fans want, it's what they want, it's what you and I want. They have to fight again. Settle this thing once and for all . . .'

In the gym ten weeks later, Michael Watson still seethed. 'Last time out I gave him a boxing lesson! I couldn't believe it when they gave him the decision. I thought, "What more do I have to do to prove I'm the better fighter?" I know now – I have to knock him out. I'm going to carve my initials on his forehead.'

Watson did not sound like the composed man I had met in the past. There was an urgency to his tone which resounded with the swirls and eddies of a fighter reaching beyond himself.

'Do you ever worry about hurting another man?' I asked.

'I know I'm doing what God wants me to do.'

Watson spoke with a conviction that Mike Tyson had never shared – even when, in the late '80s, Don King announced his fighter's conversion to Christianity and orchestrated a water-dunking baptism before the world's press at a church in Cleveland. But where Tyson's faith was at best tenuous, Watson's was resolute. I'd always been interested in the extent to which so many professional boxers professed their Christianity. Sometimes, the mix verged on schizophrenia. But Michael Watson was one of the sanest people I had ever met.

'Do you see why,' I persisted, 'some people might see a contradiction in a Christian making his living out of hitting other men?'

'Yes.'

'Does that contradiction undermine you as either a fighter or a man?'

'No.'

'Why not?'

'Because,' Watson replied with a deep breath, 'I believe that God is in my corner. He has given me a talent. Boxing is what I do best for now. I love boxing but in the end He will be the one who will decide how best I might serve Him. He will be the one to push me to victory. He will be with me on the night of our fight.'

Watson talked with a grainy fervour which suggested that he would not accept argument. He wanted to get back to trashing Eubank. While he didn't enjoy the staginess of big-time boxing, where he was expected to churn out rhetoric as smoothly as he threw combinations, Watson recognised the significance of their rematch. He described it in almost biblical terms as 'a fight at the crossroads – one fork leads to the light, the other into darkness . . .'

I wondered if he understood that Eubank himself saw the contest in such stark terms. Watson swung on his hard-backed chair and nodded. 'He says I am trying to take the food from his table, how I'd ruin his lifestyle if I beat him. All he means is that there can only be one clear winner this time.'

'And for the loser?'

'Well,' Watson replied evenly with barely a break between my words and his, 'for the loser it will mean slipping downhill.'

Watson's level gaze tilted up and away from the murky end of that 'downhill'. He was already climbing. He knew it; and I knew it. He kept talking.

'That's why this fight is so important. Eubank says it's just about money. I say it's about much more than money. Our fight is for a world title and me getting some justice after the last decision – but it's also a battle for the security of our families, for the future, for respect. Deep down, in his heart, Eubank knows all this. Maybe he's preening in public but, in private, behind closed doors, I know he's preparing – like me, he's preparing for a helluva fight . . .'

The gym lapsed into rare silence – its blows and buzzers stilled a moment – as if absorbing Watson's prediction.

'Doesn't it seem odd that you both go through the same trauma?'

'No. It seems normal to me . . . I'm a fighter!'

'And so is Eubank – whatever else he might say or do.'

'That's why it's not gonna be easy to walk right through him. I'm ready for the full twelve rounds – he's not just gonna fall over the first time I hit him. And, after the last fight, he knows I'm not falling any time he hits me. I'm telling you, if this one comes down to a war, he'll finish the worse for it. I've been to bleak places in the ring, places he has never even touched. I've fought and lost to a bodysnatcher like Mike McCallum. Eubank has not met that kind of fighter. Last time I was drained by making middleweight. This time I'm stronger and I'm gonna do it not only for me but for every other fighter out there, I'm gonna do it for the sport of boxing – I'm gonna strip Eubank of everything . . .'

Watson stared down at the logo on his chest. He was proud to have negotiated a sponsorship deal with Joe Bloggs prior to the first Eubank bout. It seemed fitting, too, that where Eubank flashed fancier designer names, Watson linked himself to one which epitomised the everyday. For if Eubank tried to look like he should've been named 'Gianni' or 'Georgio', Watson had the ease of a man content to be 'Joe Bloggs'.

As Watson glanced up in expectation of my next question I noticed the dazzling whiteness of that T-shirt – as if he was a cheeky young buck who had just flipped out of a Persil ad. I knew that, although he had a girlfriend and was the father of two children with another woman, he was again living at home with his mother. I suspected that she had a hand in those whiter-than-white shirt stakes.

On the few occasions I had phoned the Watson home I had always spoken first to his mother. Joan Watson was a soft-faced woman with a voice whose gentleness was emphasised when she spoke about the destruction of the ring. For all the support she showed her son, I heard the trepidation when she said: 'I just want it to be all over now, for the fight to be done with, and Michael and even the other boy to be home safe . . .' She made me wonder if his life might have turned out differently if Mike Tyson had had such a mother.

'Is your mother worried about you fighting Eubank again so soon?' I asked.

'My mother always worries,' Watson sighed. 'But she knows that after God and my family, boxing is everything to me. It's given me so much and I've worked so hard. Now it's my turn to become world champion – in ten more days!'

'Ten days must seem a long time when you're waiting for a fight,' I said as I recalled Tyson's similar craving for the night of his return against Ruddock.

'Aaaah, jeeezzz, the word is "slow"!' Watson laughed softly. 'It's terrible. You know the fight is coming but the sound of that first bell is so far away. In the weeks and days you wait, you sometimes say to yourself: "How long? How much longer?" But we do it, we keep on. Y'see, to fighters, these feelings become less terrible, they become . . . you know . . . familiar.' Boxing defined Michael Watson. 'But,' he thought wistfully, 'these days, they tell me it's not enough just to be a boxer. But, man, that's what I am – a fighter. I ain't no Chris Eubank . . .'

'Do you find it strange that Eubank loves Tyson?'

'I know I've got more in common with a fighter like Tyson,' Watson flared.

'Most people – especially Christians – might worry about comparing themselves with Tyson these days.'

'I respect all great fighters.'

'Even when they're heading for a rape conviction?'

'God will be the judge before me . . . who are we to judge Mike Tyson?'

'So you'd take his side against a woman's every time?'

'I am on the side of right. And, yes, I am on the side of most fighters because I know how often they get conned. But I think I'm different to a lot of boxers. I'm rooted, I'm not easily swayed. I'm not the sort of guy to make the mistakes you'll see in Eubank or Tyson.'

Watson had the kind of life outside boxing which encouraged the notion that he was more rounded than either of those men, bound up in their star-ridden puzzles and flashier addictions. It was not just our mutual love for Arsenal which shaped my own belief in Watson. There were none of the tics of fame – the vast entourages or references to himself in the third person – which better known boxers than he chose to exhibit. Watson was neither surly nor pretentious. Instead, when not facing Eubank, he was restrained. 'I'm a family man,' he confirmed, 'a son and a father, a man who knows where he's coming from and where he's going to . . .'

But there was grit, too, in Watson – a fact emphasised by his decision, after losing to Eubank, to replace his old friend and trainer, Eric Seccombe, with the high-profile expertise of Jimmy Tibbs from the East End. 'It was hard,' Watson said, 'but I have to do what's best for me in the ring now. This is a tough business. I ain't got no room for sentiment. Jimmy Tibbs is the best trainer in the game. I need someone like that in my corner. Eric's been with me for every fight for the last eight years – from when I was a kid, right through into the pros, up to the last one. It was hard to tell him. He's not happy with me. An' I understand that . . . an' . . . well . . . I think that deep down Eric will eventually understand what I've done. Nothing must stop me winning this fight. I've gotta beat Eubank.'

I could not forget how, before the last Eubank fight, I had seen Eric Seccombe tend to Watson in that very gym. He was a small bespectacled ball of a man who saw 'something beautiful' in the shades and cadences of the gym while speed-balls were being pummelled and heavy bags pounded. 'Love it, love it,' Eric muttered in cheery Cockney as he wrapped Watson's hands. 'Y'see, Michael and me,' he chortled then, 'we're boxing people to the core. We go back an awful long way together, an awful long way – all the blinking way back to the amateurs. This is our life.'

Watson no longer worked much in King's Cross – he prepared himself mostly across town with Tibbs' other fighters. But, still, Watson said, 'a gym is a gym'; and he was more comfortable talking there than in the swanky hotels Eubank favoured for interviews. 'Yeah, the gym is my place,' Michael Watson said with a shy hush as he turned to box playfully against his own shadow riding up high on a paint-peeled wall. As he moved in that stifling air he said a few more words which have always stayed with me: 'It's different here. I feel at home – this is where I belong. Yeah, I'm happy here . . .'

I went in search of Chris Eubank early the following morning, wondering if he too had discovered happiness only nine days before he leapt over the ropes. I travelled down to Brighton by train, leaving behind a grey London to arrive an hour later in brilliant sunshine. The streets were still damp but the sea-breeze was as crisp as the air in King's Cross had been filthy, matching the needles and sick dumped on the St Pancras pavement.

An aesthete like Eubank loathed such squalor. He had carved out a more refined retreat, a 'happy home' of his own which did not hammer away at inequities in his past. On the Sussex coast, instead, a few elderly ladies walked their cocker-spaniels and sausage-dogs while a shaven-haired girl flashed past them on her rollerblades with a dainty wave. The old promenade looked radiant with cream and yellow Regency buildings shining on the beachfront.

Brighton had never been a great boxing town. But there had been a repeated claim since 1990 that its most famous citizen was, in fact, a fighter. 'Well, this is Brighton at its most beautiful,' Chris Eubank agreed in his oddly piping and sibilant voice which reminded me most of Mike Tyson, his own hero from the ring. 'But I must tell you, my good fellow, it's quite wrong to say that I live in Brighton. I live in Hove – quite a bit further up the road. They are two different places. And, as you might assume, I favour Hove . . .'

'Where does Brighton end and Hove begin?' I wondered blithely, trying to explore a quintessential English subject bound up in themes of property and class. Perhaps I could yet prove to a meditative businessman like Eubank that I had the nous to appreciate his world beyond boxing.

'If you have any sort of eye,' Eubank sneered, 'it has to be obvious!'

'Which do you think Mike Tyson might prefer?' I asked, curious why a boxer who professed to hate his occupation listed a destroyer like Tyson as his favourite fighter.

'Who am I to answer that?' Eubank asked airily, before diverting the weight of responsibility. 'Who are you to ask this?'

I cleared my throat and considered the best answer to this blunt question. 'Well . . . I'm not too sure about that one . . .'

'Neither am I, my friend, neither am I!'

'Are you concerned for Tyson?'

'For Michael?'

'It's looking pretty bad . . .' I said.

'He's innocent of course!' Eubank exclaimed.

'You think so?'

'Naturally! Do you think this woman went up to his room at 2 a.m. to discuss philosophy like you and I may do later this morning?'

'Her naïvety doesn't automatically assure his innocence.'

'How well do you know him?' Eubank probed.

'I've interviewed him a few times.'

'And?'

'He was interesting, even charming . . .'

'Of course! He's the only man to whom I would bow down. The thought of him ending up in prison is . . . well . . . it's just horrible!'

'How do you think Tyson would cope in jail?'

Eubank moved onto that momentous conundrum. His hands made a black pyramid which he examined before resting the length of his long chin on the tips of those joined fingers. 'Who is to say exactly what is in the nature of a man?' he pondered, sounding as if his middle-name was Leviathan rather than Livingstone. 'Who is to say?' he asked again, beginning to enjoy himself, 'for I can speak only in accordance with my own personality, in accordance with my own knowledge. Do you follow?'

'Yes, Chris,' I replied dutifully, 'I follow.'

Eubank was a pussycat – an obtuse tabby who dabbled in minor heroics and showboating inside the ring and grand gestures and Versace suits on the outside. Despite the scorn he brought upon himself, I had always given the nod to Eubank. Unlike Michael Watson, I did not have to fight him and so was inclined to give him the space he required to weave his tortuous allegiance to the words 'in accordance with'.

'Now,' he lectured, 'in accordance with what I have already said, it follows that I can speak for no other man. I speak for myself. I am an individual. Now you may look at me and see an immaculately tailored suit and, in accordance with that and the words I use, you may see me as a gentleman. That I am.'

I visualised how the muscles in Watson's face would flex if he could have heard that speech; and the gentlemanly blast which would summarise his reaction.

'But,' Eubank continued, 'in the body and heart there is also the fighter. I may rightly be said to have this Jekyll and Hyde personality. A gentleman outside the ring, a gladiator inside it. I am these two parts combined into one. Perhaps Mike Tyson is the same – but I cannot speak for anyone else. This is correct, is it not?'

'Surely,' I quipped.

Eubank's imposing shadow stretched across the chintzy table. I choked back the laugh I might have shed on my living-room couch. In person, almost nose to nose, I decided to pay him my humblest respects.

'What five words would you use to describe yourself?' I asked. It was the sort of query which I knew Eubank loved.

He did not need much time to answer, even selecting his adjectives in alphabetical order. 'Approachable . . .' he said. 'Brave . . . devious . . . generous . . .' He pursed his lips. 'Moody . . .' And then he nodded, 'resourceful . . .'

'But, Chris,' I protested, 'that's six words!'

'I needed six.'

'But I said five words!'

'Ah,' Eubank smiled, 'but I'm the fighter. I'll settle on six, thank you.' Suitably described, the six-pack wordsmith veered away on a new tangent. 'Still, it's a terrible thing, boxing, a terrible thing . . .'

I had travelled to Brighton precisely because of that paradox. Like few fighters before him, he stressed his disdain for the profession which had proved how apt it was for 'bank' to dominate his name.

Boxing is, as he stated, 'a soiled activity, a savage blood-business'. Yet the romantic in me liked to believe that there was also a poetic glory in a fighter's courage. So I sided with those boxers who derided Eubank; for whenever he labelled boxing 'a mug's game' he was demeaning men like Michael Watson.

But I knew that, away from the press conferences and television appearances, he nurtured a passion for boxing. Anyone who becomes animated when talking about Tyson's power cannot be an advocate for the abolitionists. Eubank was interested in fighting – beyond just in monetary terms. Yet the way he lamented its worst features made me appreciate him as a fighter who might tap deeper into my own ambivalence. There were too many suckering clichés about boxing – what did it really mean to call it the 'Noble Art' when fighters were getting bashed in the brain and ripped off at every turn? I hoped then that Chris Eubank would force me to consider how much more slack I could find in my questionable fence-sitting. What, after all, was it about boxing that had snagged me so sharply that I had travelled from Las Vegas to King's Cross to Brighton as if pursuing the resolution to a significant riddle? How did you even begin to unravel an enigma like Eubank?

While he delighted in his own money-making opportunities, Eubank focused on boxing's inherent exploitation. 'This business trades on the worst emotions,' he mused. 'Look at the violence, the abuse of fighters. Look at how most boxers end up. They're damaged, they lose the money they've made, they are given so little respect. Unless you are an exceptionally strong character – someone like myself who acts in accordance with all his intelligence and discipline – boxing will ruin you. I have seen it happen too often.'

Amid the immodesty there was hurt in those words. Eubank's two older brothers, Peter and Frank, were also boxers, but they were journeymen rather than champions. They were the kind of fighters promoters called 'bodies' – opponents rather than boxers. If a fighter fell by the wayside a couple of days before a promotion, Peter and Frank Eubank were the sort of pugs the money-men would phone up and say: 'Listen, do you fancy earning some money? Yeah? There's a new kid fighting in London (or Cardiff or Birmingham or Liverpool or Glasgow . . .)' And, desperate for cash, Peter or Frank would haggle for another fifty quid before accepting the promoter's 'take it or leave it' purse. Then they'd travel to another city to take on a young prospect whose management were intent on padding his unbeaten record with the sort of durable but dispirited opponent they embodied.

'What other business would treat professionals so shabbily?' Eubank asked. 'It can break your heart to see most fighters. That's why I am determined to be different. Why I am disrespectful of boxing tradition. That history is corrupt. I am out to break its mould. I am going to keep both my brains and my winnings. How many other boxers can make that claim?'

There were times when Eubank could be unusually lucid. I thought again of Watson's more clipped observations – as if one fighter held up a mirror of words to the other's secrets. Eubank considered his rival to be another example of the misguided sap, a victim of boxing's debased myths. But Watson was an intriguing figure. Even if he revered the rituals of boxing he was too smart to ignore the trickery of his trade. It seemed fitting that Watson – the straight-talking man in the white hat – had recently overturned the most draconian piece of legislation in British boxing. Five months before, he had won a protracted battle in court against the right of his former manager, Mickey Duff, to keep him contracted against his will. Duff, for years the most powerful man in British boxing, acted as both manager and promoter to an expansive stable of fighters. The advantages Duff accrued from his dual role, at the boxers' expense, were sufficiently clear for Justice Scott to back Watson's claim of 'Conflict of Interest' and free him from a restrictive contract.

The implications were enormous. Boxers could at last acquire more equitable deals – thus shifting an antiquated imbalance. Eubank knew that, for all his patter, Mickey Duff was nothing less than an iron-balled businessman. Michael Watson, in becoming self-managed, had beaten Duff with a resilience which belied his mild manner. But away from boxing he remained a family man. Joe Bloggs himself.

Eubank, however, regarded himself more ambitiously as a mysterious icon who could 'dabble anywhere and everywhere'. I suspected that his enunciated ridicule of boxing stemmed from public perceptions that fighters are invariably thick-tongued dolts. His verbosity tried to overcome British barriers of both class and race. Black boxers were not expected to be endowed with either imagination or intelligence. I admired Eubank's desire to prove the sneering chatterers wrong but sensed the futility of his efforts. It would not be a simple task to transform himself into the Renaissance Man from Peckham. When a fighter like Eubank became comfortable with his rise it was said that he'd rejected his 'blackness'; yet if he stayed the same as when he began to box he'd be considered little more than a virtuoso street-thug.

Watson was an exception – a product of a good home and tightly knit north London family. Eubank's background was much rougher and more representative. Although he had been born in Dulwich and brought up in Peckham, which led him to numerous street crimes and detention centres, his later teenage years had been spent in a New York ghetto.

I had always been fascinated by the route Eubank took from Peckham to the South Bronx but he was reluctant to discuss the past. 'It is too much of a reminder of what drove me to become a boxer,' he said. But I persevered and the bare facts were prised from his grip.

Two and a half years apparently passed between his birth in 1966 and the next occasion he sat on his mother's knee. He was her tenth child and his father's fifth, the youngest in an amorphous bunch. His first memory was one of hostility – of his grandmother, who looked after him those first few years, shouting at him. 'I grew used to the idea of facing adversity,' he bristled, 'because my childhood was not easy. My mother eventually sent for me, but when I was seven she left for good. I was not bothered. I felt immune to love.'

'A seven-year-old boy, immune to love?'

'I saw my mother's leaving more as a chance for me to run a little wilder. You see, I was a boisterous child in Peckham.'

'Boisterous?'

'Certainly,' he crooned. 'My father worked as a panel-beater [for Ford in Dagenham]. He was away all day – I was free to do as I pleased.'

'What pleased you in Peckham?' I asked.

'I liked to steal. Other kids would take a packet of crisps and a bar of chocolate. I would lift ten packets and twenty bars. Even then I was different. There were three of us – Nasty, Sticksman and me. *The Three Musketeers* – it was my favourite film, the one I could relate to most. We moved uptown. Oxford Street. White ladies' handbags, the shops, whatever took our fancy. We dipped in and out. I say this not to glamorise that time, that crime. It was wrong, but I was young . . .'

'What about school?'

'I was suspended from school so many times. Eighteen times in one year!' Like a sly cat dipping its creamy paw into yesterday's pot of double-thick, Eubank marvelled at his audacity. He smacked his lips with satiny emphasis. 'Eighteen times! I was put into care then. But still I continued my boisterous ways. Detention centres meant nothing. At fifteen I was pulling in maybe £700 a week when the average wage packet was £60. I had the works – Italian shoes, mohair suit, money to catch taxis back to Peckham at £15 a shot. You see, we'd steal things – £80 sunglasses, designer shirts, silk ties, the best trousers – and sell them for a quarter of the price in Peckham. We were well known, for I was always fair when selling the goods we'd stolen. Robin Hood, y'know. My heart was good. It was just the circumstances which were not acceptable.'

Then, in 1980, Chris Eubank was called to the Bronx by his mother. 'She had been living there while I stayed on in London. There was concern about my rebellious behaviour, so she sent for me,' Eubank recalled in a voice suited better to an astringent headmaster than a mewling Bronx-kid.

In pugilistic folklore American fighters are considered superior to their British counterparts. But their greater capacity for violence – the mean-spirited streak in black American fighters like Tyson and James Toney – has always carried an underlying social indictment. Both Tyson and Toney, like so many boxers, had been abandoned by their respective fathers soon after their first birthdays. It seemed to me a dubious privilege to have survived deprivation and desertion to emerge amongst America's 'baddest men'. But then I was a white South African from the suburbs, from a country steeped in violence and too many hard men. I had learnt to guard against easy assumptions about 'ghetto-life'. Chris Eubank, who had seen more than me, was less reserved when dishing out short shrift to anyone who celebrated life in the Bronx.

'When I arrived in New York, I hated it. It was more than a jungle – it was dirty and dangerous. It was horrible. I realised that I needed to move out of the twilight, away from the despair of those who, you know, "have not"; I needed to "have". But, then, I was just concentrating on my own survival. I smoked my last cigarette, drank my last drink. I started to go to this gym in the South Bronx, encouraged by my mother who knew it would keep me out of trouble. And that became my life. I went to school at Bronx High and I trained like a madman in the afternoon and early evening and on weekends. I lost myself in this world . . .'

Having heard other fighters' stories of how they became enthralled by the blur and hum of the gym, I expected that Eubank would have been similarly impressed. But he chose a more rarefied version of his introduction to boxing.

'I was not like the others. I did not fall in love with the stink of the boxing gym. I was haunted more by the world outside. The South Bronx is a place of nightmares. So I trained like a demon to get out . . .'

When Eubank returned to Britain in 1989, having had four bouts as a professional in Atlantic City, he did the small round of British promoters. 'I saw them all,' he said scornfully, 'Mickey Duff and Frank Warren and every other one of their greedy breed. They were insulting. I was the fighter, I was seeking a manager or a promoter to work on my behalf – but it was as if they were doing me a favour in even seeing me. The offers they made were laughable. They are used to dealing with fighters willing to be mugged. I went instead with Barry Hearn.'

Hearn had made his fortune in snooker. Seeing the potential million-pound fights on offer, he turned his attention to boxing just as Eubank returned from New York. They were made for each other. Eubank dropped his American accent for the bizarre trot of an English toff while Bazza cranked up his Essex banter. They were hustlers together, two working-class boys from Peckham and Romford, via the Bronx and the Crucible in Sheffield, who hit upon an ingenious ploy. Running contrary to everything enshrined into British sport – from humility to clouded notions of fair play – they created Eubank's 'Simply the Best' persona, a knowing parody of the 'Bad Boy' of boxing who was only in the business for the sake of his own pocket.

Unlike Henry Cooper or Frank Bruno – seminal figures in the 'cor, blimey, know what I mean?' HP Sauce stereotype which decreed that British fighters were lovable losers – Eubank was a conniving poseur. His proverbial pegs, it was said, were in need of lowering. As Eubank admitted: 'A significant percentage of the British public has a strong desire not only to see me lose but, also, to witness me being beaten up badly. They perceive me to be arrogant. They will pay a lot of money to see me hurt. That is their right, after all.'

That public yearning had emerged the previous autumn when he had been matched against Benn – who conformed then to the popular alternative to the 'Our 'Enry & Frank' cliché. He was a gap-toothed black fighter who liked 'nothing more than a good ol' fashioned tear-up'. Benn was neither an aspiring philosopher nor a nancy-boy. There were no elocution lessons nor 'Best-Dressed Man in Britain' awards for him. He came to rumble.

Yet it was the self-same Eubank who swaggered down the aisle to Tina Turner and vaulted over the ropes, the very joker prancing round the ring who showed the most extraordinary fighting heart that night – eventually grinding Benn into submission. I thought then that, in Eubank, a fighter had emerged who could articulate all that was oppressive about boxing; but a fighter, too, capable of finding a rigour which testified to everything that was brave about the human spirit. In the end I was more wrong than right. Just when he made one feel a Wilfred Owen-ish ardour to log his valour, he took the fight-game down a new road of bluster. In the middle of his victory interview, he gasped to his sweetheart on live television: 'Love you strong, Karron,' he sobbed, 'coming home now, Karron, will you marry me, Karron, will you marry me . . . ?'; which, of course, she did. Chris Eubank transformed himself into a celebrity, slipping into a shiny domain beyond boxing.

We talked together quietly in his favourite beach-front hotel, the Hospitality Inn, sipping morning tea just after eleven, Eubank dressed in a darkly elegant Versace suit and impossibly shiny shoes. I plied him with the respectfully serious questions he most desired. He spoke glibly about Italian fashion, British politics, American film and Jamaican holidays – for he knew that whatever diversion he took I would eventually drag him back to reality. And he was ready to be pulled back. As Watson had said of him, he had only one man on his mind.

'Michael Watson is strong. He will not give in without a severe beating. I have the same feelings welling up inside me as I did before I fought Benn in Birmingham. I think it could be that tough – but I prevailed then and I will prevail now.'

'But why do you keep fighting, Chris? Is it just the money?'

'What else?' Eubank scoffed. 'You see, the glory is not worth the pain – but, for the moment, the money is . . .'

'Michael Watson speaks more about being compelled to fight for reasons other than money,' I suggested. 'He says he is also fighting for a world title, for respect, for the sake of boxing. Do you share any of those feelings?'

'Well, I am a gladiator, so I must have fire in me to fight for reasons of pride. But if you have to fight it is not something that is pleasant, it is not something a sane person can love.'

'Watson seems to love boxing.'

'Yes, but then I would class him as an unpolished man. He knows no better. But this is also what makes him dangerous. He lives for boxing. I merely use boxing as a stepping-stone to get me the place in society I require. So I enter his territory. I know that. He will come to battle. But so will I. You see, we have no choice now – the die, as they say, has been cast.'

'He says he's counting the days until he breaks your heart . . .'

Eubank smiled a sad smile, his mask slipping for once, as if he suddenly imagined how it might feel to have your heart broken. 'We'll see,' he sighed. 'We await our fate together, Michael Watson and I. Soon it will only be the two of us – face to face. Then, we will find out whose heart breaks first . . .'

Chris Eubank and Michael Watson were set to fight again at White Hart Lane in Tottenham for the WBO super-middleweight title – their championship saga again illustrating the machinations at the heart of modern boxing. The comparative mediocrity of their Earl's Court bout stemmed from the difficulty they both experienced in making the middleweight limit. Hugh McIlvanney suggested that Watson 'gave the impression that it would be difficult to lose any appreciable weight without the assistance of a carpenter's plane'. Eubank, being more strongly muscled, complained of the dehydration which had set in during the fight after months of struggle with his scales. There was no option for either fighter but to move up the divisions.

It was unprecedented, however, for two boxers to climb a weight section and instantly be offered a title fight. But, with the WBO's super-middleweight title vacant, Barry Hearn's boxers were ushered to the head of the queue. The organisation's first- and second-ranked fighters in that division were dropped from the rankings altogether – even though they had waited months for their title chance and had not suffered any interim defeats. The WBO, whose hilarious slogan was 'Dignity, Honesty & Respect', were unable to justify their reasoning – beyond the unspoken truth that they were almost entirely dependent on the money supplied by British promoters who were less sceptical of the fledgling organisation than their American counterparts.

ITV's fight audience of 16,000,000 people ignored such intricacies. Boxing's political gambits were complex and dreary. A bloody match for a world title between two British fighters who held a grudge against each other was compelling. The mood of the Eubank-Watson rematch was emphasised by the final press conference a few days before the fight. A new peak of malice was reached.

Watson reiterated that he had been 'robbed' in the previous fight – to which Eubank responded with an accusation that his opponent was 'an idiot'. He turned to Watson and scoffed, 'You lost the last fight and you'll lose again. You're a loser – go and ask your bank manager.' Watson, setting aside 'The Force' of Jesus, belittled the champion's lisp and flowery accent. Eubank stormed out, vowing vengeance.

It all, of course, made headlines the next morning. 'Ring of Hate'; 'This

Time it's War'; 'A Fight to the Finish'. The tabloids had their story – but even they could not have predicted the looming catastrophe.

There were hints of what awaited both men when I spoke to them for the last time before they entered the ring. Holding his head high in parody of boxing's age-old conceits of arrogance and nobility, Eubank strode nonchalantly towards me through yet another throng of staring faces and pointing fingers.

'I'm ready for this,' he eventually said, his mind for once not appearing to flip awkwardly through an imaginary dictionary. 'For me, Michael Watson is nothing. He is merely transparent. It's true that I have not shown him any respect but then, for a long time, I have also tried not to show him any disrespect. He made things very difficult at the press conference but I have regained my composure. He is solely an obstacle I have to surmount in order to attain a better life for myself. He seems to find my personality repugnant – that's down to him. I don't need to rattle his emotions like he is trying to do with me. But these piffling attempts of his are not working. He is riling me. Michael Watson has clearly disrespected me and so I feel more animosity than usual. Frankly, I don't care for the man . . .'

'But he looks more determined than ever,' I argued.

'Yes. But his bravery is to his detriment. This time, I know he won't even try to counter-punch. He'll be so much more aggressive. He'll press ahead, he'll be in my face, regardless of the punishment I inflict on him. Eventually, it will be too much for him, the punches will take their toll. But he'll keep coming till he falls. That's why I'll slaughter him and look exceptional in the process – and I am rarely wrong.'

'So you have no fear of Michael Watson?'

'None.'

Watson was only marginally less bullish about his own prospects. 'This is my third title fight; and I'm coming out a winner this time,' he promised.

'Third time lucky?'

'This time I won't need any luck. Just wait, you'll see, everything's going to be all right, everything's going to be great once I'm champion. Man, what a party there'll be in north London on Saturday night, what a party . . .'

21 September 1991

They made their respective entrances that night as if each had chosen to attend a different party. Michael Watson walked down the dusky tunnel and across the floodlit Tottenham pitch with the sound of reggae booming in his wake and the chant of his name rolling around the old football ground. It wasn't quite Highbury but, even for him, a fervent Arsenal supporter, it felt as welcome as playing at home again. 'Wat-son . . . Wat-son . . . Wat-son . . .' the carol came from seemingly 30,000 voices in earnest cry.

By the time the challenger was skipping tensely in the centre of a packed ring, the crowd was set to ignite. Their glee fizzed through the metal rungs of the stadium like a blue flame. Chris Eubank, as was his wont, kept them waiting. The noise flattened into a long whine of expectation as red and yellow lasers, the colour of Eubank's trunks, dipped across White Hart Lane. And then, amid all that brouhaha and dazzle, it started: the march of a man lost in a party deep within his own kinky mind.

Eubank's wide nostrils flared outrageously, as if they were at the end of a horse's head pumped full of bad cocaine. He tapped his red gloves together – not once, but twice, three times with the bunched side of one glove bouncing up and down his other fist. He frowned and cocked his head meaningfully, like 'The Thinker', as he watched the tentative tapping. For all we less transcendental cretins knew, he may have been observing the eerie transfer of lightning from one fist to the other. He nodded sagely and repeated the process, his nose sucking up air like a new hoover might do dirt.

Eubank was transfixed by his ritual and had to be pushed along by the tuxedoed Barry Hearn. A stream of leggy go-go girls wearing *Daily Mirror* T-shirts, satin shorts and killer heels each waved a large Union Jack in front of the main attraction. The fighter started to move as the bombast intensified with Tina Turner joining the romp – her 'Simply the Best' inflaming the doubters further as they rose to admonish the champion. Occasionally Eubank would pause, looking out at the yapping crowd as if he could drink in their venom and transform himself into the glowering 'Prince of Darkness' to Michael Watson's radiant 'Force'.

As he nodded again, Eubank's nose went into overdrive. His huge jaw rippled and the sculpted chest heaved. 'Yes!' I could see him thinking, 'yes . . . it's time . . . it's time to tap my gloves again . . .' Bang on cue, he placed one glove on top of the other and began to tap. We all went mad in our disparate ways – most smiling deliriously while standing on their seats, some hollering, others punching the air, a few more laughing or shaking their heads in disbelief.

The helpless smilers were mostly the numerous women at ringside. My attention was diverted from Eubank to them, to the sparkle of white teeth and red-glossed lips beaming their pulsating pleasure above spangly dresses and strappy stilettos. These were the smiles of people so lost in the fantasy of brutal glamour that they remained oblivious to the face-splitting width of their grins. There was something darkly sexual in that vast orgy of smiling, of women wreathed in rapture, their men brooding with mock profundity. While I was glad to be one of them, to be part of a pitching mob of smirkers and shouters guzzling down the juice of that moment, I tried to look a little more worldly, a seen-it-all-before kind of guy no longer turned on by the fierce allure of punches thrown on prime-time television. It didn't work. I was at one with the salivating rest. My eyes were on Eubank and my mouth twitched at its corners.

I wanted to remember the soft grain in Watson's voice as he spoke of breaking hearts, and the sad grin on Eubank's own face when he heard those words. I wanted to think of them as men rather than just fighters; but how could I in that mindless fervour? I was a sucker for it that night. And I did not want any old tactical shindig, or even a quick one- or two-rounder. I wanted the works, a wringer of fight clichés, a beaut of a bash, a brute of a struggle, a rip-roarer, a cliff-hanger, a tear-jerker, a stone-cold classic.

'It's too much . . .' I heard someone say. I knew that, rather than complaining, he meant that he could hardly bear the intensity.

Eubank had scaled the ring apron. He stood there and glared and tapped, tapped and glared. Eubank, in short, fucked with us a little longer. He had taken us to some bizarre point of no return. He was ready to squeeze it for a few seconds more. Whatever his shortcomings as a boxer, Eubank's tack enticed the kind of people who previously would never have dreamed of watching a fight. He helped remind them that it was ten o'clock on a Saturday night and they were out – and out of everything which was humdrum about the rest of their week.

And then, finally, Eubank jumped the rope, lifting the lid on the loudest roar we heard that night, as he landed and skittered backwards round its one corner in a nimble orbit. When he came to an eventual halt, staring straight at Watson, he opened his nostrils wider than ever. 'Jaysus,' the Irish reporter next to me breathed, like he was summoning forth 'The Force', 'who does this Eubank feller think he is – the Second Coming or what?'

There was hardly enough time for Eubank to ponder that possibility; for Michael Watson made his plan clear from the opening bell. He had the conviction of Christ and, as his opponent expected, The Force came at him in a hot rush, welding unyielding passion onto violence. He was 'all over Eubank like a rash', commented Barry McGuigan, the former world featherweight champion, at ringside. It was obvious that the man from Hove would have suddenly preferred to be at home, having a quiet Saturday night in, listening to his Tina Turner CDs and flicking through *Classic Cars* and the latest *GQ* fashion spreads. Instead he was being pummelled to the body and the head.

During their Earl's Court encounter Watson had paced his attacks. He would follow a flurry of activity with circular movements, keeping an advancing Eubank at bay with his left jab. When Eubank backed away, waiting for him to come onto the counter-punch, Watson would rest a little. As a middleweight, to conserve his stamina, he fought in spurts. At the heavier weight, he'd resolved to leave nothing to chance. He maintained a ceaseless percussion of blows.

The vestiges of camp from Eubank's grand entrance had been erased. There was an edgy blankness in his expression which made him look hunted. Eubank's dread, however, was not of more pain. He was not a coward – what fighter ever is? Eubank's fear, instead, grew from the realisation that he could lose for the first time. By the end of the third that trepidation had ripened.

My own appetite for the contest was jolted by the shock I felt whenever a particularly spiteful punch landed. Until you sit a few feet away from the ring you cannot imagine how hard professional fighters hit each other – the close-up sounds and sights of a fist smashing into another man's face or gut are never easy to absorb. The severity of Watson's and Eubank's hitting was sanitised on television, the impact and cruel angles of their power being deadened by the flatness of the screen. Live, their fight closed in on us with almost suffocating urgency.

Eubank was cut in the fourth. The blood trickled across his face in a thin ribbon, as if in candid recognition of Watson's early dominance. But The Force held back the balloons and streamers. He knew that Eubank would come again, that the cut could yet galvanise the champion's fight-back. The party would have to wait. Watson went back behind the jab and methodical combinations. Eubank, in turn, stepped up his own tempo, pumping out resilience and hope.

By the halfway stage they had settled on a skeletal rhythm. They laid down their bone-crunching tracks but Watson's efforts were always sharper. Eubank slid towards defeat. I thought there'd be no ignominy in such a loss. Eubank had already proved himself to be a fighter of open-hearted fortitude. He was overwhelmed but he kept banging back. That admirable persistence reminded me of his words: 'His bravery will be to his detriment . . .' He had been talking of Watson then; now, that quaint saying sounded more applicable when directed towards Eubank himself.

His corner battled to staunch the blood. They also attempted to entice a tenacity in Eubank to duplicate that pouring from Watson. But Watson renewed his offence as if indeed bolstered by divine assurance. There was a chilling zeal to his ambition. Michael Watson wanted to win but he also wanted to break Chris Eubank's heart.

As Eubank said months later, 'When I heard the bell after the eighth I was in deep trouble. Michael Watson had shown a strength which I didn't think possible. It felt unnatural. It was like facing an abnormal man. He was phenomenal. I wasn't scared of him – I suppose you might say my attitude was one which I held more in accordance with fate. You know, what will be, will be . . . if I am to lose so be it but, I kept telling myself, just go down fighting . . .

'I knew that to have a chance I had to knock him down but that seemed unlikely. So all I wanted to do for those last four rounds was to stay on my feet. I was still proud. I wouldn't quit. In the back of my mind there was a small flame, the hope that if he made a mistake I'd take my chance. "If he does anything wrong," I thought, "then I'll take that chance." The ninth passes, the tenth passes – nothing. He's on top . . . and then the eleventh came and I still don't know how . . . it happened in a heavy fog . . .'

With two rounds left Watson just had to stay on his feet to ensure himself the sweetest victory. Ronnie Davis – Eubank's shaved pit-bull of a trainer – roused his spent fighter one last time. In earlier fights I had seen Eubank instruct Davis to slap him across the face after a poor round. Now Eubank looked as if he had nothing left. 'C'mon!' Ronnie exhorted, 'it's not over yet! C'mon!'

Perhaps those small words worked some magic. Eubank came out punching and backed up a surprised Watson. 'Maybe . . . just maybe . . .' each swing appeared to say. But then, as if clearing his head after a stumble, Watson powered a right cross and a left hook to the head. Eubank went down, as weary as he was legless. White Hart Lane skipped a beat.

'He's down, the bloody fucker's down at last!' shouted the Irish writer, pulling at my sleeve deliriously.

I saw every step and movement with stainless clarity. It was as if each shot was played out with deliberate precision, second by second. Or, more likely, that the reel I now see in my head is framed by video rather than mere memory.

Eubank was on his hands and knees and I found myself standing, lost in the drama. Roy Francis, the referee, turned towards Watson as he counted out 'two', making sure that he had retired to a neutral corner. Watson hurried from one side of the ring to the other but Eubank had already pulled himself up on one knee. Before 'four' could even be said he was up, his back to Watson who was separated from him by the referee's bulky frame. And then Watson closed in on his victim. His mind must have already entered that zone of emptiness which would shroud him for so long. All his frustration and longing must have obliterated any thought – of pity or anything else. Michael Watson was a fighter and fighters ride on instinct when they see hurt in their opponent.

Watson came in for the kill. It was then that he was hit. The punch landed in a scything arc which pundits would have termed 'perfect' if it had not wrought such havoc. The impact on Michael Watson's jaw knocked him off his feet. He landed on his back. He was down and all but out.

None of us saw it then but Michael Watson's head rocked hard against the third and lowest rope. For a hundredth of a second his head may have rested there, as if cribbed in a cat's-cradle made out of an elastic band by a child. But then it snapped back, the rope inducing more of a whiplash than Eubank's right hand. Watson struggled up, looking more groggy than Eubank had done only an instant before. The bell rang – for the end of that round and, as we now know, something far worse.

Michael Watson's brain had already begun to bleed. But there was nothing for us to see. Another man alongside me, a man who'd been quiet all through the fight, started chattering, as if in prayer, 'Three more minutes . . . only three more minutes, Michael. Please God, please . . .' I saw Barry Hearn rush over to Eubank's corner. He was shouting hoarsely at Eubank, looking over at Watson, 'He's gone, he's fucking gone . . .' Eubank stared back at him vacantly, as if seeing a ghost, like he himself had 'gone' from his body.

Jimmy Tibbs and his corner were devastated. They showered water over their stricken fighter, buffing him round the face tenderly, asking 'Are you okay . . . are you all right . . .' I saw Michael Watson nod. But from where I sat it was impossible to see into his eyes. He staggered up on spindly legs for the final round.

It was the one moment we had all been waiting for, that cataclysmic finale, a blinding finish where one fighter 'takes out' the other, where a man lurches against the ropes and tries to stop himself being swallowed up in blackness, where one boxer wins and the other loses, where all our innate ferocity and misery gets buried with those punches and we supposedly come out of his knockout feeling exhilarated and drained of shabby desire. I wanted to see if Watson could survive the inevitable assault, if he could somehow drag himself from the hole into which he'd fallen. Neither I nor anyone else around me wanted our climax, that certain knockout, to be denied. The grace and skill of Watson in the preceding rounds were forgotten. He was slipping away and yet we still wanted to see a few more punches – as much from him as Eubank.

Eubank rushed towards him with flailing arms. Most of his shattered punches missed. After twenty seconds, with Watson creaking like a badly hacked tree, Roy Francis stepped between the fighters. They disappeared from view as the ring was engulfed. Hundreds of people clambered towards the ropes as if by coming close enough they could convince themselves of the truth.

The next few minutes are lost forever. I was only returned to reality by the sight of Eubank's face on a television monitor a few feet away. I watched him talking but could only hear the scuffle which had broken out on the edge of the ring between two rival groups of fans. Eubank hollered at Gary Newbon, the ITV interviewer, 'I want him tested. I want him tested to see if he has anything in his blood. Because he was too . . . he was so strong. I want his urine tested because no one can be that strong . . .' But for me, then, his words were drowned by the ringside brawl. I turned away – feeling sick with the frenzy of the night – and walked up the same aisle which Michael Watson had marched down only an hour before with the crowd singing his name.

Like one of those gaping pedestrians at a roadside accident I succumbed to the horror of the crash. I wanted to look away but I couldn't, I wanted to leave but I didn't. Through the lemony haze of the floodlights I knew that that eleventh-round punch from Eubank had been what I always wanted to see most in a ring. The kind of last-gasp blow which turns defeat into stunning victory. It was a punch, a lethal uppercut, which yanked me from my seat and left me senseless of everything but the sheer spectacle of men working feverishly on each fighter as they slumped down on their tiny stools.

When else as an adult, if not in sex or sleep, had I been so beyond the mundane? There was a difference when Arsenal scored a last-minute winner, or when I disappeared into the closing page of a book or the last scene of a film. Those moments were all imitations of life – whereas that single blow had distilled life so graphically that it conjured up images of death.

But I'd wanted to see that punch; to say that I had witnessed the most unexpected reversal in the ring. I also wanted the conclusive triumph of one man over another. So much of my own life stumbled between two different poles – one marking out a mazed past, the other peering into an unseen future – that I seldom lived wholly in the 'now'. I had felt more alive, at least in the sense of being aware of nothing but the present, in those few minutes spanning the eleventh and twelfth.

But after it was waved to an end I needed the extraordinary to be subsumed by the ordinary again. I wanted both boxers to get up, to hug and even kiss each other, to say 'what a fight, man, what a fight – but it's over now . . .'

But, still, we waited for Watson to get up.

'I don't fucking believe it . . . I don't fucking believe it . . .' a strapping man said as he snapped the waistband on his tuxedo.

'It looks bad for Michael . . . he's still down . . .' his stork-like friend said as he stubbed out his cigar against the back of a chair before craning his neck over the rising crowd.

There was no sign of Watson. He still lay on the canvas. The tall man gasped. 'They're bringing out the stretcher.'

'Nah, nah, he's just knackered . . . he'll be okay . . . won't he?' Tuxedo-man asked.

'He's not moving. Christ, I'm telling you, he's not moving . . .'

I headed for the tunnel leading to the dressing-room. As I waited outside the shadowed passage I kept hearing the same words: 'He's not getting up . . .'

Five minutes passed, then ten.

And then I saw Eric Seccombe, shaking and crying. His pale face jerked and twitched in cruel little spasms. 'No, no . . .' he kept saying. I followed his staring eyes and saw the stretcher carrying Michael Watson. His body lay still on the greying surface. I knew then that something terrible had happened. I heard Eric Seccombe cry again. 'No, Michael, no . . .'

The headline was encased in a square metal box. I remember the swish of a passing car lipping a puddle as I read the words. BOXER IN COMA. The surrounding Sunday morning hush made for an eerie fit. I stared at the headline again. There was no change.

'Pray God – Let Him Live!' howled *The Sun*'s front page the following morning, leading the tabloids' outpouring of heartache. Even the broadsheets devoted pages of speculation on Watson's and boxing's future. It appeared that everyone had an opinion to spout about boxing and whether or not it should be subjected to an immediate ban.

But the most interesting voice in that righteous cacophony belonged to the man who had come closest to Michael Watson after the fight. Peter Hamlyn was a doctor, a neurology surgeon of impeccable composure, who spent the Monday fielding panicky hypotheses whenever he was not checking the deterioration of his patient's brain. Hamlyn's primary concern, a source even of measured anger, focused not on the barbarism of boxing but on the more commonplace inefficiency which had compounded the effect of Eubank's punch.

Hamlyn explained that Watson had suffered an acute haematoma – a chronic bleeding of the brain. It was an injury seen more often in victims of high-speed car-crashes or bomb-blasts. While Eubank had rattled his brain, deterioration had occurred when Watson's head hit the rope. Whiplash caused the brain to spin wildly, activating a steady discharge of blood onto the cranium. Hamlyn stressed that the only remedy was to remove the casualty to a specialist neurosurgical unit within an hour of the brain beginning to bleed. But the brawl at ringside had delayed the arrival of a stretcher; and there were no oxygen tents or other medical apparatus which might have been utilised during the wait.

Although there was a doctor at ringside he still had to phone for an ambulance. Even when Watson was rushed from White Hart Lane, they delivered him to the wrong hospital. He had to be moved again to Barts where, more than seventy minutes after the fight, Hamlyn discovered a fast-swelling blood clot pressing down onto the fighter's brain. The injury worsened as the pressure intensified.

Hamlyn cut Watson's head open to relieve the stress on his brain. It was still uncertain whether he had saved the boxer's life. He refused to offer a hopeful prognosis. If nothing else, Watson had suffered brain damage. Hamlyn did not sound as if he expected much beyond a persistent vegetative state.

On *Newsnight*, facing Jeremy Paxman, he illustrated the impact. Hamlyn explained that the human brain looked not dissimilar to a blancmange concealed in a box. Whenever that 'box' was struck the brain rotated even though it was connected to the sides of the head by a complex pattern of thin strings which serve as blood vessels. Those 'strings' were severed by a hard punch and blood oozed from their torn ends. The brain, moreover, crashed from one side of its box to the other, sustaining internal bleeding. As Hamlyn rolled the plastic mould of a brain around in a cardboard box, a dull reverberation filled the screen.

It was simple to conceive the same heaving of Watson's brain in his own skull – especially when neurologists compared the effect of a punch from a heavyweight like Frank Bruno to a brush with a half-ton truck. The effects of that cerebral rollicking were worsened when the fighter struggled to make the weight limit. The dehydration involved in stringent weight control robbed the brain of vital fluid which would otherwise help protect it.

But Hamlyn refused to condemn boxing. He knew that fighters recognised the risks they took. He dismissed calls to abolish boxing. The only questions he would consider were those determining how best to avoid the needless delay which had so affected Watson in that crucial first hour of his being hurt. There would always be boxers, he concluded, as long as there was deprivation – just as there would always be sports like motor-racing and rock-climbing while humans pushed themselves towards perilous limits.

I could not free my own brain from Chris Eubank's assertion before the Watson fight that he knew that 'my job is to hurt the other fighter as badly as I can. When I have hurt him and he is dazed and bleeding then I must pounce. As he backs against the ropes with pain in his face I must smash my fist into that face again. He expects it, the crowd demand it. They want you to finish the other man off. And that's why I hate boxing.'

After a month, at the end of October 1991, Watson had shown the first slender sign of life beneath the thick quilt of his unconsciousness. He was going to live, Peter Hamlyn thought; but at a level of the barest subsistence. Yet, at the end of November, entering the third month of his coma, Watson showed more of the fight he had brought to the ring when he communicated through a series of eye-blinks. No matter how slight, Hamlyn and the Watson family clung to the hope in those fluttering lids when confronting the complete paralysis afflicting the rest of his body.

There was further improvement early in January when Watson was able to twitch his right arm and leg and open his eyes. That movement was repeated sporadically throughout the month so that, as Eubank contemplated his return to the ring on 1 February 1992, there was speculation that Michael Watson might pick up a steadier pattern of rehabilitation within three more months. But confidence was dented by the certainty that a painstaking path was the only way back to even partial recovery.

Unable to hear what his opponent's thoughts may have been, public attention shifted from Watson to Eubank – grieving in a way only other boxers who had shared an equivalent fate could fathom. I was preoccupied by the story Eubank told me of how close he had been to such terrain before. On that burnished September day I had spent with him in Brighton, he detailed the way in which he had saved another of Barry Hearn's fighters at the end of 1990. Jim McDonnell, a courageous lightweight, had lost an epic encounter against the great Ghanaian world champion, Azumah Nelson, a few months before he entered the ring at the Albert Hall against the American Kenny Vice. Although Vice was little more than a journeyman, this was one fight too far for McDonnell and, Eubank mused, 'he was beaten so badly that it looked as if every punch he had ever taken was sucked up again that night. He was knocked out completely. It seemed like there was no chance he would ever come round. Blood was pouring out of his nose, mouth and ears. He'd been knocked senseless. I was in his dressing-room after that fight and I was crying like a baby.

'People were running around, not knowing what to do. Even the doctors did not have the equipment they needed to save him. He was fading away into a coma and then someone said, "You talk to him! Your voice is distinctive – use it. Talk to him!" And so I stopped crying. I bent down and spoke to Jim McDonnell. Slowly, he came out of it. Boxing did that to him but he was saved by another fighter's voice. It was a miracle, my friend, a small but beautiful miracle . . .'

There were no miracles of any shape or size for Michael Watson in the ensuing weeks – until Muhammad Ali, like a ravaged god, came to visit him. The well of small-time celebrities circling Watson's hospital ward had dried up after the first month. Until then a cachet of cool had enveloped the Queen Elizabeth II wing at Barts. Gordon Burn in *The Observer* detailed how it had been considered hip by a certain sector of London's glitterati to meet at the hospital and 'hang with Michael' – before they moved on to Brown's in Covent Garden or the more street-level Phoenix Apollo in the East End. The former boxer Terry Marsh called them 'the mercenary Samaritans' as they swanned through the front entrance where the paparazzi waited. Most of the boxers who came to visit – especially the most famous, like Frank Bruno and Barry McGuigan – chose instead to enter Barts via an underground tunnel. Their presence would at least have been meaningful to the Watson family who knew the depth of Michael's devotion to the ring.

They guarded their privacy while watching the jostling for 'I knew the victim' status. A woman who had been my initial contact with the fighter visited him for eight hours every day at Barts and refused to shed her anonymity to the gaggle of reporters. The newspapers were oppressive in their desire to buy her story but she remained admirably detached. 'I don't think anybody ever stopped to ask Michael,' she said, 'whether he would have wanted to become a tragic hero . . .'

The demands on Watson's immediate family – his mother, uncle and young daughters – were intense. The estranged mother of his two little girls chose to keep them away from the hospital where he at last lay awake but still seriously ill. His mother, Joan, and uncle eventually signed an exclusive deal to talk only to the *Daily Mirror*. Despite the severity of his disability, Watson displayed an aversion to the continuing voyeurism.

But Muhammad Ali was different. When Ali finally came to Watson in February 1992, the *Mirror* detailed his sojourn with a tear in its inky eye. Yet the 'Boxers in Bedside Vigil' was concocted by London's king of PR sleaze, Max Clifford, fresh from his toe-sucking exploits with Antonia de Sancha and his earlier 'Freddie Starr Ate My Hamster' coup. Although Ali was in town to help Clifford orchestrate the hyping of a London restaurant, the symbolism of two damaged fighters meeting in hospital proved immune to questions of taste – particularly as the visit of Ali so gratified Watson that soon afterwards he began to string short sentences together and respond to basic commands.

The photographs I saw the next day in the *Mirror* appeared gravely static as Ali stood over Michael Watson. Ali's face looked like a plastic bag filled with brackish water. He tried to mobilise a smile for the camera and the young fighter staring up at him. Watson's own face was painfully thin, with none of the spark which made 'The Force' a less-than-absurd name for him at the height of his career. Ali, meanwhile, faltered through a few words of comfort and hand-squeezes. They shadowed each other, Michael Watson and Muhammad Ali, as broken mementos, both looking as distant from their former lives as the other. The cameras flashed with a light which could not permeate their filmy gaze. They were lost; and it looked from the expressions on their half-smiling faces as if they knew that truth better than anyone else.

February 1992

Chris Eubank's own deliverance resumed with a stutter – for he had spilled more than just the proverbial blood of another man. He was fated, some said, to receive punishment for what he had done, slowly, cut by cut.

When we met for the first time after the Watson fight I tried to avoid adding to his burden of responsibility. I kept up the small-talk for five minutes before I breathed the words we'd both evaded. 'But Michael Watson . . .' I said hesitantly.

'Michael Watson . . . ah . . . what can I possibly say about Michael Watson?'

Eubank looked away from me and out the window of the hotel lounge where we sat. The silence made me shift in embarrassment. I searched for words to cover the look which had settled like shiny black marble over Eubank's taut features.

'I've noticed how you always call him by his full name – Michael Watson . . .' I said.

'Yes. We want to remember him as whole again, as a complete person. He's always "Michael Watson" to me, always "Michael Watson".'

'And yet, in the build-up to the last fight,' I said, 'there was much talk of disrespect.'

Eubank raised an index finger and looked set to wag it at me in rebuke. But he held it high in the air for a moment before, changing his mind, curling it into the tight ball of his hand. 'Before our second fight,' he eventually answered, 'I said things about Michael Watson, things I now regret. I said Michael Watson was transparent, that he was nothing. How wrong could I be? Michael Watson was a superman that night – but, in the end, his humanity took over. He was just human at the end – a man whose life has been destroyed.'

Four months had passed since the fight. Michael Watson lay still in Barts.

Eubank had announced that he would fight on, saying that boxing was the lone route open to him to make the type of money he needed to 'secure the future of both myself and my family. I, like Michael Watson, am a fighter. This is my trade and I will continue to box as long as my economic circumstances dictate that this is necessary. I have to fight until I have enough money. My heart is with Michael Watson but it will not help him for me to give up my living. I've said this to people – they cannot know how sorry I am for Michael, how sorry I am for the mother, how sorry I am for the man's family and friends. But allow me to live with my sorrow, allow me to continue my business, allow me to be a businessman too . . .'

There was more sensitivity in his voice than there might appear in those words on paper. Despite his yearning to return to money-making, Eubank realised the impossibility of his plea. For, as Gordon Burn wrote, 'Few people can hear the name Eubank without also hearing a sub-echo of the name Michael Watson; flickering behind the first name these days there seems to be an ineradicable after-image of the other: "Eubank/Watson, Eubank/Watson . . ." It's like one of those flashing neon signs where the lineaments of the tubes not lit up are always visible. Except it isn't flashing: the Eubank element is still cosmic blue, hotlips pink, generating heat. But the Watson part is out and permanently gathering dust.'

I thought that I had seen enough of boxing. I had had my fill. I wanted to forget about fighters. But then, in an increasingly catastrophic plot, which could have been written to measure for a downbeat soap-opera, Chris Eubank killed a man. On 7 February, only a week after I had seen him return to the ring with a lucky win against South Africa's Sugar-Boy Malinga, Eubank's Range Rover swerved out of control and hit a motorway worker at speed. Kevin Lawlor died instantly and, once more, Chris Eubank had the smell of tragedy on his hands.

Eubank had been driving fast towards Gatwick Airport with his brother and a friend. They were late for their holiday flight to Jamaica – where the boxer was due to rest as part of his own recovery from the Watson fight. Although he was unlikely to be charged with manslaughter, the effect of another calamity on the fighter's already capricious mind appeared ominous. I could only imagine what he might see in the killing of a man he had never even met. Eubank's own brother, moreover, prepared to sue him for negligent driving.

Chris Eubank's latest brush with death happened on Friday the seventh; on Monday the tenth, Tyson was finally convicted of rape in Indiana and sentenced to six years in prison – thus joining Michael Watson in a similarly grim and restricted place.

Tyson, Eubank and Watson: so different and yet so besieged. I wondered then if they were right, those superstitious voices who claim that such trauma always comes in dark clusters of three.

3

THIS IS BOXING, BABY

THEN, AS IF TO ILLUMINATE MY OWN CONTRASTING GOOD luck, a girl phoned me. She came out of nowhere, breathing down the line, laughing like a dream, telling me that she'd just had her legs cast by Madame Tussauds, that her name was Alison. She was about to complete her post-grad degree in architecture by designing a rubber brothel in which she'd hang those legs of hers in glistening latex and plaster. I guessed then that she knew nothing about boxing. She said instead that she'd bought a book I had written, taken it home with her for Christmas and now she wondered if I'd help her meet a couple of the eminent London prostitutes described in that otherwise forgotten corker.

Well, not even Mighty Mike could compete with that scenario. My head whirled as I tried to figure out whether this might prove to be the definitive blind date with a funky south-of-the-river London babe or end up as a spooky encounter with a woman who admitted serenely that she actually hailed from, of all the hotbeds of sexual intrigue, Harpenden, Herts. After the homeboys how about Home Counties Girl? Funny ha-ha or just funny-peculiar? I played hard to get for a week or two, pretending to think more about the sombre state of boxing's hinterland than of this husky-voiced honey; and then I gave up. I met her in a bar, we got drunk and went home together. The sweet ending to our little story being that she went on to exhibit her alternative brothel while, two years on, I married her.

But in the beginning I attempted to keep her away from the ring. With Tyson in prison and Watson in a hospital bed I could hardly hold up any pretty or cerebral pictures to convince her I was embroiled in anything but a dehumanising business. Boxing was suffering and I was no longer sure I wanted to be around its terminal decline.

Tyson's appeal against his sentence had been quashed by a 2–1 majority, despite the costly presence of Alan Dershowitz in his new legal team. Reports from his cell confirmed that he was 'bitter and mistrusting'. There was further chaos in the heavyweight division as the newly undisputed champion from Brownsville, Riddick Bowe, dumped his WBC belt in the bin rather than face Lennox Lewis – who promptly fished the title out of the trash and accepted the WBC's offer to become their preferred champion.

Without a recognisable heavyweight hero, boxing has always struggled. With Tyson gone and Bowe, Lewis and the WBO's Tommy Morrison all claiming to be 'world' heavyweight champions, the fight game's stained reputation was completely shredded. The heavyweight division had lapsed into the kind of anarchy which dominated the early '80s when a collection of mugs had simultaneously flashed championship belts. It had needed a brooding Tyson to re-establish the line of ascendancy which stretched from Ali, Frazier, Liston and Marciano to Louis, Tunney, Dempsey and Johnson. Those lustrous days looked to be lost forever – and not just for the big boys either.

Michael Watson, in the harshest example, had started talking again; but he strung words together brokenly. Although he told Reg Gutteridge in *Boxing News* that 'it's a miracle – I know that I am not alone', more attention was paid to comments in *The Sun* where he professed his loathing for Eubank. He stressed that he'd barred his former rival from visiting him; and yet the bedridden Watson could not easily lift his eyes from the video of their last fight which he watched over and over again.

Eubank found unexpected solace in his trips to Indiana to meet Prisoner 922335 – as the baddest man had become known. I remember him lecturing me at length on Tyson's innocence during a public workout in a Peckham shopping centre. The man from Hove had just returned from an encounter with Tyson and, inspired by 'Michael's internal strength', he was set to put right injustices which afflicted everyone from Iron Mike to 'inner-city youths' living in Peckham and Moss Side.

But Eubank's trouble remained that too few of us believed him when he uttered his various pearls of wisdom. It was as if he spoke from neither the head nor the heart but in mere bubbles of affectation. Even when he talked plainly his words could be misconstrued. A year after the White Hart Lane fight, a tearful Eubank had offered Watson his world title belt, admitting that he had been outfought by a superior man. Watson's contempt held. So the rambling conqueror ploughed his showman's furrow, pulling in million-pound purses against paltry opposition. Across country, meanwhile, a half-paralysed and brain-damaged Watson watched him on the gleaming but silent screen.

It was not difficult to be diverted from this bleakness. So for our first six months together I skirted the edges of my boxing obsession, getting Alison to talk about other things she liked. I soon learnt more than I'd previously known about strange contemporary artists, modelling, vodka and the potential use of rubber as a building material.

But I kept slipping back into the dark – even in moments of apparent safety when the new light of my life would tell me about the big mad world of fashion. She'd point to a glossy pic of Naomi Campbell and I'd mutter, ''course I know who she is – she went out with Tyson for a while, just before Robin Givens . . .'; she'd say something about a poor but supremely talented Brixton boy like John Galliano being destined for the big time in Paris and I'd nod dumbly and say that Eubank preferred Versace even though he was from Peckham; she'd articulate the thrill of walking through the stagy gloom and into the glare of a New York cat-walk and I'd concede that it might almost be as compelling as a fighter's approach to the ring. Maybe, I mused, Kate Moss and Mike Tyson had something in common after all.

She'd wink at me quizzically, thinking, 'just what the hell has he said now? Another boxing joke? Why?'

I'd stumble on and ask her about being an architect – and then say that I knew at least three professional fighters who would choose architecture if they could one day study instead of fight.

'What's this thing about boxing?' she eventually asked.

How do you begin to explain boxing to a woman who has never given any thought to its supposedly nobler features? How do you casually tell the girl you're about to move in with that, sometimes, you stay up late into the night watching videos of men hitting each other in the face? How do you glide past the name of Michael Watson? How do you account for the fact that for every green-spined Penguin classic there are at least five back issues of not only *The Ring* but also *Boxing News*, *Boxing Monthly*, *Boxing Illustrated* and even the lowlier *KO*, *World Boxing* and *Boxing Outlook*? How do you acknowledge the fact that, essentially, you're a connoisseur of violence?

Now I'm no great fan of Mickey Rourke but, when you're getting desperate, sometimes you'll do anything. You'll even start talking about *9½ Weeks*. She'd loved it. I hadn't; but I knew ol' Mick was big on boxing.

'Really?' she sighed politely.

I meandered on about how the stubbled one had got the bug so bad that he had even given up on Hollywood in order to ply a humbler trade as a four-round preliminary fighter. The implication of this being that she was actually lucky that, even though I hadn't sculpted my body for the ring, I was not as crazy as Mickey Rourke. Fighting some tough Mexican journeymen would not be quite the same as slipping a black blindfold on Kim Basinger.

'I'm sure you're right,' she said drily.

I took that as a cue for my next move. 'He's going to be on TV tonight, y'know . . .'

'Who?'

'Mickey Rourke.'

'Is he?' she said with barely a flicker of interest.

'He's gonna be on with Jonathon Ross – and a couple of boxers . . .'

'Which boxers?' she asked more enthusiastically.

'Eubank, Benn . . . and an American fighter called James Toney . . .'

'Chris Eubank?' she laughed.

'Yes,' I admitted shyly.

'And Nigel Benn?'

'They're fighting each other again.'

'Sounds great,' she said; and I knew her well enough by then to know that she meant it. So we sat down that night, my girl and I, and watched a couple of fighters threaten each other for the first of many times.

She felt her eyes prick when Eubank spoke about Watson. She laughed when he and Benn traded their predictable sobriquets and asked why, again like Tyson, they both lisped over the letter 's'. But she said that she could also feel the goose-bumps rise at the thought of them turning towards each other at the sound of the first bell. As much as she could hardly wait to see what would happen, she wondered how they could stand it.

Before I could welcome her formally to boxing's warped world, the camera cut away to the guy who had given me an excuse to switch on the box. Mickey Rourke mooched awkwardly in his LA gym while he and Jonathon Ross swapped banalities by satellite. Ross was ensconced in his London studio where, on the garish sofas, Benn and Eubank eyeballed each other. We chuckled at the absurdity of it, my sweetheart and I, boxing pals at last.

And then, sliding alongside the movie-star like he had an ice-pick in his pocket, he came into shocking view.

'Who's that?' she murmured.

James Toney was a frightening man when he gave that look, like he had murder in mind. They called him 'Lights Out' – a defiant alias to brandish in American towns as devoutly illuminated as Las Vegas and Los Angeles. But I knew how many men he had knocked out both in and outside the ring; for 'Lights Out', too, connoted an inner darkness.

'He doesn't look too happy, does he?' she observed snappily.

'Uh-uh . . .'

'Why not?'

I tried to explain the unsettling stories of Toney's destruction. The kicked-in doors, splintered tables and smashed mirrors were rumoured to be nothing compared to the damage he might do one day. When the rage came down he was capable of anything.

Toney was the one 'world' champion who had the capacity to match Tyson's missing aura. A former crack-dealer, he retained an urge to intimidate. He spoke with the sullen threat of a drive-by shooter. His photographs and interviews reinforced that narrative – for Toney's ability to spread fear in the middleweight ranks and to simultaneously pull in the TV ratings centred on his bravado. But as we watched him fume at Rourke's side I suspected that his resentment was real. I thought James Toney might be unhinged from reality; a little like Eubank but only more so. Toney looked crazier, wilder, darker, scarier.

Yet his divergence from Eubank tugged at me more than anything. They were both unbeaten 'world' super-middleweight champions of rival boxing organisations. But the one was as layered as the other was stark. Where Eubank feigned erudition, Toney celebrated crudity. While the British dandy expressed his disdain for boxing, the American terror savoured the ferocity of his trade. If 'Simply the Best' was a showbizzy Tina Turner ditty then 'Lights Out' was a gun-pumping rap. Where Eubank enabled me to flaunt equivocation towards the fight-game's tangled moralities, Toney forced a gut-deep fall for boxing.

Eubank tried to look enviable when he instructed us to do as he did: 'To look good, to be good like me . . .' Yet I could still hear the catch in his voice as I watched Eubank's alter-ego at work. 'The Good Man' and 'The Bad Boy' epitomised this business's ability to set one extreme against the other.

I realised then that I was drawn more towards the bad guy, Toney. He depicted boxing's primal appeal with telling accuracy. Yet he was also managed by a middle-aged Jewish woman, Jackie Kallen, who, with his mother, Sherry Toney, presented a unique female front to the Lights Out camp. But, on Jonathon Ross's fluffy show, the women were nowhere to be seen as Toney spat out his insults.

Eubank and Benn were bums. He could take them both out in one night, one after the other. They were 'nuthin'. He could kill them any time the fancy took him. Toney boiled on, turning up the burners of insolence and danger, his eyes blazing in an impassive black face.

Benn came back at Toney with something about 'thick' and 'plank'; but Eubank was oddly silent. I thought, like me, he was chilled to the bone. But Eubank may have been the lucky one. While he was off to Manchester with Benn I was on my way towards the Wild West for a Lights Out face-to-face.

Suddenly she turned to me. 'Is this the guy you're meeting in Tulsa?'

'Yes,' I mumbled, 'it's him . . .'

'Oh, shit . . .' she giggled.

'Frightening or what?'

'I dunno . . . sometimes he looks like a little boy.'

'A little boy?' I replied incredulously.

'Well,' she said seriously, 'he tries so hard to look mean. But he's got such a sweet face. Maybe, deep down, he's a bit of a sweetie.'

'Maybe . . .' I trailed away in doubtful hope.

I thought of Alison as soon as I hit Tulsa. I missed her already. It was perishing and the skies were heavy with the threat of snow. The grey flatlands of Oklahoma flashed by as the taxi sped towards downtown.

'So, tell me, bud,' Hank the cabbie drawled with dubious intent, 'what's ya business in Tulsa?'

'Boxing,' I said glumly.

'Boxing!' Hank turned to grin demonically at me. 'You here for the fights?'

'Yesssssss!' I yelped back as Hank skidded across the icy island separating our side of the highway from that filled with a stream of cars sharking as fast as they could out of town.

'Oh boy, oh boy!' Hank whooped. The steering wheel spun madly through his hands. We careered back on course, hitting a hump of kerb and slithering across a mercifully empty stretch of road. 'Ain't that a gas!' Hank chortled as, bolstered by our heady escape, he pressed his foot down hard on the accelerator. 'Hell's bells, maybe boxing ain't dead after all!'

'Are you going to the fights?' I bleated while Hank switched lanes again without a backward glance. I clawed at the door handle, searching for a steadying grip as we skidded down the freezing white boulevard.

'Dead right!'

'Tommy Morrison?' I asked, hoping Hank would slow down long enough to consider Oklahoma's favourite son – the white slugger who had launched an implausible claim to be the world's most exciting heavyweight now that Tyson was gone.

'Well, Tommy Morrison is always Tommy Morrison,' Hank sniggered with alarming logic, 'but I'm watchin' someone else . . .'

'James Toney?'

'Hell, yeah! – man, I'd like to see his butt whipped!'

'Why?'

'Never could stand that type of nigger.'

I glared back at Hank. The full force of my liberal huff diverted me from the fact that we were almost flying. 'Niggers With Attitude?' I mocked in disbelief, thinking that a nut like Hank could not possibly be into original gangsta hip-hop as well as boxing.

'You got it, bud!'

'What sort of attitude?' I probed, all thoughts of an early death banished while I imagined myself as Clarence Darrow in the deepest mid-west.

'That young nigger attitude – like he's out to murder every one of us! Well, fuck him I say, fuck him!' Hank hollered in time to the swaying speedometer.

I closed my eyes and thought about James 'Lights Out' Toney as Hank and I hurtled towards Tulsa, or Hell.

'Fuck Toney,' he cried again. 'Fuck him!'

Hank's devilish cackle echoed in my head an hour later as James Toney stared down upon us with derision. His 'fuck you' glower looked to be on knife-sharpening terms with the homicidal. Toney was only one of twelve people seated at a long press-conference table in the swish Doubletree Hotel in central Tulsa; but he may as well have sat alone on Death Row.

He was dressed in black, in a hooded top and tracksuit pants. His gold earring glinted in the chandeliered light, catching our collective eye again and again. It was as if we could not tear our gaze from him, as if he had cast a deadly spell over us.

Toney had always made much of a ghetto boast that, five years before, his fists had not been enough. He'd carried a gun whenever he stepped out onto the street. It gave him protection against the crazies and other hustlers. Toney traded in white rock on the fringes of Detroit and in Ann Arbor, the college town in Michigan which had been his home for eighteen years. But the gun had also made him look cool. James Toney was a mean mother-fucker, but he still wanted to be liked.

In his last year at Huron High he was the school's star quarterback and a dealer in downtown crack. It was a slick package, telling his homeboys that he was making things happen both on and off the field. He was up for a football scholarship but it felt better to be running with his gang, the naughty 'Bad Boys Inc.', making some real money and spreading it around.

Unlike Tyson, there had been a choice for Toney. It was not just that he could opt for the football field instead of the street corner. Toney did not come from a tenement block where the stairwells were littered with bottle-neck pipes and they slept twelve to a room. He was an only child and he lived with his mother, Sherry, in their compact house. She ran a small bakery, had gained an MA in English and Drama and always ensured there was plenty of food, clothing and books at home.

The problem here, as with Tyson, and so often in America, came with the father – the lack of a father. James Toney Snr had beaten up and then shot and wounded Sherry before deserting her and their one-year-old son. He had never been back and that day haunted his boy. Twenty-three years later James Toney, the International Boxing Federation (IBF) super-middle-weight champion of the world, swore that he would gun down his father the moment he next laid eyes on him.

The beginnings of this story were not that extraordinary in the context of professional boxing. A sadistic father gone missing, ending up in jail, a mother labouring on her own, a young black boy 'hanging with the homies', getting up to no good. Even a ring greenhorn like Alison knew that the best fighters came from the street. Within the sanctum of boxers and trainers those gnarled roots were taken for granted. But Toney's life assumed a deeper resonance. This was partly because he was so matter-of-fact about his involvement in crack; more so because he was boxing's equivalent of the gangster homeboy. And no one was more feared or misunderstood in white

America than those black outsiders.

But I was sure that Toney could not be all bad. It was that softening of certainty which made boxing perennially intriguing. If I could get beyond that 'fuck you' sheen of the hardest men, of fighters like Toney and Tyson, I thought life might yield something more responsive. After all, not even a modern socialite like Eubank could match Toney when breaking down boxing's oldest barriers of gender.

In Tulsa, where he was preparing to defend his super-middleweight title against the number-one contender, Tony Thornton, the allure of Toney's female entourage was startling to see. The four of them led the Lights Out team from the front, a sleek posse like nothing else in boxing. They veiled the surrounding machismo with sumptuous style. Apart from his mother, Sherry, dressed in fire-engine red and flashing her painted nails and lips with intent, the Toney girls included Sarah, James's bright and lovely fiancée, and Jasmine, their eight-month-old baby who sported a snazzy polka-dot bow on the top of her tiny head. They sat together in the front row of the packed conference hall while their favourite man did his bad boy routine. Alongside Toney, of course, posed the blonde, big-haired, immaculately made-up, designer-dressed and Yorkshire terrier-carrying Jackie Kallen – the first woman to manage a fighter to world-champion status.

Toney admitted that he owed everything to Sherry and Jackie. His mother had put him on the straight and narrow and Jackie kept him there. They had persuaded him to trade punches rather than drugs. Toney conceded that he did not need the easy money that came from selling crack. He'd just liked it; and it sometimes felt as if it could fill up the hole where his father had been. Five years before, when he was injured on the football field and his potential career as a quarterback lay in ruins, it seemed as if he might only find sanctuary in another gun and a wider range of streets from which to sell.

But Toney had never forgotten the ring. When he was not yet a teenager and already fighting in alleyways, his mother had taken him to the local gym. 'I told James straight,' Sherry said, 'you might as well learn to fight properly. I got James boxing. It did him the world of good.'

Boxing introduced Toney to a code of masculinity which had been missing from his life. But he also learnt the loneliness in fighting one-on-one. The more distinct appeal of football and the streets lay as much in the company of other men as in the money they promised. Fighters, however, were considered to be tough guys round the badlands of Detroit. Some of them even became unimaginably rich. As solitary as he knew it to be, boxing gave Toney fresh expectation. He went back to the gym. It was then that he first saw her.

Jackie Kallen captivated him. She was white, Jewish and middle-aged. Kallen also looked wealthy, she spoke differently and he couldn't work out 'what the fuck she was tryin' to prove'. It was only later that he understood that she too had turned to boxing to fill a yearning. Kallen thought Toney was a mean-looking kid – but he interested her. He was always swearing, punching lockers and kicking over spit-buckets. Yet she also noticed his exceptionally fast hands and feet, rock-solid chin and knockout punch in both fists. Beyond Mike Tyson, few boxers can claim all these attributes. Fewer still had Toney's intensity. When his original manager, Johnny 'Ace' Smith, was shot dead in a drugs deal, Kallen stepped in smartly.

In Tulsa, Jackie Kallen stood out in the peculiar dozen seated on the Doubletree podium. Eleven men and one woman, six black and six white fight figures. It was symptomatic of boxing's incestuous circle that there were so many familiar characters alongside her. Kallen was up against some of boxing's shrewdest operators. Bob Arum presided over proceedings, oozing all the lawyerish guile and bluff charm he had brought to bear in twenty-five years of promoting fights – most of that time spent as Don King's most formidable adversary. Another of King's great enemies sat next to Arum. Bill Cayton, having lost Tyson to Big Don, now pinned his wallet to Tommy Morrison.

With boxing robbed of its premier attraction in Tyson, the way was clear for the James & Jackie Show to take over. Tulsa was merely the latest stopover in their 'Lady & The Champ' trail of glory.

Along the table Eddie Mustafa Muhammad, a friend of Tyson and a former world light-heavyweight champion, presented himself as a top trainer. There'd been bad blood between him and Kallen six months before when Toney had beaten Iran Barkley to win his super-middleweight belt. But Muhammad and the various other promoters, managers and trainers were full of conviviality once more, sprouting vivid chestnuts about bringing a classic night of boxing to the mid-west, doing their best to sell the few remaining tickets left for a promotion billed by Arum as 'The Tulsa Shootout'.

Three days before the fighting began, the quietest voices belonged to the four boxers. The surly Toney and his stolidly dignified opponent, Tony Thornton; and the two heavyweights, the unheralded Michael Bentt and the golden local boy, Morrison. But then, as if a switch had been turned on in his head, Toney began to rant. He objected to the fact that he had to concede top billing to Morrison. He was by far the superior fighter. In fact, Toney bristled, there was not a boxer in the world who could beat him. He might be three divisions lighter than the heavyweights but he could beat every single one of the podgy bums. Jackie put a manicured hand on his arm to calm him. The other 'Shootout' dignitaries twitched in their plush seats, waiting for the next Lights Out detonation.

Toney's rage was notorious. After a fight against Mike MacCallum, Toney furiously pursued his rival's fifty-one-year-old lawyer. The portly and bespectacled Milton Chawsky had suggested that MacCallum should have been given the verdict over Toney in an enthralling contest. Sending tables spinning through the air and screaming, 'You blind bastard!', Toney went after Chawsky, only being prevented from doing more serious damage by a gang of security men. 'I'm gonna get you, fat boy!' snarled Toney, before turning his tirade onto a more suitable target in the media audience – Julian Jackson, the hardest puncher in boxing. 'I won't make you wait, motherfucker!' young James whispered. He made Tyson's repartee sound like a simpering voiceover of cookie recipes. Nose-to-nose with Toney, the more sensible Jackson backed down.

Toney and his 6ft 7in bodyguard, Andre Williams, had been involved in another brawl at an Atlantic City media gathering. Williams had tried to stare down Iran Barkley, the shaven-skulled and self-styled 'automatic psychopath'. Quite why Toney needed a bodyguard when he was so intent on proving himself the toughest man in the business may have puzzled Barkley's burly trainer, Eddie Muhammad, for he interrupted the question-and-answer session in eccentric fashion. He threw himself at Williams and sent him crashing to the floor. Toney decided not to assist his giant bodyguard but challenged instead two other colourful oddballs – the promoter Butch Lewis, famous for wearing expensive tuxedos and gold neck chokers without a shirt underneath, and his fighter Bernard 'The Executioner' Hopkins who was accompanied by a couple of axe-wielding jokers dressed in black hangmen's hoods. A different security unit had to separate the scufflers – once again suggesting that a James Toney press conference was just like the wrestling. The crucial difference being that, with Toney, the violence was real.

Inside the ring, however, any resemblance to cartoon destruction was buried beneath his sublime skills. Toney was already being spoken of, and by experts other than him, as the best fighter in the world, as the greatest pound-for-pound champion in contemporary boxing. There was an intelligence to his fighting which belied the crude 'Lights Out' persona.

Yet, like Tyson, Toney needed nurturing. But where Mighty Mike had Bill Cayton and Don King, Toney had Sherry and Jackie. While the heavyweight's 'bad intentions' spun out of control, Kallen realised that her fighter could channel his fury into boxing. She and Sherry built up Toney's self-esteem, convincing him that his most destructive urges could be changed into a winning force.

Toney's breakthrough into the championship ranks had occurred in May 1991, in Davenport, Iowa, a small town on the banks of the Mississippi where the old riverside gambling boats offered the mid-west's sole response to Vegas. It was then that James and Sherry had shown the world – and proved to Toney Snr that they had made it despite everything he had done to them.

Davenport was also home to Michael Nunn, considered then to be boxing's most dexterous fighter. But Jackie thought that James might beat him. The rest of boxing had laughed at her while she manoeuvred her fighter into that supposedly hopeless championship contest. The unbeaten Nunn had held the IBF middleweight title for nearly three years. His seventh defence, against Toney, a 20–1 underdog, was meant to be his homecoming dance, a flowing reward after all those years of toiling on the road.

During the weigh-in Nunn derided Toney as a punk. He flicked imaginary fleas from the Lights Out head. As if to remind us that such crudity made the world of professional boxing different from those of golf or chess, Toney screamed: 'I'm going to kill you, you motherfucker! Gonna break your bones, gonna break your fucking bones!'

In the ring, Toney wore his favourite black trunks with a golden Star of David etched onto the left thigh in honour of Kallen. The champion was dressed in Polly-Anna white. He stood tall, with a smirk on his handsome face as he was introduced by the deeply tanned and similarly buffed ring-announcer, the aptly named Michael Buffer.

Kallen was distraught. She hugged her fighter as Buffer completed his rip-roaring preamble. He oiled his words and turned their syllables inside out. In the muggy Mississippi air, 'Let's Get Ready To Rumble' was transformed into a howling 'LET'S GIT RE-ADYYY TOOO RRRRUMBBLLLLLE!'

For the first five rounds Nunn picked off Toney at will. He thudded in hooks to the body and jabs to the head. Toney seemed outclassed – only landing a pitiful 12 per cent of his punches. But I was entertained by his audacity.

Bill Miller, his venerable trainer, was concerned. 'You've got to press him, son, otherwise we're goin' nowhere tonight . . .'

'It's all right,' Toney said, 'I can hear him. He's breathing like a freight-train . . .'

A few rounds later Miller chided: 'You're losing it, son, you're losing it!'

'Don't worry about it,' Toney retorted calmly, 'he's not goin' the distance!'

As they moved into the eighth round, Nunn was ahead on the first judge's card by three points, by five on the next, and seven on the last. Toney needed a knockout. He began by snapping right hands into the champion's face.

'He's showing you he can be hit!' Miller exclaimed as he wiped his fighter's face.

'Very much so!' Toney agreed, his slanted eyes glinting.

I admired his decorum amid such adversity. Toney came out like a freight-train of his own at the start of the eleventh. He threw five big punches at the back-pedalling Nunn. Another right upper-cut rocked Nunn and he never even saw the huge left hook which swung in from the blindside. It exploded on his chin. If there is truly such a thing as a beautiful punch then that emerged from the perfect mould. It was breathtaking.

Stretched out on the canvas, Nunn battled even to lift his head for the first five seconds. But, somehow, he hauled himself up just before the count of ten. Toney went after him like a starving Doberman chasing a bleeding rabbit. Another four right hands crashed into Nunn. He slumped forward against the ropes and then onto his knees. A white towel sailed through the air just as the referee intervened.

After pitching over with exhausted rapture, Toney made himself a platform on the ropes. He stood there with his black boots splayed on the middle rung and shouted out at the 10,000 people who had refused to believe him: 'I told you so! I told you so!' James Toney, at twenty-two, had become the world's youngest middleweight champion for more than fifty years.

Sherry and Jackie allowed their tears to fall. Mrs Toney wore a great big black hat and clung onto her son with flashing red fingernails while Ms Kallen did the same, repeating over and over: 'Oh my God . . . oh my God, you did it . . . oh my God . . .'

I liked the fact that, on live television a few minutes later, in his slurring Michigan drawl, Toney dedicated his win to the two women – as a birthday gift to Jackie and as an early Mother's Day present to his Mom, 'who has done so much to support and encourage me'. He spoke earnestly as the sweat poured from him and the women cried.

Barely an hour later, Toney told bewildered reporters that: 'Yeah, I sold crack; sure, I used a gun . . .' But before they could even phone in the latest 'Street-Thug Champ: The Next Tyson' scoop he said something different – '. . . but my mom is my idol.'

It made me smile and believe that something more complex ticked behind the Angry Man mask. Just as Eubank had done in offering up his singular marriage proposal moments after beating Benn, Toney barked out his love for a woman. But he blurred the roughest edges from being both an archetypal motherfucker and his mama's own boy. 'I've only got one idol: Mom!' he repeated. 'She taught me that if you want something, you have to work hard . . .' In return he jogged with Sherry Toney each morning at dawn and did alternate afternoon shifts in her Ann Arbor bakery – 'Speciality Cakes & Pies'. And when he was not with Sherry he was more than likely to be in the gym, with Jackie looking on.

That pattern prevailed as he added the IBF super-middleweight title less than two years later, in February 1993, in a consummate display against Iran 'The Blade' Barkley at Caesars Palace in Las Vegas.

His pre-fight exchanges with Barkley had numbered amongst the most profane in boxing history – and yet at the bell he demonstrated a talent as cool as it was precise. Toney did not run as I thought he might have done against the heavier champion. He could have used his twenty-four-year-old legs to full effect against a bruiser who was eight years older than him. But he chose to stand in the centre of the ring where he locked his radar onto Iran. He boxed as if he was playing chess against a computer, showing too much spontaneous imagination to be beaten by a mechanical opponent. His punching was pointedly accurate. He picked off Barkley with a calculating speed. Slipping beneath Barkley's punches, it was as if all his fury had been distilled into one long blue burn. Toney glowed as steadily in the ring as he flared recklessly on the outside. His resentment towards Barkley, his father and the universe in general was moulded into defiant profes-sionalism. He never lifted his eyes or his fists from the forge of Barkley's huge bald head.

Occasionally a big Blade right skimmed Toney's own sheared scalp but it would be replied to instantly with crisp counter-punching. Even when he was pinned against the ropes he accepted the shift in relaxed certitude and opened up with fabulously quick combinations.

'He's a sucker for the uppercut,' Bill Miller mentioned between rounds. Without further prompting, Toney went out and let rip an uppercut which sent Barkley's gumshield flying like he had just spat out a thick crimson wedge of gum for fear of choking. It shot out the side of his mouth with a force which bounced it across the canvas. The referee picked it up as carefully as he might have lifted an old man's dentures. As they washed the black mouth-shield I noticed that Barkley had begun to swallow some of the blood pouring from his broken nose and torn mouth.

In his corner they worked frantically to restore some of Iran's vision by softening the swelling. Even below the small dark hills of his eyes, the champion cut a doleful figure. Thick cotton swabs were stuffed up both his nostrils. His mouth hung open like a door on one remaining hinge. In the opposite corner, eighteen feet away, Toney enjoyed a light towelling down as if he had just won the first set of a game of Country Club tennis. He maintained a look of distant absorption as Miller praised his clinical excellence.

In the fourth and fifth he exhibited an astonishing range of punches – an overhand right, a left hook, a straight right, a jolting right uppercut; triple jabs followed by a fantastic hook-cross-uppercut combination; two straight right hands melting into a slicing hook, another overhand right, a second left hook and then four, five, six, seven unanswered jabs which reshaped the crumpled map of Iran's face just a little more. Miller welcomed his adroit technician back with a laudatory, 'You're taking him to school, son, you're taking him to school!'

By the start of the eighth I was not the only one calling for the end. Barkley's sore head and bleeding face were smeared in Vaseline. He looked like a mummy being wheeled out of the embalming chamber. Sherry shrugged at Jackie as if to ask the point of the fight continuing. In her mind only James's father deserved that sort of shellacking.

At the end of the ninth, Eddie Muhammad turned to his lonely champion and said, 'That's it! I'm not going to let you go back out there . . .'

'No!' Barkley growled.

'You can't see,' Muhammad sighed with gruff tenderness.

'No!' Barkley repeated – his word being less an acknowledgement of partial blindness than an affirmation of his heart size.

Muhammad glanced meaningfully at the ringside doctor as he tried to cut the gloves from Barkley's fists. Even the white tape there was reddened. At last the doctor nodded to the referee who waved it over.

Muhammad stroked Barkley's bald pate as the new champion scaled the ropes and screamed out at us once more: 'I told you so!' as if his exultant voice might carry not only to those hacks who had questioned his finesse but to the father who had left him for dead.

Sherry smiled and climbed the apron of the ring to hold him again. Ann Arbor's 'Speciality Cakes & Pies' team were on the sweetest rise.

Six months later, at the Doubletree in Tulsa, Toney refused the slow bake. He bubbled again towards the boil. The large British tabloid contingent had taunted him with repeated references to Eubank and Benn, who had just drawn a more tedious skirmish in Manchester. A middle-aged man from the *Daily Star* was especially dogged. Recalling his frivolous brush with the two British boxers and Jonathon Ross, Toney smouldered at a nation's inadequacies.

'I hate the British! Always the same! Y'all know shit about boxing! You're losers! Bums too! Eubank, Benn, the lot o' you! I'm tellin' all o' you who live in Britain, if you know what's good for you, don't come near me no more! I'm mad as hell now!'

Jackie Kallen cut in quickly with an accomplished coo that 'James wants to get in the ring with Chris Eubank and Nigel Benn – because we'd love to come out to Britain to take on Eubank and Benn in their own backyard! We're ready and waiting and I know James would put on a performance that would really please all of those great and knowledgeable British fight fans . . .'

Toney snorted his disdain, but I marvelled at the way the women worked together. Jackie continued her soft patter as Sherry rose elegantly to pass baby Jasmine into her son's arms. He welcomed his girl with a cuddle and shut himself off from the rest of us. The remainder of the press conference drifted by as the other boxers spoke courteously of Toney's abilities in the ring – while the man himself nuzzled Jasmine's ear.

At the end, as I tried to work out how best I might approach him, Toney scooped up his baby in the crook of an arm and sauntered through the glitzy ballroom. 'We're outta here, Jasmine . . .' he said. The waiting pack of hacks parted before him. No one dared step forward to talk to him.

On the main rostrum Jackie popped Pee-Wee, that minuscule mutt, into her bag and shook Bob Arum warmly by the hand. The promoter grinned as he clutched Jackie's diamond-studded mitt and gazed at her fighter scowling at the back of the hall. He knew that, after Tyson, boxing needed a new gangster-like champion. It seemed as if Lights Out was just the man for such a butt-kicking, ratings-shifting job. I studied Toney too as he kissed Jasmine on the nose.

'What'cha want?' he snarled. Leaning against a wall, embracing his baby, he'd caught me staring at him.

'Nothing . . .' I whimpered.

'Where you from?' Toney asked abruptly.

A bloodied image of black rage floated past as I considered my best answer. The options were clouded. White South Africa or, Toney's favourite damn place in the world, Britain? 'Well . . .' I thought of him being mad as hell. 'I'm South African . . .'

'No shit?' he said as he blew a raspberry on Jasmine's chubby neck. 'They still having some kind of trouble down there?'

'It's getting better,' I said vaguely.

'You live there?'

'No, I live in London –' He puckered his lips again and I added a hasty qualification '– but I don't feel one bit British in actual fact!' sounding as quaintly English as I'd ever done.

'I guess that's all right then,' Toney drawled. 'I'd love to whup some British ass – especially that fucking Eubank. I don't like that guy. I hate him! What 'bout you?'

'Yeah!' I boasted with increasing confidence, 'I hate him too!' I was lying but it felt good to talk like a motherfucker for a change.

'You ever talk to the guy?'

'Yeah . . .'

'Then you give him a message from me!'

'Sure . . .'

Toney adjusted his baby's bow. 'You tell him I say he's a pussy!'

'No problem . . .' I said with a shrug. After all, I had heard worse.

'You tell him his mama's a bitch and a ho'!'

'Hey, James, hey, that's enough!' Sherry cackled as she and Jackie wheeled over.

'Well, hi there!' Jackie trilled as she extended a hand. 'I'm Jackie Kallen.'

'An' I'm Sherry – James's mother!' snorted the woman I otherwise knew as 'Idol'. 'These other two are Sarah an' Jasmine . . .' she gestured towards Toney's two girls.

'Hello,' I said.

Sarah smiled at me as Sherry replied, 'Yeah, hello!'

'Would you like to come up to James's room and have some tea with us?' Jackie enquired. She knew that I was due to write a feature for *Esquire* about her and Toney. The PR machine was shifting into gear with genteel smoothness.

'Well, if no one minds . . .'

'Of course not!' Jackie laughed. 'We've been expecting you – haven't we, James?'

'Uh-huh!' Toney grunted ambiguously.

'Let's go then!' Sherry chided.

James Toney led the way, carrying Jasmine, as the three other women in his life followed hard on his heels, with me picking up the rear, wondering what it would be like to take afternoon-tea in Tulsa with a former crack-dealer called Lights Out.

By the time we had taken our velvety elevator ride to James Toney's suite on the eighteenth floor of the Doubletree, Jackie Kallen had decided on a late lunch instead of afternoon tea.

'Sounds good . . .' Toney growled as he picked up the room-service menu.

'No, James!' Jackie said firmly.

'Aw, come on, Jackie . . .'

'You know you can't, James! You'll thank me when you step on those scales.'

'That's what you think!' Toney grumbled. I thought how much harder it must have been for him in the previous years when he'd struggled to make the middleweight mark of 160 pounds. The closest he had ever come to losing had been against the mediocre Dave Tiberi when, after having secretly used diuretics to help him lose twenty-five pounds in a month, Toney sneaked home with a disputed split decision. The fatigue he'd shown in that fight had been caused entirely by his weight problems. He ended up spending a night in hospital, suffering from severe dehydration. From then on, Kallen resolved to monitor Toney's weight on a daily basis. But even at 168 it was hard to keep him in check.

'The day after tomorrow, James. Not too long now.'

'Easy to say,' he muttered.

'Yeah, I know, easy to say, hard to do. But you'll remember this sacrifice on Friday. You can think of today and of that night when we all went out to eat pizza and you couldn't pig out because you had to make the weight. You can take it out on Tony Thornton.'

'I can't talk to you, Jackie, not when you're about to stuff your face!'

'Sometimes I think that, one day, the kid'll break my heart,' Jackie said as Toney left to brood on Thornton in his bedroom.

The rest of us – me, Pee-Wee and the Lights Out women, settled down for our snack. Sherry and Sarah were so bound up in him as a son and future husband that their entire lives were shaped by Toney's exploits in the ring. Jackie was different. She had her own family and a separate lifestyle. But she was a player in her own right, a formidable manager on the fight circuit. And yet I still could not quite square her appearance with the coarse business of boxing.

'You know, people always say that!' she smiled over a bowl of yoghurt and cherries. 'They ask me, "Jackie, how can you stand to be so close to boxers, to be in a gym with those guys? It gets hot, it smells, everybody is – like, you know – sweaty! They hit each other! It's just so gross!".'

She paused for effect, as if an overpowering cocktail of testosterone had suddenly made her re-examine her motivation. Jackie flicked back a wave of hair, stared intently at her hands and then opened her eyes wide as she looked at me for confirmation. 'I'm pretty feminine, wouldn't you say? I mean, my nails, look at them, they're just so!'

I admired them effusively. Sherry, who'd heard it all before, patted Jasmine on the head. She strolled over to the window where she hummed faintly and tapped her own long talons against the glass.

Jackie Kallen was consistent in portraying an image which had reporters on the boxing beat reaching for their 'pretty lady' and 'glamorous blonde' lines when describing her breakthrough. She recognised the appeal of snappy copy – with her as the suburban glam-puss and Toney as the simmering crack-trader. She even allowed them to get away with their 'Beauty & The Beast' headlines. It was not unlike the 'Cus & The Kid' concept dreamed up for D'Amato and Tyson – but more provocative for the way in which Kallen took on the fight establishment as a lone woman manager. A stale whiff of sweat was the least of her obstacles.

'It never bothered me,' Jackie stressed. 'I'd just go up and hug a guy after a good sparring session. I could take the odour! You know, most fighters don't get enough hugs. When somebody from a different world from theirs comes up and says, "I'm so proud of you, you did good!" their faces radiate a kind of joy. I love that: and I love James and all my other fighters as if they were my own sons!'

Sherry persisted with her subtle drumming against the window. Tulsa on a cold Wednesday afternoon, Jackie on another roll, two more days before the next fight. Sherry looked like she had been here before. She knew that professional boxing was not just about money and fighting. It was as much about talking and waiting; most of all, waiting. Tap, tap, tap – her nails confirmed that tuneless truth.

'Whether you're a man or woman, a fighter or a mother,' Jackie continued while nodding in Sherry's refined direction, 'it's the same. This game gets in your blood. It fills you with hope and fear, elation and exhaustion. If it hadn't been for boxing I don't know what would have filled the void for me . . .'

The 'void' for Jackie Kallen came in the mid-'70s. A Jewish housewife living just outside of Detroit, she was a mother of three who wrote an entertainment column for a local newspaper. This occasionally brought her into contact with minor-league celebrities. But she wanted something more and so she nagged and nagged again until the newspaper agreed, in 1976, that she could write sports features – 'from a lady's perspective,' she frowned.

Amongst the first people she wrote about, Tommy Hearns was a gangly nineteen-year-old professional boxer from Detroit. Hearns, after eight professional fights, was then unknown. He spoke with a hesitant mumble. But Kallen saw something in him and so she again urged and cajoled until she was taken on as his publicist.

For the next twelve years Kallen sampled every facet of boxing's money-go-round as she plugged Hearns. From being a skinny Detroit ghetto kid to a six-time world champion, 'The Hitman' became the fans' favourite; a KO artist whose place in ring mythology was sealed by fights against Leonard, Hagler and Duran.

Through her work with Hearns, Jackie had developed 'an unquenchable thirst to manage a fighter of my own. I met Bobby Hitz. He was a Damon Runyon-type figure, a sweet club fighter, a white heavyweight from Chicago; one of those guys who always had something wrong with him – a sprained wrist, a broken ankle. I started to manage him because no one else wanted him. I adored him, he was my fighter. Every day I'd wrap his hands in the gym, hold his legs for sit-ups and punch his stomach with the medicine-ball. Bobby was an unsuccessful fighter and I was boxing's only woman manager. No one took us seriously.

'But this one kid always watched us. An angry kid. Punching everyone and everything. I knew the stories about James dealing in drugs but one day he came over with this photo of himself. It was a terrible xeroxed copy but he was so proud of it that, before he gave it to me, he signed it. "James Toney". That was so sweet. I said to myself, "If I become his manager, I'm gonna make sure we have only the most beautiful prints".'

'What do you think drew James towards you?'

'James wanted someone who'd care for him as a person as well as a fighter. He saw how much I cared for Bobby Hitz, even though he was never going to be a great fighter. James had also been brought up by an amazingly strong woman. There was that link between Sherry and I. I told her that I wanted to continue the work she had done, to stand alongside her in developing James as much as a person as a fighter. Now look at us. We're family! James wears the Star of David, he's standing up as an usher at my son's wedding. Sherry and I travel all over the country together. We wear the same clothes, we go on holidays together, my family and the Toneys! Isn't that right, Sherry?'

'Yeah . . .' Mrs T grunted.

'When we started out together I told Sherry and James that we could make a lot of money as long as we did the right things. Nothing else mattered. There we were – the angriest black kid you'd ever meet, hot off the street, and a Jewish housewife from the suburbs. Everyone thought we were a circus-act. He was streetwise, I was innocent. We were opposites who clicked. Yes, James sold crack, and I came from a family who don't drink, who don't drug. I've been married for twenty-seven years and all of us – my husband, my kids and I – are high-achievers. So I took James into our home, I showed him these values. I let him sleep over, I gave him the run of the house. I let him borrow the car. I'd say, "Here, James, take the Porsche!" I never doubted him and he never let me down. In fact he would watch out for me. Y'see, even though I'm forty-eight on my next birthday I'm the kind of woman who thinks without fear. I believe I can handle myself in the inner-city. James makes sure I don't step too far off-track.'

'What about your other fighters?'

'In my gym I have guys on parole for murder and rape and drug-dealing. Even out here in Tulsa, one of the guys with us has served five years for armed robbery and another has been in jail for manslaughter. But they've done their time. Maybe they're not book-smart but they've got intelligence. So I tell them to work hard, that they're wonderful, that they've got an understanding of life that they can build on. And, always, James makes sure I'm okay.

'I remember taking him to see Tommy Hearns' house. He saw Tommy's Rolls in the drive, the beautiful house, the championship belts. I said to him, "James, you can have this – all of it. I'm not blowing smoke up your butt. If you stay off the street, train really hard and listen to me we'll do it together." It's that simple – it overcame every difference between us and brought all the world titles and money and now the movie offers and everything else . . .'

Hollywood had already latched onto them. Jackie Kallen was not even worried that the studio who had bought the option were threatening to call the movie *The Lady & The Champ* – or that Cher was slated to play her. She knew that, with James Toney, she had struck gold and they could call it by any name they chose.

That dream-life began with victory over Nunn. 'James was such an underdog but he knocked Nunn out and I was so elated. I lived that fight so vicariously that I felt the intensity he felt, the relief, the joy, everything but the fatigue. We ended up, about thirty of us, in a little diner near the airport – the only place in Davenport that stayed open late. We came marching in about 2 a.m. with the world title belt and we partied! It was the most incredible night of my life.'

Since then, Toney had fought almost every other month. By the time he met Tiberi he'd defended his world title five times in eleven months. Only two other fighters in boxing history had had six title bouts in such a short period – and the last of these, Manuel Ortiz, had done so in 1943. It was hardly a typical route for the modern champion. But the boxing world's veneration for Toney stemmed from that exacting fact; contrary to other contemporary title-holders, Lights Out was willing to fight as often as he could against the toughest opponents.

While he had been soothed by Jasmine's birth, Toney still cut a tempestuous figure. Jackie shuddered when I asked her about the rumours. 'Mostly, they're true,' she said quietly. 'He has put his fist through my office door, he has shattered the mirrored wall in our gym. That's why I want him fighting so often – it keeps him off the streets and burns off that resentment. If he doesn't fight in the gym or the ring I know we're heading for trouble. James will end up fighting in some alleyway if I don't keep him busy. I used to worry that he'd slip back to the streets if he got discouraged. But I don't think that'll happen – as long as we keep winning. I dread to think what would happen if he ever lost. You see, with James, we're dealing with an extremely complex person. A man of dark mood swings.'

I glanced over at Sherry. She stood in silence, looking down at Tulsa below, listening to us talk about her son. It was Jackie's turn now, this was her interview. Sherry's time would come. She just had to wait a while longer. She flattened her hand against the pane, as if by stopping the tapping she could end the waiting.

Jackie tried for something more upbeat. 'I suppose it's that intensity which makes James Toney the most exciting fighter in boxing today!'

It was an increasingly rational assessment. With Tyson's demise a clear route had unfurled – Lights Out had the poise of a classical boxer and the vitriol to ignite expansive media coverage. One without the other was never enough. There were too many big-mouthed swaggerers who talked better than they fought; and the only boxer who possessed possibly finer versatility than Toney was a lightweight nicknamed Sweet Pea. Pernell Whitaker, the sweetest pea in the whole pod, was simply too well-balanced an individual to garner the press to match his artistry. Sweet Pea was a delight; but he neither knocked out his opponents nor threatened to cripple them. Consequently, he was considered to be a master by the cognoscenti and a bore by the peanut gallery who enticed advertisers to boxing on the small screen.

Jackie Kallen was aware of the publicity value of managing an inflammatory fighter. 'Yes,' she confirmed happily, 'we have had confrontations where he has picked up a chair and aimed it at me. I just walk away. When he's cooled down I know we're gonna talk. That's why we're indestructible. He kicks ass, while I kiss ass . . . it's an unbeatable combination!'

'And when there's trouble,' Sherry said sharply, 'he'll listen to me!'

'Oh, absolutely!' Jackie laughed. 'Sherry's the boss, really!'

'You know it! James!'

Bang on cue, he opened the door with a wink. 'We ready now, bro?'

'I saw you on television in London the other night,' I began.

'Fightin'?'

'No – you were having a quiet chat with your friends . . .'

'Who?' Toney said indignantly.

'Er . . . Eubank and Benn?'

'They ain't no fucking friends of mine!'

'I gathered that.'

'Chris Eubank's nothing but a bum! Chris Eubank and Nigel Benn are losers. They're scared of me, they're running from a whippin'.' Toney stared urgently at my tape-recorder. 'You gettin' this, man?'

'I'm getting it . . .'

'Good, 'cos I want you to put down all these words!'

'How would you plan a fight against someone as unorthodox as Eubank?'

'Well, I'd plan to kill him,' Toney sneered without missing a beat.

I had to laugh out loud. The more I saw of James Toney, the more I liked him. A dead-pan joker lurked behind the grouchy grimace.

'Don't laugh!' he demanded. 'I ain't joking. I'm gonna kill that guy! I don't like the way he runs off at the mouth!' He leaned over until his mouth was almost touching the tape. 'Chris Eubank, it's true, your mother – she's got no titties, the bitch is through. Same goes for Nigel Benn – your mama, she's just like the Loch Ness Monster.'

'Oh, James!' Sarah said doubtfully as she wiped their baby's scrunched-up face.

'It's true. Tell her, Don!'

'Uh, well, I guess, speaking literally, it's obviously not quite true . . .' I hesitated. Toney nodded at me again, as if to say 'C'mon, help me out here!'. I did my best. I knew I was acting ridiculously but I liked having him turn to me for support. 'Actually, come to think of it,' I offered, 'neither Benn nor Eubank is much of an oil-painting. So maybe there's something in it . . .'

'Yo, my main man talks! Y'see, Sarah? It's true! Eubank's mama's got no titties and Benn's is jus' that old Loch Ness Monster!'

Sarah smiled wearily at us. She was studying psychology at college. I thought that there could hardly be a more appropriate course for a woman about to marry James Toney.

'This is important,' he maintained. 'I want Eubank and Benn to hear me. I'd fight them on a "winner takes all" basis, I'd fight them on the same night – I'd bust 'em up, I'd take their hearts away. Eubank first and then his mama can suck my dick!'

'I'm not sure the British public would like you very much,' I suggested, 'especially if you keep up that kind of talk. It's hardly polite . . .'

'I've got nothing against the British – it's just their fighters! They're losers. Eubank, Benn, Bruno, Lewis. They lack guts, they lack style. Over there the women are ugly, the men are fat, chubby-looking! Now don't look at me like that, big guy. You know it! You can help me on this one, you can stir things up. Make me a hate-figure!'

'Why?'

'When I go over there I want everyone to hate me 'cos then I'll fight a lot better. They can all kiss my black ass!'

'And pay you a couple of million for the pleasure,' I said primly.

'Damn right they can! But it's their belts I want as much as the money,' he argued with a new seriousness. 'I'm a fighter from the old school, I'm a throwback to the great days of boxing. I want to unify these different "world" titles. The IBF, the WBC, the WBA, the WBO, the W-whatever. Shit, I want to be the undisputed champion of the world! Who else is like that today?'

'Tyson had that attitude . . .' I said.

'Yeah, but he ain't around right now.'

'What do you think of Tyson?'

'I think he needs a mother like I got, I think he needs a Jasmine.'

'You're saying he needs more love.'

'If that don't make me sound soft,' he muttered.

'You sound dead right.'

'Good. I feel for the brother. He ain't been as lucky as me. He ain't got the family I got round me.'

'Did you ever meet him?' I asked Toney.

'Uh-uh.'

'Chris Eubank has,' I countered. 'He even visits him in jail.'

'So what? I'd still whup him! Even Mike Tyson couldn't help him. By the time Tyson gets out I'll be moving onto a heavyweight title myself . . .'

As usual, big bad James had a plan: 'I'm moving up soon to light-heavyweight and then I'm gonna fight for the heavyweight championship of the world. If Jackie would let me, I would take Lennox Lewis right now – that guy ain't got it!'

Apart from the fact that he could fight as well as box James 'Lights Out' Toney was, I suggested, the biggest mouth in boxing.

'Yeah, you know it! From 168 to heavyweight no one can touch me.' He laughed again. 'I can tell you don't believe me. But it's gonna happen: heavyweight champion of the world!'

I was certain that Toney would never be a great heavyweight. His frame was that of a strong super-middleweight. The discipline he needed to always make that weight helped him preserve his speed and sharpness in the ring. His heavyweight talk sounded like nothing more than just bloated chit-chat. I tried to steer him away from his cherished polemic to a deeper reflection.

'Do you think about your father when you've got time on your hands, on a day like today, while you're waiting to fight?'

'I think about him only when I think about shooting him dead. I'm talking about the piece of shit who tried to murder my mother and me, the scum who walked out on us, the gun hot in his hand. I'm gonna kill him.'

'Where's your father now?' I wondered.

'Jail,' Sherry interrupted. 'The man is no good. Serving time for rape now. Grafton, Ohio. Gets out in '95.'

'So how long is it since you last saw him?' I asked Sherry.

'June 5, 1970. The day's carved on my brain. More than twenty-three years now.'

'I'll kill him,' Toney repeated.

'Can you believe it?' Sherry said as if she hadn't even heard her son. 'Toney Snr's writing letters to the press, saying that he wants to be with James. But he wants his money now he's a famous fighter. I told James I'd take him to see his father.'

'No way,' Toney said evenly.

'Y'see, James even sent him a letter, warning him to stay away,' Sherry said.

'Next time I'll spell it out with a bullet.'

'There won't be a next time. I'll make sure of that . . .'

The room was silent but for the snuffling of Pee-Wee as he slept on the fighter's chest.

'What about the fight this Friday night?' I eventually asked.

'I predict an easy win for me,' Toney said.

'I'm surprised you haven't said anything bad about Tony Thornton yet!'

'Well, he hasn't tried to diss me. I respect Tony Thornton. He's a cagey veteran. When I was a kid I used to watch him on TV. He beat lots of great fighters before I even turned pro. So he knows his way round a ring as well as anyone. He knows all the angles, all the moves. He can be real slippery and I know he's tough. But when the fighting's over he's just a regular guy.'

'They call him the "Punching Postman"!'

'Yeah,' Toney laughed, 'he's a fucking postman!'

'Different kind of deliveries to your last job!'

'Ain't pay as well as either,' Toney observed. 'But I don't need no letter to tell me that Thornton's better than most. Look, he fought Chris Eubank in Britain and he won that fight. They gave it to Eubank – a split-decision – but it should have gone Thornton's way. I take my hat off to him. I'm gonna earn him his biggest pay-day on Friday. But I'm still gonna lay some bad hurt on him.'

'Have you thought about this fight a lot?'

'I got Tony Thornton on the brain. I see his face last thing at night. When I wake up I see him again. But it's worse for him 'cos I'm the champion and he's on his way out. I'm younger and stronger than him. He's no fool. He knows it.'

'But you must have some doubts,' I said. 'You've said how canny Thornton is in the ring. What if he beats you?'

'It ain't happening . . .'

'But what if it did? You must sometimes have a little fear too . . .'

'No.'

'Even just before the fight? While you're waiting in your dressing-room? When you're walking out to the ring?'

Toney shook his head. 'It's just a strange time.'

'But what's it like?' I asked, thinking that maybe we were getting some-where previously hidden. 'What's it like to be a fighter in those moments?'

'You gotta be there to understand it,' he said. 'You get me?'

There was an inviting hint in his voice. I looked at Jackie.

'Do you wanna sit in with James?' she said brightly.

'When?'

'Right before the fight. Meet him in his hotel room an hour or so before he leaves for the arena. Be with him in the dressing-room up until the moment he goes out. What do you think, James?'

'Okay.'

I must have looked surprised because Sherry lent over and patted me on the head, just like she had done with Jasmine an hour earlier. 'It'll be okay,' she said, 'James is comfortable round you.'

'You come along an' wait with me, man,' Toney said. 'You'll taste what it's like then. A world title fight. You'll see, you'll feel it then . . .'

29 October 1993

We had waited so long for seven o'clock to come that, when it did, I knew there was something terrible about being this close to a boxer in the dark hours before a fight. A stone-cold look had settled on James Toney's face, but we could sense the churning inside him.The voice outside came again, high and trembling, skulking down the sumptuous passage on the seventeenth floor.

'Dearest, darlin', I had to write to say I won't be home anymore . . .'

I could not believe it. A few doors away, a maniac with a taste for irony played '24 Hours to Tulsa' over and over and again. But Toney was oblivious to both Gene Pitney and our high-rise joker. He sat across the room from me in a low hush, listening instead to some internal reverie. Toney had said earlier that he could already hear the thud of bone against flesh, his opponent's moan, the crowd's insatiable gasp. I thought those sounds must have grown louder for his own quiet had deepened with the waiting. Toney had been carrying this fight in his head for weeks, dreaming of it at night and imagining it by day. Now we were just two hours away from the first bell.

The minutes clicked across the red shine of the digital clock in sombre procession. Toney's eyebrows, rising and falling as if drawing in breath, offered an uneasy salute as the next digit rolled past.

7.01.

We yearned for a sign that he was ready to leave. Not yet, the fighter's gentle rocking seemed to stress, not quite yet. Toney and I were less than six feet apart. I began to feel uncomfortable with our surreal intimacy.

'Dearest, darlin' . . . Only 24 hours from Tulsa, Only one day from your arms, But what can I do?'

Finally, as if he could stand it no longer, Toney stood up in the soft gloom. He walked over to the window and stared across that stretch of Oklahoma's Bible Belt. It was no longer snowing and Tulsa looked sinister in shadowy light. Across the street, just out of sight, nine thousand people flocked together in the town's Convention Center. Bob Arum's 'Tulsa Shootout' logo stood out in neon, casting strange colours on Toney's skin.

Another town, another world title challenger. Although he was undefeated after forty bouts and still only twenty-five, how could he bear the strain, fight after fight?

He shrugged and said softly, 'This is boxing, baby. I deal with it. I ain't lost yet.' There was no fear in the sound of this 'yet'. The end of our silence seemed to lift him. More tellingly, Gene Pitney had changed his maudlin tune.

'Yeah, I gotta tell ya now, Something's gotten hold of my heart . . .'

'Man, I hate that shit!' Toney said. I watched him closely again. His face was surprisingly young and unmarked – the only scarring being above the fleshy creases of eyelid where he'd been cut badly before. Up close he no longer looked like a killer. I pictured him as a small boy, in the blue and maize-coloured streets of Ann Arbor. A serious kid, until the smiling starts and you cannot stop him for all the flashing white teeth and high-fives. The boy Alison could still see when we had studied him on TV; James Toney Jnr, protected from a rampaging father by Sherry, the mother who taught him how to bake bread in a big clay oven.

I knew that Sherry would be alone in her own room, also readying herself for the fight. She'd wear her finest clothes and jewellery and would sit at ringside with Sarah and Jasmine, almost aching for that time when it would be over and they could climb through the ropes and hug their boy again.

Toney looked at the clock once more. Another minute clicked by. 7.05 on a chilling Friday night.

He scanned his reflection in a long mirror. He was set for the night's work, wearing a hooded tracksuit and heavy boots. A solid gold choker glinted on his muscled neck. He yawned with exaggerated cool and rubbed a thickly knuckled hand over and under his chin, as if checking the quality of a razor. Then he exhaled gratefully; and I could no longer control the tremor in my right leg.

Toney strolled towards the door and, in one sweeping movement, picked up his bag. I noticed the folds of skin at the base of his shaved black head. They conveyed a vulnerability at odds with his renewed motherfucker glare. I was tempted to rub his gleaming skull for luck, to sweeten that moment and make it just a little more tender. But I was afraid I might upset him, that I would heighten the growing rhythm of his menace before he was ready. I held back for it was his world; and I felt acutely that I didn't belong.

Toney thrust his fists deep into the pockets of his top. He cocked a brow at me and drawled, 'You ready for this?'

I swallowed hard, took a step forward and said a diffident 'Yeah, I'm ready'.

'Okay,' he murmured, 'let's go . . .'

We strode soundlessly towards the glittering Doubletree elevator. Toney led the way, flanked by his two homeboys, the pair who had done their time in prison before meeting Jackie Kallen. They too were professional boxers but, not being in the same superstar bracket as Lights Out, their task was to support the champion. They brought with them a giant ghetto-blaster and stacks of CDs which would reverberate through the vacuum left before fight-time. I knew that Gene Pitney would not be found in that box – all that remained was a vanishing croon as we left his fervent fan.

We lined up alongside each other in the elevator. Anxious to do my bit, I pressed 'Lobby'. The word lit up and the doors slid shut. But only seconds later they opened again. We must have made a sight for the ageing couple, in full-evening dress, who stopped us on the sixteenth floor. According to the name-tags swinging from their reddish necks, 'Melvyn' and 'Missy' were in town for the 'Oklahoma State Agricultural Convention'. These were people primed for perpetually toothy smiling; but their shock in facing three black men and me in a Tulsa lift suggested that they were not given to debunking cultural stereotypes. Their smiles, anticipating an encounter with fellow farmers, dissolved in disbelief. Missy took hold of Melvyn's arm and shuffled back, pulling her silver-haired husband out of his nightmare.

It was like an invisible sheet of one-way glass separated us from them. We stood in stoic stillness while their eyes darted back and forth as if in search of the murderer amongst us. I was the conspicuous one, the white guy, so I guessed they wouldn't pick me.

Our youngest homeboy, a gentle-faced heavyweight not long out of jail for manslaughter, pushed the 'Doors Open' button and nodded, as if to say, 'you'll be okay in here'. Missy and Melvyn looked uncertainly at each other before they crossed the line. The sixteen-flight ride was a painstaking journey down America's cultural divide; but James Toney looked locked in a lightless tunnel of his own making. His eyes were black and unblinking as he fixed a gaze on the sealed door.

Surprisingly, our Oklahoma heroine proved herself different. Halfway down the vault, and still unravaged, Missy looked up slowly. She read the words 'Participant' and 'Ringside' dangling on our own neck-chains.

Her face softened as she gasped, 'Oh . . . the fighters!' She gestured dreamily to Melvyn as if she suddenly understood, as if she recognised a moment of sublime beauty. Melvyn was still scared but Missy whispered, 'Good luck, boys, g'luck tonight . . .' The boxers nodded briefly, in unison, like a hardcore Detroit crew remembering some ancient Motown move. I nearly clicked my fingers in delight.

Missy pursued us across the lobby, clutching my arm with another 'good luck' squeeze as if she believed that even I would be in the ring in another hour. I was tempted to linger and say 'Much obliged, Ma'am Missy', but the others were already swinging into the cement corridor which joined the hotel to the Convention Center.

The walls on that outside passage were only as high as our shoulders. After the warmth of the hotel the air was joltingly icy. The fighters pretended not to notice, turning their faces defiantly into the slanting sleet. The snow which had blown in through the opening that afternoon crunched noisily beneath our boots. On such a bleak night it felt like we were a small army unit marching on Moscow rather than Tulsa.

We were getting close, too close. Toney pushed open the entrance to a sprawling expanse. The hissing heating vents took the edge from the cold but a shiver still ran through me. Our footsteps echoed in the gloomy passage.

When we eventually turned a corner, the queuing crowd was a piercing reminder of what lay ahead. We saw them first. Our step slowed momentarily but they were even more surprised than us. Chilli-dog and Bud-devouring fans opened up a path before us, gaping at Lights Out in awe.

I heard the murmurs rising in excitement and volume. 'Look, look, it's the fighters. James Toney . . . Toney . . . Toney!' It was if there was a holy dread around him, discouraging their attempts to attract his attention. He walked steadily, lost in boxing, ignoring everyone and everything, advancing with the aloof step of a world champion. But I guessed that, for all his indifference, he was soaking this up; for it seemed like nothing but the purest respect which cleared his course as people moved out of his way, watching him with as much reverence as amazement. Boxing had given him this in the white American heartland. It made him shine in Tulsa. The folksy and beery gawkers realised the emotional and physical extremity of all he was about to put himself through. Boxing was beyond them, a world they could only experience by watching fighters like him.

And then I heard him screaming in delight. 'It's you, it's you!' he said as if helping me to identify myself. 'Hell's bells, I don't believe it!' Hank the taxi-driver shrieked. 'How ya doin', bud, how ya doin'?' He pointed at me and then at Lights Out. 'James Toney! Way to go, man! You're the champ!' As I looked back at Hank I wanted to ask him where his 'fuck nigger Toney!' diatribe had gone; but he was too busy yapping 'You're the man, James, you're the man!'

In less than a minute we were alone again and clattering down two flights of stairs and then along a maze of corridors running through the bowels of the building – which, with the pipes reverberating around us, sounded like it had begun to gurgle in anticipation of its next feed. The heat of nine thousand people pressed down on us. We moved quickly, wanting to be there, to reach the dressing-room, beyond that subterranean world suddenly filled with blinding light, television cables and bearded sound-men yelling 'Showtime, champ, showtime!' as they saw Toney approach.

Inside at last, with the door shut tight, the noise of the crowd rumbled above, like a train careering along a distant track. Toney's head swivelled round the room as if in search of something familiar. I looked at the stain-less white walls and wooden benches, the cement floor and metal-rimmed shower at the back. A small television in one corner beamed back images from the ring to which Toney would soon be called. It felt cold again.

'The waiting-room . . .' Toney sighed. There was relief in the snap of the ghetto-blaster opening up, swallowing a CD and then emitting a steely rap which would be our constant soundtrack. At first Toney just sat there, listening to the music drowning out the roar, nodding his head in time to the scratchy and booming beats, flexing his neck from side to side. He began to loosen as the hip-hop became increasingly belligerent with every original member of Niggaz With Attitude – Eazy-E, Ice Cube, Dr Dre. Hank would have noticed the stark shift in tone as Dre and Snoop Doggy Dogg paid homage to their *motherfuckin', gang-bangin' niggazzz'*.

Toney, meanwhile, had slipped into a more profound 'Lights Out' attitude. Turning his baseball cap round, he stripped off his hooded top and threw a handful of shadowy jabs at himself in the mirror. Dr Dre's 'Chronic' churned on, making the rapidly moistening room jump with every Snoop Doggy Dogg whine and sampled breakbeat. Toney ducked and slid, punching air all the time, seeing himself hit Tony Thornton.

I had been told that Thornton would be waiting next door. He knew that Toney was the favourite, that he was an undefeated world champion. But, realising that this might be his last chance to win a world title, he was in even more impressive shape than he had been against Eubank. Thornton was a terrific boxer; and lesser men than he had scored upset victories. There would be a desperation in him, too, to make it after so many years.

I wondered if Toney was thinking along the same lines. As he sat down to lace his boots I asked him the question which was, simultaneously, the most stupid and the most essential. 'How're you feeling?' I said thickly.

'Great,' he answered tersely. 'How 'bout you?'

'Good,' I mumbled.

There must have been something in my voice for he glanced at me quizzically. 'What?' he asked.

'I've been thinking about Thornton . . .'

'Why?'

'You're not?'

Toney sized me up with a look and said, with some deliberation, 'Look, no way can I lose this fight. Thornton ain't doin' shit to me. Maybe he can give Chris Eubank the runaround but I ain't Eubank. This is routine man, routine. I'll stick my jab in his face all night long, tearing him down, slow and sure . . .' Toney had prevailed against cruel punchers like Barkley and

MacCallum so perhaps it was easy for him to talk glibly of a fight less than twenty minutes away.

With his protective cup in place, Lights Out pulled on his knee-length black trunks. He resumed that punching of his own shadow. As I examined the yellow Star of David gleaming on his otherwise pitch-black shorts, Jackie Kallen breezed into the dressing-room. Wearing a glossy black outfit, complete with frills and tassels and an embossed 'James "Lights Out" Toney – Two-Time World Champion' motif, she brought a scent of expensive perfume and a glimpse of long and newly painted crimson fingernails into that staunchly masculine setting.

But even on a 'routine' fight night she struggled to curb the anxiety. Pee-Wee, who usually popped in and out of her handbag when he was not scurrying around our feet, had been left behind at the hotel. He too felt nervous in a big-fight stadium.

As Jackie spoke to me in lulling tones about the little dog, she watched her prize-fighter. His hands were wrapped in white bandages and, as the bright red gloves were pulled onto his fists by Bill Miller, Toney looked at her. While her face was immaculately made-up, his streamed with sweat.

'Ten minutes, champ!' barked the soundman outside.

On TV a tuxedo-clad George Foreman supplied some colour to the pre-fight build-up which otherwise concentrated on footage of Thornton and Toney hurting their previous opponents. Jackie squeezed my right arm as Toney slapped gloves with the open palms of his two friends. 'It's soon,' she whispered, 'very soon . . .'

Bill Miller drew Toney aside, speaking to him in a composed undertone, repeating the strategies they knew by heart, putting his hand on the boxer's taut neck, rubbing it slightly, patting him on the shoulder, moving up to embrace his head. There was something almost unbearable about the way the old trainer held his young fighter despite the fact that the monstrous ghetto-blaster pumped out Dre's death-fixated 'High-Powered' with its gun-shots and invocation to 'have no remorse'.

Each time the four-minute rap ended, the track would immediately resume. I knew that Miller hated hip-hop, with its grinding sound and mournful obscenities. He would have preferred Ella Fitzgerald or Ben Webster, even the harsher bop of Parker and more angular sheets of Coltrane. Anything but Dr Dre. But Miller loved James Toney too. He allowed him his favourite rap and cuffed him again. 'Keep your head, son, keep your head in there . . .' he said.

Toney nodded and then threw another combination. The knocking turned into hammering on the dressing-room door. 'One minute! He's on his way out!' the HBO cameraman shouted.

On the flickering television set an overhead shot honed in on the hooded figure of Tony Thornton. L.L. Cool J.'s 'Mama's Gonna Knock You Out' accompanied his march. We heard a packed stadium rise to its thudding beat. The tumult would have been frightening if our dressing-room had been otherwise silent. But 'High-Powered' started up once more. Toney turned away from the television and pulled up his own black cape. From his shroud, he stared at me slyly, as if he knew I was more afraid than him.

The door swung open. 'Showtime!' yelped the soundman above Dre's threat and the crowd's growl.

James Toney banged his gloves together hard. He looked straight at me. 'Okay,' he said, 'let's go . . .' He jerked his head towards the door, indicating that I should walk with him. We both took a deep breath. 'Let's go to work,' Toney muttered and I followed him on the long walk toward the ring.

He paced a few steps ahead as his homeboys picked up their own rap. Amid all their 'James Toney is in the house!' exhortations and the rising sea of uproar, the IBF super-middleweight champion of the world moved with silent resolution. Miller and Kallen were equally tight-lipped. They knew how much Toney depended on another world title victory. It was as if we were racing through a dream. Our shadows rode up high against the walls. The noise seemed to amplify with every lengthening stride.

'So this is what it's like,' I thought hazily to myself for the hundredth time that night; and I knew once more that boxing was like nothing else.

By the time we turned into the blaze of the arena, Toney was almost running. The television cameras were in our faces, following each step to the ring. Screaming faces craned over the stair-rails and swung out of every aisle. It was a feeling like no other, as terrible as it was thrilling.

We saw Sherry and Sarah shouting and stretching towards us as we reached ringside. Their eyes were glistening. I wondered if it was more with pride than fear. I waved back at them, feeling foolish again that I was in the spotlight with Lights Out. But Toney didn't care. He had his sights set on Thornton, already circling the ring. Michael Buffer cleared his throat for one more 'Let's Get Ready To Rumble' exhortation.

As we reached the bottom rope Jackie Kallen put her hand on James Toney's shoulder. I felt suddenly sure that he would win. I had experienced both the tension of his dressing-room wait and the frenzy of approaching the ring. It was enough. I was almost sick with relief that I would not be the one having to lift my own fists to fight.

The introductions skimmed past. I can only recall the way in which the two boxers left their corners and walked towards each other. It was a moment of grim release. They both looked as if they were glad that they were alone at last. For them, after the wait, the fighting was oddly easier to endure.

It took me a full twelve rounds to recover. I was also haunted by memories of Tyson and Watson. I had spent protracted periods with them before their last fights. With one in jail and the other still in hospital I feared that my jinx might strike again. I guessed Toney would have jeered at those qualms for, above all else, he was a fighter; one of both instinct and finesse. And his ring-sense meant that he showed Thornton more respect than he did most of his opponents. He worked at a distance, building up points in orderly rather than scintillating fashion. Thornton himself proved again that he was a highly efficient boxer. Yet he was too wary to risk everything on an all-out assault. He stalked Toney methodically, throwing a full range of hooks and uppercuts. Lights Out responded with speed and subtle bursts of counter-punching.

The result was a fight of twelve remarkably similar rounds, with Toney easily winning the last six. Thornton could not provide the test Toney needed to lift himself into the realms of savage reverie. It was, after all, just a 'routine' night in Tulsa – a snowy October night in which the champion administered, in his own words, 'a respectful beating' to an alert veteran.

When we returned to the dressing-room Toney was full of talk again. The reporters closed in on him, complimenting his ring savvy but wondering why he had not done more damage to Thornton. 'The crowd wanted blood and guts but I fought the fight I had to win,' Toney explained. He lifted his sleepy Jasmine out of Sherry's arms. He kissed his favourite babe once more before saying, 'You don't just wade in against Thornton. Patience is the key against a guy like that – patience and skill. Thornton messed up Eubank but I ain't Chris Eubank. Thornton's a fine technician but he couldn't whip me – but who can? I'm the best fighter in the world. No one can touch me! We all know it! Who doesn't?'

He came over to the corner where I stood, his question still hanging in the air, and said with a winning laugh, 'See, man, I'm not so bad. I'm real good and I'm fighting again in six weeks and then a month after that – you comin', baby? We gonna do this again?'

He took a step back, winked again and then said, with extra relish, 'An' now, baby, it's time to eat cheeseburgers, lotsa cheeseburgers . . . 'cos I'm James Toney, champion o' the world . . .'

4

OSCAR'S NIGHT

A DOZEN SMALL CAKES, RATHER THAN CHEESEBURGERS, FLEW across the Atlantic on the day Sherry and James Toney returned to Ann Arbor. As a memento of our time together in Tulsa, the Speciality Cakes & Pies duo picked out a tasty sample of apple, blueberry and cherry-bites and miniature pecan pies and stacked them high in their bakery's largest box. Then they called Federal Express.

In response to her son's mean assumption that all the men living in London were 'chubby-looking', I'd suggested to Sherry that she could probably tell, just by looking at my curvy figure, how much I'd enjoy her cake and pie delicacies. I said it in passing, in a slender moment of banter, and thought nothing of it until I opened that couriered parcel of calories.

Sherry's baking spread a roll of post between Michigan and London. I wrote back to thank her and she assured me that it was her pleasure. I whipped up Toney a compilation of rap to remind him of my appetite for the roughest stuff in his boxing oven and Jackie Kallen responded instantly with a pink card to say that my tape could be heard in her Galaxy gym while Toney beat up his unfortunate sparring partners.

Toney was happy to see that he had made the cover of Britain's *Boxing News* with an exclusive 'Mr Nasty' tag, but Jackie delighted more in the witty *Esquire* photographs of her, Lights Out and Pee-Wee. She asked for a couple of prints for her office walls and reminded me that Toney's next title defence would be in Los Angeles, where they'd also be working on their *Lady & The Champ* blockbuster. They all hoped, she stressed, that my lovely English gal and I would make it to LA. She was sure we'd have a great time 'hangin' with James and Mickey . . .'

'Mickey?' Alison asked as Jackie's soft American twang wound its way across our answerphone. 'Rourke?'

'Must be,' I said, briefly imagining that it could also be a despairing manager's reference to 'Mickey's Big Mouth' beers or burgers.

As I gazed at the slimline picture of the boxer and Pee-Wee hanging in our hallway, I tossed up the easiest of questions.

'Should we go?'

We could afford 9½ days, rather than weeks, in LA. But, on our second day, we were summoned to Mickey's. Sherry Toney gave us the wink, indicating that her James and Hollywood's Mickey were becoming thicker by the minute. It was a two-way street for both boys. While Toney deigned to punch Rourke in the face whenever they sparred in the star's private ring, a wan Mick ensured the shadowy Lights Out got his break into *le cinema*. They were soon to begin working together on a garbled film called *Bullet*. Toney would play the part of Blackjack Jones – the leader of a rabid street gang. 'I told Mickey and my agent,' Toney said, 'that I'd only play bad guy roles. I wanna be the black Jean-Claude van Damme. I wanna kick people in the head and snap the bones in their arms and legs. Those are the sorta movies I like!'

It felt like we were in the movies ourselves as we trawled through one of Hollywood's less salubrious quarters in search of Rourke's joint. The Outlaw Gym was for his and his friends' exclusive use; but Rourke's tenuous street cred was maintained by its location in a part of LA where no one spoke English unless engaging you in a cheap drug deal. We kept expecting old Rourkey to jump out of a stinking alleyway, blow me away with a puff of his sunken buttock cheeks and then, as the real clincher, slide that pitch-black blindfold over Alison's head.

But there was no sign of him even when, an hour later, we found his latest holy grail. Rourke's pristine gym was empty, except for some sweaty white hunk working the heavy bag like a peacock preparing for stud.

He sloped against a white wall, taking a breather, fondling his damp Calvin Klein vest and eyeing us like we were boxing's answer to Beavis and Butthead. I thought he was about to offer us a deal for our own mini-series. 'Yeah?' he sneered. 'Who're you?'

'We're meeting James Toney here,' I said.

'Oh, right!' He beamed a 5,000-watt tooth-capped grin.

Hunky pouted at Alison, telling us that he was an 'occasional legal adviser to Mickey', and said we could hit the bag while he sharpened up on the speed-ball. Undeterred by our reluctance, he dashed over to the pear-shaped pouch, muttering his 'work it out, work it out . . .' mantra.

I wished I could conjure for him a wide-screen picture of life beyond Mickey's gym. I wanted to describe a typical Sunday night in the Wimbledon Park Road when a steaming girl stepped out of the bath, devoid of all decorative baubles but her rosy own. Suitably buffed and primped, Alison would skip through the door and interrupt my studious surfing with the remote. As soon as my neck snapped back, she would activate her best Chris

Eubank impression. Her nostrils would flare in synch with a heaving bosom as she put one bunched hand on top of the other. She'd look at them profoundly, tapping fist against fist, thinking like Christopher Livingstone Eubank might think. Then, suddenly, legs astride, she'd vault an invisible set of ropes and whirl in a tight little circle in the centre of our living-room floor. The steam would twirl slowly from her, just like the smoke at a Eubank ringside bash, and she'd resume her snorting and tapping.

I touched Alison on the arm, about to ask her to do the unthinkable, when James Toney walked in with baby Jasmine and a cheery scowl.

'Yo! Lights Out!' the joker blared. 'How ya doin', man?'

Toney ignored him. He handed Jasmine to Sherry, lifted his eyes demurely to Alison and then walked over and punched me lightly in the stomach. 'You're back, big boy!' he grunted as he strolled over to the changing-room.

The Kallen gang streamed into the gym to watch Jackie's joy at work. They were all there – Jackie, her husband and her father, her sons and her brother, with all the wives and girlfriends still climbing the stairs behind them. Pee-Wee was right in the middle, tugging at shoelaces and woofing at heels – until he saw the spiky rubber-pronged bag belonging to Eubank's most explicit body-double.

The ensuing stand-off between Alison's latex hedgehog-style handbag and a growling ball of fluff caused great hilarity in the Kallen camp. It was then that we noticed how detached Sherry was from the others. She sat on the opposite side of the gym, writing earnestly as they laughed uproariously. In Tulsa she had also been partly removed, on the fringes of a party whooping it up in tribute to her only son. A lone black woman in a liberal bunch of white folk. It was not as if they excluded her or failed to be pleasantly chatty. She was always with them; yet she was never one of them.

Even Jackie, with her natural diplomacy and engaging warmth, could not completely bridge that space. Sherry would remain a single black mother while they were an extended Jewish family. They were from the same country, the same state even; but they came to boxing from opposite worlds. The relatives chortled on as Sherry kept writing, faster and faster.

Jackie took us into Mickey Rourke's office. She introduced us to his chic PA and also to her and James's LA agent. We sat around on Rourke's plush leather sofa while the agent grilled me on potential media assignments, trying to work out in his busy head if they should pump out as many promotional features as possible or wait until the Lights Out iron got even hotter.

He made me twitchy, that relentlessly smooth publicity gizmo. I concentrated instead on the black marble fountain bubbling away in the middle of a boxing hideaway. I thought of Sherry again, scribbling outside, and wondered what words she would leave on paper. She was more intriguing than all the agents, personal assistants, managers and movie-stars put together.

We slunk back into the gymnasium. Toney waltzed round the ring, saying, 'Hey, Ma, watch me break this sucker,' as his fiery jabs sizzled in another man's face.

Sherry looked up dreamily. 'Hey,' she said, but to us rather than Toney. 'You made it, huh?'

We sat down next to her. 'How're things?' I asked.

'Not bad.'

'Looks like you're busy . . .'

'I'm writing,' Sherry said excitedly.

'We noticed. What are you working on?'

'A screenplay . . .'

'*The Lady & The Champ*?'

'Oh no,' she laughed shyly. 'I'm doing this all on my own . . . I'm writing the story of my life. It's a black woman's story. I'm hoping to show it to a movie producer some day soon. I'm writing about me and James. I should tell you about it some time.'

'Whenever you like . . .'

'How 'bout as soon as we get outta this place? It's a real interesting tale. It'll tell you a lot 'bout James and even a little 'bout me.'

Sherry Toney, refreshed and resplendent in canary yellow, arched an immaculate eyebrow as the three of us sipped iced tea in the Bonaventure in downtown LA. Even though Skid Row was only a couple of blocks away, the glitzy Bonaventure made Tulsa's Doubletree look like a dilapidated Motel 6. The Toneys had been staying there for weeks, rising towards the stars, but Sherry had more lasting things in mind.

She snorted with the indignity of memory. 'Look, you gotta understand this one fact. With Toney Snr we're dealing with something dangerous. He's schizophrenic, psychopathic. And James knows that. He has a built-in grudge against his father. He's hated his father ever since he could walk.' She stared hard at Alison, as if to warn her. 'This is serious shit, girl . . .'

'And doesn't that worry you,' I said cautiously, afraid of angering the mighty Sherry, 'when your own son talks about murdering his father?'

'Yeah, it worries me 'cos I don't want James to wind up in prison too – though I couldn't care less what happens to his father. Like I told you last time, if he thinks he can creep back into our lives he's got another think coming. James'll kill him!'

'Are you sure?'

'Damn right! The hate is that deep. You can see it in the build-up to this next fight. I know he's got his father's face planted at the front of his brain. It's payback time for all that Toney did to him. So this boy he's fighting next, Tim Littles, he's gonna be the one who'll get busted up . . .'

'You don't have any fear when James fights?'

'No,' she said, sounding like an echo of her son.

'But I'd be a little wary of a boxer who looks as accomplished as Littles, a guy who is the number-one contender, a fighter who's also young and unbeaten.'

'Yeah – but you ain't no boxer.'

'No,' I agreed stoically.

'James will turn his rage on Littles. You see, unlike his father, he knows how to channel it.'

'But what about the other guy's potential fury?'

'James'll chill this kid. He's gonna knock him out . . .'

Sherry spoke so easily about the coming violence, as if she was as inured to brutality as her son. But her refusal to be squeamish about boxing had the strange effect of making her appear more, rather than less, compassionate. She played the role of supportive mother to the hilt, proving herself articulate in grisly boxing discourse. Sherry also transformed the Toney history into an evocative narrative, uncovering the reasons why her son turned to such a business for salvation.

James Toney Snr came from the South. 'As far as I can tell,' Sherry suggested, 'even in the South, even when he was a little boy, Toney was troubled. He told me he never had much of a father. An' he hated his mother from the moment he saw her with another man. Sex got him into strife early. He quit school at the age of ten because of a rape charge. Yeah, Toney was that kind of man even then – ten years old and up for rape! You had to know him to believe it possible.

'But his trouble really started when he moved to Detroit. He bought a gun. He robbed, burgled and pushed dope. Seems like his first wife, Geraldine, came from a decent family. Her mother was a teacher, her father a preacher. That didn't stop Toney. She fell pregnant. They married but Toney still called her a whore. He used a clock to beat her in the face – over and over . . .'

'A clock?' I chimed.

'Yeah – he beat her with a clock. In the face. He went to prison for that – eighteen months.' Sherry looked at us searchingly before she asked me an odd question. 'You know Mike Tyson's number?'

I looked blankly at her.

'You writing 'bout Tyson too. You must know his prison number . . .'

'Er . . . 922 . . . 335 . . .' I stumbled, feeling a boxing egghead for knowing such jailbird trivia.

'Yeah? Well, I still remember Toney's. A-5111652. That's why I'm gonna write this screenplay. Shake him from my mind forever . . .'

'Did you know Toney when he was in prison?'

Sherry peered down at her nails to ensure that the varnish was unchipped. 'No, but in February '67 he was paroled to Grand Rapids, Michigan. That's where I lived. I was a senior at South High. In my spare time I worked as a cashier for Mac and Howard's Supermarket. That's where I first laid eyes on Toney – not long after his release . . .'

'What did you think of him, when you first saw him?'

A look of gauzy recall filtered across Sherry's made-up face. She remembered herself at eighteen, exactly twenty-six years before. 'He was a good-looking guy. Well built with a tailored waist. He always wore shades – very much the cool dude. For three months or so he dropped by the store. He made out he was just picking up a few beers but I knew he was comin' to see me. Then, on 29 May, it was his birthday, so I gave him a candy bar. It was then that he asked me my name.'

She looked at Alison and smiled.

'"Sherry," he says, "what a pretty name!" That Saturday he came over. My mother liked him. She thought he was a gent. But my father was suspicious. Toney gave him this expensive-looking gift moments after they met. I remember what my father said after Toney left: "Too much sugar for a dime!" Y'see, my dad saw he was a con-man.'

Date-by-date, Sherry weakened and, by that December, 1967, she was pregnant and living upstairs with Toney in the small apartment above her mother's house.

'It was then that everything turned. Toney drank heavily; and whiskey made him mad. One night he tried to kill a neighbour. He got nineteen days in County Jail for that – it should have been a whole lot longer but I pleaded to get him off on a lesser charge. That was my worst mistake. It nearly cost me everythin'. He started to beat me up, usually at gun-point, keeping me prisoner in my own home.

'Then, on 24 August 1968, James was born. It was tough for a long time – until I got a decent job again. The money quietened Toney down a while. I even married him – the following August, on the ninth, in the summer of '69. But his violence came back. The police were called out again and again but he could talk his way out of anything. After four months of marriage I filed for divorce. And then it happened. He tried to murder us. I could have easily died but, on 5 June 1970, he left us there, on the floor, and vanished. Do you wonder why James hates him?'

We shook our heads, stilled by the fervour of her story. But Sherry was on a loop. Words blurred from her mouth. She told us how, from the age of five, James 'threw tantrums, punched other kids, shouted at his teachers. It got so bad that he was turfed out of one school after another. We had moved to Ann Arbor in '76 and after five or six years there was not a school in the area who would accept him. Councillors told me to send him to a school for the dangerously retarded. It was suggested that he be put on tranquillisers and anti-depressants to take the heat outta him . . .'

Sherry bit her darkly coloured lip. She blinked and lifted her head up again with a haughty sweep.

'But he was my son. I knew he wasn't retarded. I knew he wasn't mad. I knew that all his trouble stemmed from one dirty thing. He wanted a daddy. And he couldn't have one – for his was a bad man. But we had each other, James and me. We got through it. I knew some people on the school board and he got transferred to a public school outside the area. There were teachers there who cared about him. By the age of twelve, to stop him fighting in the streets, I got him boxing. I took him down to a gym. He still had some emotional problems but he had great ability too. I think even then we knew that boxing could save him . . .'

Although James graduated from high school, and received numerous offers of football scholarships, there were still snags. Badly injured, and out of football forever, he began trading in crack.

'He'd given up on boxing for a while back then,' Sherry said, as if in explanation of his behaviour. 'He fell in with the wrong crowd. Y'know the type – they carry guns, deal in drugs. He made a mistake. But I caught him before he got too deep. He ain't got no police-record. You can check on that. He promised he'd quit if I got him a job. I did. I got him to help me out in the bakery.'

'Speciality Cakes & Pies?'

'You got the taste now,' Sherry chuckled. 'I can tell I'm gonna have to fly over more of those cakes o' mine . . .'

'Mmm-hmmm!' we harmonised, before I returned to the stickier issue of those white rocks called crack. 'Is there a chance,' I asked, 'that he could go back to the street if boxing turned sour?'

'No!' Sherry snapped. 'That's in the past. It's back there with his father – in the bad old days. It's over. We're living for the future. There's no stopping James now. He's being recognised for what he is – the best fighter in the world. The boy who stepped out of his father's shadow and became a daddy himself.' Sherry looked intently at us. 'You know Jasmine?'

'She's very beautiful,' Alison affirmed.

Sherry blushed before she snorted once more. 'Yeah, okay, that's good o' you. Just don't you go calling me "Granny" now, ya'hear?'

'No, ma'am!' I gargled. 'How does James feel about it?'

''Bout you calling me "Granny"?'

'About being a father . . .'

'He loves it! He's in awe of that little girl. You shoulda seen him the last months before the birth, just before he hurt Iran Barkley so bad. He used to coo to the baby inside her mama, whispering to the bump: "Come on out, I love you, I wanna hold you . . ."'

We grinned back, reflecting on the fuzzy glow of Sherry's description. I always liked hearing evidence of a fighter as abrasive as James 'Lights Out' Toney taking time out from coercion.

'But will being a father help him as a boxer?' I eventually asked.

'Jeeeezzz!' Sherry exclaimed. 'Think what he did to Barkley. James couldn't even be there for Jasmine's birth. He made Barkley pay for that.

He's had to be away from Jasmine for this fight too – an' it ain't helped that him an' Sarah have had a temporary fallin' out. Littles will suffer for all o' that. All those questions of fatherhood drive him on in the ring. His father will be inside his head, so will his daughter. He hates the one and loves the other. But he's been a fighter far longer than he's been a father. Y'see, I know my son better than anyone . . .'

To the rest of boxing, James Toney was just a fighter, someone to revere or revile. But there was tenderness in Sherry's voice.

'I know my son better than anyone,' she repeated. 'Jackie pretends that she knows how to deal with him. But she don't; not really. When the shit flies with James there's no one but me who can control him. I speak the boy's language. I talk nigger to him. I can say that to you. You from Africa. I know you been years in Soweto, I know you listen to that hip-hop stuff too, jus' like my boy. You know how young black men talk. You know it's "motherfucker this, bitchin' ho that!". Jackie wants to pretend that James will listen to polite talk when he's mad, that he'll be a good boy if you ask nicely. That ain't true. You gotta trash-talk with these boys when you want the truth. You know that better than Jackie.'

I liked the bluntness of Sherry's compliment. But, in reality, I was even less confident than Jackie when forcing out an approximation of black rap. Instead, I nodded knowingly, my tongue hiding in its tightly shut mouth.

'Take this one time,' Sherry said. 'It was a while ago, when James was on the street. He pretended he was a gang-banger. Then the news started to spread. Because of their bad rep for fighting and that, James and his boys sometimes got blamed for things they'd never done. Word was that he and some of the others on his corner had been in on a gang rape of some poor neighbourhood girl. I didn't believe it – but I also knew that nothing is impossible.

'So I had it out with him as soon as he walked through the door. I looked him dead in the eye and said, "I got jus' one question for you, nigger!"'

Sherry banged her fist down hard on the table as she pushed her face into mine, as if I was also a wayward son. I reared back but she came closer. I could feel the heat of her breath on my pale skin. She crashed her hand against the glass table again, rattling the Bonaventure's elegant crockery.

'Did you fuck the bitch?' she snorted. 'Yes or no?'

Tummy-tucked ladies from Beverly Hills turned round in horror.

'I'm asking you again!' Sherry hissed menacingly. 'Yes or no! Did you fuck the bitch!'

The Hollywood wives gasped. Their skin-tautened stares veered from Alison to me, as if she was the victim and I the criminal. I must have shook my head because Sherry smiled calmly.

'Yeah,' she sniffed, 'he spoke plainly to me. "No," he said, "I didn't fuck her, mom. I didn't even see her. I promise you." I knew right away he was telling the truth. Jackie couldn't have done it. She's great at press conferences. But, y'know, when it comes round to asking James the essential questions, it's gonna be me who pops 'em. Not Jackie – but me, 'cos I been with him from the very start. Man, I'm his mother!'

We shared a giggle later about that shaky moment – barking out 'yes or no?' at every opportunity – but our respect for Sherry meant that giddy laughter invariably ended in rueful speculation. If Tyson had been fortunate to have a mother like her he might not have landed up in the dock having to answer that same question, framed only by a more proper set of words.

The defining relationship between a fighter and his family had begun to consume me. There were wonderful boxing mothers across the world, like Sherry in Ann Arbor and Joan Watson in Tottenham; and then there were all those absent black fathers, like Tyson's and Toney's. But, as Tyson and Eubank also knew, not every black mother was a saint; just like there were fathers who were always around.

The three brightest and newest stars in boxing were urged on by eager dads. I thought of each of them in turn – Toney's burgeoning rival, Roy Jones Jnr, from a Pensacola farm; Eubank's great pretender, Naseem Hamed, living above a corner-shop in Sheffield; and, from East LA's *barrios*, Oscar De La Hoya. The fact that they came from diverse racial groups – African-American, Arab and Hispanic respectively – embellished the attraction of comparing them to each other and to black firebrands like Tyson and Toney.

I was set to begin that contrast with De La Hoya, the ring's latest golden boy. He and his father, Joel, were on the top floor of the Bonaventure, apparently in the hotel's best suite, better even than the Lights Out boudoir. I knew that Oscar owned a face suited more to celluloid than bloodied canvas. He had the look which thrilled McDonald's and Coke when he won gold at the Barcelona Olympics in 1992. They preferred him to James Toney.

'This is the kid corporate America's been waiting for!' a McDonald's marketing man had marvelled as Oscar matched his radiant appearance with an easy charm in both English and Spanish. But De La Hoya was more than a bilingual looker who could then already slip and bang to the body with a left hook as crippling as any on the professional circuit. At nineteen years of age, Oscar also had gravitas. His mother, Cecilia, had died of cancer only months before the Games.

'Crushed by misery', Oscar had been lifted by a desire to dedicate his winning medal to her and a matching resolve to help his Mexican immigrant father escape the tiny apartment in which they'd lived so long. Before every Olympic fight, even in the final, he had knelt in the ring to pray in remembrance of Cecilia. When he won America's only boxing gold, that hallowed image lingered for the advertisers and circling fight-game sharks. They recognised that Oscar De La Hoya was the charismatic boy-wonder who might do the incredible – he could make boxing seem fantastic again. He was not the new Mike Tyson; he was a throwback to more sanctified days, to Sugar Ray Leonard and Muhammad Ali.

When you're that hyped a fight figure, you're never alone. Besides his father and uncles and cousins, Oscar De La Hoya now had a whole team behind him – from Toney's promoter, Bob Arum, to a score of marketing assistants and press officers. They ensured that Oscar's time was strictly allocated to a chosen rota of journalists. No one 'unapproved', like Alison, would be allowed up with me when I finally got the interview call from one of the LA babes running his media relations.

I waited alone in the hotel foyer for my apportioned Oscar slot. Sherry Toney clicked by in her sharp heels. At the huge glass-tombed elevator which blasted up the Bonaventure like a rocket, Mrs T turned to me. Without a flaming 'yes or no?' quandary in sight she enquired if I wanted a ride with her and another of Jackie's fine boxers – a friendly white welterweight called Bronco McKart whom I had met in Tulsa.

Careful not to convey a shift in loyalties by mentioning De La Hoya, I declined politely.

'Scares you, huh?' Sherry laughed. I wondered if she had seen me lurch from the window when we took the Bonaventure lift for the first time. I had quivered against the door, weak-kneed and gasping, while Alison placidly watched the cinemascope blur of LA sheering away in a blood-curdling rush.

'Don't worry,' Bronco shouted, 'James Toney's also scared of this elevator. He won't even step inside. He goes up in the goods lift round the back!'

'Ssshhhh!' Sherry instructed as she waved me a brisk goodbye. 'James'll kill you if he hears you tellin' everyone. He ain't no pretty-boy like Oscar . . .'

When the signal came it was with unexpected stealth. A red light shone on the bellhop's silver dais. His slick head swivelled my way. He picked up the cordless phone and, after a moment, nodded briefly, almost imperceptibly. A clever tic of his left eye made me glance at the elevator. By the time I turned back he had put the receiver down and raised his index finger. He followed it upwards with a fleeting gaze and then nodded again, more diligently this time, as if exercising the lower muscles in his neck. It looked like he was auditioning for *The Godfather IV*. I admired his technique while he repeated the silent routine, his black eyes never leaving mine. I imagined I was the Don himself, acknowledging another coded message with a twitch of my heavy lids and a mysterious half-smile.

But I must have been less impressive, for Method Man gave up on our meaningful interior dialogue. He reverted to flunkey mode. 'They're ready for you now, sir,' he sighed, 'on the top floor. Someone will meet you there.'

He bowed towards the elevator as if I had lost sight of the plot. 'Yo, Ramona! Ramona Vasquez!' he called to a sassy young chambermaid meandering ahead of me, 'hold that finger. He's also going all the way up . . .'

'To the man?' Ramona bubbled.

'*You* got it first time!' he replied snidely.

'Oscar?' she asked me for further confirmation. 'You goin' to see Oscar!' I nodded slowly again, finding it hard to snap out of character.

'Oh, baby,' Ramona Vasquez groaned. The glass doors closed on the bellman's baleful stare. 'That Oscar's got a kisser on him you wouldn't believe. It's a Hollywood face, honey. They're plastering it all over the city – all the way down there. Look, ain't LA pretty from up here?'

We had already exploded up twenty-five flights and were gaining speed. It was hard to absorb the beauty of Los Angeles' gleaming quartz as we shot along the Bonaventure's steel sides. Our lick seemed connected to Ramona's lips, as if every word she said glossed us past another hazy storey. She leaned against the lift's polished windows, clutching piles of pillow-cases to her chest, as she rattled on. 'I know what'cha thinkin',' she smirked, 'I can see it in the eyes!'

Ramona stepped towards me, waving her fist at my miserable reluctance to soak up LA's splendour at that heavenly height. I pinned myself against the exit, remembering how the Bonaventure had dwarfed the screen in *Bladerunner*. With her left hand cocked, she suddenly was Ramona the replicant.

'Yeah, Joey on the bell-desk told me!' she said.

'He did?' I drawled, stunned by Joey's premonition of my Jimmy Stewart in *Vertigo* turn.

'Sure,' Ramona breathed with minty passion, 'you also thinkin' that De La Hoya may look like an angel but he hits like a mule! He's got that great left hook! He's got it made! He's the one Hispanic guy in this fucking country who might do it all! He's a fighter, man, a foxy young fighter!' She let her fist fall. 'I think I'm in love with Oscar! You tell him my name's Ramona Vasquez, that I'm from the projects too, that I'm doin' laundry on his floor. Tell him to give me a call down the passage – anytime, baby, anytime . . .'

She flounced out on the summit of Los Angeles, overlooking the Hollywood hills and the East LA *barrios* – from where both she and Oscar came.

His face broke open into that wide smile so loved by the camera when I told him that the otherwise unknown Ramona sent her warmest regards.

'Wow! That's really nice!' Oscar blushed, the same as any kid might when hearing that a hot chambermaid had his number. He didn't sound much like a boxer. His fast patter quickly established, in a beguilingly mild Spanish accent, that his favourite words were 'wow' and 'nice'.

'She really said that? Wow!' Oscar laughed cheekily before reverting to a more ingratiating overview of Ramona's lust. 'It's nice when people from your own community approve. That reminds me of who I'm fighting for . . .'

He had begun to sound like a smoothie about to step onto the Letterman show. I had seen him chatting on TV with Jay Leno two years before, just after his Olympic triumph. He was suave enough then, at nineteen. But he was still improving in public. For all I knew his people might have already set up a plug for him on Letterman the following week, by which time he would have won what he hoped to be merely the first of six world-championship belts.

The cynics insisted that it was no coincidence that this boy from LA was called Oscar. They said that he had eyes more for the cathode rays than the ring. They claimed that, unlike a toughie such as Toney, De La Hoya was the kind of fighter loved by people who cared little for boxing. He was glamorous and cordial, beautiful and talented. He was made for Letterman, for Leno, for late-night chat about the product he was pushing.

Yet there were others who believed that he could become the greatest boxer of the '90s. De La Hoya's amateur credentials were exemplary. He had lost only one fight of consequence in 225 competitive bouts. His rare ability was conspicuous by the age of fifteen, when he won the Golden Gloves title. Three years later he even sparred with Julio Cesar Chavez, the legendary Mexican – who was then, in 1991, at his peak as he ran up the longest streak in boxing history by winning his first eighty-nine fights. Chavez, a vicious body-puncher, decided to impart some professionally stern knowledge. Outweighed by ten pounds, Oscar was hurt in the opening few minutes. But then he began to fire back. Outsiders were amazed to hear how a teenager had stood up to the Mexican. Even Chavez embraced him, wondering if they'd meet for real when the time came for his own career to end.

Looking like another Hispanic addition to *LA Law* and punching as hard as Ramona Vasquez's foul-tempered Mexican mule, how could he miss? Oscar's earning potential outstripped competent heavyweight champions like Evander Holyfield and Lennox Lewis and helped explain why Bob Arum had chosen him over Toney to headline the reopening of the famous Olympic auditorium. Arum knew that Oscar's boxing would always be invested with a wider social significance. Whenever he climbed through the ropes he did so as 'The Pride of East LA', evoking both the nostalgia of an immigrant-Mexican culture and the hopes of Hispanic America.

Oscar also placated more WASPish fears with his light skin and grace; and the money-men loved him when he ducked though the ropes clutching the Stars and Stripes in one glove and the Mexican flag in the other. It was a symbol as modernly American as a Taco Bell logo – and just as popular with the cheering throng. The screams of delight and the frenetic chants of 'Os-car, Os-car, Os-car' must have made boxing spellbinding to him.

But the crabby presence of his father, Joel, abruptly entering our room, was a reminder that Oscar fought for reasons other than ego. 'I can never forget how I began to box,' he said while looking askance at his dad. In a similar vein to Sherry in Tulsa, Joel stood behind me, hammering his thickly knotted fingers against the hotel window from where we could see their sprawling old neighbourhood.

'It was there,' Oscar pointed, 'in East LA, that I began to fight. I was six years old and my cousin would beat me up. I'd walk through the streets, crying. My father said "Enough! It's time you learned about life." He took me to the gym . . .'

That start had a familiar ring; but his father's stance spoke of more difficult truths. A pro fighter himself, Joel had dreamed of making big money ever since leaving Mexico as a boy. But there had been disappointment for him in America. A good rather than a great fighter, he'd been forced to find manual work in an air-conditioner factory. He burned with a need to get out. By 1984, the year of the Los Angeles Olympics, he was voracious in his ambition to transform his eleven-year-old son into the champion he had never been.

The De La Hoyas were inspired by the example of Paul Gonzales, another *barrio* homeboy, who had struck gold at those '84 Games. Gonzales had everything both in and outside the ring – until the fast money and fame turned him badly off track. Within a few years Gonzales was just another forgotten Hispanic boxer.

'This will be different,' Joel asserted testily. 'From the start, we've had a grip on Oscar. When he was eleven, I tell the boy I want him to be somebody, for the sake of us all. I say, "No messing up. You go to school and gym. Nowhere else." I asked a lot . . . he always obeyed.'

'But was that much of a childhood?' I asked Oscar, hoping such disobedience would not provoke a paternal cuff.

Joel's heavy hand fluttered, only to resume its steadier beat when Oscar replied after a pause. 'It was difficult,' he conceded. 'I saw how different life was for everyone else. I think about it now because I never had that freedom. I missed a lot . . .'

'He had to,' Joel rumbled. 'I'd say, "No booze, no girls – no problems." All he could look forward to was healthy food and decent sleep – he was training to be world champion.'

'But what if, Oscar,' I speculated, trying to keep a jovial dad at bay, 'your father hadn't turned you into a boxer?'

'I would have given everything to study. I'd be an architect now . . . that's what my mother would've wanted . . .'

Oscar always tried to say and do the right thing; even before America fell for him when he sank to one knee in the Olympic ring. The memory of those Barcelona moments prevailed. They tugged at corporate purse-strings but also reached beyond his Casanova pout in the Rico Suave shaving-gel ad we had seen all over town. In person, his face struggled to conceal emotion. I found myself thinking of him more as a boy chock-full of feeling than as an aspiring cultural icon.

'When I think of the Olympics,' he said, 'I remember the pressure. I wanted to win for my mother so badly. Afterwards I felt such relief. The gold was for her but my professional career is for me. And, wow, it's nice that things are paying off . . .'

We were two days away from his twelfth professional fight. The previous eleven, in little over a year, had been knockout victories against humdrum journeymen. Yet De La Hoya was about to receive his first million-dollar purse from Arum while signing a $7,500,000 deal with HBO Television. He offered another wowed reaction to all the money he was certain to make as a multiple world champion.

'Wow, there'll be too many zeros to count . . . that's kinda a nice but scary thought!'

'Scary?'

'You know what I mean . . .' Oscar stopped. Beneath that finished fantasy of moving from the *barrios* to the Bonaventure, heartache and intrigue lurked. He was living a quintessential Hollywood saga loaded with estranged money moguls and family conspiracies, with greed and jealousy. De La Hoya's perfect persona was slipping then – to the point where, in that week of his title bid, *The Ring* magazine offered a scathing portrait of their once-favourite young fighter. 'Golden Boy or Gold-digger?: The Damaged Image of Oscar De La Hoya' the cover-line screamed. The piece sketched a fanciful depiction of De La Hoya, 'full of avarice', sitting alone in a hotel room counting out $100 bills from a suitcase bulging with money. For all the hysteria of that attack on a boxer *The Ring* had once extolled as the fight-game's saviour, it was clear that De La Hoya's business decisions had not met with widespread support. Even the *Boston Globe* observed that De La Hoya's bilingualism now meant that he could say 'greedy' in two languages.

Shortly before he signed the HBO deal negotiated by his New York management team – former rock promoter Robert Mittleman and mortgage banker Steve Nelson – De La Hoya fired them. In Barcelona Mittleman and Nelson had outwitted boxing's most influential players by offering Oscar a million-dollar package – including $500,000 in cash, a house in Montebello of similar value, a $60,000 Acura NSX sports car, a $30,000 van and bonuses for his father who would also receive 11 per cent of all managerial takings. It was an unprecedented deal for an adolescent fighter.

Joel signed on his son's behalf even though they had already accepted $100,000 from Shelly Finkel, a rival manager whose outlay included $4,500 expenses for Cecilia's funeral. 'Shelly, you're my number-one guy,' Joel told Finkel at the Olympics, 'but when are you going to make Oscar an offer?' When a stunned Finkel pledged an additional $100,000 in cash, Joel's reaction was one of derision.

'We weren't going to let him take advantage of us just because he helped

us,' De La Hoya Snr snapped at reporters. 'We aren't bean farmers . . .'
Finkel was out and, against all odds, Mittleman and Nelson were in.

In the fifteen months they managed De La Hoya, Mittleman and Nelson
organised his title chance and numerous advertising contracts. Yet in
December '93, only ten weeks before his WBO shot, Oscar decided to
become self-managed and be advised only by family members. They would
handle Oscar De La Hoya Enterprises Inc. without interference. Boxing's
barons of decency feigned shock.

'Off the record,' I heard one mildly infamous promoter ask, 'do these
Hispanic guys have absolutely no fuckin' morals?'

There was additional gossip that an anonymous Latin cartel had pumped
$1,500,000 into the new company – of which Genaro Salas, Oscar's cousin
and a former postal worker, became chief adviser. On his instigation,
Mittleman and Nelson were 'iced'. The De La Hoyas, apparently, could be
ruthless when they deemed it necessary.

Oscar claimed 'no regrets about a tough business decision'. He was,
however, aware of the damage done to his carefully crafted image. 'I know
some people think I only care about money. That's not true. Boxers get
ripped off by their managers. I'm lucky. I'm self-managed. How many
fighters can say that? I want to be one of the few who keeps his millions . . .'

With that Eubankesque refrain, Oscar complained that his former
managers smothered him: 'Nelson watched every move, wanting to know
who I was speaking to and why. Mittleman moved to LA, bought a house
a block away from mine. It was like they owned me.' But possession
appeared to have shifted from one camp to another – from a white
entourage to the De La Hoya clan. Oscar was a gigantic meal-ticket for an
extended family. He belonged, even then, to others.

When I asked him what he hoped to get out of boxing, apart from
money, he said earnestly, 'Boxing needs a positive role model. I want to be
that guy. It's not that I'm trying, it just comes naturally. I want people to
say, "Oscar's a great fighter but, wow, he's really smart!"'

As Joel answered a jangling telephone Oscar moved closer to me. He
sounded agitated. 'I'm not a bad guy!' he urged. 'A few months ago I broke
down in the gym. I cried. It was a kind of sobbing. Nobody understood
why. They can't imagine the pressure. I never see my buddies, I'm never
myself . . .'

Despite the conformity of that lament, there was anguish in Oscar's
voice. 'Sometimes, I think I would choose my old lifestyle before this kind
of life. I lived just a few blocks away from the projects. Everywhere you
looked you saw gangs and drugs. But I took the clean road. And I had my
buddies. I was happy then . . .'

'And now?' I asked as Joel talked into the phone's mouthpiece, swallowed
up in his massive clinch.

'Well, I'm kinda happy,' Oscar pondered. 'Think of the money and what

I'm about to achieve. One day I'll have ten times the fun. Maybe on Saturday, when I'm world champion, I'll go back to East LA, see some buddies, even dance with a girl – wow, that would be nice . . .'

Robert Mittleman was contemptuous. 'It's all an act! The kid's a complete phoney, a stuck-up brat. If he were a pool, he'd be the shallow end.'

Mittleman mixed New York censure with homely Detroit attitude. Did he always feel this way, I wondered, even when touting Oscar as boxing's most glorious discovery?

'Always! Steve and I were smacked around continuously by the family from hell – by the father and the cousin, fucking Gerry Salas, and that scum-bag fucking piece of shit, Ray Garza, who calls himself a "business agent".'

I thought Mittleman lacked Jackie Kallen's gilded promotional touch.

'Y'see,' he moped, 'Oscar hears lots of whispering in his ear and he has the propensity to gravitate towards the worst possible people. He could have become the richest boxer ever. It's not gonna happen. He's gonna be a disaster!'

'So it's safe to say, Bob, that you feel a little bitterness?'

'Yeah, you could say that . . .'

Where Mittleman was wired and angular, Steve Nelson was portly and diplomatic. 'Oscar buckled under the pressure from uncles and cousins who wanted a slice. The bottom line is that he's made a decision which will hurt him. I don't feel anger because I don't think he knew better. He was taken advantage of . . .'

Nelson believed then that the manner of their sacking emphasised the family's manipulation. 'Oscar never told us. We heard through the relatives about the application for a restraining order against us. I was with him the night before. He said nothing – he was just the normal smiling Oscar. I tried to reach him afterwards but he was already taken prisoner. The cousin had got to him. Maybe it's an ethnic thing . . .'

There was an undercurrent of prejudice in that incessant sniping against De La Hoya; an implication that his career would be promoted better by fight insiders rather than an Hispanic family from East LA. Even if 'the cousin played the Mexican family card', it was easy to sympathise with Oscar's claim that if there had to be middlemen 'then they might as well come from home'.

While Mittleman demanded, 'Whadd'ya expect from a jerk?', Nelson had a residue of affection for his lost fighter. It helped that a $700,000 compensation settlement had just been agreed. Nelson claimed that 'Oscar's incredibly poised but he's being torn apart. Child prodigies often have dysfunctional problems. Oscar was put into the gym at the age of six, told he was destined to be a legend – his life was taken from him, he never had any choice. This could become yet another very sad boxing story . . .'

At the Olympic auditorium, Oscar De La Hoya could imagine the sadness of losing. 'I always think about it,' he confessed, 'because it would devastate so many people. And what if I lose now, on the night they reopen this place?'

The 'Pride of East LA' banners were already waving in unison with the exiled Mexican carols of 'Os-car, Me-hee-co! Os-car, Me-hee-co!'. They rose up the intimate circles of seating which made the Olympic a boxing theatre matched only for atmosphere and fight tradition by Madison Square Garden. After twelve dark years, Arum's reopening of the Olympic was being trumpeted as boxing's redemption – with Oscar its potentially divine hero.

As a boy, he had come often to the old Olympic. It was a venue where both his father and grandfather fought. 'What I remember most clearly,' he revealed, 'is that you have to put on a good show – otherwise people tear it up. They're fight fanatics.'

Joel De La Hoya looked on impassively, perhaps recalling past nights while he waited for the Olympic bell to ring. When I pressed him for his thoughts, he grunted reluctantly: 'The boy's ready.'

'What do you expect tonight?' I asked.

'We expect a good performance. Oscar knows I'll push him. Sometimes he don't like it . . .'

There was a curt smile from Oscar. 'My father never says I've done well. It used to hurt me. I would train with all my heart – and, still, nothing. I'd say, "What more can he want?" Now I know, it's best this way. I understand this business. It's hard and cruel.'

As I watched him retreat to the famous old dressing-room, his words resounded as if they'd been lifted from one of the many boxing movies filmed at the Olympic – from *The Set-Up* to *Raging Bull* – where the lead character encounters a bad fate. I saw Sugar Ray Leonard, the boxer to whom Oscar was most often compared, lean forward in expectation. He sat not far from where Gerry Salas and Ray Garza – who 'stole Oscar away' – clenched their fists anxiously. I thought of the contrasting emotions of Mittleman and Nelson, watching the boxing on television. I knew that Ramona Vasquez, too, would be glued to the screen, ready to scream for her 'baby'.

But, although the Olympic billboard had been covered in giant letters claiming that this would be 'OSCAR'S NIGHT!', it was also a night of intense suspense for others. Sherry and Jackie tried to smile while the cameras targeted their boy as he trekked towards the ring. He would have understood Oscar's words about boxing being 'hard and cruel'; he, too, would have pretended that it was better not to expect a father's praise. But where Toney had only demons for company, Oscar at least had a real dad – even if he was a man who wrapped his love in austerity. I had the feeling that one day, maybe even that night, Joel De La Hoya would say those kind and simple words to his son. James Toney would be less fortunate.

I didn't walk with him then, choosing instead to be alongside my own baby. Her hand began to moisten in mine, as thrill melted into threat. She'd read that morning how a paper-thin but brave Welsh boxer called Johnny Owen had died after a fight at the Olympic in 1980. He had not been the first nor even the last fighter to give up his life in that ring.

Toney against Littles was the second fight Alison had ever seen. The first, Lennox Lewis stopping Frank Bruno, had been a more surreal affair in Cardiff. On that occasion she had easily lost herself in the misleading diversions – in the lasers and the singing and the fact that two black British heavyweights were fighting for a world title at 1 a.m. on a Saturday morning more than fifty feet away from her. That distance had helped deaden the violence and make a serious fight feel more like late-nite live television. The equally bizarre reality that she knew the quietly sexy Lennox and, particularly, good ol' Frank from countless chat-shows also persuaded her that they were larger-than-life performers rather than mere men. I remember being surprised at how caught up she became in their clumsy drama as she yelled out loud for Lennox – mainly because everyone else was tediously mooing, 'Brooo-no, Brooo-no, Brooo-no', like he was still in pantomime.

It was not the same in the Olympic, a venue which would not allow you to forget that you were present at a real fight. Wherever you sat you felt close to the ring, perhaps even a little too close because you could see the impact of every blow to the head or body. It was altered for Alison, too, because she had met these fighters, she had laughed at their quirky jokes and listened to their wildest boasts. She'd proved to herself that Toney was that 'sweetie' she always suspected.

We had even spent a few hours with his assailant for the night, Tim Littles, on the day Sherry had regaled us with her 'Yes or No?' dilemma. Tim and his two friends spun entertaining stories about their home in Flint, Michigan, and his 'Doctor of Style' nickname. Alison liked his humility and wit when they also chatted as architect and handyman about the pleasures of bricks and mortar and working with their hands. Tim Littles told her how much satisfaction it gave him when he did a job well – and he was not talking about a task of savagery then but, instead, the simple solace in rewiring a neighbourhood building. He'd seemed just an ordinary guy, planning his own small electrical business, surrounded by his family and friends, the sort of unassuming man who instinctively knew how to put strangers at ease.

But there he stood, alone in the ring, face to face with another black fighter – that intimidating cutie, James Toney.

Alison, by then, was less convinced by the glamour of boxing. She watched the fight quietly, the shift in her emotions being marked only by the grip she exerted on my right arm. She understood the risk they were taking. She could no longer think of boxing like she'd done when chuckling at Benn, Eubank and Toney as they disparaged each other in partnership with Messrs Ross and Rourke.

Littles shaded the opening two rounds, throwing some tremendous right-handers. An unflinching Toney swallowed them like a brave boy taking his medicine. He tucked his chin into his shoulder and allowed the good doctor to go to the body next. Toney rotated away from Littles' most incisive punches with a twisting motion so that he was almost at right angles when the wallops landed. In the third, Littles caught him with a left hook – only for the champion to reply with a stiffer replica. It hurt Littles. We could see the tremor cascading down his streamlined frame, wobbling his thin legs only seconds after Lights Out had made the connection with his chin. He ducked his head towards Toney, hoping to hang on, but he couldn't stop another shocking right hand from dropping him.

We gasped as Littles pulled himself up against the ropes. He stayed there until the round ended. The knock-down had been startling; but not as traumatic as the abrupt realisation that something more terrible had happened. Alison saw the blood first. Her muffled cry made me peer across at Littles' corner where Lou Duva and George Benton were frantically trying to revive him.

It was then that I heard the rawer noise of an Olympic crowd. Duva wheeled round excitedly and literally took off in an ebullient leap when he saw the commotion around Toney. Jackie Kallen was in anguish while Sherry rushed from her seat to reach Toney's stool. A doctor was already there but you did not need to be as near as him to rear away from the long, wide and deep cut which had opened up over Toney's left eye. It was the worst gash I had ever seen, a slash so grotesque that it could have been made by a meat-cleaver. It would have needed a cement-mixer, rather than a canny cut-man, to stem the dark spurt covering Toney's confused face.

Amid the bedlam, the doctor indicated that he would allow one more round at the most. If Toney was forced to retire it could mean that his un-beaten record and world title were lost. It was the worst moment of his career.

Littles stood up jauntily, revived by the amazing news being barked out at him by his trainers. If he could keep his feet for three more minutes he might be the new world champion. We were standing ourselves, over-loading on adrenalin. Jackie and Sherry both put their hands to their faces as if to cover the sight of Toney's blood.

But we were mistaken to doubt him. Ten seconds later a huge right hand knocked Littles flat on his back. Alison's own head dropped into her hands. By the time she looked up again, Littles had stumbled across the ring and into a barrage of uppercuts and hooks. He fell face-forwards into Toney, making both of them fall. Toney was up first, ready to roll his gory credits. He finished with unbelievable brutality. Lights Out rained black rods down on Littles, whose arms slumped to his sides and left him a slack and reeling target. A sickening left hook finally brought the end.

It no longer mattered that the fight would have been ruled a 'technical draw' if it had been stopped because of an accidental clash of heads. No one had known that when the fourth round started. Toney had shown again, devastatingly, that there was more to him than a big bad mouth. He was, then, the very 'baddest man' in boxing.

Tim Littles lay unconscious on the deck while Toney lifted both arms in the air and turned slowly to his corner. Alison put her head on my shoulder and let a few more tears well. I couldn't blame her.

There is something strange and disturbing about the way boxing trades on the best and worst of feelings, making us push compassion aside in favour of another compulsive peek. By the time Tim Littles had left the ring with a plaintive shrug, Alison had dried her eyes. She was okay. She had just been overwhelmed by what she had seen, and alarmed by the depth of what she had felt for two men she had met only a week before.

The East LA girls made her smile, though, with their shining faces and shrieks for 'Os-car, Os-car, Os-car . . .'; as did the Mexican bands playing their ditties while the Hispanic homeboys tossed their 'Oscar De La Oh-Yeah' bomber-jackets into the sultry Olympic air.

'I dunno if I can stand another fight like that,' she said, 'but I'm glad we're here. I'm glad we're seeing Oscar next . . .'

She sounded as bad as me; and we were both disappointed with the tedium of De La Hoya's scrap with the WBO junior-lightweight champion, Jimmi Bredhal of Denmark. The gaunt and pallid Bredhal had promised to 'ruin the golden boy'. For two minutes it looked as if he believed his own hype. He sank right jabs into Oscar's greatest selling-point, reddening those prominent cheekbones.

And then a right cross dropped the Dane. Oscar uncorked a huge grin and stuck his tongue out in delight. But the bell saved Bredhal, as it did at the end of the second when he sagged to his knees again. With his right eye closing and red welts emerging on his forehead, Bredhal boxed on the retreat – frustrating Oscar and the baying six thousand. While dominating most rounds, De La Hoya looked nothing more than a gifted prospect learning his craft.

But just when it appeared as if Bredhal would last the distance, another uppercut knocked him down at the end of the tenth. His face was badly swollen and, at last, the ringside doctor intervened. The Olympic erupted. Oscar was world champion; and it looked as if he loved the idea of being a boxer again.

'Oscar, Oscar!' shouted a beautiful girl in the row behind ours. She wore a tight black bustier and red satin hotpants. 'He's a peach!' she swooned while blowing lavish kisses towards the ring.

'Do you know him?' I shouted back.

'No, but we went to the same school – Garfield High. He was the most popular guy! A couple of years later I became Homecoming Queen but, damn, Oscar'd left! But, who knows, maybe we'll meet one day . . .'

'What would you say to him?'

She looked wistful as she thought of an answer. And then, as if parting a cloud over his life, she said earnestly, 'I'd tell him not to believe everything people say now he's famous. I'd tell him, "Be yourself!" I'd say he gives Hispanics hope for a better America. Then,' she laughed, 'I'd ask him to dance . . .'

At the very top of the Bonaventure, a flight above Oscar De La Hoya's suite, there was a revolving bar. They called it the Skywalk. It took an hour to complete a revolution of Los Angeles. On the night Oscar became champion, while James Toney blitzed the Olympic and took twelve stitches in the process, the city below shone brilliantly beneath a rainy sky. From the inside you could no longer hear the sirens screaming or see Skid Row a few blocks away. There was just an urbane burble of conversation and blue lasers streaking across the skyscrapers which drifted past our window.

I thought again of Oscar's slightly bruised face winking with pleasure outside his dressing-room. 'Hey, man,' he laughed, 'how about Toney! What a fighter he is! What a champion! I hope, one day, I get to be a gladiator like him. This was just a start for me – guys like him, after forty-odd fights, are on another level to a baby like me . . .'

Not everyone agreed with his pragmatic assessment. Thousands of fans bound his Mexican heritage – 'Os-car, Os-car! Me-hee-co, Me-hee-co!' – just as a loquacious Bob Arum lauded him as America's greatest young boxer. The De La Hoya gravy-train was gathering speed.

At a chaotic Olympic press conference even Arum, always keen to crank out a few more bucks' worth of publicity, realised that the night belonged to his fighter. As Oscar repeated his longing to 'escape the solitude of seven weeks' training', Arum charmed the reporters. 'C'mon, guys, look around!' he gestured towards a gaping posse of Hispanic women. 'The kid's twenty-one – he's got things on his mind. C'mon, the limousine's waiting, ready to roll wherever Oscar fancies . . .'

A few hours later it began to rain softly. As beautiful at night as they were imposing, the buildings downtown darkened and flattened while stretching towards East LA – just a few miles from 18th and Grand, where the Olympic stood with its fresh coat of paint and newly minted champion. The Bonaventure bar turned slowly and, together, we suddenly hoped that Oscar De La Hoya was a long way from here, dancing with a Homecoming Queen or even a girl like Ramona, making the most of tonight, thinking, like us, 'Wow, this is nice . . .'

5

THE KING AND THE PRINCE

I N A TOWN STARK ENOUGH TO BE CALLED PLAINFIELD, AT THE Indiana Youth Center, in a room ten feet by eight, little space was left for such delicate astonishment or pleasure. All that wowed niceness had been stuck on hold for twenty-five months – and longer, much longer, for there'd hardly been contentment, let alone joy, during Mike Tyson's preceding years of freedom.

They did not keep him in a cell or behind bars. Like the other eighty-four inmates in his unit, at a prison holding fourteen hundred criminals, Tyson was locked up alone in a dorm-like room sealed by an electronic security door. He had two bunk-beds, a small desk and some metal lockers. There were no windows from which he might see a sallow cornfield spreading in the distance on the opposite side of the road, just off Route 40, on the edge of Plainfield, twenty-odd miles from the Indiana County Court where he'd heard his sentence. Six years.

If it hadn't been for the loops of barbed wire and the grey sentinel towers, passing drivers could have mistaken the horizontal building for an obscure rural high school. The 'Youth Center' euphemism garnished the pretence, with its coy hints of trouble-free recreation for a precocious community – a place to keep all those bored and wayward youngsters off the street.

Yet Mike Tyson, the oldest twenty-eight-year-old in the world, remained in jail. Under Indiana state law he had to serve at least half his term before becoming eligible for parole. Vigorous attempts by his celebrity lawyer, Alan Dershowitz, to overturn the original judgement had failed; but cracks were widening. Four of the twelve jurors who'd found Tyson guilty admitted that they might have been mistaken. 'We thought a man raped a woman,' said one, 'but it looks like a system raped a man.'

Desiree Washington provided the source of their doubt. Her credibility was damaged on two counts. It emerged that, before Tyson's criminal trial, she had consulted a civil lawyer about the potential settlement she might

126

seek from the boxer. Yet that was nowhere near as damning as the affidavit signed by a former schoolfriend, Wayne Walker, that she had accused him falsely of rape in October 1989. According to Walker, Desiree had lied to her father in an effort to avoid being punished for returning home late one night.

While those claims would be ruled inadmissible as evidence in a further appeal, they must have opened some sort of window in Tyson's head as he anticipated the possibility of an early release. But, while he waited, he maintained that he had already uncovered an equilibrium lacking in his earlier life.

Captivity in Plainfield was less like Alcatraz than he'd initially imagined. After his first few weeks inside he had said that 'every day I walk a thin line through hell'. But he learned to adjust. His daily routine was simpler and more ordered than anything he'd experienced in years. Between six in the morning and eleven-thirty at night, when the jailhouse lights were on, he could walk around, exercise, visit the library, read, meet with one visitor a day, eat his own food and earn up to a dollar twenty-five for working in the gym – where he stacked weights, handed out towels and kept an eye on the basketballs. Although it was claimed that he was doing seven hundred sit-ups a day and shadow-boxing when shut away, he was not allowed any kind of formal training. Boxing was against the rules in Plainfield, even if Prisoner 922335 had previously been a fight-game icon.

The fetid world of boxing turned without him, creaking in his absence, relying on the likes of Toney and De La Hoya to do the spinning, knowing that even they could not fill the immense hole he had left. Boxing yearned for Mike Tyson far more than he did for it.

While it was interesting to hear that his spartan existence had helped him shed three stone, dropping him ten or so pounds below his usual fighting weight, it was more stimulating to hear of the strenuous mental activity expanding the previously less than mighty mind of Iron Mike.

Yet as someone who'd heard the eloquence of which Tyson was capable, I had a link to his raw affinity for both books and ideas. There was a sensitivity in him which was not visible when he cornered another fighter or felt accosted by a thousand journalists at a Las Vegas press conference. But beyond even Desiree Washington, there were many women he had engaged in rough or forceful sex, 'bonding' as he curiously described it, who would have rejected the possibility of a higher intellectual or emotional self in Tyson. They would have scoffed at the prospect of him showing any feeling for beauty between the covers of a book.

I held on to the hope that the reverse was true – and not just because he had always been good to me. I still carried around in my head some of the more affecting words he had voiced amid the clutter of his abused and abusive personality. But nothing Tyson had ever said before quite tallied with the entries on his prison library card. These were scholarly tomes whose portentous weight would have taxed a professorial brain, never mind a boxer who barely managed to flip through a comic when I'd last met him. I guess not even the 'Ninja Kung-Fu Killers' could match the heavy-duty dudes whom Tyson pored over in Plainfield – heavyweight bruisers like Machiavelli, Voltaire, Marx, Mao Tse-Tung, Cervantes, Nietzsche, Shakespeare, Tolstoy, Dumas and Hemingway. And when he needed a distraction he would dip into a heady pile of historical and political biography – which meant that the planet's baddest man was on quotable terms with Alexander the Great, Genghis Khan, Oliver Cromwell, Lenin, Castro, Hernan Cortes and John Quincy Adams, none of whom, perhaps unjustly, had made it into *The Ring*'s list of all-time great warriors. But Mike also loved the more lyrical writers, from Scott Fitzgerald to Tennessee Williams to Maya Angelou.

He swapped bookish notes with Pete Hamill in *Esquire*. While I was stunned by his new egghead status there was something endearing about his alacrity for the cerebral joust. Of Niccolo Machiavelli, he said, 'He wrote about the world we live in. Not just in *The Prince*, but in *The Art of War*, *Discourses* . . . he saw how important it was to find out what someone's motivation was. "What do they want?" he says, "what do they want, man?"'

Voltaire, for him, was another motherfucker with a pen.

'I loved *Candide*,' Tyson confessed, hinting at an analogy with his own life. 'That was also about the world and how you start out as one thing and end up another, 'cos the world don't let you do the right thing most of the time. And Voltaire himself, he was something, man. He wasn't afraid. They kept putting him in jail and he kept writing the truth.'

But Ernest Hemingway, that carousing and brawling boxing nut, was his top literary homeboy. 'He uses those short, hard words, just like hooks and uppercuts inside. You always know what he's saying, 'cos he says it very clearly . . . he says he doesn't ever want to fight ten rounds with Tolstoy. So I say, "Hey, I better check out this guy, Tolstoy!" I did too. It was hard. I sat there with the dictionary beside me, looking up words. But I like him. I don't like his writing that much because it's so complicated, I just like the guy's way of thinking.'

I found the image of Tyson torn in an honest struggle between *War and Peace* and the *Webster's Dictionary* more impressive than the freshly inked tattoos of Arthur Ashe and Mao Tse-Tung on his upper arms. But these were Tyson's latest heroes. While I thought Ashe's *Days of Grace* a good book for Tyson to revere, and loved the thought of a bespectacled tennis player being stencilled onto his bulging bicep, the Maoist affinity seemed more contrived.

'I love reading Mao,' he enthused, 'especially about the *Long March* and what they went through. I mean, they came into a village one time and all the trees were white and Mao wanted to know what happened. They told him they were so hungry they ate the bark right off the trees! What they went through. I mean, that was adversity.'

Well, Tyson's favourite Chinese tree-eating story avoided the stereotype of a dumb boxer talking about the frisky 'Asian Babes' video he had just seen in the middle of his monastic training régime. A more generous interpretation centred on his emerging ability to accept a philosophical view of life without paranoia or rancour.

'When you die,' he concluded with Hamill, 'nothing matters but the dash. On your tombstone, it says 1933–2025, or something like that. The only thing that matters is that dash. How you live is your life. And were you happy with the way you lived it.'

Under the guidance of a visiting Indianapolis teacher, Muhammad Siddeeq, Tyson had made a further discovery in Plainfield. Like Muhammad Ali nearly thirty years before, he'd become a Muslim, a conversion which was deciphered as a militant black counter to white America. There was speculation that once released he would join Louis Farrakhan and the Nation of Islam, and change his name to Mikhael Abdul-Aziz, meaning 'Slave to the Undefeatable'. Tyson suggested less grandly that 'being a Muslim is probably not going to make me an angel in heaven . . . but I know I'll be a better person when I get out than I was when I came in.'

But good news for Mike Tyson and the Nation of Islam meant bad news for another big black man who had done time in an American jail; a man who also chanted out his own wild rhapsodies to great books and even greater boxers. Don King, I knew, was in trouble again.

And so I went to find him, in the heart of the Troubles, in Belfast of all places.

May 1994

'Danny-boy,' dangerous Don cracked, 'ain't it a fine thing to meet in bonnie old Belfast, where sweet Irish eyes are always smilin', an' a-callin' from glen to glen!'

'How you doing, Don?' I grinned helplessly.

'Tip-toparareray, tip-top-an-a-rarin'-to-go, as they say round here, one of my very most favourite places in the world, Northern Ireland, right up there with the good ol' US of A!' As he drew in the slightest of breaths with which to launch a typically understated soliloquy, I saw that King's performance was not really for my benefit. His unmistakable voice had attracted a local radio crew. They swarmed across the hotel foyer with beaming faces and eager microphones.

I could understand their fervour; for Don King, at least the first few hundred times you heard him, was a riot. It had been a while since I had last seen him in the formidable flesh, his resounding boom inspiring the godlike shock of silver hair to stand and salute his grandiloquent gibberish. And so, replenished by my break from the Don in full flow, I chortled along with the others, amazed yet again by the blistering vitality of a man who refused to concede that he had just turned sixty-two.

'Yeah, all o' you can laugh,' he testified, "cos you know it, you ain't gonna tell me you ain't heard me say it before. It's indisputable, it's undeniable, it's irrevocable and it's unbelievable, but I'm gonna say it again, right now. Yessirree, I'm the "Only in America" man. I'm back, with a bang, in beautifully beguilin' Belfast, home of the bodacious green leprechauns, those bold little fighters of yonder and yore, those symbols of the good and the great in Ireland, of Yeats an' all the poets an' even ol' Oscar Wilde. Our common heritage, y'see, like the black gold o' Guinness streamin' through the taverns and pubs of Belfast, of London, of Boston an' New York City, home to Mike Tyson, that former undisputed champion o' the world, a man unjustly charged for a crime he never did commit. Mike Tyson is innocent. But the man will return, he will reclaim his former greatness. He is our future. I'll say it again – Mike Tyson! He is the future! Mike Tyson! He will be back! An', I promise y'all, we will cross the water again, we will travel the high skies to reach the people of Britain and Northern Ireland, the fine upstanding folk who have written more letters of support to Mike Tyson than any other in the whole wide world. More letters than even Mike Tyson's own countrymen, the Yankee Doodle Dandymen I dearly love. But, notwithstanding patriotism nor any other residue of nationalistic pride, I have to tell the truth. An' I say this wherever I go, "the British are comin', the British are comin', with the Irish, they're comin' out for Mike Tyson!" More than the Americans, the Mexicans, the Japanese, the Germans, the people on these islands are doin' it for Mike Tyson. An' we love you for it, we love you . . .'

His tight little circle of pop-eyed Belfast subjects loved him back, as he got down to the more serious business of selling tickets for a fight between Chris Eubank and Belfast's own Ray Close.

'An' now we're Out for Justice!' King hollered as he celebrated the name of his latest fight promotion while proving once more that he knew a thing or two about rhetoric – seeing that it was his only real form of communication. 'Out for Justice!' King raved, 'we're all out for justice. Mike Tyson's out for justice! Don King's out for justice! Ray Close is out for justice. Yes, your own Ray "Not Even" Close is out for justice! He's out for justice against Chris Eubank. He believes he won their last fight. They called it a draw, he called it a win, an' now he wants justice. An' the man standing in his way is Chris Eubank. But this time the remorseless rematch, the surreal sequel, ain't even gonna be close because your boy, Ray Close, promises to close the curtain on Eubank. Come out and see him at that marvellous theatre of pugilism, Belfast's grand and gritty King's Hall, and back your boy all the way. It's gonna be a wonderful night, a night when justice shall finally prevail . . .'

Amongst many of those who knew him better, who had seen him at work behind slammed boardroom doors, that justice-seeking clarion call could be directed at the man himself. They did not call him 'Teflon Don' for nothing. A slithery King had evaded the grasping clutches of the law – the police, the FBI, the IRS, the County Court, the Supreme Court and the Federal Grand Jury – for so long that it was wearying even to consider the schedule of misdemeanours with which he'd been accused.

Don King had a roster of enemies longer even than Mike Tyson's book-list. They, too, were out for justice even as King agitated for the release of his prime asset from Plainfield. He could promote boxing more effectively than anyone else on earth but, still, King needed Mighty Mike out of the library and back in the ring to fortify his beleaguered empire.

His diamond-studded crown might have been slipping, but beneath the glitter the regal Don was all steel. Once you got past the mask of jocular verbosity, once you slipped beneath the 'Only in America' and 'Out for Justice' catch-phrases, the snappy crackers like 'that boy's chances of getting a shot at the title without me are slim an' none – an' slim's outta town!', you were confronted with something beyond a joke. Don King was a mercilessly smart hustler who'd do anything to ensure that he was the one loading the dice.

He'd started in business more than forty years before as a numbers-racketeer in Cleveland. He had both the brains and the toughness to shine in that gambling underworld – until he ran into the first of his legal problems by shooting dead a man who'd tried to rob his numbers-house. Acquitted on a self-defence plea, King rose fast and mean to the gambling top.

'They called me "The Numbers Czar" and Donald "The Kid" King,' he reminisced. 'I was good.'

But on 20 April 1966 he killed another man in the street – beating and kicking to death Sam Garrett while holding a loaded .357 gun in his free hand. King had run a bet with Garrett and won $600. He demanded his money but the smaller man, who weighed a hundred pounds less than him, couldn't pay on the spot. King's self-defence claim, this time, didn't convince a jury who heard that Garrett's last words were 'I'll pay you the money, Don, I'll pay you the money . . .'

In October 1967, King was sentenced to serve up to twenty years at the Marion Correctional Institute in Ohio for second-degree murder. He was paroled after four years when his lawyer had the charge reduced to manslaughter – but as King said, 'I didn't serve time, I made time serve me.' Like Mighty Mike, he had reinvented himself in jail.

'I lived in books. I escaped confinement in my mind: *A Tale of Two Cities*, *Meditations* by Marcus Aurelius, Tom Paine, the *Critique of Pure Reason*, Kant, Hegel, Mill, Machiavelli, Gibran, W.E.B. du Bois, Marcus Garvey, Freud, Shakespeare, Frederick Douglass and the Holy Bible. I've tried to emulate Douglass. He fought slavery and extolled his country, America.'

His devouring of these and other classics – 'Y'know, Homer, Dante, Aristotle and that other cat, Thomas Acquinine [sic]' – prepared King for a post-prison lifetime in boxing where he transformed promotional trickery into an artform of malapropisms and misquotations. But King's calculated mania bordered on genius in its ability to make the hard-sell.

Ten months after he walked out of a jail cell, his second career began when he persuaded Ali to give an exhibition in Cleveland to raise funds for a local hospital. Within two years he had established himself in boxing mythology by convincing the corrupt Zairean government to pay Ali and George Foreman $5,000,000 each for his 1974 'Rumble in the Jungle' epic.

King was obdurate in his desire to control the heavyweight championship. As he admitted to *Boxing News's* Harry Mullan, he never had any regrets in switching allegiance from one fighter to another. When Joe Frazier was still champion, having beaten Ali in their Bob Arum-promoted fight at Madison Square Garden, King was angling to become the main man. Chaperoned by a massive police escort, he sat with Frazier in the champion's limousine as they drove to the stadium in Kingston, Jamaica, where Foreman was waiting.

'The first round,' King marvelled at his gall, 'George hit Frazier with a devastating punch that sent Joe leaping in the air. Every time he'd strike Frazier I'd move closer to the end of the row, towards George's corner. By the time the fight ended, on a second-round TKO, I was on George's corner. When the fight was stopped, I'm into the ring, saying to George, "I told you!" And George said, "Come with me." He took me to his room. Same thing. Motorcycle cops. Sirens blasting. I came with the champion, and I left with the champion.'

In another infamous incident, King dropped Michael Dokes, one of his many 'protégés' and a mediocre WBA champion in the early '80s, only seconds after he had been knocked out by South Africa's Gerrie Coetzee. For all his campaigning zeal against apartheid, King was quick to embrace the Afrikaans champion. 'The only thing I remember about that night,' Dokes said years later, 'was being half-conscious on the floor, looking up and seeing Don King step over me to get to Gerrie Coetzee . . .'

Larry Holmes, the best heavyweight of that era, offered the pithiest summary of the promoter's attitude to fighters. For all King's playing of 'the race card', Holmes declared that 'the only colour which Don cares about is green . . .'

When told of his former fighter's comment, King claimed to be confused and hurt: 'I was a father figure to Larry Holmes,' he said, 'the only man he ever looked up to.'

'Did Don say that?' Holmes responded tartly. 'He doesn't stop. He won't quit.'

One of the few white fighters to suffer under King, the salty Tex Cobb, also quipped that 'Don is one of the great humanitarians of our time. He has risen above prejudice. He has screwed everybody he has ever been around. Hog, dog or frog, it don't matter to Don. If you've got a quarter, he wants the first twenty-six cents.'

When Tim Witherspoon defeated Frank Bruno in a WBA title fight in July 1986, King ripped off his own fighter in dollars rather than mere cents. Although Bruno's promoter, Mickey Duff, signed a deal with King which specified that Witherspoon would receive $1,700,000 to defend his title in London, the final amount for the American had shrunk to $90,094.77 when he collected his cheque for winning an eleven-round brawl. The rest had gone – after, King protested, they had paid $115,000 to the WBA and $75,000 to the British taxman. The excess $1,420.005.23 was used to pay 'training expenses', 'sundries' and, of course, Don and his son, Carl King, who'd been appointed as Witherspoon's manager.

King's continual money-smudging attracted the scrutiny of both the IRS and the FBI. In 1984 he was indicted on twenty-three counts of tax evasion while in 1991 he was investigated twice – first for taking a million dollars in claims for two bouts which never took place and then after the New York State Inspector-General, Joseph Spinelli, accused him of having direct ties with John Gotti and other Mafia family heads. He was acquitted each time.

In 1993 he quashed yet another Grand Jury inquiry into his business practices; but they kept gunning for him. When we met in Belfast, King had been given notice of a nine-count Manhattan Federal Courthouse prosecution case of 'wire fraud'. He was charged with swindling Lloyds of London out of $350,000 on a false insurance claim for a cancelled fight between Julio Cesar Chavez and Harold Brazier – scheduled as the main support to Tyson's last fight against 'Razor' Ruddock on 28 June 1991. Chavez was cut badly in sparring and ordered by his doctor to call off the Brazier bout. King subsequently filed an invoice to Lloyds for $350,000 worth of 'non-refundable training expenses' which he said he was obligated to pay to Chavez. The federal indictment against King alleged that he had faxed fraudulent contracts between him and Chavez to Lloyds – and that the Mexican had never seen a cent of the insurer's subsequent payout.

King's real problem was that his former chief book-keeper, Joe Maffia, would give evidence against him. Don felt more secure on the last occasion one of his employees had taken the witness-stand to answer such drastic allegations. Connie Harper, vice-president of Don King Productions, had taken the rap when called to the stand in 1984. Although she had skimmed $195,000 from her income when filling in her tax returns, King's actual earnings were understated by $422,000. Harper, seemingly besotted with big Don, exonerated her superior by claiming that she had been solely responsible for the deception. She was jailed for a year – by the same jury which, after finding her guilty and her boss innocent, queued for King's autograph in court. Don did his signing duty and then announced that he would be taking all twelve jurors out for a slap-up meal that very evening.

But Maffia was not in love with King. The accountant, who had been forced to resign from DKP by Big Don himself over questions of loyalty, was subpoenaed by a US Senate subcommittee headed by Republican

William Roth of Delaware. Senator Roth had begun his investigation into boxing after witnessing James Toney's controversial decision win over Delaware's Dave Tiberi in February 1992 – two days before Tyson was jailed. Roth thought wrongly that the subsequent points verdict had been fixed in Toney's favour. His research team, however, soon realised that there were more serious injustices in boxing. And Joe Maffia knew more than anyone about Don King's bulging bag of tricks.

Maffia was ready to 'reveal everything' – including the fact that King had allegedly plundered Mike Tyson's account. During the first year of the fighter's stint in Plainfield, King had apparently used $750,000 of Tyson's money for renovations to his own mansion. He had given a further $200,000 of Tyson's cash in 'consultancy fees' to his wife and sons, while his daughter Debbie had been remunerated the sum of $52,000 as the president of Iron Mike's fan-club. The boxer, through Don King's power of attorney, had an additional $15,000 of his money transferred to Debbie's husband – purportedly for no other reason than his being 'DK's son-in-law'.

Tyson was reported to be incensed when the true nature of his finances were clarified by press reports. While his conversion to Islam and literature had supposedly elevated his spirit, he was still embittered by King's treachery.

In Belfast, I attempted to broach the awkward subject.

'What sort of questions are these?' King snarled as, at six-foot five and nearly three hundred pounds, he towered above me, his weighty diamond-encrusted gold crucifix swinging on his thick neck.

'I just wondered how you felt about being subjected to another investigation,' I pandered as the radio people stepped back in puzzlement. DK was perhaps not as cuddly as they had fancied.

'Listen,' King suddenly burst into a cacophonous fit of laughter, as if he suddenly realised the absurdity of wasting any form of menace on us, 'none of this worries me. "Investigation" is my middle name, baby . . .'

'So you're not worried about any new allegations that might be made by Maffia?'

'Hell, no! It's all been said before. I've been accused of racketeering, skimming an' launderin' money. I've been told I'm a corrupter of judges, an exploiter of fighters, a fixer of fights, even a stealer of souls. Now you know that jus' ain't true. None of it. There will always be the failed and the foolish, the jaded and the jealous, who want to tear down a successful black man like me. They refuse to see that I am the true attestation of the American dream! But I am fearless, I am undeterred! I am the American Dream – inviolate, invincible, indestructible!'

'But what about Mike Tyson?'

'I love Mike Tyson!' King yelped. 'I love that brother like he's my own son! I love him! Always have, always will. And yeah, before you ask, the feelin's mutual . . .'

King's eyes glazed as he searched for a diversion; and it was then that a five-foot four-inch leprechaun of sorts, from Yorkshire, saw his chance.

'Yo, Don!' Naseem Hamed muttered, 'Don King!'

'Yo!' King exclaimed, 'The Prince is in the house!' He bounded over to Naseem and wrapped a bear-like arm around the boy. 'This kid is just so great,' King laughed blissfully, 'he's gonna go all the way. No stoppin' him now, babies – we're takin' him to America! Yessireee, the Prince is Vegas-bound. We're gonna take over the world, baby, me an' you, the King an' the Prince!'

Naseem rocked in King's embrace, happy to be his newest ring hope, oblivious to all the troubles of chuckling Don and ignorant of Tyson's immersion in Machiavelli's version of *The Prince*. His urchin Arab Yorkie face popped out of King's pulsating bosom with a smirk which said, 'Yeah, I told you all! I am the Prince! I'm gonna be a legend, I'm gonna be even bigger than Mike Tyson! I'm gonna be the next Ali, I'm gonna make forty million pounds! Don King and I, we're gonna do the business! I know it, Don knows it! Now you know it!'

I had travelled to Belfast not only to meet the King and his Prince but to talk again to the cardinal jester of boxing. Chris Eubank had flown into town on his private jet. He was still living the life.

'It's the only way, my friend,' he lorded. 'Poverty is bad. Money, for me, lots of it, is essential. I need the convenience it provides. I must have it!'

Eubank was still a moderately amusing man – even if the novelty of his monocle, gold-tipped cane, jodhpurs and riding-boots had become threadbare. He'd diversified into black Biggles mode with his World War I leather flying-helmet, goggles and chiffon scarf which he wore whenever he was seen near his Harley or Aston-Martin. I preferred him in the Versace clobber myself, but his easily lampooned arrogance still made me laugh.

In one infamous incident, he refused to step inside a new car hired for one of his many social engagements. It was, after all, only a Ford. 'Come back with something befitting my station as the champion of the world,' Eubank scolded the hapless driver. Some of the more recent, perhaps even apocryphal, anecdotes tickled me more. Eubank had splashed out on a container truck but, having failed to obtain the requisite driving licence, was reduced to sitting in the stationary vehicle in his driveway. Occasionally, as he contemplated his dream of guiding the monster down a motorway, he would honk its horn – once, twice, three times, the sound becoming more mournful with every blast.

More believably earthy was the story of Eubank showing a gaggle of television executives around his Hove palace. Twinkling proudly amid its plush ostentation he suddenly said, 'Isn't this just the bollocks?'

But the boy from Peckham tried hard to refine his aesthetic appreciation.

When interviewed in his study by an ITV camera crew, as part of their build-up to his next fight, Eubank interrupted the filming continually. He kept moving the vase of flowers behind him, undecided as to which angle would reveal its elegance best on television. I also liked the way in which Eubank instructed John Morris, head of the British Boxing Board of Control, to 'listen to this!' just before they completed a phone conversation about the contractual details of his forthcoming WBO defence. Eubank put the mouthpiece next to one of his speakers, cranked up the CD's volume and left Morris hanging on while one of Puccini's arias blasted down the telephone line. Five minutes later, Eubank picked up the phone and sighed, 'Wasn't that magnificent!'

But Eubank was back on a more barren track in Belfast. 'So,' he sighed, 'here we go again . . .'

'Isn't it getting harder every time?' I asked.

'Naturally,' Eubank snapped. 'But the only way to stay at this peak is to live the life.'

'Well,' I suggested, 'you seem to have discovered the good life.'

'Ah, in public, yes! I want to inspire others to attain my level.'

'Of course . . .'

'But in private,' Eubank laughed sadly, 'I live a different life. I live the boxing life. There is no escaping my harsh régime. No fun. No saying, "Well, I need one day to relax a little." You cannot yield if you want success in this trade. How many years have I got left in the business? One? I'd say two at the most. I'll relax into the luxurious life after all this hardship is over. Y'see, some people kill for money, some rob for money, some whore for money. I'm different. I fight for money. So, for the sake of my family's future, I have to subject myself to the hard life now . . .'

'Which must still include thinking about Michael Watson?'

'Yes.'

'I heard someone ask you if you'd swap all your money to give back Michael his health.'

'A fruitless question,' Eubank mused. 'But I did not duck the point. "Yes," I answered, "yes, I would give up all my wealth for his health . . . but on one condition! That I be given the opportunity to go out there and make my fortune all over again." That cannot be taken away from me . . .'

'What do you think about now, when your mind goes back more than two years to that night in Tottenham?'

Eubank did not answer hastily. 'I think,' he said at last, 'that this is a horrible business. Punching another man in the head with the force of two tons of pressure. I think that makes this a heavy business. I think that there's dark shit in boxing . . .'

That 'dark shit', after all his and Don King's verbal excess, was a shock. When Toney or Tyson swore it was as familiar as Oscar De La Hoya saying 'wow' or 'nice'; when Eubank said, softly, 'there's dark shit in boxing', I listened more closely.

He might even have been 'a businessman first and a showman second', but it was his third trade, boxing, which defined him most clearly.

'Michael Watson calls me garbage,' Eubank pressed ahead, 'but I still mourn for the man, for the damage I did to him. I never knew I could cause so much hurt. I didn't mean it. But man is not made for boxing. It's just that boxing is made for men. It's what we do. We want the money – and so we fight . . .'

Eubank and King, for all their shared allegiance to both hard cash and Mike Tyson, did not like each other. They visited Mighty Mike separately in Plainfield – King more often, as he was the one making money out of Tyson.

King liked to be in control, as did Eubank, and so they always clashed. It was the same in Belfast. Eubank did little to help push the fight against Ray Close, promoted as it was by King and Frank Warren. He knew that they would have to pay him his 1.25 anyway – and he was talking not about Tyson's $1.25 a day in prison but his one-two-five with all those million-pound noughts on the end.

When someone questioned him about King's past exploitation of fighters, Eubank jibed, 'I'm the wrong man to ask. I exploit promoters.'

Perhaps King would get him in the end but, in Belfast, Don seemed to have given up on Eubank. Warren, however, had just hooked up a cross-Atlantic deal with D.K. Productions and he was determined that the King's Hall would be packed with 8,000 fans and that there'd be a further fifteen or sixteen million, more even than for the previous week's FA Cup final, watching the fight on live Saturday-night television. 'C'mon, Chris,' Warren complained at the final press conference, 'you know it's a normal duty of any fighter to help publicise a promotion.'

Eubank looked disdainfully at Warren and uttered his immortal words: 'I am not normal.'

While Warren threw his hands up in exasperation I thought of Tyson saying something more ambiguous in his first TV interview in prison. On CBS's *Street Stories*, his last sentence to Ed Bradley had been the distinctly strange, 'I'm just a normal person – extremely to the extreme . . .'

Ray Close, a much more ordinary guy, did his best in Belfast. He spoke earnestly to the surrounding pressmen. He was an adequate boxer who had been the first man to blemish Eubank's perfect record when he held him to a draw in Dublin exactly a year before. Even though he had arrived at the Ulster Television Studios in a second-hand brown sedan with his young wife in the passenger seat alongside him, the twenty-five-year-old Close still had an element of surprise about him. As a Belfast boy who had known nothing but the Troubles between Protestants and Catholics, he had since become an elder and Sunday School teacher in the Mormon church of the Latter Day Saints just down the road.

Perhaps because he was not especially used to the media glare, Close started to speak in hammy rhyming couplets, which he himself had written. They were woeful, but it didn't diminish the fact that Ray was one of boxing's decent guys. And so my heart went out to him when Eubank mocked, 'Not exactly Rudyard Kipling, are you?'

Yet there was mediocrity to face, rather than triumph or disaster, when Eubank repeated his 'Great Impostor' routine in the ring. As always, it started with the smoke and the lasers and 'Simply the Best' reverberating around the hall. As a passionate crowd thundered above the music I remembered how his manager, Barry Hearn, had once said: 'When people go home at night, after seeing Chris Eubank, no matter what way the fight's gone, most of 'em will say, "Fuckin' hell, wasn't it exciting when he walked out!"'

He was right of course, for the performance went all the way downhill after his grandiose vault over the ropes. I felt my most animated, too, when Eubank entered the ring and skittered backwards. I thought of the woman I was due to marry, knowing that her nude Eubank impersonation was far better than the original.

My exposure to fighters like James Toney and Oscar De La Hoya, to the even more gifted Roy Jones and Naseem Hamed, had made me judge Eubank's limited abilities. He was still unbeaten after eight and a half years as a professional and his second fight against Close was his fifteenth world title defence in forty-two months. His 1990 battle against Nigel Benn, and the rematch against Watson, were undoubtedly amongst the finest fights seen in a British ring. He had proved then that he could reach into the shadowy corners of his resolve and somehow find the iron in his punch or chin to win. But I could no longer pretend that Eubank was a great fighter. He had ability but he was never going to be more than a boxer who could puff up his competence with the flashiest of flurries and the most bombastic of poses.

Apart from his opening strut down the aisle, Eubank's act had come to depend on his being able to sustain the uncertainty until the last possible moment – when the judges' scorecards were read out. Since the Watson fight he'd had only one KO victory, over the washed-up John Jarvis, in a hectic series of title contests which went the distance and usually ended with a controversial announcement in his favour. He did it again in Belfast, when he shaded Close in a split-decision. I wanted to believe in the more piquant theory that Eubank suffered from some kind of post-Watson trauma which prevented him from hurting his opponents. The likelier truth was that he'd lost his edge. He had even placed a £1,000 bet on himself, at 66–1, to knock out Close within two rounds. While he flailed away hopelessly he looked as if he'd forgotten all sense of timing; and, later, when he rested for long stretches of each round it seemed more certain that he was a shot fighter – a man, put simply, whose best had passed.

But he was still better than the tentative Close, who was perhaps dizzied by the news that Rupert Murdoch and Sky were about to announce their payment to Eubank of a potential £10,000,000 for a 'world tour' of eight fights in twelve months. If he kept winning, Eubank's contract would culminate in his fighting James Toney.

'On the face of it,' Eubank murmured of Toney, 'he is the most unreasonable, the most pig-headed man. But he has the most fire in his stomach, more even than Nigel Benn. Can I beat him? Where there's a will there's a way. If I take the fight, I will not be saying "ouch, that hurt!" or be looking at the referee for help. They will have to carry me out . . .'

But Belfast marked a turning-point. My interest in Eubank and his millions, in the certainty that he would be starched by Toney, had waned. A superior young British fighter had emerged and, like Don King, I skirted shamelessly away from Eubank towards Naseem Hamed.

I think even Eubank, attempting to appear above King's bluster, could sense the sea-change. Suddenly, Hamed was at the source of debate traditionally courted by Eubank. In Belfast, people were looking away from him and pointing at 'Naz' instead, asking, 'Just who does that arrogant little fucker think he is?' And they did it again when he jumped up at ringside next to his mate, Don. The King's Hall reverberated with the decanting of eight thousand boo-filled lungs as the Prince hailed his introduction by a frenzied MC.

An old Irish boy behind me wheezed in bemusement – 'For a Paki, the lad sure has loadsa cheek' – as Hamed waved theatrically to the disapproving crowd. But then, with the assurance of an established virtuoso, Naz stood on his head. The hisses sprayed into whistles which turned into unrestrained cheering when, from his ramrod headstand, he flipped over the ropes with a high double spiral of a perfect somersault which landed him on Don King's crown in the middle of a sky-blue canvas.

'Jaysus! Will ya look at that!' trilled a woman in velvet evening dress from across the aisle. 'I wish he were fighting tonight. We'd get a right show instead of puttin' up with this Eubank feller!'

Don King, meanwhile, strode around the ring, his face lit by a blazing dollar-eating grin. As the noise intensified he raised his fists ebulliently towards the rafters, no doubt dreaming of even better days and more Machiavellian nights in the ring with that snidely cherubic Yorkshire boy, that searingly cocky fighter who called himself the Prince.

He lent across our table and tapped me on the hand, as if to say 'listen to this one, pal!'. His eyes had grown big and round in anticipation of the next set of words about to pop from his smirking mouth. I looked at the shining face in front of me and remembered that Naseem Hamed, the Prince, or Naz as he was more commonly called, was only twenty years old.

'Boy,' he sniggered, as our stares locked expectantly during a pause as irreverent as it was stately, 'I'm gonna be a legend. No question about it . . .'

'A legend?'

'Yeah, Prince Naseem Hamed – legend! What'cher think then?'

'Well, gee Naz, I dunno,' I replied carefully, considering the sensation the Prince had already made as British boxing's most curious anomaly, as a champion Arab fighter from the Wincobank in Sheffield, a flash kid in leopard-skin trunks who back-flipped his way over the ropes. 'I figured you might have something grander in mind than mere "legend" . . .'

''Course I do,' Naz smiled slyly. 'Y'see, the plan's huge . . . not only do I become the greatest British boxer of all time, I become the best lightweight fighter the world has ever known.'

'And?' I prompted as Naz turned on his serious businessman face.

'And I get to earn an obscene amount of money . . .'

'Obscene?'

'Yeah, that's the word – "obscene",' Naz exhaled with a smack of his lips.

'How much?'

'I get to make forty million – that's pounds – and win three or four titles at different weights. I'm planning on me and my family living like royalty. Y'know, for me to make so much money that, after boxing, I need never work again. I can live my life as a clean person, as a great person . . . or I can go into show-business . . .'

The Prince twirled a curly straw round the rim of his glass of Coke as if to remind me that he was not a victim of Friday-night bar-room dreaming. Naz, the avowed Muslim as well as a showbiz legend-in-the-making, never touched the hard stuff. Instead, on a balmy Wednesday afternoon, we sat serenely in one of Sheffield's more elegant tea-rooms as the Prince, with his fizzy drink and chatter, and me with my questions and coffee, pondered the depth of his ambition.

Having seen Hamed at work both inside and outside the ring I did not need much convincing that, for once in British boxing, the hype might be true. His devastating speed, punching power and eccentricity made him the most talented fighter to have emerged in recent memory. The various 'Prospect of the Year' awards he had won in the previous nine months only brushed against the enormity of his potential. Even though he then had to overcome the disadvantage of being a bantamweight, one of boxing's least glamorous divisions, I knew Hamed could become a bigger name in this country than even Frank Bruno or Chris Eubank.

A series of Naz-images suggested that, beneath the gaudy lip, there was an intense and malicious wizardry to Hamed's boxing. The most pressing mind-shots were from his humiliation of the battle-hardened European bantamweight champion, Vincenzo Belcastro, during their title fight ten days before he and Don King did their Belfast jig.

I watched the fight in Sheffield with a sense of distracted wonder. There had been doubt amongst the regular boxing writers that, in only his twelfth professional bout, Hamed was ready to face such an experienced champion – a man who had been twelve rounds fourteen times before. Hamed, instead, had only fought six-rounders against opponents who rarely pulled themselves out of their perennial sparring-partner rut. Belcastro bore scant relation to any of them.

I had seen Hamed fight once before, in his second bout in April '92, when he outclassed Sean Norman in two rounds on a Eubank bill in Manchester. He was an impossibly young-looking boxer then, a Bambi-faced eighteen-year-old whose neat side-parting and strutting exuberance seemed to belong less in the professional ring than it did in a junior *Come Dancing* extravaganza. I could imagine the husky ballroom cry: 'From the Wincobank in Sheffield, representing Yorkshire in the Latin Salsa, it's the young Prince, accompanied by his lovely partner, Pee-Wee!' Yes, then, beyond the groomed dancer look, he also had that 'Exotic Crufts Pup' bounce about him. His leopardskin poncho, a supposedly snazzy variation on the crude white towel Tyson used to pull over his head when walking to the ring, was almost unbearably naff. He also relied heavily on his Eubank pastiche when he tried to make the audience sit up and bark after one of his punching pirouettes. Yet it was clear that he had a dazzling aptitude for boxing. He switched from southpaw to orthodox and back again with an ease which proved that he could box as well as fight.

But, the experts said, any decent youngster could do that against a flyweight mug like Norman; the European bantamweight champion would be very different. He would be the real test for Hamed.

They were wrong. The Italian had never been knocked down before but Hamed came out and dropped Belcastro with the first punches he threw – a gorgeous right-left combination which clicked into place within ten seconds of the bell and dumped the champion in a heap. He struggled up but the fight as an equal contest was over. Hamed had him – and he was ready to make Belcastro his squeaky toy for the night. He displayed a phenomenal mix of accuracy and evasion which meant that he was hitting Belcastro at will while seldom being touched himself. He would sometimes watch the shaven-haired Italian like a mongoose ogling a snake. Swerving away from his despairing victim's lunges, Hamed would measure the moment with agonising exactitude before striking. The force of his fists would knock Belcastro back and the Prince would almost run at him and throw five, six, seven more unanswered punches with the full weight of his body behind them.

I had never seen anything like it in a British ring. Only Roy Jones in America could boast of similarly unconventional flair. A fighter like Toney, in contrast, was one of textbook solidity. He listened hard to his learned trainer, Bill Miller, and absorbed lessons from the past. In the ring Toney concentrated on dropping his shoulder or swivelling his hip to slip a blow or add extra leverage to one of his punches. He was intelligent and controlled. But Hamed did not ever appear in need of thought or discipline. He just went with the extraordinary flood of his instinct, as if he only needed to hurl punches across the canvas to be acclaimed an artistic genius.

American reporters, for all their misgivings about Oscar De La Hoya's managerial arrangements, considered him to have a similarly free-flowing talent. But his display a few months earlier, against Jimmi Bredhal, a fighter not too far ahead in class than Belcastro, had been devoid of such brash splendour. And Naseem was a year younger than Oscar – his only problem being that he would always be a couple of a divisions lighter than De La Hoya. That weight difference would prevent the respective prides of East LA and Wincobank from meeting in the ring, but I was sure it would not stop people comparing them in the mythical pound-for-pound stakes for the rest of the '90s.

The Prince used the full twelve rounds to exhibit his ring cleverness. One of his more astonishing manoeuvres entailed him staring at poor Vincenzo's feet as he thudded home punches into his face without even looking. His dominance was so complete that, after flooring Belcastro again in the eleventh, he spat out as many needless taunts as mesmerising combinations. Naz zipped through his Ali-shuffle and placed his gloves on his hips with gloating contempt, mincing at Belcastro, before throwing his hands in the air and strolling round the ring. The previously proud European champion spent the final minutes of his reign looking a broken figure as he watched Hamed's mugging at the cameraman and laconic conversation with his own corner. Consumed by a desire to dismantle Belcastro, the Prince stripped away all pretence of mutual respect and dignity in the ring – boxing's most sentimental, but precious, tenets.

The cognoscenti were suitably scandalised. Hugh McIlvanney led the condemnation in the *Sunday Times*. Although describing the Prince as 'a spectacular talent . . . his effortless mastery of Belcastro, a seasoned pro, was an astonishing feat', McIlvanney deplored Hamed's 'eagerness to treat his demoralised victim as if he were no better than something you might wipe off your shoe'.

Even more depressing was the memory of Bradley Stone, the super-bantamweight from Canning Town, who had died less than a fortnight before after losing his British title fight to Richie Wenton. The twenty-three-year-old Stone had been, like Hamed, obsessive about boxing. He also longed to one day be a world champion. It was said later that perhaps the best moment in his short life happened in his last fight when he knocked Wenton down. But, in the same way as Belcastro had, Richie got up bravely and fought on. He won a tight decision in the end; and Bradley Stone lost his life after collapsing later that night at his girlfriend's flat. He had a blood clot on the brain and was rushed to the Royal London Hospital in White-chapel where he died the following day, on 28 April 1994.

I remembered how we had shivered at the pictures of Stone and Wenton hugging each other at the end of their fated encounter. Wenton tried to comfort the disconsolate Stone who was full of sadness after 'a crossroads fight'. There was an echo of Michael Watson's voice in Stone's speech. The only sparse comfort lay in the words of his fiancée, Donna Lawrence. She said, simply, that he had died doing something which he believed made him whole; and that he had always liked Richie Wenton.

I thought of their final embrace – and the antics of Naseem Hamed in that last round turned me cold. His belittling of Vincenzo Belcastro, a man who deserved better, seemed to ridicule Stone and Wenton too. But he fluttered innocent lashes as his Irish trainer Brendan Ingle tried to persuade reporters afterwards that Hamed was not really himself when his showboating reached its histrionic pitch. The genial Irishman claimed that his fighter was lost in his own complex homage to Sugar Ray Leonard. Naz, so Ingle's excuse went, wasn't really at the Sheffield Pond Forge during that twelfth round – rather, in his own outlandish fantasy, he was Sugar Ray outwitting Marvin Hagler at Caesars Palace in Las Vegas in 1985.

Ingle's romanticism sounded awkward when set against Naz's shameless peddling of himself as a true original. His was a view shared by ITV who, having lost Eubank to Sky, buckled their rating hopes in the ring onto the Prince's similarly brazen appeal. Only Naz, ITV rightly realised, could match Eubank's ubiquitous drawing power with viewers fascinated more by bizarre ring personae than fight strategies.

He was, however, keen to establish the difference between himself and Eubank as he curbed my tea-room reverie of his Belcastro escapades.

'Look,' he said, 'I realise I might've gone a little over the top against the feller. I was just so excited to win my first championship belt. I didn't mean to show disrespect, y'know, I was just lost inside me head. Same with Chris Eubank. I'm not out to upstage Chris or anything. We're good friends – just ask him, he's on the phone to me all the time. He once asked me, "Naz, where do you get your speed? How do you do it?" He might not like to admit it, but it's true. But he means well, does Chris. Y'know, he's always wanting to give me advice, telling me what's waiting round the corner.

'Just the other day he phones me. I'm on me mobile, sitting in the sunshine. "Naz!" he says, "I'm going to tell you something important now! You must listen!"

'So I say, "What's up, Chris?" Eubank waits a moment and then he says, all serious-like, "Naz, you must learn to absorb punishment!" I laugh, "Whaaaaat?" "Naz," he says, "it's the nature of this business. One day someone is gonna hurt you because this is a brutal trade. You must learn how to soak up punishment like I can . . ." Jeez, can you believe that! I just said, "No, no, no, Chris – you got it all wrong. I'm not you! I'm the Prince – I'm different. I ain't taking any punishment, I want to be the one doing the hitting – that's why I'm unbeatable and untouchable!" Me? Absorb punishment? Well, you gotta laugh at that one, hey?'

For all the predictable bombast, there was a more significant perspective to Naseem Hamed's rise. He was the first top-line British boxer who was neither black nor white; resulting in the tired 'cheeky Paki' digs and in misguided descriptions of Naz as Britain's 'only professional Asian boxer'. Naseem Hamed called himself a British and an Arab fighter, a Yorkshire-man of pure Yemeni stock. He was anxious to remind me of his cultural and religious background. 'It's the most important thing about me,' he urged. 'I am a Muslim, from the Yemen, but born and bred in Sheffield – that tells you everything you need to understand about me, it keeps me clean, it gives me strength, it makes me distinctive . . .'

It was also at the root of his boxing. In Yorkshire in the early '80s, when the National Front were not without influence even in the youngest playgrounds, it did not pay to be a little Arab boy, someone who could always be hooked with a 'fucking Paki' barb. Brendan Ingle had often spun the story of his laying eyes on Naz – a tiny figure surrounded by, but fighting off, three much bigger white boys. 'I was on this double-decker bus,' Ingle recalled, 'and we come to a halt outside the primary school. There's this thuggery goin' on but the smallest lad, the boy I took to be Asian, is punching beautifully, hitting all three of them. They can't land a shot on him. I said to myself, "That young fella can fight". . . '

A week later, with the coincidental power of the best parables, a corner-shop owner called Sol Hamed asked Ingle to teach his sons to box because they were 'being persecuted as Arabs'. When he met the Hamed boys Ingle was surprised to recognise the 'young fella' he'd seen from his bus window. Naseem was only seven years old and weighed forty-five pounds – but from the moment he entered the gym he fell in love with boxing.

His first hero, Herol Graham, the adroit but light-hitting Sheffield middleweight, was then Ingle's star fighter. But whenever reporters interviewed Graham, they were asked by Ingle to 'give a plug for the little Arab boy. Naz is going to be the best of the lot – he's got it all. He's going to be my real champion . . .'

After four years of intensive training, Naseem was finally old enough, at eleven, to box competitively. Much of his audacity sprung from the tough background of those early fights. They were located far from the conventional amateur circuit. Ingle took Naz around Yorkshire's pit villages where he was put into the ring with much older and heavier opponents. Because of his size and colour, Naz was an object of ridicule; but Ingle hit on an inspired method of boosting his confidence. He taught Naz to imagine that, rather than being in a pitside hall in wintry Yorkshire he was actually in sun-filled Las Vegas, fighting for a huge purse. For his first amateur bout – which he won by knockout – Naz was offered an imaginary '£400' of which Ingle claimed an equally fictional '£300' for all his years of training.

'So that's how we played it and he won almost every fight,' Ingle chuckled. 'Like when he was twelve and we're driving to a show. I says, "Right, Naz, this one's in Vegas for the world title. If you win you're getting £400,000 and you're giving me a quarter of that!" He's quiet – thinking about it, you see. Then he pipes up, "Oooo, dunno 'bout that, Brendan, a hundred grand's a lotta money!" The greedy little bastard! I tell my wife, Alma: "Hmmmm, we might have a spot o' bother with the tiny Arab!" The next night I'm working in the gym – Herol's got a big fight coming – and Naz keeps nagging me. He wants a word – "It's very important," he says. So I stop my work and Naz says, "Look, Brendan, I've discussed it with me dad – you can have the hundred grand." That was always our way – thinking big – always working towards him getting his world title shot, imagining that he could beat every fighter who's ever lived – "Kid" Galivan, Roberto Duran, Sugar Ray Leonard – he had those kind of million-dollar stars in his eyes even then . . .'

Naseem Hamed took me for a drive through Sheffield, winding down from Brendan Ingle's gym towards the centre of town in his spanking new Diahatsu – which he was already set to trade for a much more expensive American model. Our languid late-afternoon conversation was broken up by Yorkshire homeboys hailing him from the roadside and by the constant chirruping of his mobile phone. Naz's talk was of Sheffield, Las Vegas, New York, the Yemen – 'worldwide domination, starting with this country, America, and then the Middle East'. As we wound our way through his home town it seemed as if his head had travelled a long way from his father's corner-shop. With money and fame building up around him so fast, a drastic upheaval was imminent. The question remained whether he could cope with the strain of his own exorbitant self-hype.

'Things are changing so fast for me – there's so much attention since I won the European title. But I'm the best bantamweight in the whole world – no one can touch me. I'm an artist compared to the rest of them – a master craftsman. I wanna get to America and show them Yanks how to kick ass, hopefully on the same bill as Tyson when he gets out. Then I'm gonna clean up the Middle East 'cos that's where the real money is.

'I went to the Yemen and they gave people one day's notice that I was gonna spar a couple of rounds. Ten thousand turned up to see me – for an exhibition! Can you imagine what'll happen when I fight for a world title? I'm already a legend there. Afterwards the president gave me a Rolex worth ten grand – look!'

Naz lifted his left hand from the wheel. A monster watch glinted in the fading Sheffield sunshine.

'But Naz,' I sighed, 'there's a civil war in Yemen . . .'

'Yeah, I know,' he said with a diplomatic dip of his watch. 'It's a bit unfortunate, this war . . .' The Prince looked appropriately concerned for a moment and then, returning to that favoured theme of taking over the planet himself, his mood brightened. 'But things will sort themselves out there, y'know. When they do, with all that oil, I'm gonna go fight there myself – for a whack of money. Take me a whole lot closer to that forty million, all the way to being a legend – here, there, everywhere. It's happenin'. . . '

With that flourish, Naz picked up his humming mobile again. 'Yeah, yeah, sounds good – 'course I can, I can do anything I want tonight,' he crooned into the tiny receiver, the sun casting an orange glow around him, making him look strangely precocious, almost as if he was too young to be driving. Brendan Ingle's 'little Arab boy' had come a long way from the playgrounds and pit villages of Sheffield even though he was still dreaming the same reckless dream he'd had since he was seven. In his mind, the only distinction was that the fantastic had already happened – he really did believe then that he was a young Muhammad Ali, as canny at twenty as Sugar Ray Leonard was at thirty, a beaming Yorkshire ragamuffin in cahoots with Big Don King, a glittering Yeminite Royal, a legend starting to happen, destined for four world titles and a cool forty million. Naseem Hamed, at least in his own head, was already the King.

6

GUNS AND FATHERS

WE PARKED OUTSIDE THE RAILWAY STATION IN SHEFFIELD, that imaginary King and I, and watched the light over his old town bleed from yellow to red.

'Yeah,' Naz observed sagely, 'gettin' dark now . . .' sounding as if he might be speaking in metaphors rather than just standard boxing polemic.

'And I've got a train to catch,' I said.

'Back to London, then?'

I nodded as the Prince fiddled with his shades, implying that my audience with him had not quite ended. He wanted to talk a little longer. 'Top town that,' Naz said earnestly. 'Not quite as good as Sheffield, mind; but London's still pretty kickin'. I might get me a place down there soon. I been thinking 'bout it. Spread my wings.'

'You leaving Sheffield?' I asked.

'I'll never ever leave Sheffield. I might spend a week in London, another in Vegas, Paris, wherever, but my base is here. This is my home, man. I can't leave. I'm the King of Sheffield!'

'But we already knew that, Naz . . .'

'Yeah, I know, but I just like saying them words: "King of Sheffield"!'

I reached for the door. 'Well, Prince, it's been pretty good today . . .'

'Yeah, I enjoyed meself all right, chattin' an' that . . .'

'I guess I'd better be going,' I said.

'Wait, before you leave –'

'What?'

'There was something I wanted to ask you,' the Prince murmured.

'What is it?' I wondered. We were like the Two Ronnies spoofing the last scene in *Brief Encounter*.

'What's Mike Tyson really like?'

The King of Sheffield had not yet grown accustomed to his throne. Whatever legendary status he had assumed in his mind, on the outside he was still really a boy, a fan who dreamed of one day meeting his idols.

So we spoke about Tyson and all that had happened to him. Mighty Mike had been on my mind too. His final appeal had just been rejected. He would stay in Plainfield a while longer, with his books and a returning malice. Under Indiana law, with less than two years of his sentence to run, Tyson's chances of an early release depended on his completing an academic or vocational programme while displaying sufficient evidence of 'social rehabilitation'. In turning down his application for parole, Judge Patricia Gifford stressed that her primary reasons revolved around Tyson's inability to pass a High School diploma equivalency exam. His copious but unconventional use of the prison library could not prevent him from failing the test by a single mark.

'Mr Tyson's studies,' Gifford noted coolly, 'were not in any formal classroom with regular attendance. He had an instructor [Muhammad Siddeeq] coming in from the city, but it wasn't like the Indiana Department of Correction's curriculum.' They did not include the likes of Mao and Machiavelli on their syllabus. I thought it ironic that Tyson's continued incarceration resulted from his limitations as a student; if only they had asked him questions about *The Long March* or even *The Prince*.

Gifford conceded that Tyson 'has made some strides towards his rehabilitation, but it wasn't enough to shorten his sentence, or grant a new trial at this time'. While Tyson responded that, 'I feel no remorse for my actions because I did not rape Desiree Washington,' he did 'apologise for my actions during the Miss Black America beauty pageant. I also apologise to Desiree Washington, her family and the court for any pain I may have caused . . .' Yet in case such regret might be mistaken for guilt, he repeated: 'I committed no crime and will take that to my grave. But I should have been more polite. I should have walked her [Washington] downstairs. I should have been more gentlemanly towards her.'

Tyson had not anticipated success in Gifford's courtroom. 'Hey, I don't hold my breath,' he'd told Larry King on CNN the previous week. 'I accept the good and expect the worst . . .'

Yet it was the other King, Don, who felt the brunt of Tyson's anger when the boxer was asked if he'd fight again. When that query had been put to him before, Tyson had sneered, 'You think I'm gonna become a rocket scientist?' Now, having lost almost $70,000,000, he reacted with particular venom.

'I'd love to fight again under the proper circumstances. But I've been robbed, abused, lied to and taken advantage of all my life. I'm not going back into that same predicament again.' According to Bill Cayton, his former manager, Tyson was broke. To enable him to pay the massive bills owed to Alan Dershowitz, hired by Don King, Tyson had been forced to cash in his remaining two insurance policies – which would have paid him

$250,000 a year for life from the age of thirty.

When invited to reveal if he was referring specifically to King, Tyson was more cryptic: 'Don has to know that my allegiance is to Allah. Not to no other Muslim. My loyalty is to whichever individuals are loyal to me.'

Although he claimed that 'I feel good!', there was a pervasive sadness to most of his answers. 'Tennessee Williams said,' he murmured, 'that "we must distrust one another. It's the only way to protect each other from betrayal". And I'm a great believer in that. I believe everyone involved in my life, one day or another, will betray me. I totally believe that. Other people say, "No! No! No!", but that's what I believe.'

Tyson's pensive attitude extended to his comments that 'there's no doubt about it – we write our own story in life. Whatever good we do in life is going to return. Whatever ill, it'll return. There's no doubt about it . . .'

Don King may well have considered those words after his own rough day in court a few weeks later, when he heard that he would have to defend himself before a Federal jury on Lloyds' charge of 'wire insurance fraud'. It seemed feasible that King could take Tyson's place in jail.

'Yeah, I know, but I think Don will come through again,' Naz predicted. 'Mike Tyson and Don King are survivors. I think they'll stick together. And I think my future will be tied up with theirs, because King is the best promoter and Tyson the best heavyweight. It makes a lot of sense to me – Mike Tyson and Don King getting back together in boxing . . .'

'James Toney doesn't agree,' I muttered.

'He don't?' Naz said in astonishment.

'No. He said Don is the real criminal . . .'

'Wow, that Toney feller shoots from the mouth!'

'He also said that Tyson's the only other guy like him – he'll fight any-one . . .'

'Me too! I'm the third guy in the triangle. Tyson, Toney and me . . .'

'But Toney would warn you about King.'

'Why's he so down on Don?'

'It goes back to Don trying to persuade him to leave Jackie Kallen. He said some bad things about her . . .'

'What?'

'Apparently that she was white – and Jewish.'

The Prince was silent for a few moments, and then he grinned. 'But what's he really like? You know, Toney? He looks real hardcore to me. I like him! He's one top fighter!'

'We'll find out just how good when he meets Roy Jones.'

'Oh boy!' Naz jumped up in his seat. 'I know! Man, I can't wait for that fight! James Toney! Roy Jones! I reckon they're the two best fighters in the world right now.'

'But what about you, Naz?' I joked.

'Don't worry, I'm comin' up fast!' he said seriously before sinking back into the heady realms of fandom. 'Toney-Jones? Man, what a fight that'll be, what a fight!'

In the world's biggest hotel, the MGM Grand on the Las Vegas Strip, Bob Arum echoed those words. 'What a fight!' he said for the hundredth time – but with more enthusiasm than the actors playing Dorothy, the Tin Man and the Scarecrow, as they lined up again on the fake Yellow Brick Road to have their photographs taken with the next yelling family from Boulder City or yet another little girl whose face was covered in ice-cream. In the lush expanse of an MGM ballroom, Arum relentlessly 'whacked up' the interest he was going to earn on all his dreamy boxing zeros.

'We're calling it "The Uncivil War"!' he snickered. 'Toney v Jones! November 18, here, at the MGM Grand Garden. What a fight!'

'It's hardly subtle, is it?' I argued.

'Whadd'ya mean – "subtle"?'

'But, Bob, "The Uncivil War"!'

'What's wrong with it?' he asked.

'Don't you always say that Toney and Jones are two of the three best fighters in boxing today – and that the other, Pernell Whitaker, is hardly exciting?'

'Sure!'

'Well, don't such skilled boxers deserve something more imaginative?'

Bob Arum did his best to look like a man in search of absolution. His expression shifted between contrition and craving with the tick of a reforming sinner. 'Listen,' he croaked in his soft Brooklyn drawl, 'maybe you're right. We're all guilty! See?' Arum waved a hand above his nodding head. 'I've done it again, I admit it! That's my hand I'm holding up to heaven! Look!'

I considered the plump curve of Bob's mitt as he pawed the air in supplication. We knew that there were sticky confessions to unravel before another snack could be ordered from the MGM kitchen. Arum's jowly face wobbled as I summoned a priestly murmur of encouragement.

'Yeah, I've done it!' he said. 'I've cranked up the hype. I've tried to squeeze a little more juice outta these guys. Y'see, everyone loves a grudge fight – it's the simplest thing in the world to sell. Tell me a promoter who doesn't do the same an' I'll show you a loser . . . '

Arum snuck his right hand back inside his favourite trouser pocket. He jangled a couple of loose coins as if each might represent another million to be made from his biggest promotion of the year.

'Imagine . . .' he whispered persuasively, 'James "Lights Out" Toney!' The quarters and dimes clanked together as if Arum had shoved a slot-machine down his tailored suit. 'Roy Jones Jnr!' He let the grain of his voice settle before resuming his pitch with another roll of change and rush of words.

'Yes, they're unbelievably skilled athletes at the height of their powers. Artists even. But we're selling boxers here, pal, not painters. There're all those millions of pay-per-view watchers who've gotta be convinced that they should shell out some of their hard-earned dough to watch a fight on a Friday night when their wife or girlfriend wants to go out for dinner or to a movie. So we go with the hard sell. "The Uncivil War: One-On-One! Toney and Jones, toe-to-toe, two extremely violent men go at it – with, and this is the killer-plug, rage for their fathers in both hearts!" It's what this show's all about – tumultuous drama, massive personalities, a great venue in Vegas! Who could resist it?'

Arum's head swivelled up slowly. He pursed his lips as if to drink from the chandeliers dripping with champagne rather than light. He marvelled at the dazzle as he contemplated the irresistible business of a brutal fight. Then, in a sudden show of piety, the promoter lowered his gaze to the floor.

'Sometimes,' he confided, 'it gets too much. It gets ugly. It can go way beyond hype! Then, you're heading for big trouble . . .' Bob Arum rubbed his heart, shook his head and, slyly, appeared as a humble man labouring to staunch a feral tide. 'Yeah, sometimes we need to tone it down – otherwise it can veer out of control, like a runaway truck. Y'see, the best fighters in the world are very threatening individuals when the mood takes them! But I think we'll be okay this time. It was much wilder when we had Toney and Iran "The Blade" Barkley squaring off at Caesars. We called that one "Two Angry Men" and, wow, did it get hot! It was pretty ugly – all their profanity and death-threats . . .'

As if he could confront boxing's ferocity no longer, Arum shuddered and closed his eyes. In that moment, even Oscar De La Hoya's golden smile was forgotten.

But, soon, Bob was back, yanking up the war-talk. 'I'm always terrifically excited about these big fights. Duran-Leonard, Hagler-Hearns, Hearns-Leonard, Leonard-Hagler,' Arum chanted out the middleweight litany of his greatest promotions, snapping a finger in the air for each fight. 'And now we've got Toney-Jones, the fight of the '90s so far, no doubt about it! I don't think I've been as excited for a fight since Sugar Ray and Marvellous Marvin were about to do their stuff. An', you know, I see a parallel here. Jones has the same kind of smarts and speed as Leonard – and Toney, well, Toney, he's my Hagler of the '90s. What a warrior! Hell,' the Bob-Man chuckled, 'the only thing I'll say against James Toney is that when he swears too much the TV and papers can't use the copy! It's too obscene. Now what's the use of that?'

Rich Uncle Bob blinked blearily beneath the hot lights. He was a Jewish boy from Brooklyn, a former government lawyer, who'd made it in a rough business – but he was also nearly sixty years old and he looked weary. Despite his devotion to the dollar, Arum was not an unlikeable man to engage in chit-chat. As I had done with King I tried to humour him.

'It sounds as if Toney's making you yearn for a few more of the clean-cut guys.'

'Not at all!' Arum laughed. 'Contrast is everything in this game. Look at me and Don King! The good and the bad, the guy in the white hat and the other in the black. It's the same in the ring. You're always gonna need your surly gladiators – Liston, Hagler, Toney. And in all that rough you need to throw in the real diamonds – Ali, Leonard, De La Hoya. Those guys are few and far between. You're never gonna find that class of act too often in this game . . .' He shrugged. 'Listen, I love the warriors too – y'know, Hagler and Toney are great guys! It just comes natural to them to be confrontational. But, yeah, it can be easier to deal with the guys whose charisma is, well, a little less primal . . .'

Arum's voice trailed away as he gathered himself for an upbeat performance in front of the cameras. His glance swept across the ballroom, tracking the ever-growing audience, until it rested on another fighter who had slipped through a side door. Again like King, Arum was nothing if not shrewd.

'Now, there's someone . . .' I said.

'Yeah . . .' Arum breathed.

'Roy Jones,' I noted coyly, 'seems like quite a guy . . .'

'You could say that . . .'

'Are you two getting any closer?'

'Not yet . . .' Arum dead-panned, keeping his gaze trained on the prize.

'But you'd love to pin him down to a long-term contract.'

'You said it!' He smacked his lips. 'But, hey, there's trouble there too. Who knows what kind of demons that kid's dealing with – maybe it's something worse than even Toney could imagine.'

'You'd still want him?'

'Boy, in this business, you'd kill to get a piece of Roy Jones . . .'

He remained a mystery. Outside the ring his assurance bordered on the eerie. He found pleasure in appearing remote, in avoiding the bombast marketed by eccentrics like Eubank and Hamed as well as the equally worn path of menace trod by the Tyson-Toney ilk of bad boys. Depending on your response to such extreme self-possession he was either the coolest or the haughtiest fighter in contemporary boxing. I was one of the believers in Roy Jones's sense of cool. He did not readily try to either impress or intimidate other people. Rather, he kept a distance from the rest; as if he had nothing to prove to anyone but himself.

Yet everything changed when he came to fight. Roy Jones did not so much walk to the ring as prance with proprietorial lechery. The fact that he ground his swirling hips would have been putrid had it not been done with such licentious élan. Yet there was something disturbing about the sight of a young fighter finding rapture in his violence. It was harder still to believe that this abandoned body usually hosted a tranquil outsider to the boxing circus.

Rubbing himself him up against the ropes like a sleek cat on heat, Roy Jones entered the ring as if on the point of coming. He shivered like he had reached an exquisite pitch, as if boxing and fucking had melted into one. The intensity of that craving was as shocking as it was exciting. If Tyson and Toney epitomised naked malevolence – in contrast to the hoop-jumping theatrics of Eubank and Hamed – Jones represented a more curious mix. He was both the aesthete and an entertainer who recognised our need to have his savagery tuxed-up as show-business.

But, for all that raunch, a harsher skein unfurled in Jones at the sound of the bell. When I first saw him fight – in Atlantic City in December 1993 on the same bill as Toney – I was astonished as much by Jones's power as by his speed. He was like a middleweight version of Tyson at his '88 peak when blurring punches with wrecking-ball effect were thrown from a baffling variety of angles. But Jones's defence was a spectacle in itself. Where Iron Mike used to buttress his chin behind a rolling evasion of punches and that 'peek-a-boo' stance of hands held high, Roy would simply lean back and rely on his reflexes to glide him out of trouble. He was most like the Prince in that respect. Jones did not attempt to block or deflect punches. He wove out of their way as if it might be one of the easiest things in the world to dodge a fast blow hurled by a man not more than a foot away. He made it seem as if it wouldn't even matter if the punches fell like rain from his opponent's gloves – such was his ability to stay dry in any ring storm.

In Atlantic City Roy Jones fought professionally for the twentieth time, duly registering the same amount of victories with nineteen of those twenty wins coming by way of knockout. Although his bout against a trier called Percy Harris was a mis-match, it still gave Jones the opportunity to show off his pure clout. After completing his strut, he indulged in horny intercourse with both the sagging ring-ropes and the whooping Atlantic City crowd. He whipped off his jacket to reveal a nutmeg-shaded slab of muscle for a torso. Whenever Jones moved, his washboard façade rippled with a zest missing from other fighters' stockier frames.

He opened his attack with a whirring left hook and overhand right. A clownish look of alarm spread across Harris's face as he tumbled backwards. Jones did a dainty hula of dance-steps to encourage the disbelieving Harris that this was only an early-evening game before bedtime. Sad Percy struggled gamely to his feet – but his rickety movements were those of an old man preparing for a sleep as long as it was deep. Jones smiled pityingly at the ring-worn Perce before he clattered in again with frighteningly quick fists landing as much on the body as Harris's listing head.

I was surprised to see that Jones hardly used the jab – that staple punch which has fed the goals of the greatest boxers. It was as if the jab was too ordinary a punch for him. Another right chopped down on the block, whistling by in the opposite direction to a scything uppercut which had landed only moments earlier. Harris crumpled to the floor, becoming that cheap suit on a hot night. It seemed as if he would stick to the canvas but, somehow, he dragged himself up.

The second round was only marginally better for Harris. He lumbered forward as Jones zapped hard punches into his face. Then, when courage was no longer sufficient, a clipped right and a casual left hook proved too much. Harris went aground again.

Jones kept him dangling for the third and most of the fourth until, as if deciding that he had amused himself enough for one session, he let loose the last fusillade. A left hook landed a thick blanket over Harris's distress – mercifully knocking him out just as the timekeeper gonged a close to the fourth. Jones looked down diffidently as the referee pulled on his lowered left arm. But 'Little Roy', like some calm killer in a wide-screen western, knew that there was no need to gloat. His job was done. He had won without a mark being left on him. His victim looked like a hole had been blown right through his middle.

Although I did not think he was a bloodthirsty man, I saw Bob Arum glinting at ringside. That ritual slaughter was just the first in a three-fight contract which Jones and Arum had signed less than two months before, in October '92. At the start of that very month, Don King had come close to beating Arum in the hunt for Jones's signature – in a deal which would pay the fighter $800,000 for a series of bouts on King's Showtime cable network and $1.5 million for numerous Pay-Per-View fights arranged by the promoter's Showtime Event Television (SET) offshoot. The mighty Don also spoke airily of a $100,000 bonus, $50,000 in training expenses and an immediate $250,000 to be earned from a world title clash with Julian Jackson – the WBC middleweight champion. But when Jones heard that King would himself pocket $150,000 of the reputed $400,000 Showtime had put aside for his signing, he and his backers stepped towards Arum.

King was left to denounce the folksy legal team of Fred and Stanley Levin who guided Jones from their home town of Pensacola on Florida's Panhandle coastline. Like the De La Hoya family, the Levins stayed outside the boxing mainstream. They were much envied for their 'advisory association' with Roy Jones. King derided them as just another Jewish cartel wielding undue influence over one of his brothers.

'Those Levin boys are tellin' a bunch o' lies about me,' King grumbled, 'but they've made a mistake goin' in with Bob Arum. Wait till this Jones kid finds out how Arum operates – then we'll see who's left cryin'!'

But Stanley Levin, in particular, claimed an emotional bond with his fighter which went beyond business. He had witnessed the struggle between Little Roy and Roy Jones Snr; and, in contrast to the father, Levin stressed his desire to help rather than control a fighter who was then only twenty-three years old.

Levin adapted a similar principle when negotiating with promoters trying to wheedle their way into Jones's corner. Apart from King and Arum, the Italian-American Duva family had been chasing Jones for years from their New Jersey base. While Jones had fought more than once under their Main Events banner he had resisted any long-term commitment to the Duvas. He had turned down a similar offer from a fourth major promotional force in America – the rumbustious Butch Lewis. With such enthusiasm from all the big cigars of boxing, Levin was able to shred any attempt to tie Jones to a permanent contract.

He envisaged a situation not unlike that enjoyed by the young Tyson when his original management team of Jacobs and Cayton had used a variety of promoters simultaneously – without promising any exclusive rights to future fights. This enabled Tyson or, more accurately, Jacobs and Cayton to be the beneficiaries rather than the victims of manipulation. Such tactics infuriated King, Arum and the rest as they were more used to fighters and managers willing to sell almost any hold over their future for a flat fee.

Rather than fulfilling King's veiled hints of a Jewish conspiracy, Levin suspected instead that there was truth in the old line that, when it came to promoters, 'they are all devils'. Levin restricted Arum's Top Rank contract to a three-fight deal, which could be renegotiated if and when they decided to continue with his services.

Jones was one of those rare fighters with cross-over potential. His outstanding boxing qualities had already captured the purists whilst his knock-out force ensured Jones's marquee value with both the television financiers and the blue-collar fans. He was also, like De La Hoya, a 'looker' who maintained a polite reserve as smoothly as he flashed his winning white teeth; for Jones was from the country rather than the ghetto. While Toney swaggered over the most abominable bragging-rights, Jones was as content to talk about the animals he loved on his Pensacola farm. Apart from the 150 chickens running around his ranch he also owned three dogs – Blue, Dax and Niche – and a horse called Shade. When Roy Jones started to talk about his chickens, Bob Arum sighed, cheerful in the knowledge that middle America would consider him a good-looking, sweet-natured black fighter they could take to their hearts.

Yet that relaxed rural background was balanced by Jones's own quotient of hip. There was no risk of him being dismissed as some grass-chewing farmhand while he also had the capacity to look like some so-damn-cool-it's-dangerous-to-look-too-close homeboy. Jones not only knew how to wear a baseball cap with gangsta style but he listened mostly to Public Enemy, Eric B & Rakim, Scarface, Ice Cube and all those other rappers from whom James Toney picked up pointers on how to sound lethal. Roy was similarly blasé about his own gun collection and the fact that the three hounds he raised were Rottweilers rather than tiddlers like Pee-Wee.

Arum's itch to hustle along the Jones–Toney rivalry encouraged him to bring the two together as often as possible at press conferences and at ringside. While Toney threw around his weight with hefty portions of slander, Jones retained an intriguing stillness. He reacted to Toney's 'I'll moider da bum!' type jibes with magisterial derision.

Those markers of Jones's inner gravity were lit by rumour. But I had heard enough about the suffering he'd endured at the hands of his father to believe that he mined the past as a kind of insurance against risk in the present. He was convinced that his delinquent contemporaries could never say or do anything to match his father's severity.

Bound together by anger towards the men with whom they shared their names, Roy Jones and James Toney were destined to fight each other. Where one boxer had been abandoned by his father the other had nearly been suffocated. If the Toney saga was consumed by violence, the Jones soap-opera appeared more layered. Its roots lay in the Deep South, in states like Alabama and Georgia. The story of 'Big Roy' and 'Little Roy', in fact, harked back more to Faulknerian themes of identity and retribution than to the blue neon of *Miami Vice*. In the Panhandle towns of Barth and Pensacola, father and son were locked in a conflict which was less part of the modern Sunshine State than old Deep South blood gone bad.

It began when Roy Snr was born the son of sharecroppers in Georgianna, Alabama, in 1947. Life was plain and hard. He worked in the fields, went to school and dreamed of escape. Big Roy wanted to be someone, to be something better than a scuffler. But, even when the family moved to Pensacola, the struggle continued. Unlike his father, and his father before him, he graduated from school; yet when he left Washington High there was no quick reward. He looked around and saw nothing – eventually having to sign on with the Job Corps who drafted him into the army. He ended up fighting in Vietnam, a year after Muhammad Ali gave up boxing and his title to avoid the same fate.

Roy Jones Snr was also a boxer, although inhabiting a different world to Ali. He used to fight for less than $20 a night when his career started in the early 1970s. In the same way as Joel De La Hoya, he worked in the day as an electrician and boxed at night and on weekends in an effort to make just a bit more for his family. On his best night he beat another unknown fighter in a Mexican ring and was paid $1,500, the most money he ever received as a boxer.

But there was a twist to his failure between the ropes. The record books listed a 1977 fight between Marvin Hagler, Arum's unsmiling great, and one 'Roy Jones'. Although the bout ended in a third-round KO win for Hagler, Big Roy did not discourage the belief that he was the Jones who had lost consciousness beneath the magnificent fists of Marvin. It was proved later that another fighter altogether, albeit it with the same name, had lost to Hagler. I thought it strange that Roy Jones Snr should claim such destruction as his moment of renown.

Arum deflected the issue when I asked him what he gleaned from such a bittersweet anecdote. He babbled on about Hagler and Sugar Ray Leonard and how Toney and Jones were about to join their middleweight pantheon. I thought of the father instead, of how he must have died a tiny death every time he let that slice of fiction slip by. How could his spirit not coarsen whenever he avoided the question as to why he hadn't clarified the reality that he was not that 'Roy Jones' – his stock refrain being, 'Don't worry about it, print it like you want . . .'

But his subsequent record as a corner-man was less hazy. He had driven his son to the 'Fighter of the Games' award at the '88 Olympics and then guided him to a flawless 18–0 professional record before Little Roy walked out. He had also coached Vince Phillips and Arthur Williams to the point where they were contenders at welter and cruiserweight. But, shadowing the split between father and son, both fighters moved on to less regimented camps – citing Jones Snr's need to control their every move as being too oppressive to bear.

The boxing grapevine hinted that they'd endured only a taste of what Little Roy experienced. There was hearsay that Roy Jnr had been subjected to beatings in the ring when he was only a boy – that his father had used the belt and a plastic pipe on him, raising welts which scarred him. The abuse had continued for years. The young boxer was made to train for six hours every day of his life, even when he was sick, always against much bigger fighters.

The gossip was sufficiently persistent to be taken seriously – especially when set against the evidence of misuse in his son's professional life. After the Olympics, and pre-Oscar, Roy Jones was meant to personify boxing's future. His second and third professional bouts, unusually, were televised on primetime network slots. NBC were delighted when Jones knocked out two resolute journeymen, Stephan Johnson and Ron Amundsen. The fact that Amundsen went on to stretch Toney in a fight decided on the scorecards highlighted the brightness of Jones's start. And yet Roy Snr declined a lucrative NBC contract to screen further fights across America. The father argued that the network was rushing his son.

'We realise the jeopardy in this sport,' Big Roy said when asked to defend the ensuing series of palookas who made Jones's earliest adversaries look like ringmasters. As the quality of opposition decreased so the obstinacy intensified. Jones refused to consider a decent test for his son or even the possibility of their fighting outside Pensacola. Attention shifted elsewhere – mostly in Toney's direction. While Lights Out won his first world title in May 1991, Jones was still ruing the bad publicity from his first-round KO of a faker who pretended to be a Texan club-fighter called Derwin Richards

– the impostor, Tony Waddles, had never fought professionally before.

There were enough precedents in boxing history to suggest that a father was rarely the best judge in building his son's career. Where some fight-fathers are braver than their sons, others are overly cautious. The case of Roy Jones, however, was more complicated. Rather than trying to protect his son from excessive risk, it appeared as if Jones Snr was diminishing Little Roy. By stifling his son's exposure, some reasoned, the father's hold would not be undermined by boxing's twin forces of wealth and celebrity.

I was unsure what to believe. All I knew for certain was that their relationship had broken down more than two years before, on 29 July 1992, when the father shot one of his son's dogs. They had not spoken since. Within days, like a vulture after a kill, Don King was ensconced in Pensacola. He attempted and failed to woo Roy away from Stanley Levin who, with his brother Fred, had pumped in more than a million dollars without return as they tried to keep the fighter's name afloat. The conclusive victories Jones achieved in the wake of that family parting, knocking out the respectable Glenn Thomas and Harris, proved that he was ready for world title competition.

But it was said in Vegas that Roy Jones Jnr felt he needed more than his fists when he was away from the ring. It was whispered that he carried a gun wherever he went – just in case Big Roy came after him.

18 November 1994

'He'll need more than a gun to tame me,' James Toney said quietly in his MGM suite on the morning of the fight. There was no heat in his words as he sat on the huge bed, saving his energy by describing, slowly, the way in which he was going to burn Roy Jones – in less than twelve hours' time. 'How's he gonna put out my fire? I'm gonna lick him, baby, with these . . .'

Toney held up his hands, those flamethrowers for the night, and nodded at them, as if greeting their simmering power. He looked like a small boy who had just told his father he was on his way out to show the world, that no one could stop him doing just as he pleased. A few days before he had even sounded like that fidgety kid when he said, 'Roy Jones ain't fit to carry my gym bag. I don't like him. I don't like nobody.'

It made him feel better to think it was him against the world, rather than just Roy Jones.

'Yeah!' he said to himself. He bunched a fist on the bed before settling back into his lulling silence.

Toney became stranger than ever in that warped time of waiting. But, as crazy as his rhetoric appeared, I could sense the comfort he found in his repetitive mantras. 'Roy Jones's never been tested, man,' he recited, 'he's never been tested by a decent fighter. So how's he gonna live with me. How?'

The emptiness of those words on paper had a more distinct echo when he said them out loud. It was as if each rasping lilt bolstered him, as if their rhythm fenced off his fear.

'He's got speed,' Toney admitted, 'but I'll fight him on the inside. I ain't gonna give him no room to use that left hook o' his. He's only got the one hand. The right ain't nothing. An' I'm bigger than him. He ain't gonna live with my body shots. Gonna take his legs away, leave him cryin' like one o' his dogs, make that boy my bitch for the night.'

I glanced at Sherry and Sarah. Neither of them blinked. They had heard it before; and knew he sometimes said words as if they were without meaning, as if they were just sounds to soothe him while he was made to linger.

'You should get some real rest, now, y'hear?' Sherry said.

Toney grunted absently but I was already leaving. 'I just popped in to say good luck . . .' I mumbled in excuse.

'That's good o' you,' Sherry smiled.

'I ain't gonna need any luck tonight,' Toney glowered, 'I ain't gonna need it.'

Jackie Kallen, however, was ready to take any help she could find. 'You'll keep those fingers crossed for us, won't you?' she asked.

'Of course – though James has just said he won't need any luck . . .'

'Well,' Jackie breathed deeply, 'let's hope so . . .'

'Last-minute doubts?'

'No, we've always known how hard this fight will be. Roy Jones is a great fighter. James knows it, I know it.'

'He did look sensational last time out,' I said insensitively, remembering how Jones had slid away from Thomas Tate before nailing down a left hook which knocked him cold a minute into round two.

'Yeah, he's a couple of notches above the other guys out there. But so is James. No disrespect to Pernell Whitaker, but this fight tonight will decide once and for all who's the world's best fighter. So, sure, I'm feeling the butterflies. But we took this fight in the clear expectation that James would win. I still believe that. If all things are equal then I can't see any way Roy Jones can match James. He hasn't fought the same quality of guys, he hasn't shown us what he's made of when he's hurting and tired. What happens if he gets cut like James did against Tim Littles? How will he cope? Jones has never faced a fighter with the mental toughness or the sheer class of James Toney. That's why I think you've got to go with James . . .'

'Me too . . .'

Jackie bit a knuckle as she peered over Vegas under a grey November sky. 'Are you more nervous than usual?' I asked.

'Yes,' she sighed. 'But we'd be insane if we weren't feeling the nerves bite now. Especially when there's so much riding on this fight. If we win tonight, we're ready to sign the biggest contract anyone, outside the heavyweight division, has ever been given in boxing.'

'I've heard Time-Warner are offering $30,000,000 for five years.'

'I can't talk detail. I don't even want to think about it till it's all over and we've won.' Jackie shivered. 'I'm feeling weirdly superstitious today. I'm scared of putting the jinx on anything . . .'

'How's James coping with the pressure?'

'He's coping fine.'

'What's it been like being round him these last few weeks?'

Jackie pulled a little face as if, between me and her, she could say it. 'Well, you know how he can be. He's been tough work . . .'

'How?'

'He's real grouchy. It's not been the easiest. But, listen, what are managers for? I'm earning my money. And Roy Jones has to earn his tonight by going into the ring against James Toney. Who could envy that?' Jackie Kallen smiled again and dipped into her handbag.

'Where's Pee-Wee?' I suddenly remembered.

'Oh, Pee-Wee's virtually banned from the MGM. They didn't like him much last time. So poor Pee-Wee's back home, waiting for us . . .' She burrowed deeper into her bag. 'Ah,' she eventually said, 'here it is!' Holding her hand out to mine she said, 'This is for you. There're only a precious few of these about, so hold onto it . . .'

I took the card from her in surprise. 'What is it?'

'Your invite. We're having a small party after the fight, to celebrate . . .'

Late that afternoon I walked alone through a mile of MGM hotel. At last I reached the arena. They called it the Grand Garden and were already scheming on Mike Tyson's comeback fight being held there. You could smell the money they calculated on making from boxing in that space. There were enough plush green rows for 16,500 screaming fans to create just the right television atmosphere. They would be pouring in soon.

But, then, the Garden was empty – except for four guys laughing and joshing as they adjusted the angle of the hot TV lights above the canvas.

I ambled down one of the aisles to find a seat halfway along the west bank of seating.

There were five hours left before Toney would make the same walk I had taken with him in Tulsa. I thought of him sitting in his hotel room, watching the red glow of the clock. I was glad to be spared that excruciating wait. Tonight would be even worse, with Roy Jones in his head.

It made me jittery to hear the chortling of the TV technicians as they worked. But their cameras' promise of violent excitement would make the boxers' fortune.

Toney and Jones had each turned down guaranteed purse offers from

Bob Arum in excess of $2,000,000 – in favour of taking 80 per cent of the pay-per-view cut. Each household who tuned in would have to pay $29 for the evening's entertainment. Toney, as champion, would receive 45 per cent, while Jones took 35 per cent of those takings. Arum and the hotel would share what remained and make more money in ticket sales and their ceaseless merchandising. I had already bought the snazzy $19.95 MGM 'Uncivil War' T-shirt for my fashionable future wife. Each fighter, meanwhile, hoped to clear $3,000,000.

Knowing what they were feeling, I wondered if even three million was enough. Was boxing ever really worth it?

'Hey, Sugar,' one of the men yelled out, 'it ain't Showtime yet!'

I looked blankly down at him, unsure how to respond to his cheek.

One of his buddies also yelled, 'Sugar, Sugar! How ya' doin', man!' The other two had begun to wave as well.

'Jeez, fuckin' Americans,' I thought, 'can't they just leave you in peace and not ask "how you doin'?" for one fuckin' moment . . .'

'Sugar!' another of them shouted. 'Lookin' good, baby, lookin' good!'

I saw then that they were gawping at someone way above me.

'Sugar-Rayyyyyy!'

I wheeled around and there he stood, smiling that millionaire smile, wearing a beautiful suit, waving back at them. Sugar Ray Leonard looked terrific.

'Not too long now guys,' he called, 'keep at it!'

'You bet, Ray! You're the man!'

Leonard was the MGM's 'boxing ambassador' – which meant that, for a sizable fee, he would promote their image whenever they hosted a major fight. He'd always been modern boxing's golden boy, the money-making icon who set that publicity mould with which Bob Arum encouraged Oscar De La Hoya. Yet most of the fighters I knew – especially De La Hoya, Hamed, Toney and Jones – tried to emulate Sugar Ray in the ring. And not just because of his dazzle. It was the intelligence and the iron in him they wanted.

He sauntered down the long stairway. Sugar Ray Leonard looked straight at me, perhaps trying to work out if I was another potential nut who'd leap up and hug him. I tried to seem casual, to say 'Hi, Ray'; but nothing came. I stared at him.

'How you doin'?' he eventually asked.

'Good!' I nodded eagerly. 'You?'

'Pretty good.'

'Should be quite a fight tonight,' I ventured.

'Yeah, I think it's gonna be a good one.'

'Who do you like – Toney or Jones?'

'Well, they're both excellent fighters. Jones has got great speed, a lot of power. But Toney's such a precise counter-puncher . . .'

'With a great defence,' I added.

'Oh, absolutely,' he agreed.

I thought that we already sounded like old buddies, Sugar Ray and I. It was all moving so fast. I had visions of him popping in for a cheese fondue and an evening of old boxing movies with Alison and me when he was next in London. He gazed around the arena while I built up to it gently.

'You've got a new fan in London, Ray,' I said.

'Really?' Sugar replied with the wary ease of a man who'd been here before.

Using a bit of the old foxy Leonard timing myself, I let him wait.

He looked back at me. 'Who?' he said, 'who's this new fan?'

'Her name's Alison.'

Sugar's brow went up a notch. 'Alison, mmmm? Sounds interesting . . .'

'Well, actually, she's more a fan of your video . . .'

'Really? Which one?'

My mind went blank. 'Er, the one that says "work those abs!"'

It felt good to have made Leonard laugh. 'Oh yeah, *Box Out!*'

'That's it! Every morning, soon as I step out the door, she's getting down on the living-room floor, working those abs with you, baby, snapping those jabs . . .'

I was flying close to the wind with that 'baby', but Sugar laughed again. 'What about you? You don't use my workout?'

'I think when I get back to Wimbledon I'm gonna start . . .' I was using all my tricky knowledge on the hapless Ray.

'Wimbledon? As in tennis?'

'Yeah, that's the one. You still playin' the odd set, Sugar?'

'Sure, I love tennis. Playing more golf now . . .'

'Well, there's a course opposite the courts in Wimbledon . . .'

'Sounds like Wimbledon's a real happenin' place!' Leonard smiled.

'I wouldn't go that far – but, look, Sugar, next time you're over, we'll get James Toney to fly in for a set or two of doubles with us and then –'

'No, no, no! You've made a wrong call there.'

Suitably chastised by the great Sugar Ray, I felt myself flush.

'Roy Jones!' Sugar said. 'Roy Jones would be much better. I think he'd cream Toney on the tennis court . . .'

Roy Jones looked like he had dressed for the concert hall rather than the court when he stepped up onto the apron of the ring with a knowing smirk. He wore a white shirt-front, a black bow-tie and fake tuxedo jacket. All he needed was a baton to complete the ruse of a genius conductor arriving for his latest recital. But he moved to a different kind of music, to his and his brother Corey's own brand of rap. As he began to grind his pelvis in slow and dirty circles, a huge grin cracking across his face as he heard the Garden rise to his lechery, I began to worry for James Toney.

As gifted as I knew Jones to be, I had hoped some of that brilliance would dim when 'Lights Out' time descended. I thought Jones might freeze when he felt the Toney chill. I couldn't have been more wrong. Little Roy did not look like a man who'd even heard of the word 'fear'. He did not look like a boy afraid of his own father. He appeared instead to be yearning for Toney, like he could hardly wait to fight him. How scary could a sulky homeboy like Toney ever be, compared to the memory of Big Roy striding across the pasture, plastic pipe in twitching hand, screaming blue murder?

The Lights Out entourage arrived in new black satin outfits. Their logo for the evening – 'Losing is Not an Option!' – had been embossed in gold stitching above the familiar motif of a red boxing glove smashing a lightbulb. Toney himself looked most like a menacing monk, the hood of his silky cassock pulled over a shaven head. But his face was rounder than it had been the previous night, at the weigh-in, when he'd stepped on the scales. They had called out '167 pounds', a pound below the super-middleweight mark and Jones's own weight for the fight. Toney's camp had whooped and hollered as if the contest was already won.

For six weeks Toney had struggled to make that twelve-stone notch. When he'd started training he had been more than forty pounds overweight. He was bloated with talk of moving up to the light-heavies after Jones. Sometimes, usually before he sneaked in a cheeseburger, he even speculated on his skipping right up to fight the heavyweights he especially fancied. So for him to come in lighter than Jones, the IBF middleweight holder stepping up a division, was considered a crucial piece of psychology. Yet its impact had since been distorted by the news that Toney had picked up seventeen pounds in the twenty-four hours following the weigh-in. While there was nothing illegal about the world champion stepping into the ring at 184 pounds, it was bewildering that a twenty-six-year-old fighter, supposedly at his peak, could fluctuate so wildly in weight.

The discrepancy between the boxers was pronounced even as Michael Buffer roared one of his most brazen 'Let's Get Ready To Rumble' howlers. Toney stood motionless in the middle of the ring, staring at Jones, while Little Roy danced and flexed his sleekly muscled body, moving from side to side, as if to suggest the variety of angles he might use. Toney was dressed typically in black, Jones in white, Bob Arum's chosen colours. I saw the promoter lean across his wife to whisper something to Sugar Ray who, as always, smiled back.

Toney started cautiously, coming out for the first with his guard held high, not throwing many punches as he watched Jones float across the canvas, waiting to see if he'd be given the respect of a more conventional jab. While he was accurate with both a left hook and right cross, Jones also took his time. It was only in the second round that his show kicked in dramatically. He began to lead his punches with that trademark left hook, scorching a trio of them into Toney's face before the champion could even think about ducking.

Toney seemed confused by such effrontery. He was more used to slipping jabs, to firing back swift counters over an opponent's outstretched right arm. But, against Jones, whenever he tried to connect with a solid punch he seemed to miss. In the third, Jones dropped both gloves to his side and taunted Toney, who tried to feint back. But his feet were not used to moving that fast and he was jolted by another sweeping left hook. He stumbled and, although Jones missed with his next whirlwind, began to fall. Instinctively, Toney stuck out a hand to stop himself as he crashed back into the ringpost. His right glove kept the seat of his glittering pants a few inches off the canvas but, still, he was down.

Toney nodded, to show that he felt more bashful than hurt, while the referee counted. At the sound of 'eight' he came back at Jones. He even ended the round by scuttling courageously forward. But his embarrassment had just begun. I could only guess how demeaning it must have been as Jones crisply outmanoeuvred him. In the fourth and the fifth, Jones's reflexes forced Toney to lunge helplessly past him again and again. Jones would then smack the left hook in, making Toney duck down and cover up like some tormented tortoise. He looked a pitiful figure as he crouched his way across the ring.

When Toney did manage to half-raise himself away from the hook, Jones would hit him with the right hand. It was astonishing how easily Jones could snake those hard crosses through Toney's bemused guard, breezing spray from his head. Lights Out would shake his bald dome, and I could see him saying, 'No, that ain't nothing . . .'; but he couldn't kid Jones. Toney had a brief burst of more positive activity in the sixth and the ninth, encouraging two sympathetic judges to shade both those rounds in his favour – but Jones was cruising.

I dredged up memories of Toney's strong finishes. He'd knocked out Michael Nunn in the eleventh round, after he had been comprehensively outboxed for most of that fight. I could also see the corking right hand which had blitzed 'Prince' Charles Williams at the start of the twelfth in that same MGM ring only three and a half months before.

But, with no fantasy left in Toney, the tenth and the eleventh passed as Jones stayed contemptuously out of trouble. He put his hands in the air at the end of Round Ten, knowing that he had already won. Toney did the same but his gesture was filled with desperate frustration. The gumshield flashing white in his open mouth was a more significant signal. Toney had nothing left. In the break before the final three minutes, Jackie Kallen stood behind him, waxy with shock.

Hugh McIlvanney, in the seat next to mine, put a sympathetic hand on my arm. He confirmed that Jones's pounding could not have been 'more one-sided without the use of a stretcher'. Roy won the last at a trot, almost as if deciding that he had dished out enough hurt to the former champ.

But Toney's pain was not confined just to his swollen eye or bruised body. His anguish was defined first by numbers on the scorecards – 117-110, 119-109 and, worst of all, 119-108, which meant that one judge had awarded him only one round out of twelve. 'And he's only getting that mark for attendance,' McIlvanney murmured, as we stared across at Toney, stripped of bravado, hanging his shining head as Michael Buffer shouted again, '119-108 . . . for the . . . *new* . . .'

The 'IBF Super-Middleweight Champion of the World' was swallowed up by the crowd and the jubilant Jones corner.

James Toney had lost for the first time in forty-five fights. He was no longer a world champion. But, more piercingly for him, he was not even a bad man. It looked as if his heart could break as his female mourners moved in to shield him a little, as they huddled around him. Sherry, Sarah, Jackie and baby Jasmine surrounded him in a sombre circle as they reached out to touch him, their boy called 'Lights Out'.

We waited for him for nearly three hours. I was alone and did not know many of the forty-odd family and friends who had been invited to his party. I felt awkward, drinking beer and eating vol-au-vents, like some unknown stranger at an intimate wake. I even made small talk with Robert Shapiro, him not knowing who the hell I was and me trying not to ask him about O.J. Simpson. Instead, we endorsed all the nearby chit-chat about Toney – 'temporary setback . . . the weight-loss didn't help . . . he'll be back . . .'

I wanted to leave. It seemed vaguely grotesque, loitering in the hope that Toney might show his beaten face. But, at the same time, it was the right thing to do. I felt I owed something to Toney, and to Jackie and Sherry and Sarah, who were still locked with him in his dressing-room. It seemed like a small matter of respect, of paying it to all of them. The hours passed; and I thought of Jackie saying that Toney was the kind of man who'd rather die than lose. The route to melodrama, even tragedy, stretched ahead.

But then, as I imagined the worst, he walked through the door, just after midnight, with his manager and mother alongside him and Sarah a few steps behind. He pursed his lips as people started to applaud, and then stood still when the clapping strengthened. You could tell that he had made up his mind that he was not going to cry, at least not in front of us.

He let us quieten; and then he said how sorry he was to have lost. 'But I take my hat off to Roy Jones,' he mumbled.

A very beautiful Sarah put a quivering hand to her mouth, as if to ward off the tears. The silence deepened, for his new humility made us uncertain. It didn't last long. 'I gotta also say Jones did a good job of running away from my power tonight . . .'

There were shouts of support; and I smiled at Toney. He deserved that little lie if it was going to help him get through the rest of the night. It was the least we could do, to allow him to stitch back some small piece of his shattered ego.

Toney cocked his head. 'I'll be back,' he said sweetly.

Jackie Kallen's family went over to hug him. The others in the room began to queue politely. They were lining up, as if at a wedding, or more likely a funeral, to shake hands with Toney. I joined in too, at the back, and for the next ten minutes I watched him lean down to have his cheek kissed by a procession of Jewish sisters and aunts, his back slapped by Kallen brothers and cousins, and his head held by a few of his homeboys. When my turn came I put out my hand. He took it with a wink.

'Hey, big boy,' he said, 'you still here . . .'

A few more of the elderly ladies returned for another kiss and then Toney broke away for some food. My last memory of that night was an image of him lifting a plate, with Sarah on one arm and Sherry on the other.

His mother puckered her own lips to kiss him. 'I'm proud of you, boy,' I heard her say gravely.

I saw Roy Jones the next morning, just after eight, sauntering through the MGM's gigantic foyer. He had just returned from a three-mile run. I would not have believed it if I hadn't seen the sheen on him.

'Man, I can't sleep,' he sighed. He looked out at the thinning ranks of heavy-duty table gamblers being supplemented by the early-risers on the slot-machines. Rather than attending some fantastic all-night party, Jones said that he'd kept his hurting hands in buckets of ice-water before he and a few friends went out looking for some Kentucky Fried Chicken.

'Wow,' I said, 'some celebration . . .'

'It might have been, man,' Jones breathed, 'but all the KFCs were closed. I thought this was meant to be a twenty-four-hour town.'

'So what did you do?'

'We ended up in McDonald's . . . had some fries. Crazy, huh?'

I thought of the similarly deadpan way Jones had spoken at his post-fight press conference. 'Have you spoken to your father yet?' he was asked.

'Nope.'

'Will you phone him tonight?' the questioner persisted.

'I spoke to God when I got back to my dressing-room. Ain't no reason for me to call anyone else . . .'

'Did Toney bother you, with all his talk of killing you?' a new voice queried.

'Man,' Jones laughed lightly, a coldness beneath his words, 'how could he?' Had we forgotten, his level gaze demanded, that he had already been to hell and back in Pensacola?

I wanted to ask him about his father, too, that early Saturday morning;

but it felt wrong. I mentioned Toney instead, wondering if Roy had seen him after the fight.

'Yeah, we spoke a couple of minutes. Things are okay between us. The fight's over and done with now . . .'

'I saw him late last night. They had a small party for him . . .'

'Good. He showed up?'

'He turned up in the end . . .'

'How was he?' Jones asked.

'I was surprised. He said a few words, he allowed people to come up and speak to him. He was much better than I ever thought he'd be . . .'

'That's good. He was a great champion. An' he's still a great fighter . . .'

'And, best of all,' I said, 'he was a good guy in the end. He even let all the old white ladies come up and kiss him . . .'

'Man,' Roy Jones said, 'I like to think I woulda done the same thing myself.'

But then everything changed. A day later, on 20 November 1994, James Toney went out to kill Jackie Kallen. It was all her fault, he decided, the loss of his unbeaten record and that terrible humiliation in Vegas. She'd got greedy and had put herself before him. He was going to make her pay. He was going to shoot her as well as her husband and two sons.

Sherry Toney, his idol, called Jackie to warn her, to tell her that he was coming.

Jackie could hear that this time it was different. His blazing anger would not be doused. As she listened to the fright in Sherry's voice, she could hear him screaming in the background, telling his mother that he was on his way, 'that he was gonna shoot up Jackie and her whole fuckin' family . . .'

The day had begun more quietly. James and Sherry Toney had driven over from Ann Arbor to the Kallens' home in suburban West Bloomfield, Michigan, to meet with Jackie and her husband. After the devastating loss to Jones it was time for them to decide how best they might pick up the thread of his changed career. Despite the hollow inside him, Toney was calm at first. He listened to Jackie go through the possibilities, thinking of the tacky 'Losing is Not an Option' she'd had sewn onto their fight jackets. He started to seethe.

She recommended that he should exercise the rematch clause in his contract and again face Jones at super-middleweight. If he got into better shape early on, if he didn't balloon up to 210 like he had done before, if he stayed off the junk food and trained really hard, she still believed he had the ability to beat Jones. He could wipe away all the damage that had been done on Friday night.

It was then that Toney erupted. She had been the one who had made him take the fight at the lower weight, she had made him lose, and now she wanted him to do the same thing again. He'd had enough of her, he raged. He walked out of their meeting and her house. He was through with her.

By the time he reached home he'd made his choice. He was going to get her. It was then that Sherry called Jackie who, in turn, phoned the Detroit police. They took the threat seriously. The Kallen property was quickly surrounded by armed officers as they waited for the fighter's arrival.

Yet, in the end, James Toney stayed away. He kept his gun to himself.

The Detroit police went looking for him instead, having opened an investigation into his death threat. He was questioned; but they soon let him go free with only a warning for intimidating behaviour.

The following morning, while Jackie and Sherry were interviewed on television about the previous day's incident, Toney again berated her on Detroit radio. Calling her a 'ho' and telling her 'to take your money until July [when their contract expired] and then get out', Toney alleged that Jackie had forced him to fight Jones even though she knew he had flu and that he had been severely drained by his weight loss. He claimed that she was more interested in her own wealth than his health, that he resented her craving for the spotlight.

The media found it easy to side with Jackie Kallen. 'I'd be lying,' she stressed, 'if I said I wasn't hurt, I wasn't stunned, I wasn't horrified. One of the things he said was that I've only been with him for the money, that I don't care about him. I just never expected to hear that from James. I treated this kid like he's my family. We all travelled together as family, we went on holiday cruises as family. Personally, I don't think I could have done much more for him. Yes, boxing is a business but I've never taken a penny that I haven't rightfully earned. I'm sure James fights for the money also. I don't think he's in this game just because he loves the beauty of the ring.

'He said he had the flu and that I forced him into fighting Roy Jones. At the press conference and at the weigh-in he was certainly fit and cocky enough. He thought he was going to win then. No one made James Toney fight Roy Jones. He's always been the one that says he's the boss, that he calls the shots. So for him to turn round and say that I made him fight is absurd. No one makes that kid do anything.

'He's told his mother that he'll apologise if I apologise to him first. Well, I'm still trying to think what I should apologise for. For making him a millionaire, for getting him the biggest pay-day of his career? Who knows what our future holds because I just don't think the words "I'm sorry" are in his vocabulary. He can't bring himself to say it.

'But, you know, I'm a compassionate person. I'm not hard-nosed. Part of me understands why all of this happened. I know how disappointed he was having lost such a big fight. Hardest of all for him was the way he lost, the fact that he was virtually run out of the ring. It wasn't a tight fight, there was no controversy about the decision. I think that was most hurtful to him, the fact that it wasn't even close. His whole identity was crushed. One minute you're the champion and the pound-for-pound number one; and the next minute you're basically just another fighter.'

'We must distrust one another. It's the only way to protect each other from betrayal . . .'

With Mike Tyson's adaptation of Tennessee Williams tolling in my head, as if written for boxers and managers in Michigan, I decided to head for the South.

As a diversion from the Toney-Kallen rift, that partnership in which I'd once so believed, I flew to Florida. If the 'James & Jackie' story could not produce the happy ending boxing so badly needed, I could still revel in the lustre of Roy Jones Jnr. I had yearned for Toney to beat him but, at the end of the twelfth, I bowed to the reality of Jones's superiority.

While I knew I would never feel as much for Jones and his posse as I did for James, Jackie, Sherry, Sarah, Jasmine and even Pee-Wee, I knew Jones was a boxing phenomenon. I was also fascinated by the parallels and detours between his and Toney's very different fathers.

He, however, was less a fan of the Lights Out mob. 'The Toney camp thought they could rattle me,' Jones said. 'When they were checking my gloves just before we went out to the ring, Jackie Kallen's brother came into my dressing-room. He was their observer an' he starts staring at me as if he's also got some hard face, like I'm gonna get murdered tonight. That was when I decided I ain't gonna take it no more. I walked right up to him, so that our noses were almost touchin' an' I said: "What you lookin' at? There ain't nothin' you can do to stop me tonight – there ain't nothin' anyone can do, you go tell James Toney that . . ." And, man, he turned on his heel. He was outta there and so I jus' started to throw some punches, watchin' myself in the mirror, sayin', "I'm gonna hit him with this hand . . . I'm gonna hit him with that hand . . . bam-bam-bam . . . combinations, combinations, to the body, to his head." You saw me come out that night, you saw me do that little shimmy as soon I got up in the ring. I was so confident, man, I didn't even have a moment's doubt . . .'

'Did Toney say much to you during the fight?'

'Oh, sure,' Jones remembers, shaking his head in disbelief, 'I was poppin' these punches off from all different angles and they keep on landing an' James Toney's moanin', crouchin' down, "no, that ain't nothin'. . ." An' I'm breathing back, "yeah, okay, maybe they ain't nothin' but they're bouncin' off your head" . . .'

'Did you think that you might even stop him – especially when he took that short count in the third?'

'Well, I got plenty of power to take out most of these guys but, if I can, I prefer to go the distance. I feel I can learn more that way . . .'

'But against a guy like Toney,' I argued, 'even though you beat him easily on the night, you can't just pick and choose when you knock him down.'

'Yeah, he's tough, he's got a big heart. So I always felt it would go the full twelve. That's what I wanted. I didn't look for the big punch – I was content to overwhelm him every single round. I learnt stuff fighting Toney for thirty-six minutes and so I'm pretty sure that I'm gonna be an even better fighter next time round. Because, against James Toney, I reckon I only used about 60 per cent of my full potential – both in power an' precision. He didn't extend me so I know I can go up a few more levels. I've got a whole lot more to offer and I think people will be shocked when they see how much I can still improve . . .'

As a staunch admirer of both Toney's ability and passion for fighting, an abdication to Jones's majesty came reluctantly. Yet Roy Jnr had the style to cancel out Toney and anyone else – at any weight from middle to light-heavy. More even than De La Hoya or Hamed, Roy Jones looked to be in the groove.

'Yeah, "groove" is the word. Against James Toney I hit a groove all right,' Roy Jones confirmed. 'It felt like I could've fought the guy all night long – I hit the kind of groove against which he could do nothin'. I jus' wanted to prove it to him again and again – that there ain't nothin' he can do against me. An' that's what happened – simple as that. Y'see, people were surprised I beat him so easily. They kept sayin' that I hadn't been tested by a fighter like Toney – but I always knew I was better than him.

'The difference is that other people were taken in by that hard face of his, by his trash talk. All the way through the build-up he was sayin', "I'm gonna kill this boy . . ." and I think he frightened some people. I didn't take no notice. I jus' said, "We'll see . . ." I don't need to answer back to a guy like James Toney 'cos, see, I'm much more sure of myself.'

'Toney took defeat relatively well on the night,' I said, 'so were you surprised that he then threatened to kill Jackie Kallen?'

'Not really. In the ring he's a good technician but, outside, he jus' tries too hard to be mean. That never works against me. Before we fought he was talking a lot o' junk. He was gonna break my ass, make me his bitch. He wasn't into any pretty talk. I said to myself, "Okay, okay, we'll talk later – in the ring". I think James Toney's got some real problems – you take away his bad boy bluff and, well, who is he then? What you got left?'

'Well,' I answered, 'I know he's a fighter who's never had a father . . .'

'Yeah, I guess,' Jones hesitated.

'Do you know much about the story of his father?'

'The basics . . .'

'It's like I just know the basics about your father.'

'Oh, man, I'm not sure I wanna talk about him . . .'

'My father is not a bad man . . .' Roy Jones murmured, his hand covering mine in a movement as odd as it was gentle. The silence between us grew, amplified by the cries and shrieks of hundreds of birds wheeling across a blue sky.

The dirty white gulls reminded me that we were still in Florida, on the edge of Pensacola, home to Roy and his father; but, circling the far rim of the lake, a greasy black crow suggested that the story began elsewhere, in the Deep South states of Alabama and Georgia bordering Florida's Panhandle towns to the north and west, where Roy Snr had been born forty-seven years before.

From the disillusion of his family's earliest share-cropping and his own stint in the Job Corps, Vietnam and the professional ring, a father emerged; a father who turned himself into a remorseless trainer of fighters. As I remembered all that I had read about Big Roy, his son took back his lethal left and spoke again.

'I guess he decided early on to take me in hand,' he said. 'From the age of five, I understood he was determined to shape me into some kind of fighting machine. He'd drop to his knees and order me to hit him. But then he'd sway out of the way, pokin' his tongue out, the laugh stickin' in his throat. When I got tired he'd lash out – deadly as a snake. Sneaky little punches, pushes, knocking me down – jus' hard enough to make the tears fall.'

'And then what happened – later?' I asked, expecting a bleak answer, if not the severity of its telling.

'Then,' Roy Jones said, 'it got worse. You can't imagine how bad things turned out between my father and me. I ain't never felt so alone or so afraid. He'd train me from four in the afternoon till ten at night. Six hours straight, day in, day out, double that on weekends – making me fight bigger boys, four or five years older than me.

'Even now I can feel my heart rattlin', like it did every day I made my way home from school. Fear welling up 'cos he was waiting for me, out in the field, inside this damned ring he made. Whenever I made a mistake, or got dog-tired, he'd whip me with a plastic pipe. Other times, he'd take a water-hose to me – sometimes a belt . . .

'It was hell. But how do you get away from a man as big and fierce as he looked then? It ain't possible when he's your daddy. Killing myself seemed the only escape. I had this picture of me putting a gun to my head, squeezing the trigger . . . later, I got myself a knife. I carried it on me, in case he jumped me one time too many. I thought I'd end up in jail – for killing my own father.

'But, instead, most times I did as he said. I fought, and when I got knocked down again, he'd make me get up, telling me to fight back, always asking, "Well, boy, you a kingpin or a participant?" That same question over and over again, rainin' down with the blows . . .'

'And how would you answer?'
'Always the same – "kingpin . . . kingpin . . . kingpin . . ."'

When I asked if he'd mind my talking to his father, Roy Jones looked me dead in the eye, unblinking in the early-afternoon glare. 'You can talk to anyone you like . . .' he said evenly. He gave me his father's telephone number.

But Alfie Smith, his best friend, was more circumspect. 'Shit, man, you don't wanna mess with Roy's daddy,' he cautioned as we drove past the Jones's fifteen-acre spread of Pensacola farmland. The car slowed near the yellowed patch of turf where Roy's father had drilled him. Alfie shook his head, as if he could not shift the stories he had heard – or erase the day three years ago when Roy Snr had driven over to the adjoining yard where 'Little Roy' and Alfie waited. Then, the father had stared at his son for a long while before saying, 'You know, I killed your dog.' Their eyes followed the jerk of his head. The rottweiler, tied to an old oak tree, lay dead in a puddle of blood.

I had been told by another trainer that the shooting had been justified – that the dog had attacked Big Roy's eight-year-old daughter. As much as it sent a quiver through me I wanted to find the man of whom I had heard so much.

'No way!' Alfie chided when I asked if we could drop in on 'Big Daddy'. 'Don't mess with him . . .'

With Alfie's words still echoing, I slipped into my most obsequious patter when I called Big Roy myself. 'Good afternoon to you, Mr Jones,' I began. Without answer, my preamble grovelled on for almost a minute. 'I wondered, sir,' I panted at last, 'if you were still available to meet me?'

'What you wanna talk about?' he growled.

I hoped to ask Roy Jones Snr about the intensity of a father's emotion. How did it feel to lose your son after controlling him for twenty-three years? Had he watched the fight against Toney? What did he think of him that night? They were calling Roy 'The Greatest Fighter on the Planet' while he – the former trainer and manager, the father – remained locked on the outside. How did that make him feel, watching his dream develop and then sour? Did he feel guilty or angry when Roy Jnr described their years together as 'hell'? Had he known that, around the time of their split, his son packed a nine-millimetre Baretta as protection – 'because I know how my dad is'? Could they ever get over the past?

'Mr Jones,' I said, ducking as I spoke, feeling like Toney might have done when waiting for another left hook from Little Roy, 'I'd like to talk to you about boxing . . . about the good and the bad . . .'

'Mmm-hmmm . . .'

'Maybe we could, you know,' I stumbled, trying to hit an appropriately laconic drawl but sounding like just another good ol' boy, 'shoot the breeze . . . or something?'

'Sure,' Roy Jones Snr breathed down the telephone line, 'We'll kick back and, like you say, shoot the breeze . . . or somethin' . . .'

'Big Roy's not much of a talker these days,' noted Stanley Levin, Roy Jones Jnr's affable lawyer and prime adviser. 'He hasn't said a word to me in more than two years. Last time I saw him I said, real cheery, "Hi, big 'un!" He walked on by, like I was some sorta ghost. It's a real shame because if I love Little Roy like a son I also think of his daddy as a friend.

'Y'see, I've been with father and son since '84. That was when I first noticed Big Roy. I watched this man slugging his guts out to help young men, tryin' to give hope, teaching them to box. Then, I knew nothing about the trouble between him and his son.

'I'm a father myself. When I met the Joneses I'd just won custody of my son. Like now, I was high on kids, on helpin' 'em as much as possible. I started dippin' into my own pocket just to keep Big Roy's boxing programme on track. When it became apparent that Little Roy was destined for stardom, his dad asked if my brother and I would "roll the dice" with them in starting Roy professionally. We pumped in a million dollars without return . . .'

It was then, in the summer of '92, that the Jones family fractured. The shooting of Rocky, that fated mutt, marked the culmination of a struggle which had been fermenting for years. As Roy Jnr became a man, the physical abuse he had suffered was replaced by a more subtle form of manipulation.

'Roy Snr controlled his son,' Levin explained. 'It's something inside of him – he needs to dominate. And he's damn stubborn about getting his way. So Little Roy was excluded from all meetings relating to his career. I always thought that patently unfair – but Roy Jnr feared the friction if he insisted on having a say in his future. So, privately, I became Roy's voice . . .'

A curious friendship was forged between the black boxer and middle-aged Jewish lawyer – to the point where it existed as a partnership based on trust rather than any written contract. Unlike Kallen and Toney they did not have a piece of paper to tear up. For all the surface similarities between the two camps, I doubted if Jones would have gone after Levin with a gun. Yet, apart from also infuriating the promotional mafiosi of Arum, Duva and King, the bond gave Roy Jnr the confidence to free himself from his father's previously unbreakable grip.

'Big Roy and I went out drinking after the bust-up,' Levin recalled. 'I said to him, "Big 'un, your son is a remarkable man. Yet you won't say one word to him no more – and neither will he to you. It's time for you to pay him some respect, apologise, let him be a man too! Roy, if my own son said, "Dad, the only way I'm going to talk to you again is if you get down on your hands and knees and crawl to New York City" – then, dammit, I wouldn't be here – I'd be on the road! Talk to your son, make these bad times good."

'Big Roy looked long and hard at me before he sprouted one of his "parables": "Listen," he said, "once you break a plate at my table you can never eat there again.""

As hard as I tried to avoid even the smallest crack in one of his plates from the past, Roy Jones Snr kept grinding me down. The game he played was a quaint variation of musical chairs – with me left standing in confusion, and Big Roy seated elsewhere, as soon as the see-sawing rhythm of our chit-chat lurched to another stop. Whenever an arrangement for us to meet appeared settled, I wound up searching for a place at the father's table.

Our initial rendezvous, 'Big Daddy' decided, would be at night – in front of a low concrete building lost in a tract of north-west Pensacola wasteland. There, in that deserted setting, Roy Snr trained a few boys in the rudimentary arts of boxing most nights a week – but, for some reason, not that week. Two hours after our scheduled appointment failed to materialise it struck me that, perhaps, Mr Jones had not lost all sense of control.

His number was soon branded into my brain. Whenever he answered the phone we endured another stilted negotiation before he said, unfailingly, 'Well, all right, we'll do it later. Call back in a couple o' hours.' Perhaps because I didn't want to end up in a paddock with a furious Daddy, I preserved my own ingratiating charade – even when Big Roy vanished for hours on end, leaving a stream of messages with his daughters for me to 'call again in another hour or so'.

On my last night in Pensacola I even caught him at his table, eating off one of those plates from the parable – 'Well, all right,' he grumbled, 'we'll do it later – when I finish dinner. I'll drop by in an hour or so . . . we'll talk then, almost certainly . . .'

He never showed. And yet I could not stop myself wanting to pick up the phone one last time to ask Roy Jones Snr why he once said of the past: 'In the gym you'd see me with a bat. To keep the bluff on him. Time to time, "Hey boy, do this, do that!" If I gave him all those whuppings like he says, it's what he needed. If I gave him three, he needed five. If I whupped him a thousand times, then he needed it a thousand times . . .'

But I also needed to hear that he still believed in the different sentiments he had expressed before: 'Roy's got a tremendous career ahead . . . he needs to forget about this other stuff. Like I told him, "I'm satisfied being your daddy" . . . it's disturbing, though. Like they're tryin' to make this a Michael Jackson kind of story . . .'

Roy Jones Jnr, however, was not without hope that their story might end in redemption. 'Like that fight with Toney, it's over and done with,' he stressed. 'It's three years since I moved out of my dad's home, since I told him to leave me be. Now I wanna bury the past, fill up that hole between my father and me . . . '

His hand drifted across the expanse of his own home and eight acres of Pensacola land, over the lake teeming with bass and catfish in front of us, alongside the plum and fig trees shading the crested hordes of gamecocks he loved, and back towards his private basketball court filled with his yelling homies at play on a glorious Sunday morning.

'All this is mine,' he said. 'I earned it. I'm the best fighter in the world right now, I have a girl, I'm my own man, I know where I'm going . . . and I jus' turned twenty-six . . . ain't there freedom from the past in all this?'

'But what about your father, now?' I asked.

'What about him?'

'Can you talk to him yet?'

'We're talkin' . . . a little . . . y'know . . . now and then . . . '

'About boxing?'

'Oh, man,' he laughed, 'I ain't ever talkin' boxing with him again – we did that enough to last a lifetime.'

'What do you talk about then?'

'We talk in passing – when my mother's around or I call the house – little things, everyday things . . . it's gonna take time to get some place else . . . ' And then, like a dragging weight had been raised from him, Roy Jones patted me on the hand again. 'Look, understand, my father is not a bad man . . . ' He turned away to scoop up his favourite bird and then, kissing its crown, a grin suddenly slid across his face: 'Hey, anyway, unlike James Toney, I turned out all right – ain't that the truth?'

7

LOOKING ON DARKNESS

THREE MONTHS TO THE DAY HAD PASSED SINCE JAMES TONEY'S loss. He had to get back into the ring, to recover the myth which Roy Jones had razed. Toney needed to get his mouth working again, to feel the Lights Out bravado returning. Otherwise he was nothing.

For all the treachery he saw in Jackie Kallen, she understood what defeat had done to him. *'His whole identity was crushed. One minute you're the champion and the pound-for-pound number one; and the next you're basically just another fighter . . .'*

Toney could have ended up as just another fighter in prison; but Sherry worked hard on him. He tried to put some of the old boxing pieces back together. With distrust and hurt still raw, Jackie announced that they would resume their partnership – at least until her managerial contract expired in July. They chose not to disclose any details of their awkward reconciliation but Jackie, ever the PR queen, attempted to add a terse gloss in public. 'What's past is past,' she said. 'Talking about it is just like opening an old wound. We're looking to the future . . .'

I thought there was something brave, if futile, in their efforts to reunite.

'The problems are behind us now,' she continued more positively, 'everything's on an even keel.' Toney's silence, at least, remained steady.

As much as I would have liked her to be right, I was equally sure that they were doomed. 'The Lady & The Champ' story was almost over – and I hoped it would not end in tragedy.

They made a dangerous choice for Toney's return. His next fight was set for the same date, the eighteenth, and the same ring, the MGM Grand Garden, where he had been decimated by Roy Jones. More significantly, as Lights Out was still too much of a bad man to believe in karma, they selected a slick and unbeaten fighter for his comeback. Montell Griffin, who was trained by the great Eddie Futch, had been on the '92 Olympic squad with De La Hoya. He was the kind of hungry and speedy boxer most camps would have avoided as they looked to ease back into winning ways. A game journeyman was the kind of dependable pug usually selected for such an encounter.

But the Toney way, prior to the disastrous 'Uncivil War', saw him taking on and beating 'anyone, anytime, anyplace'. Before Roy Jones, the idea of Toney being endangered by a fighter even as talented as Montell Griffin would have been ridiculed.

But Toney's skill had not eroded. They also knew Griffin well. He had spent time in their gym two years before, while nearly signing as a pro with Jackie. Toney had sparred with Griffin and had never been in trouble. Moreover, Lights Out might have been defeated by a sensational, 'once-in-every-twenty-years' virtuoso like Jones, but he had been weakened by his extreme weight reduction. He was fighting Griffin at light-heavy, which would mean he'd have an additional seven pounds to pack onto his bulky frame. Lastly, by beating Griffin, it would set him up for a crack at one of his new division's titles.

In Vegas, a less-shaken Jackie Kallen flagged the fact that 'James wants a championship belt around his waist again. He wants to show everyone that it wasn't really him who lost to Roy Jones . . .'

Toney, however, came out against Griffin like a man more stimulated by the promise of popping another double cheeseburger beneath his belt. He'd made the 175-pound light-heavyweight spot without an ounce to spare and he moved around the ring with little of the zest which had oozed from him six months previously. Yet, three inches taller than the stocky 5ft 7in Griffin, he could use his longer reach to hold off the faster boxer.

Toney's belief that he had only to put in an appearance to whip up a tasty victory was nourished further in the third. A sweet right-hand counter shook Griffin to the base of his shaky boots. His legs wobbled like a fruit-packed jelly. Toney stood back and licked his lips. When he eventually did follow up with a scooping uppercut, Griffin had recovered enough composure to make Toney miss so badly that he almost tumbled to the canvas himself.

The fight settled into an uninspiring pattern. Toney chugged along at a pedestrian pace, picking up the odd good round here and there when his hands moved faster than his feet, while Griffin chipped away at both head and body. He rocked Toney momentarily in the seventh, but lacked the power to do more damage. Three-quarters of the way through the bout, Toney was ahead on all three scorecards and only needed to exert himself a fraction more to ensure success.

'You're a much better fighter than him,' an agitated Bill Miller urged at the end of the ninth. 'Quit being lazy!'

But it looked as if Toney had lost his heart in that ring twelve weeks before. Each judge awarded Griffin the last three rounds even though he was barely shading the flickering Lights Out. Griffin displayed none of the sublime ability of Jones – he just worked harder than Toney.

Kallen, Toney and I still thought he had done enough, even when we heard that there was a 114-114 draw amongst the scores. We were convinced that the 115-113 and 116-112 calls would be made in his favour.

But the unthinkable did happen. James Toney had lost for the second time in a row.

Griffin's own explanation was simple yet poignant. 'Toney intimidates a lot of guys, but I had an advantage. I'd stayed at his house so I knew that the James Toney you see out in public, in front of the cameras, is not the real James Toney. You see the real man at home – and he's a nice guy, he's not a loudmouth. He does that just for the camera. Even if he'd wanted to intimidate me he couldn't because we'd spent time together as friends. So what could he say to me?'

Roy Jones Jnr had replaced him as the world's top-ranked fighter; but Montell Griffin had only fought fourteen times before. The ferocity in James Toney had given way to numbed despair.

On a still and sun-filled Monday morning, just before noon, the infinitely happier Roy Jones Jnr set out for work. He'd also been away for three months – and you could tell by the way we ambled down some of Pensacola's loveliest streets, as if he thought it possible to delay his return to the grindstone.

'Oh, man,' he sighed as we meandered past the hushed lines of grand houses and deserted playgrounds, 'it's back to the old routine . . .'

Yet Roy Jones understood one fact better than most fighters. Even though it may seem as if the 'old routine' never changes, there are times when everything else is turned inside out – as Toney now knew. 'Little Roy' had experienced the flipside the last time he'd stepped into a ring. But even that new 'best boxer in the world' tag couldn't help him avoid the timeworn rituals on his first day back in the Square Ring gym. Roy Jones knew that the glamour of his victory over Toney had to be replaced by the tedium of skipping rope, working the heavy bag and pummelling the speed-ball before an audience of one – me.

'It's gonna be hard,' Jones suggested, 'to get back in the mood, to go through the same drill again, to pick up where I left off – like the gym on a Monday morning in Pensacola is the same as goin' in for the world title against James Toney on a Friday night in Vegas . . .' Roy Jones sniffed incredulously while he lifted a sleepy eye at another blue Florida sky: 'And, man, to top it all, it feels like I got me a February cold comin' on.'

'Well . . .' I consoled boxing's latest version of Superman, 'imagine how James Toney will feel on his next day back in the gym . . .'

'Oh yeah,' he smiled wryly.

He picked up his training gear – reminding me how Toney had snarled that Jones was not even fit to 'carry my bag' – and headed for the gymnasium. As he strode forward his head jerked towards the work-place. 'Sure, once I'm inside, I'll feel it all flowin' back. Then I'll say, "Yeah, it's good to be back, it feels real good."'

Despite his boredom as he stretched and then sat with bowed head while his hands were taped, he offered small signals. Even the exaggerated yawns, as he flexed his neck, couldn't hide the pep inside him. By the time Ice Cube's 'It Was a Good Day' throbbed across the wooden floor, Roy was banging at the heavy bag in three-minute bursts of disciplined menace. His punches gathered power and the bag swung in huge arcs. Air rushed from him in increasing volume. A hiss wrapped round a grunt – *'Tsa-huuunh! Tsa-huuunh!'* – like the noise I had heard Tyson and Cassius make years before.

Roy Jones cut an even more impressive figure than Mighty Mike at full throttle. As he swooped and pounded it became easy to recall the speed and power which had blunted Toney's machismo. The sound-system reverberated with Roy and his younger brother Corey recounting that Lights Out humbling on one of their homemade hip-hop tracks.

As Roy's echoing voice rapped out another message to the forlorn Toney, asking him if he wanted to 'do it one more time', his fists flashed simultaneously with a smearing force. If not Toney, his brutal cries seemed to ask, who else would like a taste of Roy Jones?

'What about Chris Eubank?' I queried, offering up Britain's monocled mutineer.

A shutter of indifference fell down the beaded length of Jones's face: 'I hardly know anything about Chris Eubank . . .'

'But you know that, however he's managed it, he's still officially unbeaten – that he was good enough to beat Benn and Watson . . .'

'So?' Jones retorted impassively.

'So you'd obviously be willing to fight him in Britain?'

'You tell Chris Eubank I'd take him anywhere. Man, I'd fight him inside his mama's house if he wants . . .'

It was good to hear that the Lights Out legacy had not been completely forgotten – at least Roy Jones had attempted an echo of Toney's fixation with the older Mrs Eubank.

Despite his professed apathy for Eubank, I knew that the WBO title-holder had garnered some attention in Pensacola. While fooling around at home – showing me his shadow-boxing technique against one of his dogs, or slipping into a muscle-bound pose as he stood on top of the farm's 'R.J.'-initialled wrought-iron gate – Roy Jones would offer a reminder. 'Hey, look,' he laughed, 'this one is for Chris Eubank – you tell him this one's from me to him, you tell him I'm waitin', anytime an' anyplace he likes . . .'

Yet the threat offered by Jones was so convincing that it seemed unlikely Eubank would meet him. In contrast to Hove's 'Simply the Best', Jones was 'ready to take on anyone. I'm ready for Chris Eubank, Nigel Benn or any other guy you care to mention. I'd really like to go back and fight over there. I was in London when I was eighteen years old – for the Benn–Watson fight – and I had a great time.'

'What do you remember most?'

'Oh, man,' Jones enthused, 'I just fell in love with all them pretty horses.'

'What?'

'Sure, those big police-horses . . . boy, they're so pretty!'

'Gee, Roy,' I murmur with mock incredulity, 'that's strange.'

'How come?'

'Well, it sounds like you were more interested in the "pretty horses" than in any girl you might have seen. Are you like James Toney, who thinks "all the men are fat and the woman are ugly" over there?'

'Oh no!' Roy Jones Jnr cackled, 'that's where you're wrong – I took plenty o' notice. The girls there, man, they're beautiful. Outstandingly beautiful! See – that's just another reason for me to fight in London – pretty horses, even prettier women! What better reason could there be for another look, for another trip over the ocean?'

'But your hardest fight might still be in America,' I argued, thinking of Don King's most chilling knockout artist, 'against Gerald McClellan.'

'Yeah, McClellan would be interesting. He hits harder than anyone else.'

'You think he'll beat Nigel Benn in London?' I asked in reference to King's block-busting promotion the following Saturday night which would match the WBC super-middleweight champion, Benn, against the rising middleweight title-holder, McClellan. The winner would be angling for a multi-million-dollar unification match with Jones.

'Yeah, I think McClellan beats Benn. But, maybe, jus' maybe, it's gonna be tighter than some people expect. Nigel's a real warrior, he can still bang a bit – an' I think McClellan's jaw is kinda suspect when he gets tagged . . .'

'But can Benn's own chin absorb too many McClellan punches?'

'No, probably not. Eventually, Benn will go . . .'

'Which will leave McClellan calling even louder for you.'

'Sure, he knows that I'm the guy who'll earn him some real money.'

'What do you think of him outside the ring?'

'I like Gerald McClellan – he's an okay sort of guy. He's quieter than Toney. He also likes big dogs. We've known each other a long time . . .'

'What happened when you fought – back in the amateurs, when he beat you?'

'Well, I don't worry about that. It was just before the Olympics. I was already set for a spot on the team and the selection committee were determined that the other place was gonna go to Ray McElroy. So in the National Golden Gloves I fought Gerald in the semis and they gave him a 3–2 decision. Then they gifted the decision to McElroy in the final. That's amateur politics. So I jus' said to Gerald after we fought, "Okay, good fight, we'll do it again one day" . . .'

'Did he have a lot of power – even then?'

'Oh, yeah – he's always had power. He hits real hard. But I'd fight him just the same as I fought Toney. I won't jus' be standing there waiting to be hit. I'll move, I'll give all kinds of cute angles, I'll give him a sample of my own strength. He can't soak up the kind of punches I throw. I think he'd go four, maybe five rounds and then he'd be knocked out.'

'But McClellan seems to believe that he's the best guy out there . . .'

'Yeah, it's interesting. I reckon he really does think he can beat me. But then so did James Toney. Those guys have their self-belief – that's what makes them the best guys to fight against. But, I don't see no problem with Gerald McClellan – he's just another fighter I'll beat. Sure, Gerald McClellan's a good boxer. Sure, Gerald McClellan can knock anybody out. But, after four rounds, Roy Jones kills Gerald McClellan.'

25 February 1995

Pretty horses were never really an option for Gerald McClellan. He was yet another bad man from Detroit; an unbelievably powerful hitter with a penchant for breeding savage pit-bull terriers. I had had my fill of darkness on the trail of Tyson and Toney; and so I chose to watch McClellan from a distance. He induced a shudder inside me whenever I read a sombre profile of him or saw him knock someone out.

As he prepared to fight Britain's own 'Dark Destroyer', Nigel Benn, at the London Arena, he revealed his philosophy. 'Outside the ring,' he told Graham Houston in *Boxing Monthly*, 'I'm a real soft-spoken guy. I don't say much, real quiet – but I'm an animal inside the ring. I have a one-track mind which is seek and destroy.'

Developing his bestial theme, he explained to Houston that 'a pit bull is an animal that only one person can train, it can only have one master. They hate. Let's put it like this: me in the ring with another fighter is just like a pit bull seeing another animal, you know, it's nothing personal, it's just something you have to do.'

McClellan enthused about his canine-training abilities as if he were being interviewed by *Doggy World*. 'Really,' he said, 'a dog is what you make of him. I could take a poodle and train it to be as vicious as a pit bull, not vicious as regards the damage that a pit bull can do, but a dog is what you make of it. I know some people that have got pit bulls that you can walk down the street with 'em, off the leash, and he will run up to a dog or a cat and won't touch it. But the one I have, if I let him loose in the street he would eat another dog, he'd eat a cat, a squirrel, he just hates other animals. Anything that's on the ground and moving like him, he's just got it in his mind that he must destroy.'

While I was amused by McClellan's descriptive powers, the image made me reel. The fighter saw himself as boxing's answer to that hurtling eating-machine. 'When I'm in the ring with another fighter, I look across the ring and see this guy I have so much hate for, so much desire to knock this guy unconscious.'

McClellan was remorseless, even when talking about his private life. Once he got a grip it seemed as if he would never let go. 'My favourite colour is green,' he stressed, 'and everything I own is green, my whole house, cars, everything. And there's like five different types of green and one of them is forest green. So I named my little girl Forrest.'

I told Alison this story, with the promise that our own first child would also be called 'Forest', Forest McRae, as a way of humanising a fighter who also tagged himself 'The G-Man'. 'G' for Gerald, Green and his G-Force punch. Although we couldn't decide whether green was also the colour, beyond money and envy, of psychosis, we settled down that Saturday night on our coral-shaded sofa, each with a beer in hand and ITV's *Big Fight Live* whistling down the tube.

'Don't even slip out for a pee,' I exhorted her lyrically, 'this fight is gonna be fucking awesome!' She looked at me carefully, as if to monitor the final rites of my mutation into boxing mania. 'Yeah, I'm worried for Nigel Benn. I hope he comes out of this one okay. But it'll be exciting, really exciting, as long as it lasts. This McClellan, the "G-Man", this father to Forrest, whew, is he lethal!'

Alison turned back to the screen and heard more of the same. My own bombast was stilled by ITV's matching brand. I heard how I must have sounded – but it tempered only some of my fervour.

The cameras beamed back pictures of the two fighters warming up. McClellan was lean and wiry, rippling as he threw punches in the air. Along the corridor, Benn went through a similar motion. Our screen was filled with the 'No Fear' legend adorning his woolly black cap. The camera panned down and Benn, like the G-Man, stared into the lens with serious eyes.

'Jesus,' Alison murmured as she slid down the seat, 'this could get really nasty . . .'

But, this being big-time boxing, there was also diversionary banter. They cut away to Don King and Frank Warren, the co-promotors, who had sold out the Docklands Arena with their 'Sudden Impact' campaign. Don and Frank, looking exceedingly pleased with each other, were being interviewed by ITV's 'Voice of Reason', Gary Newbon. As King waved a tiny Stars and Stripes in each hand, with a further couple of flags sticking out of his tuxedo pocket, Warren agreed with Newbon. 'It's an explosive fight! Both guys carry bombs in their gloves!'

Big Don roared his delight. 'Yes!' he warbled, 'it's gonna be a sensational fight and the British deserve the best and that's why Frank Warren and I joined together with ITV, and the voice of ITV, Gary Newbon, to bring the best in boxing. An' you're gonna see some explosive activity here an' I predict that Gerald McClellan is a miniature Mike Tyson tonight . . . yes, it's gonna be an exciting night of fisticuffs here on ITV. Don't even go to the refrigerator to get a coolie or a beer. Stand there and watch this in its entirety! Make your breaks with the break that come on between the rounds because you cannot afford to miss this. It's gonna be great, Gary!'

Gaz had already called up another hairy loud-hailer, John McCririck, Channel 4's betting clown, who did his usual rhyming routine of how every bookie and boxing writer in town had tipped McClellan to win in the first few rounds. The pre-fight betting for McClellan had hardened from 1–2 to 1–4 in his favour while it was possible to put money on Benn at 40–1. McCririck made a mockery of the risk Benn was about to confront when he twittered that 'reporters reckon the Yank will knock the chimes out of Big Benn in three minutes so I'm going to go along with the crowd and take Benn to win it for Britain! But there's going to be a primitive dog fight here on the Isle of Dogs. Will McClellan prove to be a savage, snar-lingggg pit bull – or merely a poodle? Yelp!'

We sprayed beer at the telly and swore at the fucker. Only the fighters, it seemed, were above such crassness. And then their words came through, from earlier in the week. It became impossible to romanticise even them as they endured those lonely minutes.

'Outside the ring, I'm a nice guy,' Jim Rosenthal repeated McClellan's claim as we saw him hurling punches at the camera. 'Inside I'm like an animal. It's scary feeling the confidence I have when I leave the dressing-room . . .' Rosenthal paused and then said, 'Gerald McClellan, the mandatory challenger. The champion, Nigel Benn, says, "I've fought guys who put the fear of God in me. I always put on my best performance against them".'

Rosenthal smiled at us: 'Don't go away! Benn and McClellan will be blasting off in a couple of minutes!'

By now, we were both in a lather, a mix of wild expectation and regret that we should have abandoned ourselves to the hype.

Gerald McClellan's procession up the long Arena aisle began; and I recalled a more accurate summary of his emotions than that quoted by Rosenthal. Rather than exuding the confidence attributed to him, he had admitted to Graham Houston that 'walking from the locker-room to the ring is the scariest feeling I ever had in my life. I can't explain what that feeling is. It's like I have butterflies, my heart is beating, I'm already sweating, my hands are wet, it's just a real scary feeling.' But that kind of honesty was out of kilter with the build-up of the G-Man as a killer in the ring. His fear was transformed on television into a wide-eyed endorsement of heartless certitude.

But I had to concede the irresistible power of the tightly framed shot of Nigel Benn stepping out of a dark tunnel. While the image was hackneyed, the fighter's shadow being enveloped by smoke and white light while the chimes of the real Big Ben boomed out behind him, we both jumped up and down on the settee. Bong! Bong! Bong! Despite myself, I said, 'Go on, Nige!' and Alison laughed and, in the absence of Michael Buffer, launched into her latest roaring impersonation. 'Let's Git Ready To Ruuuummbbbllle!' my soon-to-be-blushing-bride thundered in her throatiest American accent. We were not even drunk then – at least not on beer.

The fight's terrible violence, as we now know, exceeded the darkest predictions. In the opening minute McClellan, wearing his lucky green trunks, hit Benn so hard with a series of right hands that he sent him crashing through the ropes. The overwhelming anticipation of a first-round knockout might have felt like bathos if Benn had not crawled back into the ring. He pulled his feet clear of the TV cables and weaved back onto his stick-thin legs as if he himself had taken to the bottle. McClellan had to be held back by the referee before charging across at Benn. He wore a blank expression which suggested that he had his pit bull in mind. He smashed his right fist into Benn again and again. While many of those blows landed, Benn's ducking and crouching, with his chin tucked in low, meant that the majority skimmed off the top and sides of his head. Yet they still carried a wallop. Benn swayed on the ropes. The round seemed interminable but he survived by clawing and clutching at McClellan.

At the eventual sound of the bell, the Dark Destroyer looked as if he understood afresh the sentiment which McClellan had uttered two days before: 'In the ring you have to go to war and in war you have to be prepared to die. That's what boxing is . . .'

As round two began, it sounded more accurate than melodramatic as Benn returned to the battle. His right cheek had been cut and his legs were still rickety, which encouraged McClellan to flood in with punches. But it was then that Benn started to fight back. With exceptional fortitude he forced McClellan to give ground as he pummelled him to both head and body. He made McClellan blink with hard crosses to the temple. Even when he was hurt again by an answering right, Benn dug in with a left hook to the body.

It was only in the fourth and the fifth that McClellan conceded the attritional nature of Benn's fightback. His mouthguard began to slip back and forth, moving in and out of his panting mouth like a dog's lolling, whitened tongue. His defence became increasingly sloppy. He had never gone beyond the eighth round before.

As they recovered in their corners before the sixth, with the scorecards showing them to be level, the omnipresent Gary Newbon interviewed Naseem Hamed at ringside to discover his considered view. 'Great fight for Nigel,' the familiar Sheffield burr boasted. 'Now I can see him taking him out. Believe me. Two more rounds. Nigel's looking the stronger fighter now. He's took the punishment and he's coming back with a war. He's coming back with punches. McClellan's blown himself out, basically. He's thrown all the bombs he can. Believe me, it's Nigel's night. Let's get it on, Nige!'

Frank Bruno was an even more vocal believer as, in his red suit and in the seat next to Don King, he stood up and banged his giant fist down on the apron of the ring, exhorting Benn to even greater crescendos. McClellan's distress was made obvious by the way he could no longer prevent his gumshield from dangling out of his open mouth. The seventh had been a gruesome round for both men. Benn's face was distorted by a puffiness and angularity on the left side which suggested that his jaw might have been broken. You could see a trace of blood on his lips. McClellan's own movements back to his corner were slow and groggy.

But, in the eighth, collecting himself for another onslaught, McClellan speared back in for the metaphoric kill. After his unusual use of the jab, he suddenly banged in two rights to the head. Benn was trapped in McClellan's corner. He lost his balance as he tried to escape. He fell to the canvas. It seemed as if the end had finally come, as if Benn had succumbed to exhaustion.

But he rose at three. He breathed in deeply as the referee completed the standing eight count. And, just as his old enemy Eubank had done against Michael Watson, Benn fired back in his deepest crisis with a vicious right. That punch altered the course of not only the fight but the rest of their lives. McClellan faltered and was compelled to accept Benn's offer of a cheerless clinch. It was as if he knew that the worst could not be eluded.

In the ninth, McClellan's head was spun again on his creaking neck by right hooks and a long left. When he came back to hold, the crowd booed and Benn, flailing wearily at him, slipped to the floor. His head brushed the American's as he tripped and, abruptly, McClellan went down on one knee, cupping a glove to his forehead. He appealed to the ref, pawing at his head, claiming a butt, indicating that he could not continue until he had been given time to recover from a foul. But he was coaxed back to his feet and waved back into the fray. Bruno thumped the ring again with ardour.

Just before the start of the tenth, each corner streamed water over the boxers. McClellan's face had lost the expressionless mask he had shown at the outset. It had become a mass of dazed and jerking blinks which confused the ITV commentators, Reg Gutteridge and Jim Watt. Gutteridge confessed that he had never before seen a boxer blink either so rapidly or alarmingly. It looked as if he was trying to pop an invisible balloon of pressure building up deep in the sockets of both eyes.

He used his jab effectively enough for a minute but, then, another Benn right hand connected. McClellan sank to the floor, blinking all the way. He rested there as the counting began. He shook his head as if to stop the twitching of his eyes. When he got up, Gerald lifted his gloves to chest-height almost involuntarily, like a small boy showing reticent defiance. He nodded, as if to say that he was all right.

But three more rights, two straight and a last uppercut, were too much to bear. McClellan slid to the same right knee again. He put a glove on his hip and stared in front of him. But he began to blink again as the man in the white shirt stood over him, like some demented choreographer, snapping fingers in his face like he could have been counting out steps to a dance. 'Five!' he shouted, both hands in the air, 'six!', stabbing at McCllellan, 'seven!', as the boxer blinked once more, 'eight!', looking at the referee, who brought both mitts back and held up all fingers but for the littlest on his left hand. 'Nine!' he mouthed, and McClellan stayed bowed on his knee, watching the arms scissor in front of him. 'Out!'

'He's quit!' Jim Watt screamed jubilantly.

'Fuckin' hell,' I shouted as Alison bounced on the sofa, 'Benn's won!'

'He's quit!' Reg Gutteridge barked back in confirmation as McClellan got up and walked alone to his corner.

Benn was like a dervish – legs apart, arms wide, mouth roaring, head flung back as if only he could fathom the place to which he'd just been. He scaled the ropes and cried out at the hysterical crowd as he gestured towards McClellan: 'Who is he? Who is he? Who is he?'

He was a man on the edge of losing his life, a man whose hearing and sight were fading, a man destroyed by boxing. But no one, not even the doctors climbing into the ring, knew at that moment. Through the escalating tumult we saw McClellan talking softly to his sailor-capped trainer, Stan Johnson. Then he sagged delicately off his stool and onto the ground. His back was propped by the ring-post. He blinked again and then squeezed his eyes tightly together.

As Benn was engulfed by his Essex posse, Gutteridge and Watt began to discuss the slow-motion replays of the two critical knockdowns. As we watched McClellan bob down into his first kneeling respite, the theorising began. Jim Watt, a former world champion himself, a good and usually fair man, insisted with unwitting irony: 'It's a loss of heart. It was a heart problem. It was the same punches he'd been taking all night long. The chin could take the punches, the heart couldn't, down he went, head as clear as a bell, eyes as clear as a bell, nothing wrong with him – apart from the fact that that punch on the jaw had an effect on his heart. Nigel Benn has just punched the fight right out of him . . .'

As Reg Gutteridge verified that Benn's victory would be considered 'one of the boxing trade's biggest upsets', Watt broke in to wonder if it was not also a case of the bully not being able to take being bullied back. 'It's not a devastating knockdown,' he said of the second G-Man implosion, 'Gerald McClellan has decided to go on the floor, he's looked at the referee and just stayed there. In effect it's a retirement from Gerald McClellan!'

'Well, that's what I call punching the life out of you,' Reggie nearly chuckled, until he checked himself. Neither he nor Watt were cruel men. They cared about boxing and, especially, boxers. 'And he's down on the floor now, McClellan. Jim?'

'I think this could be exhaustion,' Watt said optimistically.

'I hope so,' Guttridge murmured.

'I don't think it's the punches he's taken,' Watt persisted. '[But] they'll certainly take him off to hospital overnight.'

'Oh, absolutely! Well, let's hope he's going to be okay . . .'

As with all televised championship bouts, the post-fight interview in the ring was an obligatory ritual. This one, however, was particularly lamentable. Nigel Benn was not gracious in victory as he put up with Gary Newbon sticking a microphone into his swollen face. 'Yeah,' he sneered, 'all you lot were geeing him up, giving it this, giving it that, and, yeah, I know . . .'

Newbon tried to cut in but Benn wasn't interested.

'No, now you listen to me . . . the person I'd like to thank most of all is Paul McKenna who hypnotised me and made me believe in myself. No, no, no, you listen to me!'

Newbon finally succeeded with his interruption: 'Mike MacCallum is very badly hurt, they've got a stretcher in here . . .'

Benn stared at him vacantly as the producer bellowed in Newbon's earpiece.

'McClellan,' he muttered, 'sorry, Mike McClellan is very badly hurt . . .' He tried to move Benn away so that the paramedics could get past. 'Nigel . . .' he tried again as another voice roared in his head. 'Gerald McClellan! Sorry, I'm getting most confused . . .' But, ever the pro, he pressed on with the reminder that it had been him personally, Gary Newbon, the 'Voice of ITV', who had pushed Benn back into the ring almost forty minutes before, in round one.

Benn ignored him. 'They only bought him here to bash me up, mate!' he thundered. We squirmed but Benn was undeterred. 'Now you might believe in the Dark Destroyer!'

'You made a believer outta me,' Don King guffawed beside him, 'you made a believer outta me!'

We saw Naseem popping his head round King's bulk to lend his support to 'Nige', but Gary Newbon demanded: 'Listen to me! We have a serious problem in the ring with Gerald McClellan. We have a serious problem with Gerald McClellan . . .'

By then they had already applied the heavy neck-brace to stabilise Gerald McClellan's listing head. An oxygen mask covered his nose and mouth. He was lifted and then lowered gently onto the stretcher. They carried him out of the ring. The MC, in typical *Noel Edmonds' House Party*-style, encouraged the crowd: 'How about a hand for Gerald McClellan and our best wishes for a swift recovery!'

Michael Watson was one of those who watched from ringside. But, unlike the rest, he was in a wheelchair. Who knows what might have lurched through his head in that moment. But his own injury helped another fighter even then. Having learned from the catalogue of blunders which had delayed Watson's arrival at hospital after the Eubank fight, the British Boxing Board of Control had stringently followed medical recommendations. Apart from the presence of three doctors, an anaesthetist, two teams of paramedics, the oxygen tents and other essential medical apparatus, the Board had also placed the Royal London Hospital on standby.

And then, at exactly 10.15, Gerald McClellan opened his eyes as they ran with him down the gangway. He put his hand on the oxygen mask as if to suck in more air.

'Relax, Gerald, take it easy, baby,' Stan Johnson said as he held McClellan's other hand. They neared the exit.

In the ring, the doctors turned towards Nigel Benn. He, too, needed an ambulance.

Gerald McClellan was still conscious just before eleven o'clock when they wheeled him into a hospital cubicle next to Nigel Benn's. While the neuro-surgeons examined the CT scan they had just taken of McClellan's brain, Benn parted the curtains. He stretched out and held McClellan's hand.

The two fighters were soon parted. Benn was allowed home after his own x-ray revealed that his jaw had been severely bruised rather than broken. Gerald McClellan, however, was rushed to the operating theatre. The same doctor, John Sutcliffe, who had operated on Bradley Stone nine months before, prepared for emergency surgery. His scalpel would cut a hole eight centimetres by six in the side of the boxer's scalp – for the same kind of blood clot which had killed Bradley Stone was building up an intolerable pressure on Gerald McClellan's brain.

Two hours later, just after one in the morning, Sutcliffe successfully removed the clot. 'It came out with a bit of a vengeance,' he admitted later.

While Don King and Frank Warren began the long vigil by Gerald McClellan's bed, a vigil which would be maintained by his family who flew in from America the following day, John Sutcliffe had some hope to give them. 'With Bradley Stone,' he said, 'the blood clot was exactly the same. The advantage that Gerald has is that he got here quicker than Bradley did, and his resuscitation was more complete – in that he was oxygenated as soon as he went down in the corner after the fight was stopped.'

But, still, Gerald McClellan was in a coma. Even at 3 a.m. and then, just before it became light again, at six, as Nigel Benn was twice lifted into a bath of warm water in an attempt to alleviate his frightening pain, Gerald McClellan was in darkness.

Perhaps I was hardening, irretrievably, but I felt less despairing of boxing then than I had after the Watson fight. It was not a case of my having more affinity for Michael Watson, having met him, than for Gerald McClellan. The emotion we experienced that February night in watching Benn and McClellan, even through the distorting medium of Saturday night television, had affected me profoundly and made me examine yet again my immersion in boxing. But my analysis was less tortuous, even though I could feel how deep compassion ran for Gerald McClellan, his wife and three children, including the nine-month-old Forrest.

After four straight years of exposure to the good and the very bad in boxing, to both its lustre and more pervasive grime, I held on to my most salient truth. I liked the fighters. I respected them. Once you were past their rhetoric – and even the gun collections and pit-bull breeding – I almost always found reasons to admire them. Much of that esteem stemmed from their bravery and intensity; but is was an essential vulnerability beneath those hard layers of machismo which moved me the most. Mike Tyson was often a bad man, and in the original sense of that phrase; but I could never quite forget all that had happened to him. James Toney had been unstable and unable to deal with defeat and yet, at the same time, I felt for him in his failure. Gerald McClellan had some unsavoury hobbies but he and Nigel Benn showed a tragic valour in the ring.

My affection for fighters was enhanced by the reaction of those within the trade to their latest calamity. The most sympathetic and considered voices were not those who urged that boxers should be 'protected from themselves' or who called for a civilised society's banning of a barbaric sport; rather, at least to my ears, the most tender were invariably other fighters, led by Barry McGuigan of the Professional Boxers Association, while the most reasoned included Harry Mullen, editor of Boxing News, who wrote:

'This time there are no easy answers, no get-outs. Gerald McClellan was not weight-drained, dehydrated, carrying an old injury, or over-matched, nor had he taken part in any such gruelling fights previously. He is on a life-support machine today because he boxed, and because boxing is a dangerous sport. That is the hard fact we must face, in this case perhaps more than in any of the previous tragedies – mercifully few – which have occurred in recent years. All the old arguments have been heard this week *ad nauseam*, for and against the sport's continued existence, but I doubt if any views have been changed in either direction. Boxing attracts passionate support and opposition. Its opponents are impossible to convert, while its enthusiasts, except for the most naïve among them, have long since come to terms with the sport's inherent danger. It is only defensible when every possible safety

precaution has been taken, when the risks have been reduced to a minimum, and in that context it is worth emphasising that McClellan would
not have survived Saturday night without the elaborate measures introduced after Michael Watson's experience.'

Frank Warren and Don King, for all the tackiness of those 'Sudden
Impact' posters and their promotional emphasis on both fighters' violence,
had at least done something right when deciding to pay for more than the
Boxing Board's recommended number of medical specialists at the London
Arena. They had also made up for their pre-fight repartee with a measure of
dignity and immediate financial support for the McClellan family.

Of course none of that was sufficient to provide any tangible compen-
sation for what had happened to Gerald McClellan; and yet I knew boxing
would continue and that it would do so with a graver sense of responsibility
for its only moral assets, the fighters.

Ironically, Chris Eubank's prospective first opponent in 1995, Ray Close,
had already been a beneficiary of boxing's increased vigilance. Of course
Close, being a fighter, felt more like a victim when the British Boxing Board
of Control refused him permission to meet Eubank in a deciding third
bout. They had been due to clash again in Belfast on 11 February, a fortnight before Benn–McClennan, when Close failed a routine CAT scan
which all boxers were obliged to take before any major fight. Although
Close appeared to be in excellent health, and had not suffered any overt
damage in the ring, the scan detected a number of 'abnormalities' on one
side of his brain. Rather than expose him to further peril, the BBC with-
drew not only their sanction of Eubank's defence but Close's licence to box.

One Irishman's bitter twist of luck became another's good fortune. Steve
Collins, a dedicated pro from Dublin who had fought mainly in America,
was offered the Eubank fight. After years of unsuccessful striving from his
base at Marvin Hagler's old gym in Boston, Collins had returned to Ireland
and finally won the WBO middleweight title – on the night Naseem
Hamed had so belittled Vincenzo Belcastro.

His move up to super-middleweight to challenge Eubank was resched-
uled to take place in the village of Mill Street in the south-west of Ireland
on 18 March, the night after St Patrick's day. Sky TV, if not Eubank, were
happy with the improved quality of opposition and the likelihood that a
passionate evening would be ensured by Collins's vocal Irish support. Until
then they had been let down by Eubank's 'World Tour' which had seen him
shade decisions against a line-up of anonymous fighters like the Brazilian
Mauricio Aramal, Sam Storey, also of Ireland, and, most infamously, an
American, Dan Schommer, who had only boxed twice in the preceding
three years. Yet Schommer clearly outfought Eubank. All the British boxing
writers who had travelled to Sun City in South Africa to cover the fight

considered Schommer the winner by three or four rounds. Somehow, perhaps because he was still then the WBO's most lucrative champion, Eubank received a unanimous verdict and retained his title.

The root of these difficulties could, like James Toney's, be found on the scales. Before the weigh-in at Sun City, Eubank had been forced to endure a seventy-two-hour fast in order to make the twelve-stone limit. For his next fight, a decisive victory over Henry Wharton in Manchester, the Board had monitored his weight at regular intervals to ensure that his reduction was consistent rather than drastic. They would do the same again for his bout with Collins.

The Irishman, however, had already settled on a different kind of warfare, one which was dedicated to 'fucking up' Chris Eubank's mind. Eubank himself had stressed somewhat dubiously that boxing was '85 per cent psychology and 15 per cent durability'. Collins was resolute in his desire to win the first battle, that '85 per cent cracker!'. It had begun at an even more unusually rumbustious press conference six weeks before. Collins accused Eubank of 'forgetting his African roots' by trying to 'epitomise English uppishness' with his outlandish dress-sense. Eubank was incensed, telling the Lord Mayor of Dublin that he could 'fuck his city' and hissing at Collins that, still a few weeks before Benn met McClellan, 'this is now kill or be killed . . .'

Run-of-the-mill stuff, possibly; but Collins had a more inspirational trick to turn. The weigh-in attracted an astonishing 3,000 people to the Green Glens Stadium in Mill Street, and the locals lapped up the showbiz trappings without any awareness that Eubank was on the verge of refusing to fight. Collins had announced that, like Nigel Benn, three weeks earlier, he had been hypnotised. He would fight Eubank in 'a trance' which would enable him to shrug off ordinary barriers of human fear and pain.

After the weigh-in Eubank told his promoter Barry Hearn and trainer Ronnie Davis that the fight was off. For the next four hours he insisted that he would not change his mind. Hearn and Davis threatened and pleaded until, at last, at 10.30 p.m., on the night before his twentieth world-title defence, he agreed reluctantly to fight. With his claims of hypnosis, Collins had spread long shadows across Eubank's own mind.

'I wanted to call the fight off,' Eubank said in his final pre-fight interview. 'That's why I would call the fight off now if I could – because I'm going into unknown territory. In the forty-three fights I've had in the past I've always known what I'm dealing with. I don't know what I'm dealing with tonight. I'm fighting someone who is mechanically –' Eubank searched for the right word '– er . . . orientated. And that is just an unknown area. It's not fair that I should be put in such a situation . . .'

I had entered a more comfortable patch of unknown territory. As much as I loved boxing I'd begun to weary of the endless rounds of fighting. While

Eubank and Collins exchanged psychological barbs in tiny Mill Street, I stayed in London, my ring resilience on the wane. The fact that Gerald McClellan's blinking face drifted in and out of my head at the most unexpected times did not engender enthusiasm for yet another super-middleweight title scrap.

So, instead of travelling to Ireland or even staying in to watch, we went out on the town with our friends. I was having a fine old time until the others mentioned the fight. I insisted that I was blissfully content to keep on drinking in our Sky-less pub. Alison knew otherwise.

'Come on,' she said, 'I know you really want to watch it . . .'

'Not especially,' I wavered.

'Well, I do!' she persisted. She was encouraged by the rest to race outside and find the nearest pub with either cable or a big dish. She dashed around while I tried to talk about something else, hoping that she'd be back soon with some punchy news.

Thirty minutes later, we'd found our way to a diamond-geezer pub in a Bloomsbury back street. Upstairs, it was Lads United as the boys vied with their 'Youuuuuu-bank!' and more popular 'Steeee-vohhhh!' lowing.

Chris Eubank revved his Harley Davidson, 'a 1975 Shovelhead worth £10,000' on a massive podium high above the ring. A blistering firework display spelled out 'EUBANK' in ten-foot-high letters as he flared his nostrils. I shook my head at Alison – this was one Eubank entrance which she would not be able to emulate.

Steve Collins, meanwhile, sat like a Jesuit priest in a corner of the ring, his head hooded, eyes tightly shut, ears clamped to a Walkman, mouth whispering over and over again, hypnotically of course, 'new champ, new champ, new champ'. He never even got to see Eubank's Harley – which must have further disconcerted the Simply the Best joker who had grown used to his rivals gawping at his arrival.

As early as the second round, Collins revealed the extent of his mental powers. After Eubank had dropped him with a hard body shot the referee turned to usher the champion away to a neutral corner. By the time he had returned back to start his count, Collins was up. 'No knockdown!' Collins bellowed. The ref hesitated in surprise and then, as Collins headed for Eubank, allowed the fight to proceed – thus robbing Eubank of a point.

Collins's tactics, such as they were, entailed the application of unrelenting pressure. He would also punch with both hands. That was the extent of the 'Celtic Warrior's' attempt at subtlety. Yet Eubank, who preferred to fight in spurts, was upset by Collins's incessant work-rate. Although he did hurt him with some powerful single shots, he was unable to fend off Collins with more meaningful combinations.

In the eighth round, Collins surprised Eubank with a straight right to the midriff. Eubank was down for the first time since Michael Watson had dropped him in September '91. While he tried Collins's con of disputing the knockdown, Ron Lipton administered the standing eight count. Eubank fired back angrily and pushed Collins on to the ropes, only to be stung again by a sharp right.

By the end of the ninth, according to Ronnie Davis in his corner, he was at least three rounds behind and in need of a KO. Suitably scolded, Eubank raced from his corner and, within ten seconds, had knocked Collins off his feet.

Despite the fact that Collins grinned at his trainer and listened intently to the numbers, rising at nine with an affirmative nod, he looked a certain stooge for the Houdini-like Eubank. But, in an inexplicable stint of dilatory posing which seemed to define his post-Watson career in the space of two perplexing minutes, Eubank surrendered both his title and unbeaten record. After missing Collins with an amateurish haymaker, Eubank went walkabout. He shouted 'Come on!' to Collins no less than nine times, as if counting off a series of lost lives, gesturing at him with a snarl and a cock of his right hand. Collins did the same as his head cleared.

I thought of the way Toney had torn at Tim Littles in LA, of the ruthless frenzy shared by Benn and McClellan, and most of all, of Michael Watson, and I wondered if Eubank had any of them in mind as he backed off and postured at his hurt rival. But, more probably, he just felt shattered and in need of a quieter night.

Ronnie Davis slapped him hard in the face as he went to his corner with his hand held high. 'You're going to regret that for the rest of your life,' Davis promised. 'Whadddya think you doin', fucking about like that?'

For once in his life, Eubank was silent.

'Stop fuckin' about!' Davis yelled again.

But in the last six minutes Eubank could do nothing beyond imitate the dragging strut of a melancholic peacock. Even he knew that the words 'new WBO Super-Middleweight Champion of the World' would follow the 115–111, 116–114 and 114–113 judgements. Ever the deluded poet, Eubank said later that 'when they raised his hand I thought of Kipling's poem *If* and said: "Here I am, a mortal man at last!"'

My own heart, even with the Guinness singing in my veins, was with Eubank as Steve Collins made a grandiose statement in the ring: 'I had no doubts I was gonna win! Those people who did doubt me I forgive you. It's not their fault. Don't believe the hype! Believe in the man, Steve Collins. I'm not just the best Irish fighter ever, I'm the best pound-for-pound in the world. Roy Jones, who's next?'

His name was Antoine Byrd, that next opponent for Roy Jones, on the same night, 18 March, but eight hours later, in Pensacola. Byrd was the number-one IBF contender but Jones stopped him after two minutes and six seconds with an eruption of blows as powerful as they were swift.

Comparing Collins to Jones was akin to setting a stone against a diamond. Roy was both a harder and much more beautiful fighter. I knew he would beat Steve Collins and so I was more interested in his and Stanley Levin's admission that Gerald McClellan had been their 'dream fight' – and yet, in an initial gesture of support for the stricken fighter, they donated $200,000 from the night's gate money to McClellan. They had also persuaded HBO to match them dollar for dollar.

Gerald McClellan remained oblivious to Stan's plan. After twenty-one days, he had come off the life-support machine. His doctors in London had also reduced the strength of drugs needed to block the swelling in his brain. And, although he remained in a 'controlled coma', he had shown signs of being able to respond to touch on both sides of his body. His condition was described then as being 'serious' rather than 'critical'. John Sutcliffe thought he would live – but he was even more sure that McClellan would suffer brain damage and be left both blind and deaf by his appalling injury.

'What I'm trying to get the boxing world to understand,' Levin waxed across the Atlantic to *Boxing Monthly*'s Glyn Leach, 'is that Gerald was not one of our fighters, he didn't fight on HBO, but the boxing world needs to step in and try to do something for this young man. I also hope that what this will do when some people start to scream "Abolish boxing!", maybe this will say something about some of the people involved in boxing. That maybe there's more character here than the outside world believes . . .'

Chris Eubank, too, showed more character than we might have believed when he was interviewed on Sky soon after returning to his dressing-room that same night. 'You know what?' he asked with a smile. 'I say that I've had forty-three good nights. I've had twenty world-title fights. Nineteen successful ones. This . . . this one I've lost. But I've had a good run, I've had a good time. You know, I'm not complaining. They say to me that this shows me I've got to stop the quixotic behaviour. I have to start thinking down to earth. That's not a bad thing. I've had a good run . . .'

I liked him more then than I had ever done. I also knew that, two days later, for the seventh time, he would fly by Concorde to America to be one of Mike Tyson's last visitors in prison – that, as one career in boxing wound towards a close, another was about to resume.

25 March 1995

They were ready to crawl all over him.

Mike Tyson, Prisoner 922335, would be released from the Indiana Youth Center in Plainfield at dawn – one day short of three years since he had begun his six-year sentence. It was hard to know which Tyson would walk through those jailhouse doors. Would it be the reflective Muslim who prayed five times a day? Or would it be the broke and acerbic man who asked, 'Where are all those guys I gave Rolex watches to? Where are all those people?' Would it be the alienated activist who stressed that 'white society will not allow blacks to be their equal because blacks were once slaves of white slave-masters . . . maybe I should even consider settling in Africa since America has become an asylum, especially for blacks . . . look at what they have done to me'? Or would it be the humbled, wiser Mike who said, 'I swear on everything that I did not do what they said I did. But maybe some of the other things I did, things I did not get punished for, maybe this is all payback. All the things going back into my early years. I guess I can't get mad about the way things turned out'? Would it be the malcontent who'd told *Ring* magazine that, since imprisonment, 'Mike Tyson hates the world'? Or would it be the chipper philosopher who'd asked in confinement, 'Did you read *Cyrano de Bergerac*, the guy with the big nose? He was a soldier and they said to him, "If you're such a good soldier, where are your medals?" And Cyrano said: "I don't need medals. I wear my adornments on my soul." I read that and I went: "Wow! That's me. That's me." '

But, to the world outside, he was still mostly a fighting-machine, a money-maker, a ring ogre who would again terrorise the heavyweight division, a guy who had wags asking on late-night chat shows: 'Which would you rather be – Mike Tyson's first opponent or his first date?'

Don King, naturally, had plans for his own first date with Mighty Mike. He had a fat sheaf of fight contracts for Tyson to sign, pieces of paper which would tie him back in with Don King Productions, Showtime and the MGM Grand and earn him a reputed $300,000,000. For his first fight alone, King guaranteed that Tyson would be paid $20,000,000. 'All this and more', King promised, would be revealed at a 'Coming-Out' party that night at Tyson's Ohio mansion.

Floyd Patterson, Cus D'Amato's first heavyweight champion, a fighter who made it to the fight-game pinnacle twenty years before Tyson, once said: 'In boxing, when you've got millions of dollars, you've got millions of friends . . .' Tyson, it seemed, had countless people, besides Don King, who claimed to be his 'special friend', the one who knew just the path he should follow to freedom. Of course, there were the curious celebrity visitors – the likes of Whitney Houston, Bobby Brown, Spike Lee, Betty Shabazz, Shaquille O'Neill, MC Hammer and even the parents of Michael Jackson. Fighters from Riddick Bowe to, naturally, Chris Eubank also talked to him in Plainfield – as did the promotional voices of Butch Lewis, Rock Newman, Eddie Mustafa Muhammad and the more mysterious Akbar Muhammad who had apparently been sent by Allah to guide Tyson back into the ring.

Even King did not know which way Tyson would turn when he left prison. Although the fighter had appointed his old friends John Horne and Rory Holloway, both on King's payroll, as his co-managers, there were at least four other cartels who had raised money on the assumption that Tyson would link instead with them. That scrum of rival promoters and various other factions headed by powerful players in boxing, the Nation of Islam,

Wall Street and showbusiness had begun to mass at the prison gates, as if in vigil for Iron Mike. Tyson, apart from finally completing the entire works of Homer and Mao, had supposedly studied in detail both the Koran and the genetics of pigeons. He had also enhanced his already considerable knowledge of boxing's rich and exploitative history – and yet none of that could have prepared him fully for the attention surrounding his release.

As Butch Lewis warned him again, before undoubtedly offering his own services, 'They're gonna be crawlin' all over you, baby . . .'

They began to move at exactly 6.10 a.m. Tyson was surrounded by a heaving pack of black men, with Don King still the most visible as he jostled in the early morning chill for a place just behind the right shoulder of Mighty Mike. In contrast to King's silver shock of straightened Afro, Tyson wore a white kufi prayer cap. He was dressed in a black Islamic-style suit and a pristine white shirt. His face looked lean and placid. He had grown a close-cropped beard. Tyson appeared a more thoughtful, even distinguished figure compared to the twenty-five-year-old who'd shrugged and sneered in his bulging Armani suit when they led him out of that Indiana courtroom.

It was said that his future would be defined by the route his waiting motorcade took as it passed the prison gates. If Tyson's limousine went left it would mean he was heading for the local mosque where he would pray with Muhammad Ali and his newer Islamic confidants. If the cavalcade tacked right, as King suggested, he would be driven to an airfield where a private jet would whisk him away to his sixty-six-acre estate in Southington, Ohio.

As the world's television cameras followed the procession, Tyson's limo turned to the left. He had chosen the prayerful road; but his future remained uncertain, for Don King still travelled with him.

Mike Tyson, however, had made at least one positive decision. In Ohio late that night, the fighter asked King and all the promoter's invited guests to leave his home – where Big Don had laid out an ostentatious spread including pork, shellfish and champagne, all of which were forbidden by Islam. As King tried to argue, Tyson pushed him softly towards the door and said, 'Don, listen to me, the party's over . . .'

8

DEATH AND THE MAN

TYSON ALWAYS UNDERSTOOD WHY PEOPLE CLAMOURED TO
see him, why they scrambled to be near him. Those closest to him
wanted his money, but the rest of us were looking for something different.
In May 1986, Mike was only nineteen when he nailed it down in ten words:
'People want entertainment, intrigue. I give them what they want . . .'

Yet the teenage Tyson's clipped accuracy only unzipped the most basic
steps of all he brought to the dance. The more layered if disturbing truth
remained that Tyson had little control over the lurching tango of his life.
That was why we found him intriguing. We never knew what he would do
next, or to whom. It was difficult to follow the veering curve of his mind.
Would he be happy or sad? Would he want to box or party? Would he be
surly or sweet? Who would be his latest cheerleader, his promoter, his
manager, his trainer, his bodyguard, his head-flunkey? Who would grab the
most cash out of Tyson's money-machine? Would another girl be in trouble
again? Outside the ring there were enough distracting secrets to keep us
guessing, to imagine him as the darkest of stars.

Between the ropes, if entertainment is the opposite of boredom, Iron
Mike was a performer of immeasurable power. He made us fix our eyes on
his terrible capacity for violence. When it was over, that excitement faded
into a kind of unsettled fascination. Where did Tyson find such ferocity,
what must have been done to him to make him that frightening? He grew
tired of talking and so left us to put words to his punching. And when
prison came, he was even more silent, even less accessible. His grim mystery
grew and the enigmas of his brutality became increasingly tangled. Tyson
the rapist, Tyson the raped. Mighty Mike and Muslim Mike. Tyson the
criminal, Tyson the victim. Tyson the damned, Tyson the saved.

'I think Mike Tyson belongs in a cage,' George Foreman said after the
younger fighter had been accused of raping Desiree Washington. 'I think he
needs to be sheltered like you should shelter a lion or a tiger. You lock him

up, except when you want him to come out and jump through a few hoops. When that is over, you lock him up again.'

Three and a half years later, Tyson's Islamic instructor, Muhammad Siddeeq, suggested that he was 'one hundred per cent different. He's on a different path. He's not reached an angelic state, but he's still a wonderful person.'

Although he recognised our craving, Mike Tyson never had any particular inclination either to entertain or intrigue people. It just always ended up that way.

Bill Cayton spoke tartly when asked what Tyson might do outside Plainfield's prison walls. 'I don't know what game Tyson is playing,' Cayton moaned. 'Tyson, in his own way, is very devious. He's capable of many surprises. My personal feeling is that there's no way of knowing what Mike will do, because he doesn't know. I think that Tyson lives day to day. People come to see him in prison and he tells them what they want to hear.'

John Horne usually disputed every word uttered by his WASPish predecessor as Tyson's co-manager. But he echoed at least one of Cayton's sentiments. 'Every time somebody went to Indiana to see Mike in prison,' Horne snorted, 'they came out swearing to God and to everybody else that they've got him. [But] when you're behind bars you'll come out of that cell to see a jackrabbit if it came to visit you.'

While Horne, Rory Holloway and Don King claimed to be in control of Team Tyson, they must have shivered whenever they heard their man speak. They couldn't stop the bleak words falling from his mouth. During his CNN interview in jail with Larry King, Tyson hinted sternly that he was ready to rid himself of 'detrimental influences' – a quote which an eager press assumed he aimed towards King and his entourage. But if Don was out then who could possibly be in? King's competitors would have found scant room in Tyson's heart when they read the iconoclastic views he expressed to Nigel Collins of *The Ring*.

'When it really comes down to it,' Tyson said, 'I really don't have anybody I want to go to. I've been alone all my life, and every time I accept someone in my life, they've fucked me. [*Tyson laughs*] Who do I really want to go to? I'll always take care of Camille [Ewald]. Now, she's ninety years old. Come on, odds are not on her side. As long as she is all right and my little daughter is all right, I don't give a damn about anything. Me? My life is useless. I don't give a damn about my life. That's why I'm so successful and everything, because I don't give a damn.'

Even when Collins asked him a straight boxing question, concerning the identity of his likely trainer, Tyson retained his desolate focus. 'I hate everybody, man. I don't know. I hate everybody because he'll train me today and train another guy to fight me tomorrow. This is a joke. There's no loyalty in this business. This is like the mob, like the highest-paid gun. Who gives a fuck about Mike Tyson? Give me a break, all right. Who actually cares about my well-being?'

That uncertain next chapter of Tyson's strange story was as compulsive as it was affecting. I felt for him but I wondered, too, about Desiree Washington. How would it make her feel to know that Tyson was free, at least in the most simplistic sense of that word? For all the scathing doubts expressed about her character and the civil suit she'd instigated against him, I'd not seen her grinding on about Tyson on the chat-show circuit. I'd not read any book or gawped at any mini-series about her version of that night in Indianapolis. Perhaps they were coming; but if they were she was moving slowly in hitching her ride with the rest of the heaving band already on board Iron Mike's wagon of profitable liberty. All I really knew about Desiree is that, since showing up in court, she had gone to ground. It was said that her studies were suffering, that her life had been turned into 'a dirty peepshow', that she was in long-term counselling.

But shamelessly I, like the rest of boxing, only had eyes for Mike. Who would he choose next? Who would promote him and who would he fight first? Who would he allow to make those many millions with him? Who, in other words, did he despise the least?

Bob Arum had limited hopes of his own; and he was cannier than King's other adversaries when he appealed to Tyson's solitary mood. 'Don King is so untrustworthy,' Arum began with a familiar beat of his drum, 'he's starting to run out of suckers and in the boxing world that's almost impossible. Mike Tyson doesn't need a promoter in the first place. Baseball just screwed up an entire season in the battle over free agency. But here's Mike who has that opportunity because right now he is a free agent. How can he not take it? He could get to me and fight Foreman. He could go somewhere else and have another big fight. He could go from promoter to promoter, remain in control and make the most money. He could even fight a King fighter. The thing is, he is what is in demand – not King and not any one promoter.'

The Muslim posse of promoters, headed by Akbar Muhammad, Bilal Muhammad and the former world light-heavyweight champion Matthew Saad Muhammad, set out to secure Tyson's signature with more concentrated ambition, trusting that he would select fellow Islamic traders above boxing's soiled old school of Arum and King. 'It's not over, this is round one,' Bilal had snapped at Don in the midst of that dawn hustle to usher Tyson to his prayer meeting.

But Shelly Finkel, Evander Holyfield's promotional adviser, was more prescient. He stood back from the whirl of speculation surrounding Tyson's release. 'Don King,' he murmured knowingly, 'will do whatever is necessary. He knows how to exploit your weak spot. He knows how to position race in the discussion. He's big and he's loud and he knows he can be intimidating. Most of corporate America knows King was a numbers guy, knows he killed two people, but they also know he can make money for them. And he knows how to convince them. Then, he can walk around the block and tell a street kid anything he wants to make him believe with a whole different vocabulary. With Tyson, like before, King will do whatever is necessary . . .'

Five days after he walked out of Plainfield, Mike Tyson held his first press conference in more than three years. It lasted all of sixty-two seconds, for that was how long it took Tyson to pay homage to both Allah and Don King. Allah came out on top, for he was given the overwhelming share of Tyson's praise. The three boxing Muhammads vying for his interest with King were not even allowed to hear that spiritual message. Before Tyson appeared to make his minute-long speech, the surprised and mournful trio of Akbar, Bilal and Matthew were asked to leave the room, as was Harold Smith, another notorious promoter who claimed that he represented an Indonesian cartel prepared to pay Tyson $45,000,000 for his comeback fight.

King had won. After his holy incantation, Tyson confirmed brusquely that we all knew that Don was the best promoter in the world and, consequently, that King would be in charge of staging his return to boxing. With that he was gone – and ready to spend a chunk of the money King had heaped on his table.

The entourage was in place, hands were cupped and outstretched and Don King was a smiling and roaring man again. Team Tyson were back, with the bang coming not from Iron Mike's mouth but from the explosion of dosh he began to both rake in and scatter around his old haunt of Las Vegas.

Within weeks the rumour-mill was chomping down the crisp cash news. Tyson was making money faster than even he could spend it. In his first six years in the ring, from 1985 to 1991, Tyson earned and then lost $70,000,000. Yet on that fifth day outside his Indiana jailhouse, Iron Mike signed a couple of contracts which conjured back half of it in a flash. He did not even have to bunch his fist before he picked up the pen to scrawl his name on pieces of paper linking him with Showtime's pay-per-view television network and Vegas's MGM Grand Hotel & Casino.

The $20,000,000 from Showtime and the $15,000,000 from the MGM were just 'sweeteners'. Thirty-five mammoth ones for starters. Mike could expect at least another mighty twenty million on the night he actually ducked through the Grand Garden ropes to fight the first carefully plucked pug. In exchange, he agreed to fight six out of his next eight bouts at the MGM and allow Showtime exclusive television rights.

Don King, as always, did not do badly himself out of the lucky-dip. On 24 May the MGM gave King a 'no-interest loan' of $15,000,000 for him to buy 618,557 shares of hotel stock at $24.25 a pop. Five million dollars from the gate receipts at each of Tyson's first three fights would pay back the loan, ensuring that none of King's own money would ever be risked. In the killer sting, King convinced the MGM to insert a guarantee that his personal stock will be worth at least $48.50 a share when their contract with Tyson expires on 25 September 1997 – meaning that King will double his 'loan' and clear a certain $30,000,000. No wonder Don looked like he was about to burst into a chortling rendition of 'Somewhere Over the Rainbow'.

As Bob Arum said, 'King is one of the greatest salesmen of our time and he showed it this time. It's the worst deal for a casino in history – [that's] how it was described to me.'

The shock-haired one would have whooped slightly louder than Kirk Kervorian and the rest of the MGM board the next day. The MGM's share-price rose another 2 per cent when it was announced that they had acquired the cruel services of Mr Tyson. SET, Showtime's P-P-V arm, had done their own sums months earlier. On the basis that Tyson would fight twice before the end of the year, they expected a 100 per cent increase in their 1995 revenue – with Tyson being responsible for generating around $190 million of the $396,000,000 they thought would pour through their bulging system.

Mike did not appear to be burdened by those whopping financial forecasts. But he also did not seem impelled to renounce all worldly possessions in a state of religious serenity. Instead, the thick sheaves of dollars were turning hot in his hand. He began with a $4,000,000 cash payment for a home in Vegas, even though he would live mainly in Ohio. At Chaisson's Cars he selected five spanking top-of-the-range BMWs for his boys, including a custom-built convertible which cost $500,000. They then moved through Versace, Bernini, Armani and the Caesars Palace shops with a little snap to their step.

The reporters swooped in after them with sniping beaks. Wally Matthews, the New York boxing writer most reviled by King and John Horne, was particularly vitriolic. 'Here, in Sodom-in-the-Sand,' he ranted, 'Tyson doesn't stand for crime. He stands for cash. That is why the MGM Grand was willing to fork over some $20 million in a signing bonus for Tyson's next six fights, even if the opponents are all coming out of Don King's garbage dump of used-up heavyweights. And that is why Showtime kicked in a similar number, after having given over their airwaves to King and his cronies for the past three years. And that is why, after Tyson went on a spending spree this week in the Forum shops, a cone of silence dropped over every jeweller and suit salesman in town. As one store manager told me: "A guy spends two hundred grand in my place, I don't want to say nothing to tick him off." These humble merchants wish only that a few leaves fall their way from Tyson's money-tree.'

Matthews warmed to his polemic. 'Tyson did his bit at Versace, where he spent something like $200,000 treating himself and his entourage to suits, sports coats and those garish red-and-gold silk shirts once worn by gypsy fortune-tellers or the accordion player on the Lawrence Welk show . . . no one, of course, would speak on the record about any of this. Team Tyson takes extraordinary security precautions. Someone even called Versace's main office in Milan to make sure that every Versace employee zipped his or her lip. Like Don King, these outfits thrive on repeat business. Like King, they want Tyson as a steady customer.'

Matthews also disclosed that, as part of their pact with the supposed 'Baddest Man', the world's largest hotel planned to erect 'a life-size statue of America's Favourite Ex-Con outside the MGM Grand Garden, where Tyson is soon to resume his career of knocking men senseless while wearing his underwear in public . . . [Tyson's] only contribution to society over the past four years was an uncontrolled sexual rampage at a beauty pageant he was attending as a so-called black role model. Considering the emptiness of Tyson's words, the sham of his purported "conversion" to Islam and the ludicrousness of his claim of having "developed his mind" during three years in prison, the statue should be hollow, like a chocolate Easter bunny. This guy said he was changing his religion and his life. He wound up changing his hat.'

In *The Ring*, Jeff Ryan was filled with similar spleen. 'It is still unsettling to write about the Grim Raper's release from prison because it's hard to believe that a bum like Tyson can be convicted of rape, get sentenced to six years, and then be released in half that time just because he turned the lights out at ten every night and didn't leave any streaks when he mopped the dining-hall floor. Of course, this is America . . .' he said, before suddenly cascading into a hopeful prediction that Tyson would unify the heavyweight championship.

As much as they hated Tyson and his swaggering coterie, boxing buffs like Matthews and Ryan could not help themselves. They were riveted by the prospect of seeing Mike fight again. The momentum of Tyson hysteria appeared unstoppable. Even an attempt by James P. Jajuga to introduce a bill in the Massachusetts State Senate which would block Tyson's return was quickly shredded. His proposed Bill No 426 tried to implement a law that no boxer would be able to fight professionally if he had 'previously been convicted of a felony that included the use of physical force or sexual offence'. It never went beyond an initial reading. Corporate America had invested too much money in Tyson for politicians to consider a banning order.

While Tyson disappeared from view, to prepare both body and mind for the more savage exigencies of the ring, Don King went back to work. His was a headier task. He was ready to complete his coup, to take over boxing again, no matter what the rest of the world tried to do to either Tyson or him. Don had the typically sumptuous plan mapped out in his head, with Tyson's opening fall-guys, his dumb white pawns, already in place.

Lou Savarase was in monastic training at the Fulton Fish Market in Manhattan. He was doing his best to convince King that he was a real-life Italian-American Rocky by pounding his punches into 300-pound slabs of

DEATH AND THE MAN

tuna. 'I only work with dolphin-safe tuna,' the big and breathless Lou muttered, 'gotta be politically correct' – as if Don The Shark might be sufficiently flipper-friendly to care.

From Massachusetts itself, the even bigger and whiter Irish-American Peter McNeeley was often tagged 'The Great White Hopeless' even though he personally rejoiced in his own 'Hurricane' and 'The Medfield Mauler' nicknames. After signing a contract with Don King Productions, McNeeley had been elevated to the WBC Top Ten Rankings – although he preferred an alternate justification for his steep climb. In his last fight, he'd become only the fiftieth man to knock out the infamous Frankie 'The Suitcase' Hines in Hot Springs, Arkansas.

McNeeley and Savarase were both begging to be hit on the chin by Mighty Mike. Don just had to push the button on one of them. Who would it be? Hurricane Pete or Tuna Lou?

Don King, of course, was thinking three moves ahead. He would manoeuvre Tyson into a world title shot within a year, in Mighty Mike's third comeback fight, and then build on their mountain of MGM and Showtime money to make even more as they unified the heavyweight championship. It would be just like the good ol' days of Tyson's first terrifying reign; only better as they would get even richer while turning up the screamers.

Boxing had disintegrated further in Tyson's absence. There was chaos wherever you looked. The fight-game's flagship division was the most pitiful. A jovial and burger-munching forty-six-year-old grandfather, a perennial sparring partner and a bored and fat slacker were strolling around calling themselves the 'Heavyweight Champion of the World'. They were about to be joined by a fourth incumbent because the grandad had given up one of his two titles in order to avoid fighting a serious contender. The couple of pretenders whom King put up for that vacancy were even worse, having had their share of drug problems and woeful performances in the ring.

George Foreman was the old man and the IBF champion; Oliver McCall, one of Tyson's former punchbags, had become the WBC's journeyman version of a world title-holder; the talented but desperately unmotivated Riddick Bowe stretched the WBO belt around his hefty waist; Bruce Seldon, a china-chinned mediocrity whom both Bowe and McCall had blasted in the past, would fight the washed-up Tony Tucker for the right to claim the WBA crown Foreman had surrendered. Big George wanted to meet a German called Axel Schultz rather than fight a more faintly dangerous rival. Even the WBA took umbrage and so, with a careless brand of diplomacy, Foreman gave up the championship he'd snatched sensationally from Michael Moorer in November 1994.

The historical significance of Foreman's victory over Moorer had been clear. Having originally won the title in 1973, Foreman was the link between Sonny Liston and Mike Tyson. He was a fighter who spanned four decades of television-driven boxing. In that time he had reinvented himself. The unsmiling ogre ballooned up into a chuckling charmer. Foreman had also been in the other corner on that African night in 1974 when Muhammad Ali was at his very greatest. For his secondary role in Ali's 'Rumble in the Jungle' legend alone, it was difficult to begrudge Foreman his own extraordinary night against Moorer twenty years later. He'd been on the receiving end of Moorer's beating for nine long rounds. Then, in an instant, everything was turned inside out. Moorer's guard slipped and Granddaddy hit him with a terrific right. He only needed that one punch to squash young Michael. Moorer shrunk like a cheap meat patty hitting the buttery pan. The biggest burger of them all had ended up back on George's plate.

With his chubby old codger jokes and 'Punching Preacher' appeal, Foreman made a mature and homely counterpoint to boxing's arrogant juveniles. But the nostalgic glow faded. Big George's second championship saga soon added yet more grease to the sport's tainted reputation.

The heavyweight scene shifted dramatically back towards Don King. Six weeks before, in London in late September 1994, Oliver McCall at last stepped beyond Tyson's squat shadow to stun Lennox Lewis with a devastating knock-down. The referee stopped the fight in Round 2. A wailing and hysterical McCall had become the WBC's latest king. Yankee Doodle Don was even more jubilant than his fighter. Apart from winning $450,000 on a Vegas bet that McCall would beat Lewis, Don was almost manic with glee that he had won back at least a portion of the heavyweight title. Without it he knew he would never land a free Mike Tyson.

Just over six months later, two 'world' heavyweight champions, Moorer and McCall, had mushroomed into four from five. Foreman, McCall, Seldon or Tucker and Bowe – who'd since lifted the previously ignored and still meaningless WBO version. It was a bauble Bowe was on the verge of relinquishing because he felt, like Michael Moorer (a WBO hero before him), that it was hindering his career. Being WBO champ, of course, meant that none of the three other 'Alphabet Boys' would rank Bowe in their top ten – even though he was still regarded as the best heavyweight outside of any jailhouse wall. Boxing was a mess.

But at least Don King was radiant again. He had thirty million waiting for him in a MGM safe and Iron Mike was back under Don's own lock and key. King's next shimmering ball of confusion was set to roll in Vegas. At the MGM Grand, McCall would fight the forty-five-year-old Larry Holmes, who had once been a great champion.

In 1988, when he was a veteran coming out of retirement, Holmes had been KO'd mercilessly by Tyson. But Holmes, ever the pragmatist, had seen enough of Tyson even then. He predicted Mike's miserable fate with precision. 'I think that in four or five years he'll be out of the picture. He'll be in jail,' Holmes said of Tyson in January '88.

Seven years on Tyson was out and Holmes had a chance to become a 'world' champion again. I doubt if even sharp old Larry could have guessed that one. Boxing had become an absurd mix of ironies and travesties.

In support of the worn McCall v Holmes WBC clash on 8 April 1995, Bruce Seldon ('The Atlantic City Express') and Tony 'TNT' Tucker would square off in their unwanted WBA epic. It sounded awful; but Don King foresaw 'another astounding double display of championship fisticuffs!'

Luckily, I had already made plans for the night.

We were married that day, Alison and I, far from the desert. The sun shone beautifully, everyone looked happy, we said our vows, kissed, got a little drunk and then I let slip that my new wife was so hiply post-modern that she didn't even want to know where we were going on honeymoon. She wanted me to surprise her. It was like we were getting married in the late '50s and I had suddenly been transformed into a decisive and lantern-jawed husband wearing a gleaming suit and tie. I kind of liked the idea – especially as I had heard that there was a Caesars Palace in Luton, a mere ten miles down the road. A honeymoon at Caesars, in lovely Luton, sounded just the job for a romantic couple newly knotted in Hertfordshire.

Of course I reverted to slack-jawed predictability and, as everyone expected, we went to America instead.

Once there, I snuck a glance at the papers the morning after our first night of marital bliss. We were still thousands of miles from Vegas but I couldn't help myself. I was burning, mildly, to find out who'd won on Don King's double-bill of 'astounding fisticuffs'.

The reports were not complimentary. In a shabby performance, Oliver McCall had creaked home against the ancient Larry Holmes to retain his WBC title. Bruce Seldon, who blurred the increasingly fine line between being a bum and a second-rate champion, had become the new WBA supremo after a dull struggle against Tony Tucker. Although he was believed to be somewhere in Las Vegas, Mike Tyson remained in hiding.

With a relieved sigh, I shut the paper and my mind to the ring. We went down to the beach and I forgot about the decline of boxing for the next couple of weeks – until Alison suddenly looked up and murmured on our honeymoon's last Saturday: 'Did you remember that George Foreman's fighting tonight?'

Of course I did; and naturally, as any new husband might, I accepted her suggestion that we watch the fight together on HBO. 'If you really want to . . .' I said graciously.

We had an elegant candle-lit dinner in a restaurant looking over the sea; and I only had to bolt the last few mouthfuls of crème brûlée. 'We've gotta get back for the boxing,' Alison explained to the bewildered maître d' as we flung him our dollars. I knew we were going to be happy together.

But she was less exhilarated an hour later. 'I don't believe it!' Alison fumed. The room was dark but for the bluish blur of the television and a huge moon shining down through the open window. The wind blew gently in off the ocean and I took another drink as she shook her head sadly at the TV.

On screen, George Foreman's face was swollen and dejected. His eyes were already covered by dark glasses. Across the ring, his twenty-two-year-old opponent, Axel Schultz, looked fresh and unmarked. For twelve painful rounds, the young man had thudded blows into the grandad, proving himself too quick and too strong. Schultz was not a great fighter but he was competent. If Foreman was too bulky to be dismissed as a shadow of his former self, he was more like a forlorn Michelin Man who could do nothing beyond wading forward into punches. He rolled into them as relentlessly as the breakers did on the shore outside. He soaked them up to the point where they bruised and reshaped his rubbery flab. George was too proud to even think about going down, but Schultz was a decisive winner – until the scorecards were read out.

It was a split decision but Foreman was still the IBF heavyweight champion of the world. 'I don't believe it,' Alison repeated with eyes glassier than poor Axel. 'How can they do this?'

I could hardly believe it myself; but I reached for that line James Toney had once said to me in a different hotel room across America. 'This is boxing, baby . . .'

'I don't care,' she said, 'it's still wrong . . .'

But she did not turn away for long. As farcical as it had become, boxing still had that capacity to drop a dirty great hook inside your head and reel you back in with steady purpose. I helped spread her interest in the ring; but there was something else about boxing which drifted in and spun a net around her heart. Alison had become more than just dutifully supportive in encouraging me to press on with this book. She'd become a kooky boxing nut herself. She started to buy *The Sun* because it included more fight coverage than any other national newspaper. I would rustle my *Guardian* at her, turning to the Women's Page as a point of principle, but she was oblivious. I'd hunch over an article pondering the absence of 'media heavyweights amongst women under forty in post-feminist British culture' while Alison laughed at the sassiest boxing gossip. 'Guess what?' she'd interrupt my musing. 'Paula Yates wants to mother Mike Tyson!'

I'd try to sneak a glance over her shoulder but she would have already flipped to the next Exclusive.

'Look! It's Naz again . . . mmm . . . that's quite interesting!'

I'd succumb to the addictive curiosity. 'What?'

'Naz says he's staying at super-bantamweight for the next few fights . . . and . . . oh . . . yes! He got another parking ticket in Sheffield! He kept saying to the guy writing the ticket, "Don't you know who I am?"'

A week later Alison abandoned her Chris Eubank impersonation. She'd so perfected it that she only had to flare a nostril for me to know what was coming next: her 'Simply the Best' routine. But she moved on. The steam curling round her was familiar. Another day, another bath. She had a towel wrapped around her lower half. I was confused by the mirrored sun-shades she wore at five past eleven on a Monday night. It seemed mildly kinky to me. But, as she began to mince, I started to laugh. I could tell that she was moving back into her jokey boxer mode. She nodded and lifted her nose, rocking back, scrunching her face like he did, getting his bad dancing down pat. She spared me his incessant smirks and concentrated on shimmering across the room in jerky symmetry. Naseem Hamed brought to life! She was the same weight as him but about half a foot taller and, fortunately, much more attractive. But why the towel? When she'd taken the piss out of Eubank she had done it with naked honesty. Modesty and a Naz impression seemed way off kilter.

I was a tad slow. The towel was meant to be a kilt – just like the one Naseem had worn, with dark glasses, during the entrance to his last fight on the outskirts of Edinburgh. The Scots had loved the gesture, bursting into passionate renditions of 'Flower of Scotland' when Naz backflipped his way into the ring. They'd yelped with delight as, like Cheryl out of Bucks Fizz, he suddenly whipped the kilt off in one flowing motion to reveal boxing trunks made out of streaks of leopard-skin. It looked like a manic tailor had taken a pair of shears to the cloth and cut his shorts to shreds. They had been slashed into a straggly, flesh-revealing leopard-skin skirt which any self-respecting transvestite would have considered carefully before slipping on in the loo at Madame Jo-Jos.

Alison, Wimbledon's answer to Vivienne Westwood, understood the style at work. What could I do but whistle admiringly when she ripped off her fluffy towel-cum-kilt to expose a perfect copy of that leopard-skin skirt made out of creamy strands of toilet paper. Her streaky 'Prince Naseem' outfit ruffled and flared provocatively, with not even a protective cup in place, as she emulated Naz's somersault over an imaginary set of ropes. This did not seem like ordinary married life. I loved it but, still, I shivered guiltily. What had boxing, or I, done to a sophisticated woman?

Although Alison had been inspired by the fashionable razzmatazz of his walk to the ring, Naseem Hamed had shown at least some restraint on the night he unveiled his skirt 'n' shades special in Scotland. He was still outrageously cocky and garish, of course, but, by his standards, there was an undertow of muted respect in all that he did. He reminded me most of a boy making quiet quips at a funeral in an attempt to cheer everyone else up, to remind us that sometimes there was vibrant truth in the most obvious of clichés. If life was to go on, as we knew it would, we might as well keep on wise-cracking to stop ourselves going mad. His words and gestures were not always the most tasteful, but Naz's sentiments were meant to be as sincere as they were wacky.

Naseem remembered Gerald McClellan that night. It was exactly a week since The Prince himself had said excitedly after the fifth round of Benn and McClellan: 'Now I can see him taking him out. Believe me. Two more rounds. Nigel's looking the stronger fighter now. He's took the punishment and he's coming back with a war. He's coming back with punches. McClellan's blown himself out . . .'

On 4 March, Gerald McClellan was still hanging on in a coma at the Royal London Hospital. Seven nights after fighting Nigel Benn, his body kept on struggling to breathe. Like Naseem I could still see that image of McClellan sinking to the canvas, his eyes blinking, while the television lights glistened on his favourite green shorts. On each upper thigh of his boxing trunks there was the embossed name of one of his children, 'Lil' Gerald' on the left and 'Forrest' on the right.

I doubted if that was why Naz had hacked chunks out of his own spotted pants the following Saturday night. But the American fighter still flickered through his head. It had not helped that his own trainer, Brendan Ingle, had been in McClellan's corner against Benn, that Brendan had been closer than anyone when Gerald first began to shut his eyes in pain.

Ingle, who had been with Naseem for fourteen years, noticed the inevitable effect on his prodigy. 'No one knows Naz better than me,' he said the day before Hamed fought Argentina's Sergio Liendo at the Livingston Forum near Edinburgh, 'and I've noticed that there hasn't been quite the same bounce in the boy this week. We haven't actually sat down to discuss McClellan but I know it's been on his mind. Naz is so quick and clever he hardly ever gets hit, but seeing McClellan in that state has brought it home to him just how dangerous boxing can be – and that's no bad thing. If it makes him more careful, that's fine by me.'

It also made him more considered. Naz had begun to realise how closely the media would scrutinise his reaction at such a grief-stricken time. Even if he had his new set of shorts, he had to tone everything else down. ITV were under the same orders. Although they trumpeted loudly that 'Saturday Night is Big Fight Night', they were less fevered in hyping a bout so soon after they had shown one man almost kill another on live television.

Even the excitable Gary Newbon was subdued as he entered Naseem's dressing-room an hour before the fight. Naz grinned rather than smirked as he snapped his fingers like a young Count Basie counting out the beat to the show's opening tune. 'I'm so relaxed,' he crooned to Newbon, 'I'm ready to do the business . . .'

Gaz seemed shocked by the absence of typical boxing ferocity. 'Brendan,' he asked the smiling Irish trainer, 'why is this lad so relaxed? He's expected to be focused and tense at this stage . . .'

Before Brendan could repeat his adage about Naz being this way ever since he had met him, ever since he was a tiny seven-year-old boy dreaming of stardom, The Prince shouted out his own answer: 'I'm cool,' he sang, 'I'm cool!' He turned to the camera to give ten million viewers the benefit of his boxing wisdom. 'Don't try this at home,' he warned, 'it's totally professional.'

He was more chilling than cool in the ring. Liendo was a tough and durable fighter who had not been stopped in fifty fights. In the opening round he proved that he had come to compete. He sunk a right to the body and then even managed to tag a couple on Naz's jutting chin. Hamed did not blink. He fired back instantly. A right uppercut hurt Liendo. But the Argentinian was a brave man. He attacked The Prince as soon as the bell for round two sounded. But a louder gong clanged in his head a minute later. The Prince unfurled a sweetly anaesthetising left hook. Liendo's lashes fluttered helplessly as he fell. But, somehow, he remained sufficiently alert to shift his collapse into a crouch. It was an incredible recovery in the dizzying space of so few seconds. But his resilience was badly mistaken. As Liendo pulled himself upright, Naz almost shook with pleasure. He pumped his arms back and forth before charging in again with a right which realigned Liendo's motion into a tottering stumble.

He stood up at five and watched the referee take the count up to eight. Even without the memory of Gerald McClellan hovering over the ring, it was evident that Liendo was a beaten man. But the Belgian official stepped back to allow Naseem his unnecessary KO. It was a vicious punch which we should never have seen. Liendo himself had already looked away in the direction of his corner, as if pleading for mercy. He was too dazed to notice the huge arc of another left hook until it crashed on his chin. The power of that punch stretched Liendo on his back, as unmoving as any Hollywood corpse.

For a horrifying moment we thought that the worst had happened and something even more terrible had happened to Liendo. But then he began to move. They helped drag him to his corner. He sat on his tiny stool. After a while it became clear that Sergio Liendo would be able to walk out of the ring on his own trembling legs – and so Brendan Ingle could ease his stringent efforts to check The Prince's celebrations.

After knocking out an opponent Naseem usually shifted into his Americanised Yorkie accent to say words like, 'Ooooo, bay-beee, it hurts to be this good!' But he was more earnest when asked to assess his latest destruction. 'I thought the referee should have stopped it after the first knockdown. I just hope [Liendo's] nice and safe . . . I want to dedicate this fight to Gerald McClellan . . .'

Naseem had come some way since he'd belittled Vincenzo Belcastro. I thought there was hope that he could pull himself out of his otherwise ceaseless addiction to a life of bombast and flash. But it was hard for him. He had only turned twenty-one the month before and he was about to become a millionaire in his next fight. As his brother Raith said, 'We're building an empire round him . . .'

On billboards and in glossy magazines, Naseem and a gleaming Audi were pictured alongside a caption which read: 'They're Both the Most Powerful in their Class'. At the bottom of the ad, a zany copywriter had added, 'If you see either of the above, exercise due caution . . .' With all the money he was making in the ring, and from such endorsements, it was difficult for Hamed to stop his head being turned.

He spoke at length about his desire to avoid 'temptation'. Although he was spending more and more time in London, dancing in clubs and strutting down Savile Row, Naseem still lived with his parents above their corner-shop in Sheffield's spartan Wincobank. 'My parents are proud of me,' he told Geoffrey Beattie in *The Guardian*. 'They're proud to see their son up there. Their advice to me is to live my life cleanly and not give in to the temptations of life. When people meet me they say I'm totally different to how I appear on telly. When people see me on the telly, they see a cocky, arrogant, brash fighter who just wants to win, but then when they meet me they think that I'm just very normal . . . I've never tasted alcohol in my life, because of my religious beliefs, and it's helped me with my boxing. It's kept me out of trouble. And I can't commit myself to any girl at the moment. Boxing comes first. I don't want the public to believe all the hype. I do know that I'm talented but that's because I've been blessed. I've got a gift from Allah. Allah has always been there for me. I always carry a small Koran with me in my sports bag. I need Allah . . .'

I thought of Naseem when I heard Mike Tyson say, 'I just want to pray and fight, pray and fight . . .' as he readied himself for his own return to the ring. There were echoes of Tyson in Hamed's life; not just in their Islamic faith but in the way their brutal skill meant they were always something more than ordinary. Yet The Prince said people thought he was 'very normal' when they met him; Iron Mike said 'I'm just a normal person – extremely to the extreme . . .'

There was a difference. While Naseem still yearned to be considered extraordinary, to become 'legendary', Mike wished above all else that he might become mundane. But how could he when he was making thirty-five million a few mornings after handing in his prisoner's tag? How could he when he felt so isolated? While Mike had lost Cus D'Amato and had always been without a family, Naseem still had his own eccentric mentor, Brendan, his eight brothers and sisters and his cherished mum and dad back in

Sheffield. He had a home, which was not perhaps the word Mike Tyson most commonly reached for when he looked around his new $4,000,000 joint in Vegas.

There was much talk about Don King bringing The Prince and Mighty Mike together on the Tyson comeback bill at the MGM. Naseem himself was desperate to see Vegas. He was also a big enough Tyson fan to wish that he might fight in one of Mike's main supporting bouts. Two months after he crushed Sergio Liendo he fought again with even more relish, as if hoping that Don King would not be able to resist his magnetic attraction.

Enrique Angeles was a relatively talented and still ambitious young Mexican – and yet he lasted no longer than Liendo did. On 6 May, at the West of England Showgrounds in Shepton Mallet, after fifty-five seconds of the second round, Angeles hit the canvas for the first time in thirty-one professional fights. I watched the fight on tape a few days later, and was amazed again by Naseem's booming power. His punches cast an almost comic spell over his opponents. An intoxicating right hit, followed by a fast left chaser, looked like it had flipped the lid off the stunned Enrique's head. He crumpled to the floor like a hapless drunk who could no longer defy gravity. Angeles did not even try to get up. Watching the damage again in slow motion drained the dregs of humour. The clownish prancing of Naz could not hide the fact that he had a punch which might ruin another man. In the trade they described him glibly as a 'lethal finisher'. I began to fear that the little jester from Sheffield might yet strike a blow which would suck out the life from a lesser fighter. But Naz had his mind fixed on fame rather than death.

Hamed's destruction of Angeles had been speedier than his grand approach, which saw him sweep through a blazing sheet to pose and strut in a blinding shimmer of lasers and fireworks. We could just make out his leopard-skin skirt flapping in the centre of the blaze. Ten minutes later, after the smoke had cleared, he almost decapitated Enrique Angeles.

As the video skipped through his latest victory shuffle, his eighteenth straight win, I thought Naseem Hamed was on the verge of becoming one of the world's very best fighters. He spelt out the meaning of danger to hordes of small, dark men dreaming their dreams in steamy gymnasiums from Bangkok to Bogotá, from Los Angeles to Mexico City. He knew it; and he liked the feeling, thinking that he was unbeatable. 'Oh, baby, that was a beautiful workout,' he quivered. 'All hell broke loose. He weren't intimidated, but once those beautiful punches landed with that awesome power, baby, he just couldn't take it . . .'

6 May 1995

While The Prince celebrated his ripening violence in Shepton Mallet, with spring turning into a blistering English summer, it was strangely cold in Las

Vegas. The day before had been even worse. A rainy Friday in Vegas, in May, was never meant to be an uplifting experience. But around two o'clock on Saturday afternoon just as, eight hours ahead, Naz marvelled at himself live on satellite, the sky above Caesars Palace cleared a little. The four fighters gathered themselves for the coming struggle, still aware of a dank chill in the air.

Even under patchy blue and grey cloud, Las Vegas looked and sounded like Little Mexico. Around Caesars, where Bob Arum's 'La Batalla!' promotion was being held, the sombreros bobbed and the Mexican bands jigged as the mostly Hispanic crowd moved towards the arena. It was a public holiday in Mexico, a day they called Cinco de Mayo, a date selected by Arum in an attempt to accentuate the Mexican heritage of the fighters on his bill. Despite the festivity, I felt a tightening inside my fajita-ed stomach.

'La Batalla!', the battle, had been sold to even more pay-per-view homes across America and Mexico than the fight between Roy Jones and James Toney less than six months earlier. I knew the reason. There was a rivalry which had fermented for years, a tension stretching across issues of class and culture, of ethnicity and machismo. Hard and spiteful questions were to be answered in the ring. It was one of those 'crossroads' fights for two very different but evenly matched boxers. They were both champions in the same weight division, representing opposite sides of Los Angeles, symbolising distinct strands of Mexican immigration to America.

My interest and concern centred on Oscar De La Hoya. I had nothing against Rafael Ruelas, setting his IBF lightweight belt against the WBO version held by De La Hoya in a rare unification bout. He was a good and chivalrous man, a fine fighter whose story was matched and deepened by that of his brother, Gabriel, who would defend his WBC junior-lightweight crown on the same bill. I liked the look of the Ruelas brothers. They were solid and true, professional fighters trying to brighten their futures amid the murky perils of the ring.

But, still, Oscar was my boy, one of the boxers I'd followed for more than three years. Even before the Olympics of '92, I'd guessed that he would be one to watch, that the mythology was already in place for him to emerge as the decade's defining fighter. He had charisma, talent, looks and luck. Yet after the open-hearted confusion he'd confessed to me at the top of the Bonaventure in March '94, I did not feel that I really knew him. He remained a paradox, a sweet and polite guy full of the unresolved intrigue which Tyson said we so liked.

Oscar was 'The Golden Boy' and yet, beneath the glitter, it was easy to sense the strain. His rich stardom was muddied by loss and distrust. He had never recovered fully from either his mother's death or the stigma of firing his managers just before he lifted his first world title – that awkward victory over Jimmi Bredhal.

He was also more sensitive than most fighters when considering the grind of the game. 'It's a tough and nasty business,' he stressed just before the Jones–Toney shindig, 'and I never escape that fact. There're a lot of people you have to keep away from, a lot of people who want to bring you down. There're cheats and critics wherever you look. That's why I think about getting out of boxing as soon as I've achieved my ambitions. You know, I still have that hope of being an architect . . .'

'Why don't you do that sooner than later?' I asked.

'I can't,' Oscar said with a curious smile. 'Not yet . . .'

'Why?' I persisted, remembering how Joel De La Hoya had brooded over us at the Bonaventure. 'Is it because of your father, of some fear that you'd be letting him down if you stopped boxing?'

'No,' he responded instantly, 'I'm fighting for me. I want to win six titles in six different divisions. I'm gonna beat the very best guys out there. I want to do that. I might even go all the way up to middleweight in the next few years. I'm as tall as guys like Toney and Jones so I reckon I can go up and take on some of the bigger boys. That's what drives me, to become one of the greatest fighters ever . . .'

'But . . . ?' I prompted.

'But,' he grinned his Rico Suave shaving gel grin, 'it's not easy. There're always questions about me, the same old questions.'

'What sort of questions?'

'You know – they ask if I'm a golden boy or just a gold-digger. They ask if I'm good or bad. They ask if I'm a fake. They ask if I've had it too easy. They ask if I'm tough enough to take on the hardest punchers.'

'And how do you feel when you hear those questions?'

'It isn't always fun. Even the nice questions – I've heard them so many times. People ask the same thing over and over again. But you have to listen and answer and try to keep smiling. It's like this crazy big loop. Training, press conferences, interviews, public appearances, fighting, more talking into the camera, more questions. There's a lot of pressure. All the time I can feel it, building up, pressing down on me . . .

'A lot of people are waiting for me to lose so that they can turn around and say, "oh boy, we told you so!" It's been that way for a long time now. So maybe I'm getting used to it. I found it worse at the Olympics. Now I'm hardening myself. I think I've matured since I first became a world champion. I'm a much better fighter, a much stronger person. I still want to be that role-model I've spoken about before. I know how many Hispanic kids are out there, living in poverty and danger. I want to be the guy they can look up to, the guy who proves that they can get out and do something with their lives. I want to be that guy.'

Oscar spoke with conviction; but 'role-model' talk always seems to come wrapped in bubbles of PR puff. I was more interested in the irony that Oscar had largely been shunned by the hardcore boys he yearned to inspire. Arum's relaunching of the Olympic had failed because De La Hoya had not been able to draw large enough crowds from the Hispanic neighbourhoods adjoining the old building. The fight aficionados were not willing to pay high prices to watch an unproven boxer they suspected Arum had manufactured – especially against hand-picked Danish and Italian patsies. They preferred to drive into Inglewood to see half-a-dozen fierce contests between local fighters who would have been unknown to Hollywood boxing fans like Jack Nicholson or Jay Leno.

For the Latino gangs and *barrio* homeboys drifting through East LA, Oscar was too pretty and marketable a celebrity for their caustic tastes. They expected their role-models to be desperados rather than aspiring architects. They loved boxing but they liked their fighters to be broken-nosed brawlers rather than straight-up cuties like Oscar.

'Yeah, you're right,' the shining example admitted with a twinkling smile. 'I think the Hispanic fight fans will only really like me once they see me suffer and come back swaggering. They want to see me bleed, maybe lose a tooth or two, and come back spitting fury. They're very macho . . .'

'But at least their girlfriends like you,' I murmured in sympathy.

'Aaaah, yeah, and the girlfriends are usually so very pretty!'

'So what do you do?'

'Well, you know,' Oscar blushed, 'women are just so great . . .'

'But you'd like to get the boyfriends cheering too?'

'Oh yeah! I'd like the whole cross-section. From the sweetest girl to the toughest guy. Y'see, the girls are attracted to the fame, the money, even the smile. That's great. But the Latino fight fans are the hardest in the world. To get their respect you have to prove that you're ready to die in the ring. They want you to be a warrior. That's why they love Duran and Chavez – those guys have been through so many fights. They've proved their machismo over and over again.'

'But, beyond the machismo, do you think about the dangers that thrill those fans?'

'Yes.'

'Do you think about the damage there is in boxing, the fact that a fighter can die in the ring?'

'Well, I try to think instead about winning. I don't want to die in a fight. I'm not out to win the respect of the hardcore LA fans at any cost. I'll get their respect in my own style. I reckon once I've beaten all the toughest Mexican and Hispanic fighters out there they'll take me to their hearts. They're very loyal. But you have to earn their loyalty. When you're a baby like me you can't expect they're just going to drop a Chavez for you. How can you drop a legend who's been in the professional ring ninety-five times before, a guy who has only one loss on his record, for a guy who has only had fifteen fights? It's not going to happen just like that. It takes time. Maybe at the moment they even like a guy like Rafael Ruelas more than me because as a pro he's been around a whole lot longer, he's a guy with more than forty fights. I'm still below those guys in the eyes of the Hispanic fight fans. I've got to go out and beat them before I can call myself a great fighter. I know that, they know that. It's no problem.'

'Do you think there's resentment because you won a world title after only twelve fights – when some of the great Hispanic fighters of the past had forty or fifty bouts before they got a chance?'

'There's some of that – absolutely. But the people who really know boxing accept that I've been fighting for years. I had about five times the amount of amateur fights as a guy like Rafael Ruelas. I've not just come to the ring in the last couple of years. I've been there thirteen, fourteen years now. The way I look at it, there are two stages in boxing. I've been through the first, I've climbed the learning curve, and now I'm in stage two. I think I'm just about able to beat anyone they put in the ring against me. It's taken a while but I've reached that point. I look forward to fighting some of those very tough guys they're always talking about – Molina, Hernandez, Ruelas, even Chavez. If I fight only the best then I know the respect will come. I'm ready to win and yeah – if that's what it takes – to suffer a little too . . .'

Between the professional ropes there had always been a sense of uncertainty around Oscar De La Hoya. The claims of greatness Arum made on his behalf after two or three contests irked the fight fanatics. They saw too much hype and too little substance. There were also doubts about his chin – Oscar having been knocked down by two light-hitting journeymen in Giorgio Campanella and Narciso Valenzuela. The fact that he rose from the canvas on both occasions to score immediate KO victories only served to highlight the inadequacies of his opposition. If De La Hoya could be floored by such nonentities, the question scornfully ran, what hope would he have against the top-line names he now mentioned?

My personal scepticism waned when De La Hoya moved up and fought at lightweight. He lifted the WBO crown with an almost casual display of power. I was mightily impressed by him at the MGM on the two worst nights of James Toney's career. De La Hoya knocked out Eric Griffiths in three destructive rounds just before Toney lost to Jones, and then out-pointed the highly respected Puerto Rican John-John Molina when Lights Out was shut down against Montell Griffin.

Molina had a 36-3 record and had not been defeated for nearly five years. But De La Hoya decked him and went on to dominate a gruelling championship fight despite the other man's determination and skill. It was Oscar's first serious test, and he sailed through it with spinnaker-swirling assurance.

But, two and a half months later, he surfed a much higher and more menacing wave. Rafael Ruelas v Oscar De La Hoya. 'La Batalla!', a fight of certain violence, a struggle which would settle the future of both fighters.

Rafael Ruelas was only twenty-four years old but he had won forty-three of his forty-four fights; and even the single blemish had been less a clear defeat against Mauro Gutierrez than a mistake of following his corner's count. While his trainer Joe Goosen shouted 'seven . . . eight,' Ruelas rested on a knee, waiting for 'nine' before he stood up on steady pins – only to see that the referee had been a beat ahead and had already called 'ten'. He had made an elementary mistake in not watching the man who mattered. In the rematch, Ruelas easily outpointed Gutierrez to straighten that kink in his otherwise perfect résumé.

Although Ruelas had been knocked down on numerous occasions, particularly in the early rounds, he was noted for his resilience and sheer persistence. He always came back stronger, being one of those men who refused to give in, an action fighter who crowded his opponent and battered him on the inside, close to the body, always staying in range so that he might take as many shots as he landed. Ruelas was a likelier role-model for the Hispanic crowds than the ornate Oscar.

Rafael and Gabriel Ruelas were also closer to the roots of their followers than De La Hoya. The Ruelas boys were from a family of thirteen children born to poor farming parents in the Jalisco mountains of southern Mexico. Gabriel was ten months older than Rafael. They spent the earliest years of their life picking corn and garbanzo beans on land near a town called Yerba Buena. When they were aged nine and ten, in 1980, they were sent to live with an older brother in California. They swapped their beans for candy and went from door to door, selling small packets of the stuff for twenty-five cents a bag.

On one of those candied missions they knocked on the door of the heavily coiffured Joe Goosen who was then already training young fighters. The Ruelas boys went down to the gym with Joe. They both turned professional while still in their teens. Rafael had his pro début as an eighteen-year-old featherweight, not long after Gabriel's own start in September 1988 when Bob Arum hailed him as 'the next Duran'. They fought primarily on the West Coast, basing themselves in the southern Californian suburb of Sylmar, just outside LA. Gabriel's own record was a similarly impressive 40-2, having lost only to the brilliant Azumah Nelson and being forced to retire against Jeff Franklin when he fractured an elbow. A few months before 'La Batalla!', they became the first-ever brothers to defend their respective world titles on the same bill when, on 28 January at the MGM, Gabriel scored a second-round TKO over Freddie Leberatore and Rafael stopped Billy Schwer from Luton after eight bloody rounds.

Rafael was the quieter of the two, a modest guy who avoided the conceit and threat hawked by boxers like Hamed and Toney. But he carried a small grudge against the angel-faced and golf-playing Oscar.

'I think all boxers should get into golf,' De La Hoya had said when mentioning that he often played a nine-hole course at his training camp in

Big Bear. 'Boxers make good golfers. They have great hand-eye co-ordination. It's there. The timing, everything . . .'

Ruelas knew that a passion for golf belonged more to the pampered Anglos of Beverly Hills than the Hispanic workers and hustlers of East LA. According to Ruelas, Oscar's infatuation with the game was an indication of how far he had removed himself from boxing's blue-collar base. 'We don't play golf,' Rafael muttered, perhaps recalling how Joel De La Hoya had once scoffed that he and Oscar were not 'bean farmers'. He looked unusually angry as he suggested, 'After this fight Oscar might want to take a rest and consider a career in golf. His heart is obviously not in boxing. It's just something he does for the money. He'd rather be out hitting golf balls.'

Ruelas's resentment towards De La Hoya was bound up in that fight-game perennial – money. Although he had beaten Oscar twice in their three amateur contests, he'd only been paid $400 when he first fought professionally. The Golden Boy, in contrast, picked up a cool $75,000 – and bonuses worth a million dollars for signing with Mittleman and Nelson. While Ruelas's earnings had increased after forty fights to the point where 'La Batalla!' would earn him a million-dollar purse, Oscar was guaranteed a minimum of $1,750,000 for the fight – with additional revenue to come from pay-per-view receipts.

'If he hadn't won that gold medal,' Ruelas argued, 'there would've been no Oscar story.'

De La Hoya had his own opinion. 'I view Ruelas as awkward,' he said, 'he has bad balance, always lunging with his punches. With that bad balance, when I catch him with some good shots he'll fall over . . . he really doesn't do much thinking in the ring.'

'Who is he to judge me?' Ruelas jeered, stressing the disparity between his forty-four bouts and Oscar's mere seventeen fights. 'When we fought as amateurs and when we sparred before the Olympics, I learned he's not very strong up here,' Ruelas motioned, tapping his heart. 'I learned that he doesn't like pressure, which is what he's going to get. He's always crying about "pressure" and he's always gotten it from me – and he'll get it again. Things came a lot easier for him. Maybe they came too quickly, too sudden. People also say Oscar's chin is questionable. His chin is not questionable. It's already been shown that his chin is not the greatest. When he went down from those guys who can't punch, it removed the question. I'm going to hurt him. I'm going to knock him out. The Oscar story will be over – in very dramatic fashion.'

A leaden evening sky had not yet turned black. Rafael Ruelas sat alone in his dressing-room. His head was lowered, eyes anchored to the small television. He watched his brother fight, knowing that soon he and Oscar De Le Hoya would walk to that same open-air ring.

Gabriel Ruelas defended his WBC junior-lightweight title against a scrawny Colombian boxer called Jimmy Garcia. In his previous bout, Garcia had been systematically punished by the WBA champion, Genaro Hernandez – a superior body-puncher already lined up to meet the winner of the De La Hoya–Ruelas clash. Hernandez won all twelve rounds. It took Garcia weeks to recover and he remained inactive for the next five months.

But Jose Sulaiman, the WBC president and Don King's head-honcho amongst the various boxing bodies, remembered that after the Hernandez fight, Garcia 'came up to me and told me the belt he dreamed of and treasured was the green belt of the WBC and how he had always wanted to fight for it. He asked me to forgive him for fighting for another version of the championship, saying that he had really needed that fight, but then he pleaded with me not to rule him out of fighting for our belt.'

Incredibly, in his very next fight, the WBC awarded Garcia another title crack. He had just over a month to shed thirty-two pounds and by the time he entered the ring against Gabrial Ruelas he was severely weakened. His punches were feathery brushes which Ruelas ignored while thudding combinations to Garcia's head and body. In the opening round he landed forty-three heavy blows on Garcia's listing frame. From then on Ruelas cruised, winning every round except the eighth, as he snapped Garcia's head back and forth as if it was attached to an elastic stand.

'Walk through this punk,' Joe Goosen encouraged Gabriel, 'he's got nothing left . . .'

The worst memory I have of the fight is of Garcia leaning back helplessly over the ropes as, yet again, his head is jolted with a sickening crack. Ruelas hurt him repeatedly but Garcia would not sink to the floor. Although there were no knockdowns, Ruelas's dominance was so complete that the three judges awarded him a number of 10-8 rounds – normally used only when a fighter is made to take a count.

While Garcia had no chance of recovering, the referee allowed the fight to continue, his justification being that the Colombian kept punching – if that's what you could call pawing arm-movements so despondent it looked as if Garcia was wading through chest-high mud.

Ruelas, frustrated that he could not bring about an early finish, exerted even more pressure in the tenth. The hammering was so overbearing that, at the end of the round, Ruelas grinned at Garcia. It was not a sneer or a smirk, more an unexpected smile of admiration and pity. Ruelas's expression was one of disbelief. 'Why?' it seemed to ask of Garcia. 'Why go on?' I don't think Jimmy Garcia even noticed.

Mitch Halpern, the referee, called in the ringside physician. Dr Flip Homansky stared into Garcia's vacant eyes, as his father and trainer screamed for him to continue. Homansky allowed him to get off his stool when Garcia nodded twice that he felt able to fight on. The doctor gestured to Halpern that he should stop the fight if Ruelas landed one more big punch.

After twenty-five seconds the inevitable happened. Ruelas banged two cruel rights on Garcia's jaw and Halpern leapt between the fighters. The slow butchery had ended.

Two minutes later, in a doleful echo of Gerald McClellan, Garcia collapsed in his own corner. He was unconscious when they laid him on the white stretcher. His father rubbed his hands together nervously, not knowing what to do next. They lifted Jimmy up and carried him out. Six minutes after the fight had been waved to a close, the paramedics slid Jimmy Garcia into the back of a waiting ambulance.

Gabriel Ruelas stood on his own in the ring, looking out into the crowd, a fallen angel if ever I saw one.

'La Batalla!', naturally, continued. Oscar De La Hoya was the first to head down the long Caesars gangway. He was dressed in a black cape. The hood was pulled down as if in deference to the cold night and some boos framing the cheers. Jimmy Garcia, an oxygen mask strapped to his face, was almost forgotten.

Rafael Ruelas seemed tense as he entered the ring a few minutes later, jogging to the strains of a Mexican polka. His trunks were red, white and green, the colours of the Mexican flag, while De La Hoya wore a bottle-green pair – both of which I thought were prettier than the leopard-skin skirt flashed that same evening by young Prince Naseem.

Ruelas wore his pencil-slim moustache while Oscar favoured a rough stubble which, with his severe crop, made him look more like a fighter from the '50s than a modern Hollywood icon. Oscar had also set aside his dollar-churning smile and the tiny Mexican and American flags which he used to wave in each glove while being introduced. He had his fight-face on, blanking out the bulk of support being voiced for his opponent.

The white-tuxed Michael Buffer thundered his rumble greeting and added a convincingly Latino growl to his 'Rafael Ruuuu-elllll-aaaaaassssss!' and 'Oscar De La 'Oyyyyyy-aaaaaaaaaaa!' roar. Even if he looked like Dex out of *Dynasty*, the Buffer-Boy sounded as if he was auditioning for the part of Manolito in *The High Chapparal*.

Rounds one to three were always going to be vital – for Ruelas was at his most vulnerable during the opening stanzas. He was a notoriously slow starter. Even when winning the IBF title from Freddie Pendleton, Ruelas had been knocked down twice in the first three minutes.

He tried to compensate by rushing at Oscar, who made him miss badly. De La Hoya snaked in long leads with fierce concentration and an authority absent from his earliest appearances in boxing's championship class. Ruelas swung wildly again and De La Hoya forced him to wince with a hard counter. They clinched and Ruelas tried to lash out as the referee parted them. De La Hoya's glare was icy and all the more unnerving for its sudden appearance.

Oscar moved even more fluidly in the second, shaking off his past rigidity to jab and glide and hit with smooth power. He tracked a fast combination with a perfect left hook, as precise and rollicking a punch as he could have wished to find. Ruelas lay on the canvas, his face full of shock. He managed to claw himself up after eight long seconds – only to be sent back again by a big Oscar right. Dishevelled and broken, Ruelas nodded out of habit as Richard Steele counted. Oscar hummed in again and, in another moment, it was all over. De La Hoya's final assault was blocked just as it began to gain savage momentum.

Richard Steele put his arms around Ruelas who had slumped against the ropes. The tall black referee held the fighter, as if his embrace might be a comfort.

Oscar turned and ran towards his own corner. His face was lit by the most naked kind of joy. He'd won. He'd won. Bob Arum rocked in dark-suited delight. He'd won. He'd won. Oscar put a red glove to his white slashed mouth and raised his head to the starless heaven. He kissed his glove and gave thanks. He was one of only two boxers in the world to hold twin-versions of a world title. Oscar De La Hoya, the WBO and new IBF lightweight champion, had truly arrived, establishing himself that night as one of the most dynamic fighters in contemporary boxing. But more than that, Oscar was young and happy – and alive.

Jimmy Garcia died thirteen days later, in the early hours of Friday, 19 May 1995. He was twenty-three years old. He lost his life trying to win a green belt in a fight for which he was due to be paid $20,000. Gabriel Ruelas, the champion, had been promised $300,000.

They operated on Garcia's brain thirty-five minutes after Gabriel Ruelas's last punch. At the University Medical Center in Las Vegas they cut into his scalp even before Rafael and Oscar came out for round one. Surgery to remove a one-inch blood clot took two hours to complete. The doctors called the injury by its increasingly familiar medical name – subdural hematoma – and hoped that their work had been successful.

For five days, Garcia fought and faltered and then rallied again. Gabriel Ruelas was at his bedside, praying with the Garcia family. Jimmy's father, Manuel, had urged him on during the fight. But there had not been enough strength in the sad-faced boxer to repel Ruelas. Fathers and sons were never meant to work together in boxing. Yet, in that starched hospital bed, Jimmy managed to squeeze his father's hand. There had been hope then. They waited, murmuring to Jimmy and Jesus, for another sign of life. But the coma deepened.

In a heartbreaking conversation with *Boxing Monthly*'s Jack Welsh, Gabriel said, 'When I first saw Jimmy, no matter what the doctors kept saying, I knew he wouldn't make it. The way I saw Garcia, I really saw a dead body in front of me. His eyes never opened and he remained comatose . . .'

They switched off the life-support machine at 1.43 a.m. that Friday morning; and when Gabriel Ruelas heard the news he began his grieving. 'I wish it was me who died, not Jimmy,' he told Welsh. 'I was so glad I was able to talk to his parents. His mother, Carmen, said Jimmy had promised he would bring back the title before he left Colombia for Las Vegas. He wanted to make some money and buy his family a nice house. He wanted to do things for his people. Me, I'd already done what I wanted to do. So I wish I was in his position instead. Garcia wanted to get married, live better. Well, I have a wife, Leslie, and a ten-week-old son, Diego. I tell people I've already been rich from boxing . . .

'A month ago I was talking to Leslie about Gerald McClellan. He had a blood clot removed from the brain, too. He'll never fight again but he might be able to live a normal life one day. All fighters think it can happen to us, but we still go on. That's the hardest thing. But I never thought about this. I never thought it could happen to me. I remember in the last press conference at Caesars, I said that I had trained very hard for this fight and I haven't seen my son for seven weeks, so somebody will have to pay for that. Jimmy Garcia will have to pay for it. Oh, I regret saying that.'

Gerald McClellan, three months after his fight with Nigel Benn, was alive and back in America. He was still unconscious in a hospital in Michigan but he would live – even if he was almost certain to be blind and partially deaf. Nigel Benn had not yet been able to bring himself to visit either McClellan or his family. He said he would not be able to 'look Gerald's mother in the face' while he remained a fighter.

Gabriel Ruelas tried. 'I had to make peace with them,' he said of the Garcia family. 'I thought it would be extremely more difficult than it was, considering the family being wracked with grief. Garcia's parents were very gracious. I couldn't have blamed them if they were different and I didn't expect them to be like that . . . at first it was hard to talk. Mrs Garcia kept staring at my hands. Right then she wasn't able to talk to me but later she said she was looking at "the hands that killed my son". Mrs Garcia made up for everything before we left when she gave me a warm hug. She said that whenever she sees me fighting on TV, she will see Jimmy and pray for me.'

Leslie Ruelas spoke with harsher eloquence. 'When I used to look up in the stands,' she explained to Welsh, 'I'd think there are some sick people out there and they want blood, not a good fight. If somebody doesn't get hurt, they seem disappointed. I'd say, "Gabriel, let's move to Mexico, we can be farmers, we can do anything." Boxing is a very sick profession, but it's what he's good at and I can't take away his love. Gabe would never be the same.

'I have to be proud and happy at what Gabriel and Rafael have achieved with their goals in a sport that is marred by politics and very violent . . . [but] I have never liked boxing as a sport. If it was a technical thing, and nobody got hurt, that would be fine. But when people are trying to smash each other's heads in, I have to say, no, no, no . . .'

If boxing in Las Vegas had become a graveyard at night, it was still a circus by day. Five days after Jimmy Garcia died, a jubilant Don King addressed the assembled masses at an MGM press conference.

'We are grateful,' he hollered breathlessly, 'to Kirk Kerkorian and his MGM associates for putting us back on the Yellow Brick Road, on our way back to the world heavyweight championship, on what will be truly the richest sporting event in history.'

Dandy Don was flanked by two fighters, one black and one white, Iron Mike and Hurricane Pete, the bad man and his tomato can.

Having pipped 'Tuna' Lou Savarase to the hot plate, Peter McNeeley reacted to the idea of fighting Tyson with affable enthusiasm. He was bolstered by the promise of earning over a half a million for the privilege. 'This is my life,' he warbled as if he'd at last reached the Land of Oz. 'I have no other job. I'm the busiest fighter in New England. All my last eight fights, going back to last July, have ended in the first round. Boxing fans in Las Vegas and the rest of the world will learn how hard I can really punch when I knock out Mike Tyson in ten rounds on 18 August.'

Tyson, dressed in a black suit and white panama hat, looked thoroughly amused. He admitted later that he thought McNeeley was 'kinda cute'. But there was little affection in his voice when he was asked to respond to comments that his talent had begun to erode even before he was jailed. 'My skills slipping?' he mocked. 'Who are these people? Whoever said that never said it to my face. Most of these critics have never boxed. And I know they never fought me, so where do they get the authority to tell me I'm not the same fighter?'

Don King grinned his mad and roiling grin, teeth almost dancing in his mouth as he bumped up the jive-talk. 'Ooooo,' he chortled, 'you can tell. He's back. The man is definitely back! This is history in the making! Don King and big-time boxing are back! An' Mike Tyson has resurrected us, he's brought me back to life! Without Mike I was dead and buried . . .'

When they at last got round to Jimmy Garcia, the reporters were more interested in Tyson's reaction to George Foreman's argument that professional fighters should wear protective headgear. Despite the fact that head-guards tend to make boxers complacent and, much more seriously, reduce their line of vision against blows swinging in from the side, Tyson cut to the core. For him, boxing was nothing without danger.

'If we started using headgear,' he stressed, 'we might as well end boxing. Things happen in boxing. It's been happening for a hundred and ten years.'

Tyson was unequivocal about his own commitment to the ring. 'When I was released I went straight back to the gym. That's what I do. I missed the régime of training more than I thought I would. As I said before, I'm here to do one thing – to do my job, which is fighting. I do nothing else but prepare myself to become heavyweight champion again.'

Rather than entertain or intrigue people, Tyson wanted to be respected for, at least in his own head, he was just an ordinary guy trying to make it in the ring. He still wanted to be a fighter, a great fighter. He'd always wanted that. Only boxing could give him happiness.

I remembered how Mike had once had his own heroes. Boxing icons. He'd always liked the toughest Latin fighters. I had not forgotten the little story he'd told to Wally Matthews in 1991.

'I thought [Roberto] Duran was the greatest,' Tyson said. 'I was at the fight when he fought Davey Moore. I was waaaaay up at the top of Madison Square Garden. You know what was great? Me and my friend snuck all the way down to the bottom. I was like a fucking groupie. We went down there and saw Bobby Chacon, Eusebio Pedroza, all the fighters in the front row. We went up to them: "Hi, how you doing?" . . . I was happy that night. I went down there and I was kissing those guys' asses, all those fighters I admired.'

Still half in love with his memory of the young Roberto, Tyson recalled that 'I never wanted to hang out with Duran, because I liked him as my idol. I didn't want to see his bad points. Sometimes I try to do things like Duran in the ring. Like I'm in a fight and I'll think, "I'm gonna feint like Duran and go to the body". And I know I don't do it like Duran, but I try. I can never picture anyone doing that with me. I swear. I can't imagine any kids ever looking up at me. I just can't imagine it.'

In 1995, when young black boys in America said, 'I wanna be like Mike,' parents invariably hoped that they were talking in Nike-speak about Michael Jordan rather than Mike Tyson. Jordan, who had begun his own comeback to basketball just before Tyson left prison, was still an American sporting legend, a 'role-model' without parallel. And yet Tyson had won the adulation of the most disenchanted and disenfranchised. They saw Mighty Mike as being an extension of them; he had been fucked by America but he was coming back with blazing fists and millions of dollars.

Despite his knowledge of pigeon-genes and *The Great Gatsby*, Tyson remained the ultimate homeboy, still that 'baddest man on the planet'. Iron Mike's name was dropped on countless gangsta rap records, his face plastered across T-shirts from Brooklyn to Compton, an 'I'll Be Back' promise scrawled below his huge neck. His sombre menace had been enhanced rather than dissipated by his time in prison. After a four-year stretch in the cooler Mike Tyson had, ironically, become even hotter.

At the MGM, as Don King looked down at him with dollar-ringed love, Tyson himself was more ambivalent when asked to consider his iconic status.

'I'm not a good guy,' he mumbled, 'I'm not a bad guy. I'm just trying to get along and survive. I'm involved in a sport I love, but it's a sport that doesn't love me. I'm looking forward to doing something. If I do become a role-model, okay. However, I can't do nothing but be Mike Tyson, nobody else.'

A month later, on a sweltering Tuesday afternoon in June, Mike Tyson went back to New York. Brownsville was still too rough a quarter to host Don King's and the Reverend Al Sharpton's 'homecoming party' for Mike; so they chose Harlem. The dissent surrounding Tyson's visit meant that they also had to scale down plans for a full-blown party, settling instead on a glorified personal appearance. From different perspectives within New York's black community, Tyson was either the inspirational 'Iron Mike' or a convicted rapist who had yet to apologise for his crime.

As the tension and temperature climbed to ninety-seven degrees on Lennox Avenue, three hundred people crammed into a small tent hastily erected outside Sylvia's restaurant while a thousand more looked for a way in from the street outside.

'Remember the lady who drove her two children into the river in South Carolina?' the Reverend William Crockett yelped below a white banner which read 'Harlem Salutes Mike Tyson & Don King'. 'Mike Tyson didn't do that. Remember Timothy McVeigh, who blew up the building in Oklahoma City? Mike Tyson didn't do that. Remember Jeffrey Dahmer, who ate the people and put them in the refrigerator? Mike Tyson didn't do that . . .'

It was hardly the start which Team Tyson had been hoping for – and they must have been relieved when the praise of Mike became more strictly biblical in tone. Each new speaker seemed intent on making some reference to the parable of the Prodigal Son and, by the time it was Tyson's turn to take the mic, Al Sharpton was pumped up enough to burble his strange 'bring forth the fatted calf' remark.

Tyson took the hint and stood up in his brash white suit. He waved lamely and accepted questions from a group of people which the *New York Daily News* ridiculed as 'sycophants and psycho fans'. It made a change from the usual bear-baiting boxing-press jamborees in Vegas.

'Mike, do you still give away turkeys at Thanksgiving?' and 'Mike, I just want to tell you that African-American women love you,' were the kind of queries and comments which popped up invitingly. Even when Bill Tatum, editor of the local *Amsterdam News*, admitted that the celebration of Tyson's freedom in Harlem had 'divided blacks in this city', he cranked up the volume of laudatory noise by declaring his personal belief that 'Mike Tyson, after all, is a hero who has come home! He is one of our brothers!'

When, however, a journalist finally broke through the heaving ranks of disciples to ask Tyson about regret, Don King erupted. 'Sorry?' he shouted.

DEATH AND THE MAN

'Sorry for what? What are you talking about? C'mon man!'

Would Tyson renounce violence against women, another voice enquired.

'He doesn't have to,' John Horne snapped. 'I won't sit here and let you disrespect him like that!'

The Tyson entourage swept back into their limousines to be driven to the Apollo Theatre on 125th Street where, in a 'Mike Tyson Rally', the fighter pledged a total of one million dollars to diverse charities. He also donated an immediate $200,000 to neighbourhood causes ranging from a youth foundation to a sports club for young Puerto Rican boys in the Bronx.

Yet Jill Nelson, who had formed an 'African-Americans Against Violence' lobby group, was unconvinced by such largesse. She was one of seventy-five black women from Harlem who set up a vigil on Lennox Avenue to protest against Tyson's renewed heroism and against violence in a society where 'a woman is battered every fifteen seconds'.

Tyson had declined an invitation to speak at the gathering; and Nelson had since learned that, instead, he took his posse to Chavonaltos in Manhattan where they tried on various suits while fans gaped at them through the glitzy store windows.

'You have a nerve,' the black writer Carol Taylor seethed at Jill Nelson. 'I love Mike Tyson and he has a right to redemption.' Returning to the scriptural messages so popular amongst Tyson's supporters, Taylor shouted again at the other women, 'You who are without sin cast the first stone!'

But Jill Nelson was unrepentant. 'I am deeply offended,' she said, 'that Mike Tyson felt shopping was more important than standing with our community to protest about violence against women. It goes to show that he's not on the path to redemption, but on the path to pay-per-view . . .'

18 August 1995

Tyson was paid $25,000,000 to fight Peter McNeeley, a boxing bum whose fight statistics were so contrived they bordered on the criminal. Apart from the fact that he was a big white Irish-American who was certain to lose, McNeeley had been chosen as Tyson's first opponent because of his record. Thirty-eight fights, thirty-seven wins with twenty of them coming in the first round. Don King loved that kind of CV. It helped him sell the fight to his potential 'two billion' pay-per-view watchers around the world.

King once said that, in boxing, 'everything you hear is a lie'; and so it was with Peter McNeeley's credentials as a boxer. Although it was true to say that he had beaten thirty-seven men in the ring, it was more pertinent to know that fourteen of McNeeley's victims had never won a fight between them. As *Boxing News* revealed a week before the fight, his opponents' combined record consisted of 168 wins, 366 defeats and 15 draws – a success rate of 30 per cent. Most of the pugs were total unknowns. The few familiar names were of the ilk of Ron Drinkwater who had been retired for fifteen years before he was exhumed by the McNeeley camp in 1993. The grey and sadly parched Drinkwater was knocked back inside a minute.

McNeeley was sufficiently encouraged to turn to Tyson at the final press conference and warn him that 'I'm going to wrap you in a cocoon of horror.' It was a great line, which even Tyson loved; but, ultimately, it only helped whip Don King into a state of near-hysterical excitement. 'People all over the world, from Ireland's Belfast to New York and Chicago, will be decked out in green,' he promised. 'The leprechauns will be dancing from glen to glen, the chaps will be singing Irish lullabies and the shamrocks will be shining!'

Turning to laud each fighter, while a dejected Tyson mouthed 'bullshit', King hit more ecstatic heights. Of Peter McNeeley he said, 'few boxers have fought lesser opponents with greater skill'; while 'thanks to Mike Tyson I have been resurrected. I was dead in the media cave, but I came back to life and rolled away the boulder. This is going to be the biggest event in the history of sport! That is a fact. This is not a fight, this is a global happening! Call your cable operator now! Hurry! For the first time ever two billion people will watch on pay-per-view these two great gladiators get it on in the ring at the MGM Grand Garden Arena! That is a fact!' Less a fact than a mildly massaged statistic; and yet Tyson-McNeeley was set to shatter all pay-per-view records despite the fact that it would cost most Americans almost $50 to watch the carnage on TV.

Boxing Illustrated's editor, Herbert G. Goldman, was more laconic than King in assessing the fight's historical significance to the rest of us: 'Well, if you're the type who watches every minute of the O.J. Simpson trial, a boxing fanatic, a Mike Tyson addict, and the sort of guy who doesn't mind tossing fifty bucks into a stripper's G-String, pick up the phone and order . . .'

In London, Harry Mullan was more disturbed by King's relentless selling of the Tyson-McNeeley extravaganza. 'As editor of the sport's trade paper, *Boxing News*, for the past eighteen years,' he wrote in the *Independent on Sunday*, 'I frequently find myself a spokesman for the pro-boxing faction. This time, though, along with everyone else who has trotted out the ritual arguments in defence of the too-often indefensible, I have to climb out of the bunker, hands in the air and squinting in the sunlight. What is taking place in Las Vegas is as immoral and wicked as a public hanging, and the fact that McNeeley is skipping to the gallows is no justification. He will be butchered – probably within a round and certainly within three – and the harder he is hit, the more comprehensively he is battered, the louder the 16,000 capacity crowd will howl their approval. There must be decency and dignity in boxing, otherwise no one with a grain of humanity in their soul could ever watch it, but little will be in evidence at the MGM Garden Arena.'

Mike Tyson walked to the ring in his black executioner shorts and boots, with only a ferocious scowl and a white towel around his bare neck for company. After the histrionics of Chris Eubank and his Harley-Davidson and Naseem Hamed and his leopard-skin skirt and shades, there was a stripped-down chill in Tyson's return to basics. He was back.

The fight lasted eighty-nine seconds, which meant that Tyson earned $280,898.89 a second. As soon as the bell rang, McNeeley charged across the ring like a crazed bull. His head was down and his arms flailed furiously, as if he knew that his only chance was to surprise a rusty Tyson with an early punch. He succeeded in bewildering Tyson for a moment. Mighty Mike seemed uncertain on how best to cope with McNeeley crawling all over him until, after eight seconds, the old instincts took over. Tyson clipped home a punch and McNeeley fell down – only to instantly jump up with, in Hugh McIlvanney's words, 'the briskness of a jogger who was ready for his orange juice'. The Hurricane-Man stormed back at Tyson and was almost blown away by the wind of Tyson's rushed misses. But as soon as Mike found a semblance of accuracy, the fight was over. A couple of mistimed left hooks and a swift and shuddering right uppercut went to work inside McNeeley's spinning head. The Medfield Mauler pitched against the ropes and then tumbled to the canvas like he had reached home after a long night on the Guinness.

McNeeley, however, was ready for one more. Back on his feet he held his gloves high to indicate his desire for another slug at Mike. As Mills Lane went through the mandatory count, he noticed that Tyson had not moved to a neutral corner. But, as Mills turned towards him, he saw another example of boxing's unpredictability. McNeeley's trainer, Vinny Vecchione, known as 'Curly' because of his bald dome, hurled himself into the ring in the eighty-ninth second, knowing that such an action would immediately disqualify his fighter. Vecchione had seen the full impact of that Tyson uppercut and he could imagine what was coming next.

As boos and chants of 'bullshit, bullshit' cascaded down from the cheap seats, the $200 rip-off cushions at the very top and back of the arena, Curly was certain of his actions. 'I feel a responsibility to Peter and I thought about Jimmy Garcia. I did the right thing to save Peter. He's only twenty-six and he's like a son to me.'

'I stick by Curly,' McNeeley confirmed, 'he's like a father to me. But I told you I was coming to fight and I took it to him. I don't feel bad about anything. Vinny did what he thought best for me, but I could have gone on fighting. I wasn't hurt and Mike knew I was in there with him. You can be sure about that. I was no frigging pushover!'

Tyson had already left the ring with a curt, 'I felt good in there tonight. Thank God we both came through it healthy. I've still got a lot to learn, a lot to go through . . .'

Don King, meanwhile, exulted in the present. 'Tonight I gave you sensation! Spectacle! Peter was raining blows from all directions. Nobody has gone for Mike like that. It was the most terrific altercation mankind could wish to see! Who cares how long it lasted?'

9

THE CINDERELLA MEN

I WAS TWENTY-THREE YEARS OLD WHEN I LEFT JOHANNESBURG
for London, still young enough to imagine that I understood the vagaries
of a culture I'd followed from a six-thousand-mile distance. In the English
autumn of 1984 I could delude myself into thinking that I had as good a
handle as anyone when comparing the square grit of the Arsenal back-four
with Morrissey's daffodil-waving. I liked Martin Amis and Paul Morley. On
alternate Thursday evenings I sat through Nicholas Roeg triple-bills at the
Everyman and whole episodes of *Coronation Street*. I wasn't sure if I got the
full drift of either, but it hardly mattered. I didn't know anyone in London
and so I could pretend. Sometimes, in letters I found painful to write, I
tried to tell my mother and father that I'd fitted seamlessly into a strange
country.

But Frank Bruno always made me wonder. I remember watching him on
Sportsnight during my earliest months in England. In a curious way he
made me feel homesick for South Africa. It had not been long since I'd left
the hot classrooms of Soweto, a township rubbed raw by a descending State
of Emergency. I was still coming out of the personal confusion entailed in
having to explain *Silas Marner* to township students more familiar with
political detention than literary nicety. Seeing Bruno fill up my tiny TV on
drizzly Wednesday evenings in a Shepherd's Bush bedsit uncorked the
memories, bringing back those mornings of loaded teaching and afternoons
left hazy by hard drink.

My Soweto boxing friends and I had heard about Bruno, 'the big black
English guy', for he'd won twenty-one consecutive fights, all by knockout,
in his first two years of professional fighting. We were vaguely interested in
Frank, but more fascinated by stories coming out of America. Cus D'Amato
and his furious teenager, Mike Tyson, were already being spoken of in
smashed shebeen allegories of destruction and power. As we drank we
talked more about the few clippings we had collected of D'Amato's Catskills

clan than the news that, in May '84, Bruno had been stopped by James 'Bonecrusher' Smith. Like American fight fans, township boxing experts, 'fundies' as we called ourselves, knew that British heavyweights were never meant to be much good.

By the time I reached London, Bruno was on his first comeback trail and making me queasy with nostalgia. After his disastrous loss to Bonecrusher in the last round of a fight which he had dominated, Frank started over by squeezing some hapless saps picked specifically for that purpose. I had not been in Shepherd's Bush long when Bruno, born up the road in Hammersmith in the same year as me, began cracking heads like eggs again. On 25 September 1984, he scrambled a perennial loser called Ken Lakusta early in the second round and, six weeks later, fried another no-hoper, Jeff Jordan, in the third at the Albert Hall. The Frank Bruno show was back on the road – but I was bemused by the sight of his wheels being banged on once more.

The BBC were willing accomplices in the charade. They helped create the routine which became so tediously familiar. As soon as Frank had bowled over another victim he would lean over to greet Harry Carpenter. The venerable commentator clearly knew his way around boxing, having been at ringside nearly twenty years before when Henry Cooper twice fought Cassius Clay in London. Yet Carpenter was prepared to play the smiling straight man to Bruno's polite barrow-boy patter. They developed a slapstick routine as cuddly and predictable as any of the big lugs selected to fall at the size twelve feet of young Frank.

'You know what I mean, 'Arry?' was then on its way to being patented into every Bruno answer, becoming a slogan embedded as much into British society as boxing. Bruno, having been exposed between the ropes, was emerging more as a phenomenon of light entertainment than the ring. I was probably fucked up after twenty-three years of life in South Africa but, still, I squirmed whenever Frank an' Harry 'did the business'. My mind may have been diseased by the difference I saw when moving between the suburbs and the townships but, on the other side of the world, I felt the unease creeping back whenever I listened to the black boxer's and white commentator's chattering exchanges. The words they said to each other were banal enough, but I suspected all kinds of prejudice to be lurking beneath the amused white reaction to our Frank.

While affection and warmth were intended, subtle variations of condescension could be sensed in the descriptions of Bruno both in the pub and the tabloids. Frank was 'a right laugh' and 'Britain's favourite black man', he was 'a sunny sort' and 'a hugely impressive physical specimen'. His interaction with Carpenter did not readily counteract those chestnuts. The hammy dialogue played on their most basic differences in an effort to raise the easiest of chuckles. White Uncle Harry was bespectacled and mildly cerebral, portly and lightly plummy with his measured eloquence; Black

Frank was big and bumbling, shining with sweat and earnest endeavour, offering up his ''Arrys' and boxing metaphors with the purest Cockney and deepest of 'Ho-Ho-Ho!' chuckles.

I was hardly alone in questioning the way in which Bruno was consistently portrayed. For every roaring party of adoring 'Brooo-no, Brooo-no!' fans there would be at least one concerned liberal critic worrying away at the stereotype the boxer appeared to perpetuate every time he called out to Harry for approval. 'Where's 'Arry?' Bruno once famously asked as soon as he had registered another crushing victory.

Yet even when Carpenter retired, Bruno retained the soundbites and good cheer lapped up by interviewers from Des Lynam to Gaby Roslin. In those later years I saw Bruno show a reflection and intelligence away from the cameras which underlined the simplistic nature of my original perceptions. Bruno was not the media victim I had imagined. His own insight into his celebrity persona was bitingly acute. Slowly, I came to realise that Bruno was actually more in control of his image than either Eubank or Hamed – despite those fighters' respective attempts to depict themselves as erudite and legendary. Bruno was able to filter the side of himself which he felt best suited to both the ring and the coarsening demands of being a television personality. Unlike Chris and The Prince, Frank had few illusions and no pretensions; and out of that clarity, however crude it had once seemed, came a self-awareness missing from other boxers' more exaggerated ambitions.

But, eleven years before, I was less convinced. I knew then that British boxing had been dominated for years by a cartel, the same chain of men who had their shackles firmly fixed on Frank. The names were old and familiar, even to a South African like me. Mickey Duff. Mike Barrett. Terry Lawless. Jarvis Astaire. For a decade and more there'd been no choice for any British fighter who hoped to earn a living in the ring. Even if the rules of the game were unfair, and they could feel themselves choking on the accompanying cigar smoke, they were compelled to deal with the Duff syndicate.

Mickey Duff had been in boxing longer even than Don King, having learned his various tricks from the slanderous rivalry between Jack Solomons and Harry Levene who ran boxing in Britain in the 1950s and '60s. Mickey was masterful in his ability to manufacture a fighter out of nothing. Bruno, however, had something. Although never an instinctive fighter, he was big and strong. He had a hurtful jab and concussive force in both fists. Almost as significant, being a charming man, he could sell that easily marketable personality to Harry and the rest of us.

Duff had the BBC in his pocket, locked into a contract stating that they would only screen fights promoted by him. He, in turn, would stage any major Bruno fight at Wembley, where both the arena and stadium were controlled by Astaire. Together with Barrett, whom they ultimately ditched, and Lawless, who acted as manager and trainer, they worked long and hard on their lavish dream – creating Britain's first world heavyweight champion this century.

The Duff-Bruno plan first unfurled on 17 March 1982, when a twenty-year-old Frank made his professional debut at the Albert Hall. He knocked out his first 'body', known otherwise as Lupe Guerra, after two and a half minutes of round one. Thirteen days later he fought again at the Wembley Arena, a venue which would soon become a home full of old fighters and hopeless journeymen to him. On 30 March he set the Duff pattern in the kind of stone from which his body seemed sculpted. He upended the unheralded Harvey Steichan in one second less than the time it had taken him a fortnight before.

After the shocking setback against Bonecrusher Smith, Duff went back to his customarily safe matchmaking principles and produced seven straight mugs for Bruno to down. Don King delivered the WBA champion Tim Witherspoon to Wembley on 19 July 1986; and lifted that notorious million and more from his American fighter's purse after watching 'Terrible Tim' batter an exhausted Bruno to an eleventh-round TKO. Four fights and a couple of pantomime seasons later, Bruno was summoned in 1989 to Las Vegas where he failed to take the undisputed heavyweight crown from Tyson. Bruno lost on a fifth-round TKO. A further four fights in the next four years saw Bruno manoeuvred into yet another opportunity – and he troubled the WBC-holder Lennox Lewis in Cardiff until he succumbed once more to a TKO defeat, this time in round seven. It was the same old Frank, the same old story.

When required to separate a series of skittle-like opponents from their senses there was no better fighter than Bruno. He was as magnificently conditioned when thrashing a rusted Jesse Ferguson as he would be when facing The Boogie-Man's former sparring boss – Iron Mike himself. But as soon as he climbed up to championship level, the disparity in ability would eventually tell. Bruno was sufficiently forceful to hurt Smith, Witherspoon, Tyson and Lewis. But as soon as his stamina waned he left himself wide open to brutal attacks. He was too brave a man ever to take to the canvas. Instead, he would fall back against the ropes like a short-circuited robot and absorb blows on his defenceless chin until the referee halted the mechanical slaughter. They could not knock him out but, in the end, Bruno's conquerors unplugged his world-title fantasies.

After the loss to Lewis it had seemed inevitable that Bruno would retire – and yet soon afterwards he announced, on the front page of *The Sun* that he would fight on. His young daughters, he said, had begged him not to give up. Being a good father he could not disappoint them. His perpetual quest for a heavyweight title resumed with a string of bouts against 'credible opposition' – i.e. 'Boogie Man' Ferguson, Rodolfo Marin and the gargantuan Mike Evans. Between March 1994 and May 1995 that dismal trio lasted less than a combined total of nine minutes against Bruno. World-title try number four, against the WBC's Oliver McCall, had already been negotiated by Don King and Frank Warren when Evans was reduced to a mass of lard in a Glasgow ring.

Same old Frank, some sneered, same old story. Yet the sub-text had changed. Bruno had given up pantomime. He was a little meaner and dirtier between the ropes while, in the gym, he became the old bloodhound trying faithfully to master a couple of new tricks. Bruno had to learn the boxer's most reflex action of automatically clutching and holding when hurt. But they could only alter so much for Frank continued to shape his majestic physique into even more formidable chunks of bulge and ripple. Bruno remained the body-beautiful and doubt prevailed that such a muscle-bound frame was suited to twelve rounds of boxing where speed, fluidity and timing are often more important than sheer power.

The real shifts in the Bruno saga were political rather than fistic. Managed now by his wife, Laura, Bruno had politely parted from Mickey Duff. The once overwhelming Mickey had seen his hold on British boxing erode beneath the pressure of Frank Warren – a man who had travelled the most extreme of paths during the previous Bruno eras. After being the first promoter to succeed in loosening Duff's stranglehold when he struck a deal with ITV in the 1980s to rival Mickey's old-pals act with the BBC, Warren had since made and lost a fortune in between nearly dying after being shot by a 'mystery gunman'. The aspiring killer was initially thought to be Terry Marsh, but the disgruntled former boxer was acquitted later of all charges in court. While the identity of his most dangerous enemy stayed a secret, it became public knowledge that Warren had been made bankrupt and was being investigated by Companies House for his role as a director in numerous business transactions.

But Warren had moved in step with boxing in the mid-'90s. He had not lost his smart touch. With one inspirational gambit, he swept all his pieces onto Don King's side of the board. His association with DKP instantly assured Warren of his status as the most powerful player in boxing outside America. Frank and Laura Bruno knew what Warren, through King, could do for them. They castled the increasingly vulnerable Duff. Apart from the Don, Warren could also bring the Brunos an even more attractive television package than that offered by ITV, who had seen off the BBC with some wild spending.

ITV had lost Eubank to Sky but had emerged from their disappointment with the ratings-success of Benn-McClellan, Bruno's latest comeback and the Prince Naseem explosion. But when Hamed blitzed Enrique Angeles, he did so on Sky rather than ITV. Realising that Eubank could no longer produce the viewing figures they required, Sky had turned eagerly towards Warren and his trio of stars – Hamed, Benn and, now, Bruno, whom they believed might yet lead them to the biggest man of all, Mike Tyson. The sums of hard cash offered to Warren and his fighters were astronomical. While obviously beneficial to the star boxers' bank accounts, the Sky deal caused much misgiving – not least in our household where there was an outbreak of hand-wringing at the thought of paying out £21.50 a month to Rupert Murdoch for boxing and football matches which had once been ours for free. But, the suckers we are, we called up Videotron the day after the Warren sale was announced. Within a week, we had a snazzy green cable adding some colour to our front garden as it piped in yet more pictures of boxers hitting each other in the face. We were lost, and we knew it.

We also knew that the implications for all British boxers – from The Prince downwards – were enormous. If Duff, Barry Hearn and Frank Maloney could barely compete with the Sky-lined Warren, small promoters were fated. Any young fighter with a modicum of talent was drawn towards the lure of Warren's massive promotions where anything up to fifteen fights would be staged in a single night.

Sky's coverage of boxing was a distinct improvement on ITV's, and yet they could not obscure another truth. The cherished grassroots of the sport were being yanked out. If a fighter had not hooked up a deal with Warren and Sky after half a dozen professional bouts he could be considered a non-starter. The days of honing real craft in the ring were gone. Even the freakishly gifted Naz was certain to be affected. While his fame had grown steadily, his move to Sky inevitably slowed the process. Most of the nation, unlike the hardened addicts amongst us, had yet to shell out for the pleasure of 'going cable' or, worse still, hooking up a dish on the roof.

Eubank had regularly commanded audiences of 15,000,000 on ITV. In 1995 Sky were happy if they pulled in a quarter of those viewers. While the pro-boxing lobby always warned that the fight-game would go underground if legislation was introduced to curb its violence, it seemed that Sky had done more than the abolitionists in driving boxing off the mass-market screens. Without coverage on terrestrial television, ordinary boxing in Britain seemed on the verge of becoming an even more tangential and obscure activity. Increasingly, it appeared to all but the hard-core fan as if there were only four boxers left in this country – Chris Eubank, Nigel Benn, Naseem Hamed and, still the biggest of them all, Frank Bruno.

For Alison, being English, Frank Bruno was the most famous man in Britain. He was one of the very sweetest and nicest men alive. Even though she had more of a patriotic taste for it than me, I was happy to drive us to Wembley on the early Saturday evening of 2 September 1995. Beyond the fact that he once made me think of South Africa, I had never felt emotionally involved in Bruno's career before. But, as the fading sun spread long streaks across the road leading towards the stadium, I felt Alison's anticipation. We wanted Frank to win. We hoped it would be fourth time lucky.

On our first honeymoon night we had missed Oliver McCall's last fight; but Bruno hadn't. He had been at ringside at the MGM to see McCall scuffle past Holmes. Bruno was convinced he could beat the erratic WBC champion. I began to believe him during the extended build-up to their fight. Accompanied by his huge entourage, McCall seemed to spend as much time playing croquet on the lawns of his Hertfordshire hideaway as he did working in the gym. Boxing traditionalists were similarly horrified by the news that McCall was surrounded by his wife and children – although McCall dismissed speculation that he was being softened up by claiming that 'hell, me and my kids talk about me beating up Bruno all the time . . .'

McCall also introduced a darker undercurrent. He reiterated that Bruno had spurred on Benn during his destructive attacks on McClellan. 'This is a fight for vengeance for me, for my friend,' McCall promised. 'Gerald McClellan is a close friend of mine . . . and so I'm very happy that Mr Nigel Benn will be helping Bruno because I will try to take him out and try to do what he's done to my friend.'

The tabloids whipped themselves into their customary lather. 'I Will Turn Bruno Into A Vegetable' and 'Sick' headlines screamed across the back pages the following day. While tempted to fine McCall, the American's threat to jump on the next plane home if he had to pay 'as much as one penny' encouraged the British Boxing Board of Control to gloss over the bad feeling. John Morris, the Board secretary, made the dubious claim that McCall's words 'were open to misinterpretation and were misunderstood'.

There was no mistaking the jingoism at work during the overblown laser show which followed the fighters' departure from their dressing-rooms. Bruno and McCall walked down a slanting, hundred-foot tunnel of light. Postcard snaps of Britain and America were beamed above their heads in green laser. For Frank it was Big Ben, the Houses of Parliament, Churchill's 'V' for Victory sign and a massive bulldog as 'Land of Hope and Glory' resounded. Oliver McCall, his tearful face contorted with feeling, and a silver hair-haloed Don King were sent out to the ring with images of Marilyn Monroe, Abraham Lincoln, Elvis Presley and the Stars and Stripes shimmering to a booming 'Born in the USA'.

The fight itself was as predictable, if less sensational. For ten rounds Bruno ground down a leaden McCall with determination rather than skill. It was oddly uninvolving until the last six minutes when a fatigued and desperate Frank did what he had never done before – he clinched and grasped as McCall began to hurt him. When Bruno survived the last round we knew that, at last, he had his world heavyweight title.

Alison gave into the goosebumps and a glistening of her eyes as Naseem and Nigel danced around the exhausted Bruno. The fireworks exploded and, yes, again, 'Land of Hope and Glory' reverberated. Eleven years and one month on, Johannesburg and Soweto and even that tiny Shepherd's

Bush bedsit seemed far away. I thought again of all the people I had left behind, especially my township boxing connoisseurs who would have been as stirred as we were to hear Frank Bruno crying at ringside. He remembered all those who'd ever questioned his 'whitened' relationship with promoters, BBC television commentators and a *Sun*-waving army of fans.

'It was tough in there,' he cried, the tears rolling from his swollen eyes, 'but I love my brother, I'm not an Uncle Tom, I love my people, I'm not a sell-out, I'm not an Uncle Tom . . .'

The Sun stripped back the poignance. 'Arise Sir Frank!' they crowed on their front page the Monday morning after the fight. Below their banner headline they splashed a large photograph of Bruno dressed in a white suit and dark glasses. His lips looked sore and bloated. He attempted a half-smile while holding the '*Sun* Knighthood' plaque. It was impossible to know what he was thinking for his eyes were covered by the heavy shades. My guess was that he had Iron Mike and many more millions in mind – for Don King and Frank Warren had already agreed that Bruno's first defence would be against Tyson at the MGM in March 1996. That gave Bruno six sweet months to savour his world-champion status.

Chris Eubank, meanwhile, had six hard days left. On the following Saturday night, 9 September, he would discover if he still had the strength to hold onto the good life he so revered. Before a crowd of 25,000 at the Pairc ua Ciamh football stadium in County Cork, Eubank would again cross uncertain terrain. Steve Collins, with his renewed hypnotic talk, was still weaving spells across Eubank's clouded mind.

'If you want to lose your life,' Eubank warned Collins, 'if you want to cheat by using schoolboy tactics, it's down to you. I'll have no remorse. If Collins chooses to go under hypnosis and doesn't wake up that's down to him. His family should not look at me. I'm doing a job. If he wants to mess around with his basic instincts, the buck finishes with him – not me. I'm knocking him out. I intend putting him to sleep for ten seconds in a concise, clinical way. There will be no boxing match as such, no contest. I will not hold back.'

The Boxing Board of Control did not restrain themselves either as they slapped an immediate £5,000 fine on Eubank for his 'unsavoury comments'. It was a small burden to add to his expanding list of financial quandaries. Keith Miles, his former manager in the late '80s, had instigated a £5,000,000 lawsuit against Eubank, alleging that the boxer had honoured only eighteen months of their four-year contract. Miles claimed that Eubank had made £15,000,000 out of boxing and that, as his contracted manager, he was due a third of that figure. The Inland Revenue had also taken note of Eubank's career earnings and extended a more serious threat over the fighter's future. Eubank admitted that he owed 'a huge amount', a sum which would ruin him if he did not carry on fighting.

Eubank's fine talk about breaking the mould by getting out early with his massive savings intact looked distinctly grubby. At the height of his career even his most casual spending was breathlessly reckless. He would think nothing of spending £200,000 on an Aston Martin or flying to New York on Concorde for an afternoon's worth of shopping at Sachs on Fifth Avenue. Eubank's Concorde bill had risen to £29,000 a year. He also felt able to rent a permanent suite at the Grosvenor House Hotel, across the road from Hyde Park. For hosting his occasional jaunts to London the boxer paid the hotel an annual fee of £40,000. He was also happy to declare that he spent £90 on each set of his Versace underpants. Knowing him to be a fastidious man, I imagined that he changed his underwear sufficiently often to rival even Tyson as one of Versace's favourite clients.

It was all good knockabout stuff and helped keep Eubank's name in print even as his taste for boxing soured. Unfortunately for him, Eubank forgot to put away even a fraction of his ring revenue for the sad day when the tax man came knocking. 'My parents were not accountants,' he said despondently when it was revealed that, early in 1995, he was struggling to cough up the £2.2 million he owed in back-taxes. When asked why he had not set aside at least a percentage of his vast payments for the irresistible Collector, Eubank looked hurt. 'I'm not versed in these matters . . .' he murmured.

Yet sympathy for Eubank was curdled by his enduring contempt for other boxers. After losing his WBO title and unbeaten record to Collins he had shown some grace even when coating himself in Kipling: 'Here I am, a mortal man at last . . .' But he quickly reverted to type and began to ridicule Collins for his 'legalised cheating'; and when he returned to the ring he selected the most miserable opposition he could find. He earned £700,000 for first-round victories against the unknown Bruno Godoy and the even more woeful Jose Ignacio Barruetabena who was knocked out in fifty-five seconds.

Eubank was capable of great lucidity when jeering at boxing as a 'blood-sport'. And yet he seemed bent on finding himself the most helpless of opponents, men who were so pitifully equipped to defend themselves that any sense of danger they presented was directed only towards their own health. Eubank defended his choice of bloody pickings as sound business sense even though we already knew that he was not particularly 'versed' in such matters.

Instead of boosting his reputation, Eubank's scandalous opposition diminished his standing. Although he had done more than anyone, even Frank Bruno, in bringing boxing within the posing pages of the Sunday colour supplements and the grinning chatshow circuit, Eubank had since become a weary joke. His jaded punch-lines had been heard a dozen times too often. Everyone knew about the monocle and the jodhpurs, the reliance on 'in accordance with' catchphrases and floundering philosophical waffle. As both a fighter and a novelty celebrity, Eubank's time was slipping away.

But the man who still paraded and primped to 'Simply the Best' seemed oblivious to that maudlin truth. I both laughed and sighed for his sake when I heard the story of how, one sunny morning, Eubank took to the streets of Brighton for his hated stretch of roadwork. He ran along the main promenade and was heartened to see that a large crowd had gathered at the roadside. They began to cheer and applaud and he accepted their plaudits with the resigned sang-froid of an old royal waving to the excited plebs. He kept running, his feet moving faster and faster beneath him as he absorbed their adulation, too preoccupied with his own fame to notice that people had turned out instead to watch the Tour de France reach Britain for the first time in history. As the gleaming cyclists hissed by on the opposite side of the seafront, acclaimed by the watching crowd, Chris Eubank jogged on. The crowd ignored him but he was happy, surprised at such a good turnout for one of his low-key training runs. He was on his way to being a champion again.

To make the money he required to 'maintain my excellent lifestyle', Eubank needed to beat Steve Collins in their WBO title return and then go on to face Nigel Benn for a third time. Collins had defected from Barry Hearn to the ever-expanding Warren camp where Benn was also ensconced. Neither Warren nor Don King were willing to work with Hearn. Faced with such a limited choice, Eubank made another of his 'strictly business' decisions. He cut all promotional ties with Hearn and declared himself self-managed and willing to work with any other promoter who could make him a last few big cash fights. Unsurprisingly, Frank Warren won the bid to stage Collins-Eubank II which meant that the Irishman would receive his first million-pound purse while the hard-pressed Eubank had to settle for a mere £400,000.

After he had flattened Barruetabena in Whitley Bay on 29 July, Eubank gave voice to his delusions, promising that he would soon be back in the hot money seat. 'Collins, you're getting knocked out,' he mouthed grandly into the Sky camera. 'Benn, you're getting knocked out. James Toney, come down from light-heavyweight, you've insulted my mother once too often . . .'

Although we perked up at the mention of our shy American pal, Toney, it said much for our gathering disinterest in Chris Eubank that there was no grinding of pearly gnashers when we realised we would miss his crucial rematch with Collins. I accepted it as a radiant sign that we would yet get out of this blurry boxing maze with our sanity restored.

While Eubank and Collins fought in Ireland, we partied hard in Poland. At our friends' wedding, we hurled down the vodka before offering up the conga as a British contribution to the more evocative Polish songs and handkerchief-wielding folk-dancing instigated by the bride's family. Alison even forgot the fight; but I knew that I was not the only boxing fan amongst the contingent of male guests from London. We slunk back to the tables to ponder the outcome of Collins-Eubank as our English girls danced round the Poles.

According to our watches they would be just about ready to approach the ring, with Eubank having to stroll there first in his unaccustomed role of challenger. We snorted at the news that Eubank was so determined to win that he had even introduced something he called the 'power-strut' into his road routine in Brighton. He must have wondered where all his followers had gone as he power-strutted along the cycle-less promenade. 'What a dickhead,' we said, 'what a guy!'

Suddenly, the idea of watching Eubank win back his world championship fight in Ireland while we were at a wedding in Krakow seemed an agreeably surreal way to spend a Saturday night. We spoke enthusiastically about going in search of a Sky-carrying satellite, thinking that no one would miss us for an hour or so. Besides, I'd seen every one of Eubank's previous twenty title fights either live on TV or at ringside. Why break the habit in Krakow? If his career was to end that night I wanted to see his final act as it happened.

Our plan festered as the band cranked up the beat. Eubank or Collins, Collins or Eubank, the words to a Polish love-song seemed to run as the liquor hummed through my head.

Yet the minutes slipped by into hours. We rocked on in our wedding chairs. It no longer mattered who won. On a summer night in Krakow, as the music flowed on, the supposed importance of Chris Eubank beating Steve Collins was impossible to sustain.

Twenty-four hours later, we sat shattered on our sofa. The video whirred slowly as we watched an even more haggard Chris Eubank slump down on his small wooden stool. It was the end of the eleventh round and he looked distressed. Even through our half-shut eyes we could tell that the commentators were right. Steve Collins had too much for him. From the moment he came rushing out at the start with his head down and his arms pumping furiously, the champion had been relentless. Eubank was bewildered and beaten.

'You've got to knock him out, Chris,' Ronnie Davis said quietly to Eubank. He did not slap his fighter in the face as he had done so often in the past, he did not swear at Eubank and ask him what the fuck he was doing fucking around like a prat. Ronnie knew that the end was coming. They needed a miracle. 'You've got to knock him out if you're gonna win this one,' he said again.

'I'm trying,' Chris said earnestly, 'but he's been coming all night . . .'

There was a plaintive tone in his voice, as if even he knew the inevitable. He was going to lose again, for a second time. The mystique was broken, the Chris Eubank phenomenon was about to close.

'He's been coming all night,' Eubank repeated in mournful disbelief.

It would not have been Eubank, however, if there had not been one last twist at the bell. A split-decision was announced to an incredulous and baying crowd.

The first judge's scorecard was read out in Eubank's favour. By then I was wide-awake, bug-eyed at the prospect of the most outrageous example yet of Eubank larceny. If nothing else, he kept us guessing to the very end.

But, soon, it was truly over. Collins had won on the two remaining scorecards. Eubank turned away in subdued despair, brushing aside the hand of the man who had just beaten him again. It was finished and he knew it. It was his time to be alone; not only a mortal, but a humbled man at last.

In the end boxing was cruel to everyone – even Chris Eubank.

At twenty-one, eight years younger than Eubank, and still unbeaten, yet to be threatened, Naseem Hamed imagined life would always be easy. He believed he was a divine choice, destined to live only for greatness. Pain belonged to men like Steve Robinson, the fighter Naz would meet in his first world-title fight three weeks after Eubank had lost his last.

They called Robinson 'The Cinderella Man'. It was easy to see why. You only needed to look at his serious face or into his sad brown eyes to know that he was a man to Naseem's boy. He had loved and ached, he had been defeated, more than once, both between and beyond the ropes. Steve Robinson had a family, he'd had a menial job before he made it in boxing. He had suffered and struggled; but he was tough and honest and had done better than anyone might ever have dreamed. His was one of those stories I repeated to myself when thinking about all boxing had done to Michael Watson, Bradley Stone, Gerald McClellan and Jimmy Garcia.

On 15 April 1993 Robinson had been on the dole again, a twenty-three-year-old black Welshman from Ely in Cardiff. Only weeks before, in a final effort to turn himself into a decent professional boxer, he had given up his £52-a-week job as a packer in Debenham's Cardiff warehouse. Until then his record in the ring had not been one to fortify faith in his future. Thirteen wins, nine losses and one draw.

Robinson appeared to be a younger version of Chris Eubank's journeymen brothers. He had boxed all around the country, and abroad, against more experienced and favoured 'house' fighters whose shining résumés were always in need of another win. Of his nine defeats, Robinson thought he had won more than half but the judges, swayed by the home crowd or the bigger name, invariably gave the decision to the other guy.

Yet, as is the way with boxing, his luck suddenly turned with the misery of another fighter. Early on that Thursday afternoon in April, at his mother-in-law's house, Robinson pondered his problems over a now legendary plate of pie and chips. The phone rang. It was a call for him, for he was too poor to have a telephone in his own home. The news was thrilling and terrifying.

Ruben Palacio, the WBO featherweight champion from Colombia, had been tested at a medical in the north-east of England and found to be HIV-positive. He was the first world champion to be diagnosed as a carrier of the virus. Before fight-insiders could react fully to the implications of AIDS infiltrating a bloody business like boxing, there was a substitute to be found. An ITV slot had to be filled and the WBO had a sanctioning fee to collect. Palacio was stripped of his title and sent back to Colombia on the earliest possible plane. His challenger, John Davison, and an emergency opponent would contest the vacant championship.

The fight was just over forty-eight hours away and would be held in front of Davison's vociferous fans in Washington, Tyne and Wear. Davison had been preparing for months and Robinson hesitated at the thought of entering the ring the night after next. But Ronnie Rush, his Trinidadian trainer, was insistent. They had to take the fight, it was the hope they had not even dared express.

And, being a quiet and thoughtful fighter, Robinson listened and eventually nodded. 'Okay,' he said, 'let's do it . . .'

Steve Robinson, the Cinderella Man, did it. He won a split decision against the local star and became a world champion. His purse that night was £12,000. By his second defence, against the highly touted Colin McMillan, he was earning £250,000 a fight. Robinson was a voracious champion, driven by hunger and resentment. Because of his 'Cinderella' start in boxing and the nine blemishes before, Robinson never received the plaudits he felt he was due. The London critics travelled to Cardiff expecting that, every time, he would be shocked out of his good fortune and returned to the weary infantry from where he came.

But Robinson defended his title emphatically on seven occasions – most notably against the stylish English trio of former world champions, McMillan, Paul Hodkinson and Duke McKenzie, all of whom were tipped to have too much class for the Welshman.

'I should have the respect by now,' he said softly when I spoke to him. 'I'm probably the best featherweight in the world right now. My achievements as champion should be judged – not my early career. Records only tell you so much. But it's always been this way with me. The win over Davison was called a fluke. McMillan was supposed to be some kind of Sugar Ray Leonard and yet when I beat him they questioned it. They said he had an old shoulder injury. Hodkinson was the guy they said would strip me. He was a great fighter, too much for a journeyman from Cardiff. When I knocked out Hodkinson they said it was because he hadn't fought for a while. Even when I win, I can't really win respect. They prefer a guy like Frank Bruno. He's more their style, living in London, going on the telly, a big funny guy doing the pantomimes and stuff. That ain't my style. So where's the story for these reporters, where's the flash they need? Maybe that's why the national press are waiting for me to get beat. But, boy, they been waiting a long time. Now these same people think that Naseem is their saviour. But tell me. Who has he beaten? I don't see Colin McMillan, Paul Hodkinson or Duke McKenzie on his record. But they just go on thinking he's the man. Man, how do I get that respect?'

The trouble for Robinson remained that he was more artisan than artist. His success depended on graft rather than craft. But for his tenacity, he was just another ordinary bloke; a worker rather than a genius, a Cinderella Man to The Prince.

To the paymasters in the Sky executive suites, there was no doubt as to which fighter held the most public appeal. Even though Robinson was the world champion about to defend his title for the eighth consecutive time before an adoring crowd in Cardiff, the London advertising men knew how to spin the sales coin while hyping the contest. 'See The Prince Become King' they promised.

It appeared from the start as if the men who always matter most in boxing, the money-men, were determined that Naseem should get his way. Although he had never fought before at the nine-stone limit, the WBO installed Hamed as their number-one featherweight contender. They also insisted, no doubt with half an eye on the hefty sanctioning commission such a fight would make them in Britain, that Hamed would be Robinson's mandatory challenger. They gave the champion sixty days to fight Hamed – a tactic which slotted perfectly into Frank Warren's agenda for The Prince.

While Robinson wanted the fight he felt that, as the holder, he should have been the one to dictate its timing and purse negotiation. He would have preferred to have put back a struggle with Hamed for at least another year, to strengthen his stake in a million-pound skirmish. But, against the combined onslaught of Sky, the WBO and Warren, he was left helpless. In the meantime he did battle in court with his former promoter, Barry Hearn, whom he had left for Warren. Having also lost Eubank and Collins to his rival, Hearn concentrated on salvaging some of his heavy losses from Robinson. He wanted £150,000, a sum which could not easily be tossed aside by the Cardiff fighter.

Once, he had thought he was a Warren favourite. He'd since seen that, in the promoter's eyes, he could never compare to Hamed. Robinson was not a stupid man. He knew how much he risked by facing Hamed. But he ended up signing a contract which he felt was worth less than 50 per cent of what he deserved. What could he do? As they kept telling him, he had no choice.

I liked Steve Robinson but I was no different to the rest of them. Instead of travelling to his unglamorous gym in Cwmcarn, just outside Newport, I took the easier trip to Yorkshire. I turned away from the Cinderella Man and back to the little Prince.

At four-thirty on a balmy Tuesday afternoon in Sheffield they had just hung the brightly coloured bags. He walked through the door. I was surprised to see how small he looked in his plain white vest, blue boxing trunks and new trainers which squeaked every time he took a step.

He flexed his neck and shoulders in his best miniature Tyson impression as they cranked up the drum and bass on the gym's sound-system. He began to shadow-box. It was hot and he did not spare himself. Sweat speckled his forehead and ran down the back of his thin neck as he moved up and down half the length of the gym – pumping his arms aggressively as he walked forward and then glided backwards, boxing on the retreat. Lost in a dusky fight world of his own, he grunted and hissed as he fought. He spat out salty insults like 'chicken' or 'sucker' while peppering his imaginary opponent with spicy jabs.

Then he did something curious. He threw his short arms in the air and stuck out his tongue while shuffling his feet with blurring speed. I was mightily impressed – surely this was Ali taunting Foreman in '74 or Sugar Ray Leonard mocking Duran to the point of '*No mas*'? Finally, he dropped down onto his haunches for a breather. He looked over at me with a grin.

'Who you fighting?' I asked.

'Well . . . you know . . .' he blushed. 'I been fighting that Belcastro feller again . . .' he mumbled in a broad Yorkie-ragamuffin accent.

He couldn't have been more than ten. His white and veiny skin had turned pink in the broiling gym. 'So that means you must be . . .' I started to say.

'Yeah, I'm Naz today.'

'I should've guessed,' I said.

'You waitin' for him? You waitin' for Naz?' the boy asked breathlessly.

I nodded.

'Naz's always late . . . he's The Prince, y'know . . . an' Brendan's gone to Ireland today so who knows when he'll show up. Anyways, pal, watch this!'

I watched my small friend relive Naseem Hamed's finest performance in the ring, his heckling dismantling of Vincenzo Belcastro eighteen months before. The tiny boy said 'take it, baby, take it!' and 'pow-pow-pow'. He sounded like a small-fry John Woo as he ignited his piston-like punches. He swivelled his hips and sniggered, rolling back like a limbo-dancing stripper. Bending from the waist so that his head stretched towards the painted yellow lines on the floor, he stuck his right glove out. He looked me dead in the eye and leaned further back, moving his hand back and forth in the crude wanking gesture Naz sometimes flashed just before he knocked out his opponent. I felt my age then, shocked by his saucy cheek.

When Alison did her Naseem impression I thought it was gracefully humorous, a jesting acknowledgement that we'd never end up in big-time boxing or showbusiness, that we could never shake our stuff in public like the shameless Prince. But watching the boy I realised how much she censored. He was a far more thorough copyist. He left nothing out. When he was not sliding his hand back and forth to the side he was rotating his pelvis, jabbing it in and out, sighing 'oooo, so good, I am the man, I am so great, you know it!' like he knew what he was talking about. I looked away, turning over that 'Kids these days!' shock-horror headline in my dazed head.

'Bam-bam-bam-bam, cha-cha-cha,' the kid cried. 'Hey, feller!'

I looked over at him quizzically.

'Bam-bam-bam-bam, cha-cha-cha, bam-bam-bam-bam!' he shouted in his high voice as he blasted and scythed blows through the muggy heat. He had reverted to full fighting mode, pouring the punches in, making the air shimmer with his combinations, an entranced glance shifting between his feet and me in the corner, as if I was Brendan and he was Naseem. 'Wha'cher think then?' he asked.

'Brilliant,' I said truthfully.

Again, he reddened slightly. 'Brilliant? Really?'

'Definitely.'

'You a reporter then?' he said, perhaps imagining a colour feature on his agreed lustre.

'Not really . . .' I deadpanned.

'Well, I know Naz if you wanna meet him,' the boy murmured proudly.

'What do you think of him?' I wondered.

'Brilliant,' he repeated as he stared down at his own gloves.

'Is he training today?' I asked my skinny expert.

'Dunno, I ain't seen him for a while. They say he's training at night, y'know, like at midnight an' stuff. Does he know you're here, pal?'

'No,' I admitted. 'I thought I'd just turn up.'

'I dunno if he's gonna show then. Maybe he's in London.'

'Maybe,' I said.

'Hey, it's okay! Stick around anyways. You might learn something, pal.'

My cheery chum skipped away towards the green canvas ring at the top of the gym. Although Brendan Ingle and Naz were both away, the usual procedure had begun. They wanted to fight here, all of them, they always wanted to fight. An unknown older man ordered the oddly varied collection of boxers into the ring. Apart from my Naz-impressionist, there were a couple of other small boys and a few men in their late twenties, guys who worked out in the ring to help keep the V in the shape of their bodies when they were not earning a living as bouncers or security guards. In between those opposites, some of Ingle's young professional fighters ambled across the crowded canvas. Used to mass-sparring sessions, they were accessible rather than patronising towards those sharing their space.

Ten of them moved around the ring, kids trying to hit the weaving men, amateurs working with the pros in a cramped loop of fighting. It looked like chaos at first, a bizarre mutation of the lonely toil I had seen from Mike Tyson and Roy Jones in America. Hamed had told me that he still sparred with the rest of the Ingle camp, that he had always done it Brendan's way. He worked with heavyweights and flyweights, he hurt the big men to the body and ghosted away from the fast lunges of the lightest boys, showing a power and speed which we knew Robinson would never be able to match.

The Welsh champion prepared for Hamed by also boxing fighters of varying weights. But I doubted if any of them would have quite the force or quickness of Hamed. Robinson had decided further to train with both southpaws and orthodox boxers. But he would not have been able to switch them as often as Hamed could flit between the two styles. I thought there was nothing the Cinderella Man could do to ready himself completely for the flaring madness, the magical aptitude Hamed had for the square ring. He was going to be punished while he lost, for Hamed had the most incredible compound of fists and feet, of leverage and evasion. Beneath the garish complexity, Hamed had swallowed whole the most simple pretext of boxing. Hit and avoid being hit yourself. Everything he did between the ropes centred on that most basic but outrageous ambition. Hit hard and avoid being hit back. It looked easy when he did it.

High on the wall behind the ring I saw the familiar sign: 'Boxing Can Seriously Damage Your Health.' The fighters boxed on, preoccupied instead with their sparring. They were joshing and working, proving that, at least to them, boxing could be fun. If Brendan was their master then The Prince was their guide. I watched my tiny pal almost wag his tail in delight as he circled and barked like he'd been born to this yard. A black bouncer stepped towards him to tap him on the shoulder with a bunched glove. The mini-Naz ducked under it and came out grinning on the other side to pop a fizzy left into an exposed solar plexus. The black guy mixed a laugh into his muffled groan. The little chap waved his arms in the air and winked at me – as if he already knew what Naz would do to Robinson.

As the call came for them to switch partners I turned to leave the gym. 'Bye, feller!' the boy said as he faced up to a wiry welterweight. 'See ya, pal,' he chimed as he began to dance, his eyes on the other fighter's feet, 'see ya!'

Outside, I looked at the church opposite and then back at the grubby St Thomas Boys Club, which had once been the vicarage's village school. For years there had been the same old National Front slogan daubed on the garage wall adjoining the gym. No one cared. The white, black, Asian and Arab boys didn't give a fuck about the NF or even about the hand which had crossed out the 'Boys' in 'St Thomas Boys Club' and inked in 'Queers' instead. They lived for boxing inside those peeling walls, beneath the thick steel girders from where those tinted bags hung.

Wincobank was a rough neighbourhood, short of either riches or enchantment. It did not look like the easiest place in which to grow up in England. A trio of thin and dirty-faced kids lounged on the corner across the street, sharing a fag. They were probably a year older than the boy boxing inside. They stared at me blankly until one of them began to jerk his hand at me in that sneering memoir to masturbation. I was probably as old as the three of them put together but, still, their hostility bothered me. I pined for my chatty pal inside but knew that it was time to press on.

I passed the sullen children, ignoring the boldest of them as he flicked the cigarette stub in my path. They watched me in silence as if to welcome me to Wincobank, or Wancobank as they probably would've mouthed at me if I'd faced them. Naseem Hamed knew boys like them when he was still at school, boys who might've leered 'Paki, Paki, Paki, dirty Paki bastard', at him until they learned that he could fight better than anyone else. Although he was insistent in stressing his Arabic heritage, he was more ambiguous when distancing himself from the young Pakistanis and Indians he remembered from his past classrooms.

'I'm not Asian,' he'd said to me, 'so it's an insult when people don't see me as an Arab fighter. My family are from the Yemen, we're Arabic people. We ain't Asians, man! My roots are in Arab culture but I'm British-born and bred. Listen to my accent. It's Sheffield through and through. I'm proud of it. I got the best of both. British and Arab – so I always looked down on those people who just said "Paki, Paki," at me. They know nothing about my culture, my people. They should listen to me talk, I ain't got no Pakistan accent.'

He probably did not mean any offence, but Naz's limited political subtlety did not even stretch to his sexuality-and-celebrity discourse. 'Don't get me wrong,' he told *The Sun* as he prepared to fight Steve Robinson, 'I love girls. But there are problems with being a household name. Being twenty-one is hard. You have to keep women at arm's length. Basically you don't want to fall into the same trap as Mike Tyson. But come on. Are you really expected to believe that girl went to his bedroom at two in the morning because she wanted to get a picture of Tyson for her dad? If she had come to my hotel bedroom at two in the morning, well – but th/ am a bit more on the ball. I have my head screwed on. No girl will ev/ me off or pull any strokes. Women are so devious it's untrue . . .'

We sighed, Alison and I, and stepped back from The Prince. H/ a breathtaking mastery in the ring, but I was tired of the mouthy/ as I walked the three-hundred-yard hill to the corner-shop ab/ lived with his parents, I felt weary of stepping through th/ stood outside the plain shop and the Hamed home I was/ Alfa-Romeo and Wrangler Jeep which Frank Warren h/ were both gone. I guessed The Prince was away, probab/

on a new suit, or driving around the posh part of Sheffield looking at Trevor Francis's 'mansion' which he was planning to buy as soon as he'd whipped Robinson.

Naseem Hamed was lost in conceit, even more than his most famous contemporaries – De La Hoya, Eubank, Jones, Toney and Tyson. I no longer needed to hear him say again that he was 'extraordinary, a legend in the making, a millionaire at twenty-one, about to make another forty big ones, a Yorkie Arab babe-magnet, a Prince about to become King . . .' We'd heard it all before and, sometimes, a hundred times is enough, even if the words are more true than not.

On my way home again, I smiled at the scowling young boys Naz had left behind in Wincobank. They eyed me warily, saying nothing. The disquiet I'd felt when first seeing them had gone. I wondered what would happen to them in the years to come. Unlike the Naz fan in St Thomas they did not seem to have much hope left, even after only ten or eleven years of life. They looked to be weighed down by trouble. For all their frazzling precociousness, at least Naseem and his pal had found a way through despair. They had discovered themselves in boxing.

It seemed more than a year since Naseem Hamed had driven me around these same streets, waving to the lost boys who hailed him from the roadside. When I reached the bottom of the hill and the end of the road leading away from St Thomas's, I thought of the curious words Brendan Ingle had said of The Prince only a few weeks before. 'If he doesn't go mad, he'll go all the way . . .'

Hamed had no doubts about his own sanity. 'When I win the title,' he said, 'I won't go berserk. I have the speech ready . . .'

30 September 1995

'Hamed, Hamed, who the fuck is Hamed?'

Alison and I shivered as the rain began to fall. All around us people were standing on their £100 seats, eyes blazing in the dark, mouths painted red if they were women and coated in beer if they were men. They were excited as they shouted, banging their boots on the plastic chairs in time with the angry chant, as if they were at war with some threatening Ayatollah from the East.

'Hamed, Hamed, who the fuck is Hamed?'

They spat out the 'Hamed' with seeming bitterness, although they might just have been trying to impress each other with the loudness of their voices. But when more than three-quarters of a packed 16,000 crowd at Cardiff Arms Park screamed the same word with the same mock religious frenzy, it was hard not to assume a disgust in every disgusted *'Hamed, Hamed'*, to think every grating *'who the fuck is Hamed?'* query was bound up in hatred of his perceived foreignness, his difference from a white Welsh crowd.

Steve Robinson was black but he was Welsh. Even if he'd been from Sheffield it would have been difficult for them to conjure a similar malevolence from a name like Robinson, from a yodelling 'Robinson, Robinson, who the fuck is Robinson?' song.

But The Prince was not the most sensitive fighter in the world. I guessed that the spit and spleen showering down on him would roll off the backs of his leopard-skin clad entourage. He was surrounded by them and so free to dance to his extended hard-stepping Jungle ditty. He didn't need to answer to anyone. He knew he was The Prince. He was cool, he was relaxed even as he somersaulted over the ropes. He had been living this moment in his head for years. He looked like he had reached home as soon as his feet hit the canvas.

Steve Robinson appeared less comfortable. A protracted fanfare wasn't his style but he was too sweet a man not to go through the bluster he knew everyone else wanted. He seemed vaguely embarrassed having to step out of the smoke made by a roaring laser-etched Welsh dragon before following the lead of a goat called Jenkins. The goat was the mascot of the Royal Regiment of Wales and, being a patriotic sort of guy, Robinson accepted Jenkins as a sacrifice he could put up with if it pleased his more nationalistic followers. But he seemed happier when listening to Bob Marley hymning him towards the ring – although 'Natural Mystic' sounded a more appropriate description of Naseem.

For the first round alone, Robinson managed to quell at least some of Hamed's innate mysticism. He blocked most of the shorter man's punches behind a high guard held so tight in front of his face that it might as well have been pinned together by a bolt. Hamed couldn't get through, his blows bouncing against the shiny yellow gloves of Robinson.

Twenty feet away we had a strategic duel of our own to somehow see through the massed ranks of hysterical fans standing in the few rows ahead. The cheaper seats creaked even more indignantly. 'Who the fuck is Hamed?' had given way to increasingly desperate and no more charming shouts of 'Fucking sit down, you wankers!'. But the draw of the fight was too much. They stayed standing in front, threatening a riot behind.

A more scientific ruckus unfolded inside the ring as, from the start of round two, Hamed began to dismantle the courageous champion. He stood square on, taunting Robinson with his arms slung low and his chin poking out invitingly. Although he was tagged by a single left he just laughed and unloaded a burst of his own, topped by a right uppercut which made Robinson shudder. As the drizzle continued the steam rose from the fighters' bodies. In the third and the fourth Hamed swayed out of reach with infuriating ease, snapping back to land blows from a bamboozling set of angles. One uppercut began from just above the ankle while lefts slanted down even as he veered away to the right.

By the start of the fifth Hamed had thrown 298 punches to Robinson's measly 92. But as soon as he tried to open up, Robinson would be forced back into his crab-like scuttle. Hamed hurt him as much with speed and accuracy as power. Robinson's face had begun to mark and distend by the time Hamed hit him with four mean blows to the head. A ringing left-right-left combination was followed by another unanswerable right uppercut which dropped the Welshman for only the second time in his long career. Robinson whimpered inside and Hamed heard it. The Prince was set to mete out the gruesome fullness of his promise.

Throughout the long beating, Hamed mugged and mocked as if he was Muhammad Ali and Robinson just another bum who'd never be Sugar Ray. He talked to the silent champ all the while, saying, 'Who's stronger now, Steve?', goading Robinson to fight back furiously so that Hamed could chop him down again. Blood seeped from Robinson but he refused to give in to the cruelty. Hamed made him miss repeatedly with laughable scorn in the seventh before, mercifully, it ended with an astonishing jolt in the next round.

The left hook was so quick that it took a couple of seconds for the full impact to filter down the length of Robinson's wiry body. By the time his feet were whipped from under him by the slippery force of the blow it looked as if all the breath had been taken from his body. He was so badly shaken that the referee did not even bother to count. He waved the fight over to the fury of the crowd. They had not seen the speed of the punch. They thought that Robinson had slipped. But the fighter knew better as he limped back to his corner. He had almost been cut in half by a single hook.

Robinson's tears were of frustration and pain. They smeared the blood across his face. Even Naseem was moved by the champion's fall. He would not let Brendan Ingle halt the flow of his praise as he held Robinson close. Brendan tried to remove the gumshield from his mouth but Naz shook his head. 'You boxed great,' he said in an effort to comfort Robinson, 'you were strong, man . . .'

Brendan joined in the chorus: 'Steve!' he said, 'you deserve everybody's recognition – yes!' But Robinson was inconsolable. His head stayed bowed in defeat. He remembered what it felt like to lose – but he had never been beaten so badly.

Naseem Hamed had already turned away to look for a mirror in the Sky replays on a rain-splattered TV monitor. As he'd predicted, he did not go berserk as the Sky announcer congratulated him. He was ready to deliver his world-champion speech.

'I was too strong, too fast, too good,' he sighed in homage to himself. 'As you know, tonight's the thirtieth, and I've become King. But I'm not changing my name yet. I remain Prince!'

Thirteen days later, on Friday the thirteenth, two more Cinderella Men returned to the ring. Drew Docherty and James Murray were not the kind of fighters who would ever have dreamed of speaking about themselves as royalty. They were linked to The Prince in the same way that all small men fighting in Britain were forced to look at Naseem Hamed and know that he had everything they would love. Docherty, the British bantamweight champion, was closer than most – the year before he'd been mentioned as a prospective rival for Hamed. He was held up as the kind of rugged pro who would test a flashy kid to the limits of his ability.

In the wake of Steve Robinson's startling destruction, I was surprised to see how gaunt Docherty appeared on screen in contrast to my fresh memories of Hamed's compact power. Where Docherty and his opponent for the night, Jim Murray, conformed to type, being painfully wiry and bony-faced, Hamed had the thick legs and strong upper body of a middleweight. By moving up to featherweight to win his first WBO title, Hamed had put two divisions between himself and the Scottish boxers about to contest the British bantamweight title. Docherty and Murray were angular streaks compared to Hamed's solid muscle.

It began with me flicking back and forth between channels, from the end of *Have I Got News For You* to the start of *Roseanne*, using the adverts to slide over to Sky to take in the introductions of Docherty and Murray. I was more excited about explaining the grisly irony of the fight's setting than in telling Alison much about either boxer. I knew a little of Docherty but less of Murray for he was just one of the many names tucked away on the inside pages of *Boxing News*. I was more familiar with the faintly grotesque 'boxing and black-tie dinner' promotion. Four hundred guests had paid between £50 and £80 for a four-course meal and four fights.

I had once been asked to attend one of these events, and had been disturbed by the clinking of expensive glasses and the tinkling of knives and forks playing an eerie soundtrack to the sight of two men punching each other. Although I rarely made any noise myself at fights, I was disturbed by the silence during the boxing and the polite applause at the end of every round. I never went to another, for the civility only made boxing appear more savage.

The Docherty-Murray promotion, however, was different. Terrace chants swelled towards ringside from the back of a ballroom in Glasgow's Hospitality Inn. For £30 'Boxing Only' tickets, three hundred fans were given standing room behind the penguin-suits and dinner-dresses seated at the elegant tables. Their bullying chants and rhythmic hand-claps reminded us of the menacing atmosphere we had experienced in Cardiff. The Sky cameras focused more on the angular and shirtless fighters and the dressier guests at ringside. We tut-tutted and flicked back to *Roseanne*.

After fifteen minutes we were back on Sky for, during the commercials, I had seen a replay of Murray dumping Docherty with a left hook. But the British champion got back to his feet with a sharp nod and fought on. He was not going to go under without a fight. Another hard battle had begun.

'This could be interesting,' I said, flipping to another channel, thinking that we'd return for the last rounds, the telling championship rounds.

Twenty minutes on, locked into *Newsnight*, Alison said, 'This is boring – let's see what's happening in the fight . . .'

With a nudge of my finger we were back in Glasgow. Docherty and Murray had entered the middle rounds. The bout had settled into a long and brutal exchange between two evenly-matched fighters. They lacked the glistening command of The Prince but the austere closeness of their contest took a grip on both of us. Our casual Friday night-in mood slowly darkened as, once more, we gave in to the boxing. I felt like an old junkie who, having fixed-up out of habit more than need, just because some stuff was lying round the place, remembered why he'd got hooked in the first place.

It was a pitiless but moving encounter. The two Scots fought bravely, each as remorseless as the other. And yet the little nods they gave to each other, the brief touching of gloves, the intense respect in every watchful shift of their eyes told another story. It was not the same story we had seen in the needling humiliation of Steve Robinson. The bantamweights were not derisory fighters like Hamed or Eubank. They were serious, deadly serious, and all the more humane for the way in which they both tried their hearts out.

Beyond the severe intimacy of their fighting, the £30-roarers were sounding less compassionate by the round. The drink had kicked in and the words were sung less with love than spite. *'There's only one Jim Murray, only one Jimmy Murray, one Jimmy Murray . . .'* was accompanied by stubby fingers jabbing at the handful of Docherty supporters, outnumbered by almost ten to one.

Murray and his backers came from Newmains, twelve miles to the south-east of Glasgow. My grandad had been born near Newmains but I could imagine that, today, the Lanarkshire neighbourhood would make Wincobank look like Wimbledon. Newmains was riven by unemployment and violence. The area's steel industry had long been decimated, with hard drinking since overtaken by heroin as an escape for men the same age and much younger than the twenty-five-year-old James Murray. Staring at his ravaged face as he sat on the stool, I did not think then, 'Well, at least Jim's got his boxing.' I was more interested to know if he could pull off the surprise he had suggested at the start when he knocked down the more seasoned Docherty.

His trainer, Dave Douglas, was visibly agitated. 'Jim, you'll need to win this round out of sight,' he shouted, 'out of fucking sight! Do you hear me?'

Above the blaring din of *'There's only one Jimmy Murray'*, the boxer looked straight ahead. His last words were 'Right, Dave . . .'

They came out for the twelfth. Docherty's white shorts were stained by blood, some of it his own but more having fallen from Murray's face which was cut below the eyes and across his nose. They moved slowly, Docherty with an almost languid tiredness, Murray with a starker brand of exhaustion. The final punches were not those which did the damage, although they sent Murray to the canvas for the first time. A left jab scraped the top of Murray's shaved skull and a weak right cross landed on his chest. Murray went down, crouching on his hands and knees while the referee counted the old numbers. He knelt so that the boxer could hear his voice more clearly. Across the ring, his face replete with the strain of a vicious fight, Docherty stared at the kneeling men, willing it to be over.

Jim Murray blinked and shook his head as if he might be able to free his mind of the lowering and blackening pressure. He was already close to death as he lay on his side and the Sky commentator yelled, 'Friday the thirteenth couldn't be more unlucky for James Murray.'

They removed his white gumshield but his left leg began to twitch horribly, as if it wanted to run off and find a life of its own. They tried to hold it down but only succeeded in transferring the tremor to the rest of Murray's body which began to flutter and then shake helplessly. The doctor crouched over him as Jim's mother, Margaret, clutched at the ropes. 'Jimmy, get up!' she cried. 'Please, Jimmy, get up!'

Thinking only that their boy had lost a twelve-round fight, that Murray was a Protestant to Docherty's Catholic, that they were from Newmains while their hated rivals were from Condorrat a few miles away, they began to riot. The bottles and glasses and chairs flew and fell from the air like the rain and the abuse we remembered from Cardiff. But it was far worse in Glasgow. There was a deeper intolerance at work, a sectarian violence which went back generations. As the dinner-guests fled, the women screaming and the men wide-eyed in fright, the commentators and officials ducked beneath any table they could find. Glass sprinkled down on them. The fighting spread from the back of the ballroom towards ringside.

It was another night of boxing and violence, only more so, only worse.

The riot was more rare than another death in the ring. James Murray died at 8.50 a.m. on Sunday, 15 October 1995, when the life-support machine was switched off by doctors at a hospital in Govan, Glasgow. He had been 'clinically dead' for more than thirty hours. The fighting amongst the crowd, as disturbing as it had been at the hotel and on screen, had not caused Murray's death. His ruin had happened in the ring. Boxing had killed him – rather than senseless crowd violence or its underlying causes of jobless poverty, prejudice and stupidity.

Although he claimed it was a sad coincidence, and that Murray's death the previous day had not influenced his decision, Chris Eubank announced his retirement from boxing on Monday, 16 October. 'My almost continuous fight schedule,' he said at a hastily assembled press conference, 'and the difficulties making weight have taken their toll and I need a long rest. My opinions have been made known on numerous occasions and a move to light-heavyweight does not interest me. I have, therefore, decided to retire, almost at the pinnacle of my career. Whilst I would have liked to retire as a world champion, I hope I will be remembered as the boxer who helped change the face of boxing – someone who created interest in the sport and who also set standards for so many others to aspire to . . .'

I doubted if we had seen the last of Eubank but, on that Monday morning, he looked like a man who had had enough of boxing. I knew the feeling – as did Frank Warren, who had promoted the fight between Docherty and Murray.

'It is very difficult to justify boxing,' Warren said that same day, 'when you see terrible injuries like those and the damage it does to the families.'

Although I was more detached from James Murray than any of the preceding boxing tragedies I'd seen in four years and a month, his death moved me like no other. I was not alone. There were over a thousand mourners at his funeral. The cortège was covered in flowers sent from seemingly everyone in boxing, from Frank Bruno to Frank Warren to Sky TV. The scenes at his burial were heartbreaking, especially the pictures of his mother and Drew Docherty at the graveside; but I think it was the gruff tenderness in his father's voice which lingered the longest.

'Wee Jim,' Kenny Murray said, 'was a brave man. Jim Murray was the finest man I ever knew. And he was a boxer. He was proud to be a boxer, to be fighting a champion like Drew Docherty. So keep boxing and stay off drugs. Remember: Jim Murray did not die with a needle in his arm. He did not die up a backstreet.'

10

THE SOLDIER-BOY

January 1996

A NEW YEAR AND THE SAME STORIES REELED THROUGH MY head.

In the beginning I wanted to celebrate boxing. I planned to write about the bravest and the most skilful fighters, describing their big heart and sparkle. I'd heard their voices lilt and seen the sweat slip from their faces to the floor. I thought there was something beautiful and poetic in the solitary way they both prepared for a fight and then, afterwards, held each other in relief. Boxing was as much about the fluttering sigh at the back of a fighter's walk to the ring as the cruel exchange of punches. It was about the way in which, in the gym, you might listen to the lithe skipping of feet or the sizzling pop of leather as an old boxer made the heavy bag twirl on its glinting chain.

When I started, I thought this book would reveal how I found colour and hope in boxing, across terrain that Joyce Carol Oates once said had 'nothing that seems to belong to daylight, to pleasure'. I was a sucker for the relentless severity she detailed, for her belief that, 'at its moments of greatest intensity it seems to contain so complete and powerful an image of life – life's beauty, vulnerability, despair, incalculable and often self-destructive courage – that boxing is life'.

Yet these stories now touch as much on death. It was not meant to end up this way. I originally planned to call this book *Showtime*, believing that I would string together an amusing necklace of ring baubles, shining vignettes which decorated my journey into the gaudy but still illustrious world of big-time boxing. I would play the white South African stooge, kicking back with the baddest homeboys, buddies together whether we came from the suburbs or the ghettos, from Johannesburg or the Bronx, East LA or Wincobank, via Soweto and the Yemen. Like The Prince, I would not go berserk at the first sign of trouble. I felt relaxed, I felt cool. I had the speech ready. Boxing was as scintillating as it was serious. It was

253

both fantastic and absurd. Don King! Chris Eubank! Naseem Hamed! Frank Bruno! Were these men not entertainers? Was boxing not, as Dandy Don himself coined it , 'Showtime'?

I was aware of the dangers of boxing. They did not deter me. I was not a boxer. I have never been, nor ever will be, a boxer. At a distance, the violence lent ballast to the melodrama. I knew that Spanish-speaking fighters had a word for knockout which meant 'the little death'. I remembered that Muhammad Ali called any darkening of his senses in a fight 'the Near Room', a place where 'you can see neon, orange and green lights blinking, and you can hear snakes screaming'.

I did not think of myself as thirsting for gore but I accepted the basic ferocity of boxing. I think it captivated me, more even than the outlandish character and wild drive of fighters from Toney to Tyson. I hated violence outside the ring but, between those thickly knotted ropes, the brutality became expert rather than malicious, a force of terrible grace when a fighter welded his power to boxing's most ancient finesse. It was a lie. The feelings of beauty only came later, in black-and-white photographs which sucked out the ravaging malice and ugliness of any given moment in the ring and turned them into stunning, and stunned, reflections of emotion. I gave into the silent deceit because it helped me go on, it enabled me to take another fix, allowing me to drum up another dodgy metaphor to report the way in which one man knocks another unconscious.

After the death of James Murray it again became hard to cheat the truth. I repeated the questions even though I knew the answers. How many more fights did I have to watch to 'understand' boxing? How many more men did I have to see maimed and killed to reach a coherent conclusion which could shut a book? How could I not turn away from boxing? I could not shake from my mind some of the words Hugh McIlvanney had written the week after Nigel Benn had ruined Gerald McClellan nearly a year before.

'Where does all this leave those of us who get our thrills on the safe side of the ropes? For me, strangely, the genuine shock, sorrow and guilt felt over the sufferings of Gerald McClellan have not removed the desire to watch fights, especially when the world's best are coming off their stools. It is, at times, an appetite as worrying as an addiction. But most addicts pay with their own health. It seems worse when the cost of a high is met by others. Am I entitled to go on seeking the fix? A lot of voices chorus no, and sometimes I think my own is among them.'

The perennial arguments between the abolitionists and the pro-boxing lobbyists were obsolete in the weeks and months following the loss of Kenny Murray's son, 'wee Jim'. The British Medical Association called for an immediate ban on boxing even though they realised that such a demand would not be implemented. The British Boxing Board of Control continued erroneously to compare boxing to motor-sport, mountaineering and even rugby in an effort to suggest that they were policing a sport less precarious than many others. Opinions remained intractable.

Eight days after Murray's life-support machine had been turned off, a BBC studio audience were asked to vote on the banning of boxing; 57 per cent were against a ban, 25 per cent were in favour while 18 per cent were undecided. After watching a debate on *Panorama* between Roy Hattersley and Barry McGuigan, they were asked to vote again. The change was negligible: 58 per cent against, 28 per cent for and 15 per cent unsure.

The Board had already dredged up their latest report on the *Safety of Boxing*. A few days after the Docherty-Murray fight, John Morris, the Board's secretary, insisted that the timing of the report was 'coincidental', that there was 'no knee-jerk reaction' to their findings. He was right about the last bit – the commission to investigate the hazards of boxing had been set up eighteen months before in response to the death of Bradley Stone. The panel of independent neurosurgeons and boxing doctors advised a twelve-point plan which the Board, in another slow lift of the leg, claimed would be ratified at the annual general meeting in May 1996. At least they could not be accused of putting excessive snap in their decisions.

There was, however, both concern and thought in their main proposals. The most significant was their stipulation that Magnetic Resonance Imaging (MRI) brain scans, replacing the less sophisticated CAT scan, should be made compulsory for every professional fighter in Britain. Boxers would have to pass a stringent MRI test each year. They would lose their licence to fight if the smallest irregularity was discovered. It was also felt necessary to extend the medical suspension period from twenty-eight to forty-five days for any fighter stopped in a bout. All weigh-ins were brought forward to twenty-four hours before a fight in an attempt to allow the boxers sufficient time to recover from the draining impact of shedding pounds.

The fighters themselves were sceptical, particularly those who scrambled to make a living from the ring in six- and eight-round fights in lowly halls and on the undercards of better-known boxers. They saw money being taken out of their pockets, as did the small-time promoters who did not share in any revenue from Sky. A passionate group of licence-holders met in mid-January to protest against the imminent rulings. They claimed that it was impractical and costly for an obscure fighter to show up for a weigh-in a day before he fought. What if he lived in London and his measly bout was to be held in Sunderland? Who would pay for his accommodation that night? Why should a fighter mildly hurt in a four-round contest be barred from earning another pay-cheque for the next two months? A rugby player, they said, could be badly concussed one Saturday afternoon and yet be found in a scrum the following weekend. The last 'accident' to occur in a six-round bout had occurred twenty years before – why should they be persecuted for the damage done in twelve-round fights? Who was going to pay the minimum £450 for an annual MRI when a CAT scan had cost only £160?

'I'm absolutely in favour of MRI scans,' stressed Pat Cowdell, a former professional and now a minor promoter, 'but the Board must pay. The cost of medicals will drive kids away . . . and the game just can't afford that.'

Frank Warren, to his enduring credit, moved in before the Board could dither further. He stumped up an immediate £400,000 to ensure every British professional fighter's first MRI scan. I was mightily impressed by Warren's generosity. While he had everything to lose if boxing went under, I sensed that Warren's payment stemmed more from the authentic distress he had experienced during the McClellan and Murray tragedies than from cynical pragmatism. Even if he was certain to recoup a sizeable proportion of his outlay during Naseem Hamed's next few fights and from the Bruno-Tyson showdown in Vegas, Warren could have gained similar plaudits by shelling out a quarter of that amount. Instead, his altruism signified the depth of feeling for the future of fighters like Jim Murray.

In Warren's office in Hertford, I was struck by his rising emotion as we recalled some the dark nights he had promoted in boxing. We began with Bradley Stone. Warren had managed Richie Wenton, the fighter against whom Stone lost his life in April 1994. 'I was in the corner for that fight,' Warren told me, 'for the first time in at least ten years. They were both incredibly brave. Afterwards, in the dressing-room, we were happy because Richie had come through a gruelling fight. An' I looked up and saw Bradley at the far end of the room. I went over to him. I'd often promoted him. We always got on fine, me and Bradley. An' so I asked him, "How are you, Bradley?" And he said, "I'm fine, Frank. Richie's a good fighter." I said, "Never mind, son, maybe next time . . ." He died the next day . . .'

Warren then spoke about Gerald McClellan. He could still remember how he and Don King watched the boxer drift away into a coma. 'We were alone in a hospital room with Gerald,' Warren said. 'Don was slumped in a chair, stricken with shock, saying over and over, "This is bad, man, this is tragic!" Yeah, Don is a driven man. Even in his mid-sixties he is consumed by the next deal. But that night he was distraught.' Warren hesitated, as if unsure how all of this would sound in print, two boxing money-men grieving over one of their lost fighters.

But we moved on grimly to James Murray. 'For me,' Warren said, 'the death of Jim Murray was by far boxing's saddest moment. Murray and Docherty were two young small-hall fighters, guys who were not at the top of boxing. They had not reached Gerald McClellan's level. They were fighting for so much less. They were trying so desperately to make something of themselves. For me that's what makes it even more moving. They were scrapping for their lives, living for boxing.

'Like Drew Docherty, James Murray was a decent, good, honest young man. You could not believe the misery there was at the funeral. The whole town was there. I said then you could not defend boxing. I felt terrible when James Murray's parents came over to me. I did not think I could look them in the face. But they were adamant. They had lost their son to boxing but they would not hear a word said against it. They said that boxing had been everything to Jim.'

I believed him. I'd grown to like Warren, even though I knew that, despite the serious health risk, he was sometimes not averse to helping faded fighters climb back into the ring to make more money for him. He allowed me to make my barbed comments about Don King, too, conceding that The Don described himself shamelessly as 'The Recycler'. In his own more restrained way, Warren was an enterprising recycler himself. The bottom line for him, as for all boxing promoters, remained the deal.

Yet, if I usually preferred to deride all promoters, even they gave me hope that something had been learnt from boxing's list of recent tragedies. Frank Warren was not heartless. He spoke more poignantly that anyone about the lost and damaged British boxers from the last five years. Michael Watson. Bradley Stone. James Murray.

While Warren was right to say that they would have wanted boxing to continue, to point to the encouraging words of Jim Murray's father, he could not exonerate the rest of us. We watched men endanger their own lives. If, in the eyes of his dad, Murray had died a more dignified death in the ring than in some back alley, it did not justify our watching him lose his life.

I also doubted if you could condone our interest in the men who had, effectively, killed their fellow boxers. I wondered why I needed to follow the careers of Gabriel Ruelas and Drew Docherty with the kind of scrutiny I had not shown before their fatal encounters. There was only sadness, rather than poetry, in the pain they showed on their respective returns to boxing.

On 1 December, Ruelas was overwhelmed in the fifth round and made to relinquish his WBC super-featherweight crown to Azumah Nelson. As great a fighter as Nelson was, Ruelas had offered a shambolic performance. 'I could see Jimmy [Garcia] in the ring,' he said. 'I saw the person that I wasn't fighting. I knew something was wrong even before the fight. I just wasn't there. I didn't feel right. I was thinking about Jimmy and I paid for it. I could not get him out of my mind. When I looked across the ring, I saw Jimmy . . .' Ruelas had donated his considerable share of the pay-per-view receipts of the Nelson bout to the Garcia family – and yet he could still not unclamp the guilt.

In January, Drew Docherty fought well in losing a twelve-round decision to the WBO bantamweight champion, Daniel Jiminez from Puerto Rico. At the end, while he was being congratulated on his valiant performance by the Sky team, Docherty was distraught. Something besides the loss of a boxing title scattered across his mind. 'I wasn't only fighting for myself tonight,' he said. 'I was fighting for . . .' In the sob of his voice, the name disappeared.

I did not need to see him suffer to imagine what he felt inside. But I watched on and thought how, once, a friend had described me as an 'emotional voyeur'. It had been a passing remark, and yet it hit home. I tried to gloss over the awkward hurt but later, on my own, the words seemed to burn into me. I knew why I could not just flick them away. They were not without truth. The darker the subject, the steadier my gaze.

The only hope, if that was the right word, seemed to be that I did not thrill to the agony and the chaos. It did not excite me. It turned over my heart, seeing boxing show men their need for tears.

On 21 October 1995, the week after Jim Murray died in Glasgow, Gerald McClellan turned twenty-eight. Three months on and the news from Freeport, Illinois, was gloomy. McClellan was blind, brain-damaged and in need of medication to numb bewildered depressions which made him cry and thrash at the air with his useless fists. He required constant nursing, having suffered two strokes and a coronary since he'd emerged from his two-month-long coma. His family had split apart in a bitter conflict to secure 'custody' of him. There were angry squabbles over the little money left in the 'Gerald McClellan Medical Trust Fund' while convoluted conspiracy theories were launched. Don King, inevitably, was near the centre of the controversy. According to rival factions, King was either leading a campaign against the McClellan sisters or else was subject himself to an extravagant conspiracy cooked by the FBI, who were intent on jailing him.

The former fighter, meanwhile, swayed gently in the blackness of his room, oblivious to everything around him.

Ironically, the whispers of wrong-doing only underlined the extent to which King and Frank Warren had spent money on behalf of McClellan. For once, even the boxing press seemed to agree that Big Don had done more right than wrong. King produced receipts which proved that he and Warren had paid $226,758.19 in 'out-of-pocket' expenses to the McClellans. He stressed that a further $250,000 in contractual fees had been honoured – although McClellan's purse for the fight had shrunk to $50,000 by the time his lawyers had been forced to pay off his former trainer and manager, Emmanuel Steward and John Davimos. It seemed a meagre amount to trade for a loss of sight and reason.

McClellan had defied the earliest and bleakest prognosis which indicated that, even if he came out of a coma, he would never be able to walk or talk or even hear again. Although he could manage all three functions, they were framed by his blindness and the fact that he could not understand what had happened to him. In his sister Lisa's words, 'The back of his brain is dead so it's not telling his eyes he can't see. He always thinks it's night time or he's in the dark.'

Lisa and her two sisters, Sandra and Stacy, provided round-the-clock care for Gerald – having won charge from their father, Emmit. At his custody trial, Gerald McClellan's assets were revealed to be $255,000 with an annual income of $10,000 from 'unknown sources'. His father predicted that the medical trust fund would run out sometime in 1996. There was not much money left to fight over. But, for Lisa McClellan and her sisters, their caring for Gerald was not bound up in cash. They were there for him out of love, to ensure that he never felt alone in his darkness. They were there to protect him, to keep him out of sight of the media. They refused all requests to visit Gerald whether the promised cheques came from television or tabloid journalists.

'Gerald has always been a real proud person,' Lisa said. 'We agree that Gerald wouldn't want to be seen. It's not a matter of hiding Gerald; it's just we don't want to betray him.'

But they could not alleviate his confusion. Gerald McClellan could not comprehend the lack of light in his life, he could not remember even fighting Nigel Benn. He thought his last fight had been against Julian Jackson. He believed that he was still a top-line boxer in training for his next world-title bout. He was coming back, better than ever. He had his pride. He insisted on being dressed only in designer gear. There he sat, in the dark, dressed in his silk shirts and Filas, wearing cologne by Karl Lagerfeld. He couldn't see the difference but he instructed his sisters that all his clothes, as before, should be green, his favourite colour, the colour of money, the colour after which he had named Forrest, his little girl. He was still Gerald McClellan, the world-famous champion boxer. In his head he was still 'The G-Man'.

Gabriel Ruelas and Drew Docherty both lost when they returned to the ring after participating in boxing catastrophe. Richie Wenton was even more distraught and gave up by turning away to the corner midway through his comeback bout. But Nigel Benn was different.

In the immediate aftermath of Gerald McClellan's coma, Benn was both restrained and tender. But, as the days disappeared into weeks, anguish yielded to boxing instinct.

'I'm sad,' he said, 'I'm very sad it's happened. But I'm not going to struggle [with] the past. It happened. It's very tragic. It could've been me but, listen, I can't sit here if every day I think about what happened. I'm gonna get hurt. I wanna keep that same – not The Dark Destroyer but The Warrior, I wanna keep that same intention. If I start losing that, I ain't gonna be in the ring.'

Benn admitted that he had contemplated retirement – for a day, or two at the most. 'I wanted to retire, y'know but I just can't see it happening. Like I said, I got an angel on [this] side but I got a devil on that side. An' the angel's saying [in a fey whisper] "Oooo, I'm so glad you're retiring!" And the devil said, "You ain't retiring, mate!" I really wanna be with the devil, man . . .'

When McClellan was still in the Royal London Hospital, Benn had flown with his children to Las Vegas for a desperately needed holiday. Surrounded by the pungent boxing scent of that desert town, Benn began his recovery from a terrible night. As if in answer to the blackness which covered Gerald McClellan, Benn went downtown to find a tattoo artist who could ink in a huge sun across the wide expanse of his back. The pain of the needle must have been intense but, after a fight with 'The G-Man', that huge sunburst of a tattoo felt like a kind of pleasure to Benn.

'Gerald McClellan hit me with the kitchen sink, the bath, everything,' Benn remembered with his winning brand of metaphorical matter-of-factness. 'I've never ever experienced pain like that – not even in a street-fight. I've never experienced pain like that in all my life. Never, never. My jaw felt like it was on me shoulder when he hit me, y'know . . .'

Having dredged the murkiest depths of both body and mind, Benn had more opportunity than any of us to mythologise his hurt. He had a right to the most voluminous vale of tears, to bury his head in his damaging hands and just howl for all he was worth. After fighting McClellan, Benn could have done anything and I think most of us would have understood how he had been driven to the outermost reaches of physical and psychological suffering. But Benn had a better grip on reality, even at its darkest pitch, than more ordinary people. He knew something that I still had to learn. It did not matter how much you might try to internalise remorse or even pontificate over the troubles of others. No amount of silent hair-tearing or verbal wailing would change anything for anyone else. You could only change and face up to yourself.

Benn's contrasting ability to deal with trauma in such basic fashion was bluntly endearing. 'After the fight,' he said, '[McClellan] was lying in one hospital bed next to me and he put out his hand. I just kissed his hand and I said, "Um . . . I'm sorry, Gerald, but, y'know, this is boxing . . ."'

Five months after that exchange, Benn went back to the very same ring at the Wembley Arena to fight again. He defended his WBC super-middleweight title against the Italian, Vincenzo Nardiello, on 23 July 1995. With an inky-blue sun shining on his brown back, the ghosts had long since departed, burnt off by the glare of a Vegas tattoo studio. Benn was ready to rumble again.

He thundered, in all seriousness, '[Nardiello's] gotta come with TNT in both hands. And if he ain't got TNT he's going home . . . when I get into the ring with him I will give it to him. I don't care. I'm determined. Let him know. Send him back to Italy. I'm telling you, I'm determined to go out there and have a war with him!'

The film of Benn training for the Nardiello fight was frightening. Sky's amiable commentator, Ian Darke, tried to lighten the footage by telling us that Benn ate fish for breakfast and drank half a bottle of neat honey a day. But the camera could not lift its unblinking eye from the dramatic sight of Benn punishing his gleaming body. An enormous weight had been bolted to his head. His eyes looked like they might pop out onto that plate of fresh fish as he heaved the iron ball from the ground with the strength of a vein-branched neck. His face contorted in a spasm of rapturous agony as he hoisted the weight up and down, up and down, as if locked into some mysterious S&M contraption which bridged the misty gap between pain and pleasure. Then he roared into an astonishing series of one-armed press-ups which he rotated with a puffing train of 'sit-ups'. The latter consisted of Benn elevating himself from a lying position into a sitting stance and on into an upright stand and back down again in two-second steamers of strain. Eerie grunts and cries rushed up the length of his body and out the black tunnel of his mouth. It was if he had never fought Gerald McClellan.

Unsurprisingly, Benn beat Nardiello, forcing the Italian to surrender a minute and a half into round eight. Threatened by the voracity of Benn's appetite for combat, Nardiello put in a curious performance of complaints and face-pulls, landing light kisses on Benn's lips and eyeing the referee constantly in a search for a way out. In the end Benn knocked him down and, as Nardiello protested at the unfair use of force against him, the Italian corner threw in the old white towel.

Benn was mildly put out. 'From the second round he was huffing and puffing,' he moaned. 'I was whacking him to the body. I wanted a proper fight – he was showboating, kissing me on the lips . . . so I said, "Let's go with the flow, kiss him back." That's it – but no tongues, definitely. But I'm looking for someone who can give me a fight . . . get someone who's gonna bang me, knock me down, hurt me. And then you'll see me come back!'

Ian Darke, on Sky, said the obvious and plain name of the best fighter in the world – 'Roy Jones?'

Nigel Benn smiled and lowered his dreadlocked head. The sun rippled on his back at the sound of that most brilliant star. 'Roy Jones . . .' Benn sighed in delight. 'Roy Jones to me . . .' He stopped again and considered. 'I don't mind being number two to Roy Jones. I think he's a class act and I'd really like to fight him. He'll frighten me, Roy Jones, and that's what I need – somebody to really, really frighten me. I'd be up for that fight like a mother . . . so please, God, Don King, Frank Warren, HBO, if you can get that fight on I'll fight him in his – no, in my backyard. Roy Jones is the only one who's gonna give me that real fear. He's gonna put the fear of God up me.'

Roy Jones was the only fighter in the world who made me shout out to Alison. 'Watch this,' I'd burble in disbelief, 'watch this . . .' Whereas I was normally apologetic at hogging the video again for 'research purposes', a

Roy Jones performance cranked up my evangelical fervour. Jones was the one boxer who made me literally instruct Alison to take mental notes. I knew she, an artist herself, would understand. 'Look at this guy, look at Roy Jones,' I'd rhapsodise. He was a bewitching marvel across the canvas, a genius of deception and, yes, of destruction. If only everyone who described *Raging Bull* as the best film of the '80s knew Roy Jones. As indelible as those black-and-white images of DeNiro as Jake La Motta had been, as alluring the sweep of music into celluloid during Scorsese's ring sequences, they were as stylised as Roy Jones was original. In lustrous colour he shimmered with an artistry which left me as breathless as his most competent opponent.

Alison got it. Whereas she had been around boxing long enough by then to watch a fight with a dispassionate glance, Roy Jones made her blink. 'Wow,' I'd say as, after James Toney, he whipped Antoine Byrd in one round, Vinny Pazienza in six and Tony Thornton in three. 'Let's see that again,' she'd say more calmly, as if by watching it once more she would be able to unpick his secret. We couldn't. Even in replay he was too quick, too dazzling for us to break down his movements into architectural tiers of thought. He was a smearing symphony of blows, an almost musical gush of smudge and riff, lick and thrash. He played the other boxers as if they were different instruments over which he could rap.

After he had dodged and then razed Pazienza in Atlantic City in June '95 with an astounding display which culminated in a crescendo, not so much of combinations but a seamless spiral of punches, Jones just grinned. 'He tried hard to beat me up in there but I have an awesome defence. I can sit in that corner and make a guy hit me all night, but he ain't never gonna hit me clean. I made him keep punching, working himself out and when he stopped . . . here come Roy!'

Roy came with — at least we saw in slow-mo — a spectacular left uppercut, a hook, then a right and left uppercut, another right and one last left which dropped Pazienza. Jones even retained some modesty after such a demolition. 'I'm not like James Toney or Mike Tyson who go out there and say they can't be beat,' he stressed. 'Anybody can be beaten on a given night, but a man who controls himself is a powerful man. I'm cool. You ever see me lose my head?'

Against Tony Thornton, the fighter Toney had faced when I'd walked with him to the ring in Tulsa, Jones again kept his head and looked almost invincible in the process. On the night Naseem Hamed rivalled him for flair during his victory over Steve Robinson, Jones dispatched the helpless Thornton with an explosion of thirty or more unanswered punches in the first forty-five seconds of round three.

After thanking God and his fanatical home crowd in Pensacola, Jones laughed and promised, 'If a guy makes a mistake against me, it's ding-dong!' Before he went on to compare himself to one of his beloved roosters he

shouted out, 'Be careful, Benn, I'll get you like that!' and, more enig-
matically, 'This is for everyone in the chicken business!'

Asked what he meant, Jones drawled that, 'A good rooster is a rooster
who fights like myself or Salvador Sanchez. A good rooster keeps right on
top of the other rooster, keeps him fighting the whole night!' The
distinction between Roy and a rooster, of course, was that the boxer only
allowed his rivals a few rounds a night. 'Yeah,' he agreed, 'I'm in boxing to
have fun. I'm having fun myself, God is good to me and I'd like to see the
world come together in unity . . .'

The last remark, it soon turned out, extended to him and Nigel Benn.
'You go tell Don King I'll take that fight any time. Nigel Benn's a great
warrior, that's why I want the fight!'

The problem, however, remained that Jones and his adviser, Stanley
Levin, were not prepared to give King any options on fights beyond a
unification title bout with Benn. King was also determined that a scrap as
momentous as Jones-Benn would only be screened on his Showtime pay-
per-view network while Roy and Stan were connected to Don's most
despised foe – HBO.

A month after he had crushed Thornton, Jones said that he was willing
to strike a separate deal with Benn which would force King's hand. 'That's
what I'd like to do,' he said. 'I hear about Don King offering $25,000,000
for me and Benn. He can come up with $10,000,000 apiece and we can
fight' – without offering any long-term control to King.

Jones had a new scheme to punt. He envisaged a night of British and
American warfare, where he fought Benn and his two boxing pals, Alfred
Cole and Derek Gainer, took on Frank Bruno and Naseem Hamed. 'I want
the three-fight package,' he told Claude Abrams in *Boxing News*. 'My bros
must go with me. I must have some cover if I go to another country. Bruno-
Cole would be a good fight. Let's make it a great night. I've seen Hamed.
He's a pretty good fighter but Gainer watched the fight against Robinson
and said he could beat him. Derrick don't turn anyone down. Bruno can
punch, but Cole has more skills. That will balance out into a good fight.
Me and Benn – enough said. I like Benn and that's why I want to fight him.
It's a sportsman challenge. [But] they can't speak for themselves. They can't
make their own decisions without King. We can. They don't have the
power. They're denying the public of some great fights . . . people want to
see something which is intriguing to their minds. Something which will
look good . . . I really like the biggest challenge out there. When I fought
James Toney, it was a project. Benn is a project because he is a warrior and
he will be a tough fight for me. I really believe Benn wants to fight me. I
have a lot of faith in him. I respect him.'

He also respected Merqui Sosa, knowing that the tough Dominican had
never been knocked down before. But, on 12 January '96, Jones floored and
then lambasted Sosa after a couple of minutes in the second round. It was

another chilling and almost futile exercise. With the Benn bout sealed in politicking, there was no one left for Jones to fight. There were calls instead for him, a super-middleweight, to challenge Mike Tyson at heavyweight. But Roy Jones was no fool in the ring. His dreams lay beyond, in giving up boxing for professional basketball.

'Boxing is not a challenge for me now,' he explained. 'The only challenge is Nigel Benn and he won't return my phone calls. He doesn't want to fight so there's no challenge. There hasn't been a boxer who's played in the NBA – I want to be the first.'

After trying out with the New York Knicks, Jones even suggested that he might move to London to play for the local Towers in the English basketball league. As if in preparation Alison decided, apparently on a whim, now that she had given up her boxing impersonations, that she too would try her hand at basketball. Whether in deference to her, Roy Jones or Michael Jordan, I found myself heeding her new desire. On Valentine's Day, with an irrepressible surge of romance, I bought her a basketball and a Chicago Bulls vest. She loved it; and I thought that, along with Roy Jones and even Nigel Benn, we might yet get out of boxing.

Her name was Caroline Jackson. She was only twenty-five years old but she had enough iron in her soul to bend him. She was calling him in, telling The Warrior that his time was up. Benn knew that she had his number.

'Caroline wants me to stop,' he said at the beginning of March, only a few days before he was due to fight South Africa's Sugarboy Malinga in Newcastle. 'After the McClellan fight she'd had enough. She wanted me to quit. I promised her I would stop soon, by the end of this year [1996], and I will not break that promise. She's been with me through everything. She's made me what I am today. An' she's told me, "Don't retire and then come back!" She said if I retire and come back, she'll leave me.'

After enduring a particularly harsh divorce from his first wife, Benn was afraid of losing Caroline. He knew there were only months left before she forced him to choose between her and boxing.

In forty-five fights Benn had lost only twice, to Michael Watson in 1989 and to Chris Eubank the following year. His defeat of McClellan had transformed him into an iconic figure in British boxing. If the rare likes of Hamed and Jones had more talent than him, there were few fighters who could ever hope to match Benn's desire or courage. Hamed and Eubank needed the glitz of being able to prance round non-boxing circles while Jones yearned to prove himself on the basketball court. But nothing exhilarated Benn more than fighting. The McClellan calamity had immersed him even deeper in boxing. Caroline Jackson, I thought, was the one person who might save Nigel Benn from himself.

In anticipation of his next WBC super-middleweight title defence, Benn salivated, 'I'm up for it – big time! I'm up for Sugarboy. I just hope Sugarboy is up for me . . .'

Thulane 'Sugarboy' Malinga was no chicken himself. He was thirty-six and, supposedly, on the slide. Benn had already beaten him four years earlier, lifting a controversial ten-round verdict in Birmingham, an even more fortunate victory than that sneaked by Chris Eubank over Malinga only a few months before in 1992. But Roy Jones had stripped Malinga as ruthlessly as if he was a limp stick of sugar-cane from Zululand, hacking him down in a shockingly one-sided contest in '94. It appeared doubtful that Malinga would ever be the same fighter again.

Benn, in homage to his Geordie support, wore black and white as he stepped into the Newcastle ring on 2 March to defend his WBC super-middleweight belt for the tenth time. His hair was braided with his usual dreadlocks. The 'No Fear' legend he had introduced against McClellan again garnished his Newcastle-striped trunks. But, much to our surprise, the flair oozed from the older man. Sugarboy peeled out zesty jabs which made Benn's eyes water as his head snapped back repeatedly in the opening four rounds. It was only in the fifth that the champion found some of his acclaimed power. After Malinga had hurt Benn with a jab and a left hook, the old Dark Destroyer pulled out one of his sworn party-pieces. A right hand crashed against the sugar-man, sprinkling a light glaze over his handsome features as he sank to the canvas.

But, with twenty seconds left to the bell, Malinga rose again. As they squared off in the centre of the ring it was noticeable that, despite the knockdown, Benn's face was the more damaged. His right eye was swollen and closing for the night. His mouth had started to fatten under the shuddering impact of Malinga's stiff jab. Benn eased through the rest of the round, waiting for another space in which he could whack Malinga without being hurt himself.

By the seventh, the Zulu fighter again speared his jab into Benn's grimace as if it had the piercing force of an assegai. A small cut opened up in the bruised valley of Benn's hilly eye, impairing his vision even further. He battled to move his head away from the combination of left jab and right cross. By the start of the twelfth, even though he had fought back hard in the preceding two rounds, Benn needed another of those boxing miracles prayed for by sorry cornermen. He had to find a KO to survive another night as champion.

Yet Malinga was awarded the knockdown when a weary Benn missed with a punch and briefly touched ground as a right followed the sad curve of his slip. It was enough for the ref to give Benn a standing eight count and ensure that Malinga won the last round by a 10–8 margin instead of the more customary 10–9 mark. Benn, his bloated and bleeding face offering its own violent record of the fight, had the look of a well-beaten loser. He put his arms in the air at the finish but his gesture was as perfunctory as

Malinga's mirrored motion was ecstatic.

In keeping with the irrational fancies of modern boxing, Chuck Giampa, a judge from Las Vegas, split an otherwise obvious decision. He must have been suffering a fit of blindness himself to declare Benn a 114–112 winner – when the two other official scorers at ringside had Malinga an easy 118–109 and 115–111 victor.

At the sound of the word 'new', as in WBC champion, Sugarboy broke into a keening ululation as striking as the sight of Benn's head plunging down. But, to the very end, he was an almost unbearably brave man. As the foaming Showtime MC, Jimmy Lennon Jr, hailed him from the centre of the ring, Benn suddenly reached out to take the Sky Sports microphone. His hands were bare but for the white bandages wrapped around the jutting knuckles and extending up beyond each wrist. He lifted his right fist to ask for silence. That same eye was a tumid red slit while the left was white and wildly staring.

At home, Alison and I slunk down into our seats, preparing for the worst, for a last stuttering lament. But, again, he surprised us. Although his voice cracked, he spoke clearly.

'Thank you to everyone,' he said, 'for supporting me through my career. Hold on one minute . . . can I have a quiet moment, please? I think I've done my bit for British boxing. I fought the best. I fought everyone. I've never avoided anyone but I came down here tonight and, Sugarboy Malinga, he prepared good. We've got to take nothing away from him. I'm not going to make any excuses . . . but . . . now . . . it's time to call it a day . . .'

Benn stopped, his voice lost in a muffled crying. I looked over at Alison and saw that her own eyes were big and teary. I didn't want her to guess I might be about to do the same. I turned back quickly, swallowing manfully, hoping we could yet avoid a watery hat-trick.

Benn's father had stepped forward to hold him. Ten thousand people sighed in unison. But the former Dark Destroyer, the vanquished Warrior, had turned away from them to stretch out to Caroline Jackson. She was as elegant as the ringcard and Union Jack waving high-heeled girls had been tacky during the previous hour. But it was the steady look in her eye which touched us the most. She gazed upon the man who made her heart ache.

As he held her hand, Benn spoke a sentence of almost delicate precision. 'Without this woman here, beside me, I would not be here today.' The emotion kicked in and chopped his speech into an earthier chunk. 'When I was going through a breakdown over my wife and everyfink, this is the girl who picked me up through everyfing.'

The boxer dropped to his right knee as he reached for his next line. He stared up in adoration at the woman and said, 'All I can say to you, Caroline: will you marry me?'

If we had been watching a movie we would have groaned, but this moment felt like raw and unscripted intimacy. Alison was crying and, to stop myself, I laughed almost hysterically and repeated, 'I don't believe this!' After three funerals and one ringside wedding, where next would boxing take us?

It felt like the sort of sad but ultimately hopeful night on which this book should end. I thought I might have my last page as I watched the two hug each other between the ropes. Nigel Benn smiled and said sweetly, 'Thank you, everyone. Well done, Sugarboy. All the best. Thank you all . . .'

Arms wrapped around each other, they ducked their way out of the ring. Praise cascaded around a quivering arena.

Sugarboy took his turn at the mic. 'Thank you, thank you,' he echoed. 'You are the great, you are the great, God blessed me,' he called out towards Benn as he followed the tattooed sun still shining on the beaten boxer's back. 'First of all I would like to thank God who gave me the strength to beat the great champion like Nigel Benn. Nigel was the great champion. I salute you!'

As if I had been writing this at my most fevered, the South African's 'I salute you' shout was heard the moment the camera cut away to the sight of Nigel Benn leaning down to embrace Michael Watson at the end of the front-row aisle. Watson was seated in his familiar wheelchair and able to lift his right hand to pat Benn. It was two months short of seven years since they had fought each other, since Watson had scaled his finest moment in boxing to shock the then unbeaten Benn and stop him in the sixth round. Their glittering fight had foreshadowed all the Showtime-type events that have since dominated British boxing throughout the '90s.

As they looked at each other in Newcastle, they shared an unknowable moment. Winded by it all, we gasped at the two vanquished men. But, still, they were boxers to the core. They did something natural and irresistible. They bunched their hands and punched each other, fist to fist, fighter to fighter. And then Nigel Benn was gone, with Caroline at his side, swept along by the No Fear entourage which had led him to the ring just over an hour earlier. Michael Watson remained in his wheelchair, facing the ring, lost in boxing, even then.

4 March 1996

Two nights later, in Detroit, in the freezing darkness, I began to skid. The road sliding beneath me was covered in a glassy sheet of black ice. As the car started to spin I could see the snow falling heavily across the windscreen, twirling in strands like the thick white string I'd once used to make a top dance on its metal point. The two sides of the highway were covered in pretty banks of snow. They rushed towards me as I tried to stop myself braking, feeling the steering wheel slip helplessly through my gloveless and block-like hands.

Just as I braced myself for the crash, the tyres found a grip against the roll and the car weaved across the full width of six lanes. I cut into the path of a massive container truck bearing down at high speed. It came looming and screaming out of the blackness, headlamps blazing, masses of snow-spiked tyres swerving smoothly away from me and onto the outside track where it hurtled into the distance. It was out of sight before a new monster-truck swept up behind me, testing another frayed nerve.

I shook with cold and shock as I clutched tightly at the wheel, concentrating like a drunk trying to walk a straight line. It had been one of those days. Up at six in the morning in London, stuck in an underground tunnel at seven, endless queues at Gatwick at nine, a delayed flight at eleven, a yelling baby in the seat next to mine on the left, a huge fat guy with a 'monster cold' and symptoms of a bad cocaine comedown on my right, *City Slickers II* on screen and, finally, a teeth-loosening landing made long overdue because of 'inclement conditions'. After thirteen hours I was half-way there.

'Whaddya doin' back in America again?' the black immigration official asked as he eyed the coloured entry stamps in my South African passport. 'You tryin' to take a job from one o' my brothers?'

When he heard the name of James Toney, his attitude changed from hostility to hilarity.

'Toney, huh?' he chuckled. 'No kidding?'

'No sir,' I smiled dutifully.

'Well then,' the man said as he pressed his ink pad down against the last page, 'I reckon you're in for a bumpy ride. This James Toney feller is a real wild card. Got a lot of guns, ready to shoot you up, just like he said he was gonna do with that manager of his. I'd watch out if I were you. If Toney don't get to you first, the weather surely will.' He closed my passport and smiled broadly. 'Welcome to Detroit . . .'

I thought I'd be out of Detroit and in Ann Arbor within an hour. But the jokers handling my suitcase had other ideas. At first I thought it was lost or that it had been stolen. I hung around while they looked and checked and yawned again. It was nowhere to be seen, it was gone. I had visions of my meeting James Toney and then moving on to Las Vegas and Mike Tyson in the same sweetly smelling clothes the big man in the plane had already stained when he dropped his spicy chicken pizza in my lap. But, then, abruptly, they found it. It was listed as 'an unidentified black bag', but they were certain it was mine. The only problem was that it had been delivered to a different terminal. It would take a couple of hours to be picked up and driven back to the international arrivals section.

'Why don't you wait a bit, sweets,' the weary woman at the baggage counter suggested, 'you could have a bite of pizza or something to pass the time.'

For five hours I drank coffee out of the same paper cup and watched airport television. By 9 p.m. Detroit time, which was 3 a.m. on Tuesday morning in London, the weather warnings were dire. Big-haired announcers smiled down and said, 'Folks, it's kicking up a real storm out there so don't even think about going out unless it's a hell-fire emergency. Driving conditions are treacherous and worsening by the hour – so hang on, it's gonna be a rough night. In short, Burt, the message is stay home! Burt?'

I didn't wait to hear what had happened to Burt or to see if my case would turn up. 'Don't worry, hon,' the lost property lady promised, 'we'll send it on to you in Vegas. If you're goin' anywhere tonight you'd better get movin' . . .'

Even James Toney sounded anxious when I called him to say that, finally, I was leaving the airport for Ann Arbor. 'You take care comin' out here,' he muttered, 'it ain't no easy drive tonight.'

I was bolstered by the softness in Toney's voice. He sounded young and gentle – the exact opposite of what my friendly immigration man had predicted. 'How did you do the other night?' I asked, remembering that Toney had fought three days before, on Friday, 1 March, in Indio, California, against a journeyman called Richard 'Stoneface' Mason.

'I won,' he said with a little smile in his voice.

I offered him a juicy line to devour: 'Was it easy?'

'Real easy. I pretty much did as I liked. I moved real well. Six straight wins now. I'll tell you all about it. You're coming to see me at a good time, Don, I'm on my way back.'

He sounded so sure and so earnest that I smiled back into the phone. 'That's good to hear. We've been a bit worried about you . . .'

'No need,' he said. 'I got my mind back on boxing.'

'That's good,' I repeated, trailing away, thinking of the journey ahead.

'Okay,' he grunted.

'Okay. Guess I'll see you and your mom soon.'

'Yeah, but go careful, man.'

'I will.' I sounded like I was talking to my dad.

'An' jus' call me and my mom if you hit a problem,' Toney urged.

'Okay,' I promised.

'See ya, man.'

'See you,' I said.

The nightmare trip suddenly seemed worthwhile. I was not alone in Michigan. I had flown here for a purpose. James Toney was my favourite guy in boxing, the bad man who was more tender than he looked. As I stepped out into the snowy night, bending my head against the wind, I did a small skip across the carpark. The weather made me think of Hank, the taxi-driver who'd driven me through Tulsa a couple of years before on my way to meeting Toney for the first time. 'Fuck Toney,' Hank had moaned before yelping in exultation when he saw the boxer walk alongside me towards the dressing-room.

Toney had that effect on people. I could still see the little old lady called 'Missy' in the Doubletree Hotel in Tulsa as Toney and his crew, including me, stepped into her elevator. It had also snowed that night. Toney's hooded black tracksuit and heavy boots lent an extra edge of menace to his appearance. But Missy had looked into his face when she realised he was a boxer. I could still hear the echo of her 'Good luck tonight, boys, g'luck' as she took courage and called out after us.

I had thought often of that night. The wait in the hotel room and then the dressing-room. Dr Dre and Snoop on the CD. Toney turning to me as the TV technicians yelled 'Showtime, champ, showtime!' I had not forgotten the sound in his voice when he said, 'Let's go to work,' nor the way in which he had jerked his head, telling me that I should walk with him to the ring. It had been a rare moment, a bizarre privilege to feel the crowd's wild heat and noise, their rising fervour, as we walked down the long corridor until we could see the ropes ahead. Toney had revealed more to me about boxing that night than anyone had done before or since. He had shared some of his most secret fears and yearnings in Tulsa and, as he was always such a proud man, I never stopped feeling that I owed him something for that favour. He'd trusted me and I knew how much that meant in a world as sneaky and leery as boxing.

Jackie Kallen had also trusted me. She had been instrumental in helping forge that bond between Toney and me. I liked her and she had never been less than charming while helping me understand the schemes of boxing as a billion-dollar business. I admired the way in which she'd defiantly shown her made-up face to all the old boys in the trade and how she and Toney trashed the doubters year after year.

And yet, in boxing, because this is a tough and dirty enterprise, there are always sides to be taken. The acrimony is invariably so bitter that it becomes impossible not to be drawn into a whirlpool of dissent. You could feel the rage and suspicion swirling at the heart of the break between Kallen and Toney. I knew that I could not move from one to the other, playing people off against each other in the search for balance. You could not write about boxing from a 'balanced' perspective – there was too much emotion to detach yourself from everyone. And, in boxing, anyone who was anyone had a glinting axe to bury in the back of some sucker who had tried to knife them in the past. Take your pick, they all seemed to say, you with the axes or the knives?

The discord between the Kallens and the Toneys was more layered; but when it came to a choice between a manager and a fighter, I always knew which way I'd lean. I had already heard Jackie Kallen's version of the split through countless clippings as she worked the media with typical vivacity. The silence from the Toneys, especially Sherry, was more provocative. I wanted to hear their story. In my heart, I was always with them.

I left a message for Jackie that I was on my way to Michigan, that I would be happy to talk to her, but she never called back. I think she knew as well as I did that I would end up with the Toneys. I was on my way to Ann

Arbor rather than to her home in West Bloomfield. It was the simple route, the boxing way. I was with James and Sherry, the boxer and his mother.

As snow fell steadily across Detroit International, I asked the Alamo man the way to Ann Arbor. He looked at me mournfully, as if I might be mad. 'Just head for Chicago,' he mumbled.

'Which way to Chicago?' I queried feebly.

'Thataway,' he said, pointing towards the darkest part of the sky. 'Just head for the snowstorm. That's Chicago at the bottom of it.'

'How long do you think it'll take me?'

'To Chicago?' he laughed. 'Tonight?'

'To Ann Arbor.'

'Well, Detroit to Ann Arbor ain't gonna take you more than half an hour on a good day . . . but, it ain't a good day out there no more. There's snow in Ann Arbor, buddy. Tonight, who knows what's gonna happen?'

I thought I might kill myself trying to drive the thirty-odd miles that night. Even at a fifteen-mile-an-hour crawl through the snow and over the ice my car moved like a nervous little dog forced to wear skates and take to the rink. I imagined Pee-Wee, Jackie Kallen's famous mutt, curled up in front of the fire. I doubted if I would see Pee-Wee in the furry flesh again. Sherry had already told me that the relationship between his mistress, Jackie, and her and James had soured beyond the point of redemption. Both sides were still listing from the damage. There was no going back, Sherry said over the phone, to the good old days.

Everything had changed on the Vegas night, sixteen months before, when Toney lost to Jones. Within days, after his threat to kill Kallen had been splattered across America beneath the recurring 'gun-toting ex-crack dealer' descriptions, their differences appeared irreconcilable. Sherry tried to play the awkward role of peace-maker between James and Jackie but I had memorised the division which separated her from the managerial clan. Alison had made me see how Sherry was consigned to the fringes even though she travelled everywhere with the Kallen crew. She sat back, letting Jackie take the lead. But I knew that, all the time, she was watching and thinking, seeing how things might turn out for her and James. For the boxing press, the story lay elsewhere. It was 'The Lady & the Champ', the 'ghetto-gangster' and the 'suburban Jewish mother', the 'James & Jackie Show' where he kicked, and she kissed, ass.

For years the personae paid off. Kallen showed a marketing guile and tough business sense which was more than the equal of any other manager in boxing. Toney worked hard in the ring and he kept winning against some fine fighters. He also harked back to a better time when champions would fight anyone who challenged them. His cool bravado between the ropes sharpened his crude image on the outside. But there was hurt in him which went deeper than the scowling and the swearing.

Since losing to Jones and then Montell Griffin, his trouble could be charted in the bulging contours of his thickening body. Problem multiplied on problem and it seemed as if he put on another fleshy handful of pounds every time something else went wrong in his life.

While he and Kallen agreed to see out the remaining months of her contract, Toney fired his long-time trainer, Bill Miller, after the surprise loss to Griffin. Miller had criticised Toney in both the American and British media, claiming that he had become 'lazy' and 'unfocused'. Toney replaced him with Eddie Mustafa Muhammad, a trainer whom he had engaged in vitriolic altercations in the past – most notably during the notorious build-up to his defeat of Muhammad's former champ, Iran Barkley, in 1993. Three months later Toney terminated what he and Sherry called his six-year 'dollarship' with Kallen.

The traumatic themes carried over into his private life. His marriage in May 1995 to Sarah, his girlfriend of many years and the mother of his beloved Jasmine, broke down over Christmas. His new manager, Stan Hoffman, an amiable Jewish man from New York who had found his way into boxing via the music business, admitted that James and Sarah were in the midst of 'extremely painful' divorce proceedings which would inevitably spill over into a tussle for Jasmine. Although Stan was as likeable as Jackie, repeatedly telling me that I was 'a doll' and 'a sweetheart', it was hard to gloss over the pain in his fighter's life.

Toney was ridiculed by outsiders as just another flame-mouthed bully who'd been humbled by boxing. They said he was condemned, a fighter who had already seen the best days of his life. They predicted that only more distress awaited, for Toney had too much mouth to disappear quietly. He was struggling again, reduced to being just another fighter on the comeback trail.

But, for me, even in defeat, there was more than just antipathy and bad luck about the Toney story. James and Sherry had become more complex and fascinating. I cared about them even more than I had done when Toney had been such a dominant fighter.

I counted the slow miles, one after another, until I saw the first sign for Ann Arbor. The snow still fell. It was just before midnight which meant dawn was approaching in London. Alison would still be asleep but, at last, twenty-four hours on, I'd made it to the home of the man who still called himself 'Lights Out'.

It was a shock to see them again. It had been a long while since the last time, since I'd watched Toney greet the queue of elderly Jewish ladies and broad black homeboys which had formed in an MGM reception room after he lost to Roy Jones. They had given me that unforgettable final image to carry away – James, flanked by Sherry and Sarah, holding a plate of food, as his mother leaned towards him and kissed his cheek. I could remember the words, 'I'm proud of you, boy,' as if she had just said them out loud.

Sherry had become even thinner. She looked fit and smart but I sensed the tiredness within her. It had been a hard time since Roy Jones, a 'nightmare', she said. But she was still smiling at me, nodding and talking faster than ever. James was quieter, if no less friendly. We said our hellos almost shyly, exchanging winks, shaking hands, patting each other on padded arms. While Sherry and I spoke a mile a minute, James sat in silence, nodding and grunting his agreement, occasionally sniffing back the start of a cold.

I was surprised by the size of him. I had read all the stories of Toney packing on weight but it was different seeing him in person rather than in mere print. While I would not have called him fat, even behind his back, there was no escaping how big he had grown. His face was the most conspicuous marker of an emerging heavyweight body. As a middleweight the flesh had been pinned back over his cheekbones. It had since spread to cover his face in a style more chunky than gaunt. Being a meaty type of guy myself I sympathised. I thought we looked okay, Toney and me, big boys rocking back, feeling strong at the weight. But he had to go into the ring, not me. He had been a middleweight at twenty-two whereas I had last been one at eighteen. He was a little shorter but he now weighed more than me – and it looked more like solid bulk than muscle. Yet it was not only good eating which had thickened and widened our bodies. We were both getting old. I was thirty-four and, even if he was only twenty-seven, Toney was at an age which slid away quickly in the ring. If, in odd moments, I had caught myself humming maudlin songs like 'Funny (How Time Slips Away)', Toney was even more acutely aware that his years as a boxer were closing in. There were fighters ten years older than him who were still boxing, and George Foreman was battling on almost twenty years down the line, but Toney had always told me that he wanted to be out of the ring by the time he was thirty. I doubted if that would happen. I could visualise him five years from now, using his savvy to elude a younger man. But I did not think we could easily bear the thought of Toney becoming a veteran in the ring. He had to make the most of what remained of his prime years, he had to become a name to mention again in the same breath as Jones and Tyson. Like Sherry, I knew that he would only find his happiness between the ropes. Toney was a boxer and everything he did was defined by boxing's stark realities. You could tell he was a fighter just by looking at his sore hands or at the scars around his eyes and the flattened plane of his nose.

His face was made to look even rounder by a black Russian-style hat. Its furry rim lifted often enough for me to see the two diamond studs in his right ear, each bought to represent his previous world titles. They glinted in the wintry light, symbols of a better time.

On another arctic Ann Arbor morning, the snow drifted from a grey sky. We were in search of a steaming breakfast. Sherry drove us across town in a giant Land Cruiser which ate up the black ice as smoothly as the sound of Marvin Gaye seeping from the stereo. 'Let's Get it On', 'Mercy, Mercy', 'What's Going On' and 'Trouble-Man' had never sounded more apt in the company of a fighter, a man who had once worked these same tree-lined streets, selling crack, flashing his piece at the homies from the other side of town, the 'hood-side' as Sherry tagged it.

The warmth of the journey and the sweet voice of this particular 'Marvelous' Marvin lulled us into an unusual silence. We stared at the glacial beauty outside as the songs surged on. 'Ain't it pretty?' Sherry murmured while we muttered 'very' and 'yeah!'. Our minds were elsewhere. I fixed on the typical American breakfast which awaited – the fruit and juice, eggs, bacon, sausage, tomato, mushroom, pancake, waffle and coffee extravaganza – and wondered at the irony of my interviewing James Toney over a heaped plate of food. The state of Toney's expanding girth had consumed more column inches in swingeing articles than there were inches on his waistline.

'Yeah,' Toney sighed, reading me like he might absorb the grease-splattered contents of an old menu, 'I know what they're saying. Everybody's written me off, sayin' I've had too many fights too soon, that I'm shot. They're sayin' I'm fat, that I'm finished.'

Toney's words fell fast and clear from his mouth. I switched on the tape-recorder in my coat pocket and squirmed a little in the back seat. It's never easy to hear a fighter, especially a fighter once as revered and feared as Toney, dissect his own decline. While the boxer stroked his beefy chin, I remembered all the great James Toney fights there had been over the preceding five years.

'Yeah,' Toney sighed again, interrupting our reverie, 'fat and finished – that's what they're sayin' . . .' He looked over his shoulder at me and I prepared myself for the inevitable verbal explosion following such blatant disrespect.

'Well,' Toney eventually said with an unexpected wink, 'we know different. So let them say what they like. It don't matter. I'm gonna show them the real James Toney. I'm comin' back, baby, better than ever. An' this time, I'm coming back in Lights Out shape. I'm gonna tell you all about it – soon as we get you some breakfast . . .'

Sherry settled on the Marriot. 'It's got a little bit of class,' she said. She drove us right up to the front door. 'I'm gonna let you pretty ladies off here,' she laughed, 'so you don't get your dainty little feet wet . . .'

'Aw, Ma, don't call us pretty ladies no more,' Toney moaned. 'You dissin' me and Don. It ain't right!'

'Sure it is,' Sherry sniggered. 'I'm the one doin' the drivin'. An' I know you two would get all strange on me if you had to walk in the snow. So, out! I'll see you inside.'

Toney and I shuffled into the foyer where he cocked an apologetic eye. 'My mom's a tough lady!' he whispered.

'She's great,' I said as the boxer's beeper went off again.

Toney looked down at the telephone number on his pager. 'Another one calling me,' he said slyly.

'You going to call her back?' I enquired enthusiastically.

'Nah,' Toney yawned as he leaned over the hotel's indoor bed of plants. 'I'm cooling off on women right now. I'll leave all these Ann Arbor ladies to you, man, you can take them . . .'

'I'm married now,' I said.

'Oh yeah. Me too. Dunno for how much longer though . . .'

I looked down at the circle he had drawn in the sand and waited, saying nothing.

'You heard about me and Sarah?' Toney eventually asked with the wavering voice of a heavy-hearted man.

'Yes.'

There was a hush between us. He looked away.

'How you coping?' I asked.

'Well,' Toney turned to face me. It looked like a yellowing loop of old family film ran just beneath the surface of his eyes. 'To tell you the truth, it's been real hard. You know what I'm saying?'

'Yes.'

'Hurt me more than anything anyone done to me in the ring. Me and Sarah, we were real close. We had us a baby. An' you know how much Jasmine means to me. But it's over between me and Sarah. All I got to look forward to is trying to get Jasmine back.'

'How often do you see Jasmine?'

'Man, if I'm not training in LA or in Vegas, I see her every day. She's my baby!' Toney exclaimed. 'She stays with me and Mom a few days a week and on the other days I go over and play with her.'

'Which means you see Sarah every day?' I said.

'Every single day. It ain't easy. But I made my mind up. It's over between us. With women now, for me, it's hi and bye – with a little bit of heat in between. I'm trying to think about nothing but boxing now . . .'

'But you loved Sarah,' I ventured.

'Yeah,' Toney nodded. 'I loved her. Even now, I'm there for her when she needs me. Like early this morning, just before we came out with you, I had to go over to her place. Sort something out for her with the car. It ain't easy to bear. It's painful.'

We pushed our faces back down into the plants, knowing that there was not much else either of us could say.

'What you two boys, doin'?' Sherry snapped as she breezed through the door.

'We waitin' for you, Ma,' James said.

'Good. Now, let's go eat, boys . . .'

James ate breakfast with Sherry and I; but it was not the boxer who demolished a cooked breakfast as well as a short-stack of syrupy pancakes in an exhibition of merciless finishing. While I did most of the eating, Toney did most of the talking. He entertained me with a stream of anecdotes about boxing and other fighters with a good cheer at odds with his outdated image as a mean-spirited former drug-trader. I decided again that James Toney was one of the sweeter men in boxing. He'd still got a mouth and a half on him, of course, but James and Sherry showed me a kindness which ruined Toney's reputation as boxing's perpetual bad guy.

And, for those who had described him as a lost victim of the big buffet burn-out, I was relieved to see the fighter eat the kind of moderate breakfast which champion boxers watching their weight have consumed over the years. Even though he was coming off that sixth consecutive victory and taking a few days' rest before returning to full-time training, it looked like discipline was back near the top of the Lights Out list of priorities. While I munched on, Toney pushed his plate of food aside and picked up his favourite subject – the restoration of his ring glory – with a light smile.

'Look,' he grinned, 'I'm feeling great again! An' so I ain't gonna worry about anythin' people say about me. Why should I? I'm only twenty-seven years old and I've got one of the very best records in the game. Fifty-four professional fights. Sure, Roy Jones beat me fair and square but there's just no way that the judges should have given the decision to Montell Griffin. So, really, my record should be 51-1-2. But, this is boxing. They gave a gift to Montell. I got fifty wins, two losses, two draws. It's there in black an' white. I would love to be 54-0 but all fighters lose at some point. An', you know what's best of all about my current record?'

'What?' I asked between mouthfuls.

'Man, it's real cool! 52-2-2 is exactly the same record as Marvin Hagler had as he neared his peak. Marvin finished at 62-3-2 but it's just great that, right now, I'm at the same point as he once was. That's my kind of fighter . . .'

'Hagler was great,' I burbled, 'but he was different to you – he always stayed at middleweight.'

'Yeah, I know what you're saying. I've not always prepared myself to the very best of my ability. I know better than anyone I've had some big trouble with weight. But I got my mind focused on boxing again after all the shit.'

'Are you tired of still answering questions about you and Jackie?'

'Man,' he objected, 'I'd rather not bring Jackie into our conversation. Bringing Jackie up is just giving her more publicity. I'd rather not do that. Jackie's not in my camp no more. It ended with Jackie last year on 18 July. So Jackie has no business between me and you. Jackie, whatever she might say, did not make me. I made her. My conscience is clear. So I got nothing more to say about her. We had our thing together for six years. That's it. It's over!'

'Did you really want to kill her after the Jones fight?' I persisted.

'Yeah, I wanted to kill her. She betrayed me for the dollar sign. That's all she wants – the dollar sign. An' that's not me. I want other things in life besides just money – I want realness. But I ain't gonna say anything else bad about Jackie. She's got her thing, I got mine. We ain't at war with each other. When I see her now, it's "hi" and "bye". Nothing else. That's the way it's always gonna be. I'm cool about it now. I got me a whole new career, a new thing, a new crew. They're a lot better. With Stan [Hoffman] and Eddie [Mustafa Muhammad] I'm on my way back to the top!'

'But, for most people, there's still a big question mark over your weight.'

'For my last fight a few days ago, I weighed exactly two hundred pounds. But I'm gonna go down the divisions again. Don't worry about my weight! I'm gonna get it off, I'm gonna knock it off, I'm gonna keep it off. See, I got a plan for 1996. I'm gonna get back to light-heavy. I'd like to fight 'em all in that division – Henry Maske, Darius Michalczwski, Montell Griffin and even Chris Eubank in London if he'll come out of his retirement. But, most of all, I want Roy Jones. I want him bad!'

It was an intriguingly tasty Lights Out roster of hoped-for fights, with his Jones wish running true to the typical Toney campaign of fighting the very best; but the light-heavyweight names he mentioned still surprised me. Six weeks before Toney had been angling to fight Evander Holyfield in a heavyweight contest at Madison Square Garden.

'Yeah, damn right I was! I'd love to fight Evander. He was a good fighter but I'd whup him. I'd jus' be too sharp and quick for a guy like Holyfield. But he backed away from fighting me. Well, that just motivated me to get back down to cruiser and then all the way down to light-heavy.'

'That's at least twenty-five pounds away,' I countered.

'Yeah, it's gonna be a task. But it's a task I'm ready and willing to take. I was in the gym yesterday, a couple of days after a fight, an' I'm back in the gym again today. My mom's right behind me. She wants me to get a light-heavy belt off Roy Jones to end the nightmare we've been through since 18 November 1995.'

'Does it bother you to talk about that night?'

'No. It used to. But it don't hurt me no more. Roy Jones fought me when I was at my very worst. I had to lose forty-five pounds in less than a month, I had flu, I was coming out of a period of inactivity. It was the biggest fight of our lives but I just didn't get myself into shape. I wasn't right for that fight. I believed I was gonna beat Roy Jones. I was sure of it. But at the end of the first round I could just feel my body go. All my strength went outta me. My body felt like it was all shook up – and Roy hardly laid a glove on me during the first. I knew I was in serious trouble, that I was in no fit state. I got no complaints against Roy Jones. He did what he had to do. He showed up and he won clearly on the night. He beat a shadow of the real James Toney . . .'

'Well, he did more than just show up – Roy Jones is a great fighter!'

'No, Don, you're wrong on that one. I gotta set you straight. I been in the ring with the guy. Roy Jones is a good fighter – but he ain't a great fighter yet. He's fought nuthin' but washed-up bums since he took my title.'

'But he's got such speed, such power,' I argued.

'He's got speed, yeah, but he's no quicker than Michael Nunn used to be. An' as for the power, he ain't got so much. He didn't hurt me in that fight. He ain't even the best fighter I ever faced. Mike MacCallum is the best guy I've fought. He was trickier than Jones, he hits harder than Jones. An' I beat Mike all right – but I was in shape. That's the key. If I'm in shape I can beat any guy out there!'

James Toney, like all great fighters, only had to convince himself. My protest faded. He was entitled to whatever belief it took to persuade himself that he could beat his nemesis. And, beyond my admiration for Roy Jones, there was a hankering. What would have happened if an even better version of the Toney who'd destroyed Barkley had turned up at the MGM? Jones himself had told me that even a lethargic Toney had been his hardest and most skilful opponent.

'A return fight between Roy and me is certain to happen,' Toney insisted. 'Who else is he gonna fight? There's no one out there for him but me. He ain't gonna make it in basketball. That's a joke. He knows it. I've got unfinished business with Mr Jones!'

'What about those pundits who've said that Jones has got the style to beat you every time?'

'I'd say they're wrong! I'd say they're making a fuckin' mistake! Next time against Jones I'm gonna be in helluva shape, I'm gonna be gettin' straight down to business. I ain't gonna rest until I get that fight. That's how I'm gonna redeem myself – by beating Roy Jones!'

'And Montell Griffin?'

'Well, that fight hurts me more than the Jones loss. I know I won but the judges robbed me. It was a terrible decision.'

I explained that Griffin had claimed that he had not been intimidated by the 'Lights Out' myth because he knew that 'the James Toney you see out in public, in front of the cameras, is not the real James Toney. You see the real man at home – and he's a nice guy, he's not a loudmouth'.

When I repeated Griffin's words, Toney showed the first sign of his notorious temper. He banged his fist on the table and shouted, in definitive loud-mouth style, 'He's talkin' shit!'

Toney breathed deeply, calming himself: 'Montell Griffin's a good person but he was intimidated by me. I like him but it pisses me off when I see that he's got a win over me. I've had seven fights since I met Roy and I should have a 7-0 record outside the super-middleweights. Montell's a fine boxer but next time I'd knock him out. He knows that so I don't think he's gonna meet me again.'

'Does it cause you any heartache when you see, after losing to Jones and Griffin, that you no longer make any of the pound-for-pound ratings – especially when less than eighteen months ago you were considered to be the world's best fighter?'

'Those ratings don't mean shit,' Toney sneered.

'But it must've been a good feeling to top that list.'

'Yeah, it was cool when I had all the praise, but look at Marvin Hagler again. He got no credit for so much of his career. I've had my share of praise over the years so it don't bother me that they're giving it all to Roy Jones now. I know what'll happen when we meet next.'

'What about Eubank?' I said, uncertain about perpetual rumours that the monocled mutineer would abscond from his newly discovered acting classes in Hove and climb back into the ring.

'Yeah, Chris Eubank is a real possibility,' Toney laughed. 'They say he's training again. Man, I'd like that fight!'

It was a fight that had been discussed countless times before. There was no conviction that even if he did end his retirement Eubank would choose to meet a recharged Toney.

As if it was something he thought I might be expecting, Toney dug into his faded bag of abuse. Clearly, he considered it time for us to resurrect one of his more cherished subjects – his attitude towards British fighters, starting with the man who liked to call himself 'Simply the Best'.

'Do you have any respect for Eubank?' I asked coyly.

'I have no respect for Chris Eubank,' he snarled on cue. 'It ain't personal, it's business. Eubank would be an easy fight. I expect to knock him out. He ain't got enough of a chin to take one of my shots. Nigel Benn hurt him and I hit harder than Nigel. Me and Eubank won't go five rounds. Against Nigel, Eubank was hangin' on like an octopus. I won't let him hang onto me.'

'And you'd be happy to fight Eubank in London?'

'Anywhere in Britain! I don't mind fighting over there 'cos I'd bring my guns and shoot everybody over there! No! Don't laugh, man! I'll do it!'

'What is it about the British?' I asked in mock-seriousness.

'I didn't say I don't like all British people. Some of them are real cool. You married one. It's just their fighters I hate. British fighters! Oh boy, you gotta laugh! They're bums! Straight-up bums! Bruno's a straight-up bum! Lennox Lewis is a bum! A big bum! Eubank's a bum! Benn's a bum! He lost to that old guy, Sugarboy! The bum loses to another bum!'

'Benn was never a bum,' I moaned. 'Against Gerald McClellan, even you had to concede that Benn was a great fighter.'

'No!' Toney said indignantly, his eyes opening wide in fake protest. 'Nigel was knocked out in the first round. Gerald whipped his ass but the ref gave him so much time to recover. If that hadn't happened, Gerald wouldn't be in the position he's in today. Gerald and me would've had a super-fight.'

'Were you a friend of Gerald?'

'No, never,' Toney grunted again, shutting down space for cheap sentiment. 'Me and Gerald never got along. I'm sad about what happened to him. I feel for the man. But I gotta say that I never liked Gerald. He used to say he beat my ass in the gym at Kronk. That ain't true! I was always so much better than Gerald! I've got the video tapes to prove it. When we get home I'll dig them out and I'll show you how I mastered Gerald McClellan!'

'But do you think of him now – lost to boxing and even ordinary life?'

'I do,' Toney said quietly. 'Gerald is blind and shot. I've just read this *Sports Illustrated* article where they talk about his sisters and father fightin' over the little money he got left. An' Gerald's jus' sitting there in darkness. It's a tragedy . . .'

'And boxing did that to him.'

'It don't bother me at all. The cold truth is that Gerald was not in shape for that fight. He was never able to go for more than four or five rounds. I go twelve rounds without even blinking.'

'But when you think what's happened to some of your contemporaries over the last five years – Gerald McClellan, Michael Watson. Michael was in shape the night he fought Eubank.'

'No one's ever completely safe in boxing,' Toney said evenly. 'But I'm not fighting just for me. I'm boxing to build up Jasmine's bank-balance, so that I can make her future safe. I'm willing to take any risk in the ring for her sake.'

James Toney leaned over and tapped me lightly on the hand.

'Tragedies happen in boxing. But, baby, that ain't gonna stop me. I ain't ever thought about quitting. Not even when I saw Gerald lying there. There was never a doubt in my head. The way I look at it, you gotta die somehow. So I fight on, I fight on . . .'

We swept through Ann Arbor, the wheels of Sherry's Land Cruiser crunching across thawing stacks of snow. Murky sunshine filtered across town. Winter, not only in Michigan but in James Toney's life, could not last forever.

His beeper jumped repeatedly on the dashboard. Mr Toney, plainly, was a popular man in his hometown. Sherry laughed. 'Yeah – with the ladies! Always the ladies! Look at that beeper jump. Man, that's a Mexican jumping bean if I ever saw one! Ladies phonin' all the time!'

'It don't matter, Ma,' Toney said. 'I got only one thing on my mind! Boxing, boxing, boxing. I got my focus back. That beeper can beep all it likes . . .'

As we turned into the rich cul-de-sac where they lived, Sherry amused me again with the story of how, when they first moved into their high-flying professionals' neighbourhood, the couple next door phoned the police. Seeing Toney leave his new home every day in a variety of flash cars, with beeper in hand, they made the predictable conclusion. Young Black Man + Cars + House + Beeper = Drug Baron!

'Yeah, you got it!' Sherry shivered. 'They got the police over here, saying that James must be a drug-dealer to live in this part of Ann Arbor! Well, they know who he is now. Everybody else round here – doctors, lawyers – are big fans of James now!'

Once inside his home, there could be no mistaking James Toney's trade. Everywhere I looked there were signs of his success in the ring – from the trophy cabinet hosting his various championship belts to the boxing paintings on the wall to the library of fight videos seen in every room. In the basement there was a makeshift gym filled with boxing gear and gleaming weights.

Toney was happiest at home, talking boxing, telling me how, two weeks before the fight, Tyson was set to destroy Bruno a minute into the third round. 'Don, if you wanna make some money in Vegas,' he advised, 'put everything you got on Tyson early in Round Three! Remember, you heard it here first! Mike is back to his best. I'm tellin' ya, you're gonna see a ferocious Tyson again!'

Although Eubank had been the one to visit Iron Mike in prison, I knew that Toney and Tyson were more alike. 'Yeah,' Toney grinned, 'me and Mike have always had some trouble outside the ring. But inside those ropes we're the same. We love to fight, we love to take on the best. They're writing Tyson off even before he fights Bruno – but you'll see, he's gonna be back, just like me!'

'Have you spent much time with him lately?'

'Yeah, I hang out in Vegas with Mike. When he came out of jail, we bumped into each other. We were at the Odyssey Record Store in Vegas, around two in the morning. Me and my people, him and his people. He was amazed when he saw me. He said, "Damn, you used to be a middleweight!" He couldn't believe it! He's a cool guy, a good guy. Same old Mike. We started kickin' it, did the strip clubs, went over to his place, stayed up all night . . .'

Before I could open up that disturbing image of Tyson and Toney descending on Vegas's strip-joints in swaggering tandem, Toney was up and running with his ultimate dream.

'Y'see, much as I like Mike, much as I think he's a great fighter, I know I can beat him in a year or two. My deepest wish is that I fight Mike Tyson on my thirtieth birthday for the undisputed heavyweight championship!'

'Shit, James,' I said with a slow shake of my head, staggered by his unshakeable belief, 'you don't really think you could fight Tyson?'

'No doubt about it! I know I can beat Mike Tyson! There are two guys out there I respect. Mike Tyson and Riddick Bowe. They're my boys, I like them both. But I wouldn't fear them in the ring! I'd love to fight 'em!'

'What about a Tyson-Bowe fight?' I asked the Ann Arbor oracle.

'That's a tough one. Tyson is great but Bowe is also tough. I think it all depends on the shape Riddick shows up in on the night. Mike would definitely be ready for him. That would be a great fight!'

'And you see yourself as being ready for the winner?'

'Absolutely! Mike's gonna go out and clean up the heavyweight titles. Then he knocks out Lennox Lewis. That guy's just a bum, a straight-up British bum! Then it's Tyson-Bowe!'

'And, meanwhile, you . . .?' I prompted.

'Meanwhile, I go back down in weight. I beat Roy Jones at light-heavyweight. Only once I've done that will I be ready to go back up to heavyweight and fight Mike Tyson. Until then, I'm only thinking of me and Mr Jones. Look, let me show you a couple a things . . .'

We spent the rest of the morning watching promotional videos of the build-up to Toney and Jones's previous 'Uncivil War' encounter. It was a surreal experience, sitting on a plush sofa with the fighter, watching Toney on his own enormous television screen spit out threats and warnings to Jones in the weeks leading up to their fight seventeen months before. Toney checked himself with intent, laughing at some of his own lines, nodding meaningfully when he promised to 'whup' Roy Jones and retain his IBF super-middleweight belt. James Toney did not look like a man haunted by his worst loss in the ring; instead, licking his lips, he looked hungry for boxing, like he was starving to fight Roy Jones again.

'Next time,' he pledged as the images flickered across the TV in a bluish blur, 'next time it's gonna be different . . .'

He looked up at Roy Jones as a voice from HBO hyped their '95 'Fight of the Decade!'.

'Yeah, it ain't over, baby, it ain't over!'

And it was still not over a couple of hours later as, in his favourite Ann Arbor gym, a sweat-streaked Lights Out pounded his body back into shape. His eyes glistened and a huge grin cracked across his streaming face as he worked, putting in the hours again, mouthing his mantra, 'Get it off, knock it off, keep it off!', feeling the pounds melt away as he reheated his boxing dream. He winked and beckoned towards me. The steam rose off him as he wiped the sweat, but not the smile, from his face.

'You go tell 'em,' he whispered, 'they better watch out. I'm gonna be better than ever! I'm gonna shock the world again! Whoever wants a taste of James Toney, I'm ready! I'm back, baby, I'm back!'

I was heading for another place of fantasy, for the MGM in Las Vegas. 'You better watch the time,' Sherry said in the voice of the mother she had always been to James Toney. 'I'll drive you back to your car but first I got something for you – from me and James.' She smiled secretively as she opened a door of the Land Cruiser. 'We got you a couple of gifts. You ain't never forgotten us. You've come all the way to Ann Arbor to see us – almost breaking your neck in that damn storm. We appreciate it. So this is for you.' Sherry handed me a green woollen ski-cap. 'Keep you warm on the drive back to the airport,' she said shyly.

While I thanked her she pointed out the familiar 'Lights Out' motif on my new hat – 'See, it's one which we've just done – "James Lights Out Toney – Two Time World Champion".'

'I really like it,' I said.

'Yeah, me too. It's the first time we've done it in green. It's a real nice colour.'

I thought suddenly of Gerald McClellan, the G-Man. I knew that he would be dressed in green again that morning – not too many hours down the highway from where we stood. The goodness of Sherry Toney, and all the memories I had of fighters like her son and Gerald McClellan, threatened to overwhelm me for a moment. I thought of all those people who, even if they cared about me, had scoffed at my writing a book about boxing. If they had been with me in Ann Arbor they might have changed their minds about the supposed emptiness of everyone in boxing.

Yet, before I could get too philosophical about a green woolly hat, Sherry pulled out a whole bag of tricks. There were specially printed photographs of Jasmine, of James and Sherry, of the three of them together at the little girl's third birthday party. There were videos of Toney's winning fights since he'd lost to Griffin and piles of newspaper clippings. But, best of all, there was a white box tied down with a pink ribbon.

'I think I know what this is, Sherry,' I laughed.

'Yeah, well, I know you like 'em.'

'Speciality Cakes & Pies?' I said as I untied the bow.

'You got it. I know you gonna be in Vegas for a couple o' weeks an' you ain't got your baby with you. I know what you boys are like. So these'll stop you going hungry for a while.'

The cakes were piled high, as before, in layers of Apple and Blueberry and Cherry Bites and mini pecan pies. 'Mmmm,' I said, 'my favourites.'

'Yeah, well, don't you eat 'em all in one sitting,' Sherry scolded as we climbed into the car.

'James looks like he's really determined to lose the weight,' I suggested as I closed the lid again.

'Yeah, I been telling him for a year. He gotta get down to light-heavy. He knows it. It's just been a fact that, all through this nightmare, he's taken to the table too often. Y'see, when James gets depressed, he eats. He don't drink or take drugs. He simply eats – a lot.'

'He's much bigger since I last saw him,' I said tentatively.

'Oh yeah!' Sherry snorted. 'Man, there's no two ways about it. He's had a real problem. An eating problem. It's still there. But he's getting it under control. He just can't let up. He's got to stay in shape all the time – he can't afford one more binge because it'll set him back. He knows the score. He's gotta get back down to 175 pounds. He'll do it. Y'see, we're getting things straightened out at last. He's got out of Jackie's clutches and now he's made the break with Sarah.'

'He told me a little about it.'

'That's good,' Sherry sighed. 'I knew he could talk to you. But you can't push him. He'll talk about it when he's ready.'

'He told me how painful it was for him.'

'It is. But it's healthy he can admit it now.'

'How do you feel about the divorce?' I asked.

'I'm glad!' Sherry snapped. 'I always said the only thing Sarah was good at was spending all of James's money. Boy, the way the stuff runs through her pretty fingers!'

'I thought she was studying to be a psychologist?'

'I'll tell you a couple of truths about Sarah. I paid for her tuition for four separate college courses. She didn't finish one. She didn't want to work at anything but spending money, buying clothes, going out, having a fine old time. She's bad news.'

'But James loved her,' I said.

'You're right. He really loved that girl. He gave in to her too much. You know James – inside that hard shell he's real soft with the people he likes. Sarah knew that, Jackie knew that. They played him. Even just before the wedding they were doing it. James got married on 21 May last year and he paid for everything. I kept waiting for her parents to call. But no, not even for the wedding dress. They stayed quiet. Sarah went to Jackie about the dress. They convinced James he should be the one to buy her a $7,000 wedding dress. He did it – and then he got his heart broken. He's no angel, I know he does some wild things, but those two women have not helped him. You see James sweating to drop all those pounds? The way I look at it, he's sweating to shed the influence of those two, of Sarah an' Jackie.'

'And what about you,' I asked. 'How are you dealing with it all?'

Sherry accelerated a little as she swallowed and brushed the hair from her eyes. 'Well . . .' she said, 'you know me by now. I'm gonna write it out of my system. I just ain't been able to work very well lately – the pressure has been so intense it's been hard to concentrate, to reflect on everything. But I got this feeling that things are turning. I think I'm gonna be ready soon to write my book about me and James. I'm on a mission with that book. Man, I can't wait to see Jackie's face when she reads it!'

'So she knows you're going to write about her?'

'Oh yeah! Jackie's got a degree in journalism but her eyes popped out when she saw the synopsis. "What's the matter, Jackie," I said, "didn't you think I could write?" No, Jackie did not think I had it in me. She thought

I was just like all the other boxers' mothers she knew. She thought I was a true watermelon. She would tell people that we were friends – remember? But we weren't friends. We had a six-year dollarship not a friendship.'

'Did you think that even before the Jones fight?'

'You know I did. A week before the fight she called James "a worthless piece of shit" behind his back. She said he wasn't doing all the publicity to make that fat pay-per-view cheque. I knew all about it. I didn't tell James. How could I? He was going into the biggest fight of his career and his manager's bad-mouthing him. I held my tongue. I stayed on my own, knowing the truth.'

'Did you think he was going to beat Jones?'

'I had the fear that night. I could feel it so bad. I had the call in LA two weeks before the fight. The chills went through me. I'd gone out for a run in LA. Everything was fine until I reached the top of this hill. It was then that the chill came, it went through me like a cold dark spirit. Like a premonition you feel if someone in your family is about to die.'

'Did you tell anyone?'

'I told my lawyer,' Sherry said in her beguiling American way. 'But he couldn't do anything. What was he gonna do? Sue that spirit? He advised me not to say anything to James. But I never would've done that. I kept it to myself. But it felt like death was coming.'

'And then,' I said with a deep breath, 'James threatened to kill Jackie.'

'Worst day of my life,' Sherry recalled. 'That brawl with Jackie was worse than the fight with Roy Jones. I put my life on the line for Jackie. I went out of my way for her. So many times before I'd been the one to hold them together, to keep the camp intact. I'd drop everything, leave my bakery, rush over and try to patch things up because Jackie did not know how to handle James. She tried to be his mother, to take my place. All the while she was making a million dollars out of him in the ring. Jackie would make a deal and then tell James about it afterwards. She'd control him like a puppet. But, still, I tried to help her. When he left that day, saying he was gonna shoot up her and her family, I phoned her. I warned her that he was coming. I knew he wasn't going to kill her, he was just mad with himself. But I was watching out for the both of them. I didn't want Jackie to get frightened.'

'James can be a scary guy,' I said.

'Yeah – but she's a drama queen,' Sherry mocked. 'Nothing happened. James didn't go near her but she was on the phone right away to the domestic and international media. I was with her the next day. She was sticking her chest out, bragging about it, saying, "My life's been threatened – aren't I brave?" It was a set-up between her and the press. James called her a 'ho' and she started crying, going "Boo-hoo, boo-hoo, now he calls me a whore!" But a 'ho' means a hustler where we come from. Jackie turned it round. I'll give her credit. She's good with the whip of the tongue. She knows how to handle the press. She made James look like a laughing fool, like King Kong. She's a middle-class white damsel who set him up. You can print that as it stands!'

'How did James react?'

'Terrible. The worst thing was that Jackie tried to turn him against me. I did not have to call her that Sunday but she used it. She tried to convince him that even I had turned against him, that I had taken her side. She almost managed it. He looked like a motherless child that night – so lost, so angry. I have never seen anyone so bereft. He thought I was shielding Jackie, that I was supporting her instead of him. He was very angry. He was raging. But, in the end, I got through. He listened. I said, "James, right is right and wrong is wrong! You know where I stand. You know how Jackie slides with words." He saw what had happened. He understood why I had done what I did, that Jackie milked it for all it was worth.

'Jackie was getting fifty calls an hour from the press. It was preposterous! My brother calls me from Washington. Front page of the *Washington Post* – "Gun-toting crack-dealer goes to manager's house, threatens to blow up manager's family". He said to me, "Sherry, what the hell is going on?" I told him straight. Y'see, Jackie plays the defenceless white lady to the hilt but she's very cunning. Her only problem is she thinks she knows everything. She don't listen. She thinks she's smarter than us.

'I told her once, "Jackie, there is one thing you have to understand about my son. James is a soldier-boy. Pure and simple. You know what that means? It means he'll go out and always fight his heart out for you. He'll die for you in the ring. But if you cross him, he'll kill you. He's a soldier-boy. He's on a mission." She just thought it was crazy talk. It was not. It was the truth. That's why she'll never find another James Toney as long as she lives. Few men are made like him. He's a soldier-boy – even now.

'But, for a while, it looked like she might beat him. Y'see, "The Lady & The Champ" turned into Fay Wray & King Kong. Print that for me – please. It's the perfect analogy for Ms Jackie Kallen. She was Fay Wray and she treated my boy like some dumb King Kong! An' that ain't true, you know it ain't. She might be Fay Wray but he ain't King Kong. He's my son, he's James Toney.'

II

NOTHING IS FOREVER

F ROM THE OUTSIDE, AT NIGHT, THE WORLD'S LARGEST HOTEL
looked most like a green beast, glowering over Las Vegas with fluores-
cent greed. Gerald McClellan must have been exultant when he fought
here. The G-Man knocking out someone inside a huge emerald green hotel
– it might once have been his idea of heaven.

But, on the inside, I knew that two weeks could feel like an eternity in
the MGM Grand. I had a room on the twenty-second floor. In the hope
that a radiant view would break the monotony, I pulled back the curtains
as soon as I arrived. Two hundred feet in the air, set against a black sky,
Vegas shone with a beauty which was hard to find even in the most brilliant
sunlight. I could see almost halfway down the Strip, right up to the
exploding glare of the MGM's main rivals, Caesars Palace and The Mirage.

But as my gaze swung back across the gleaming vista it locked with that
of Mike Tyson. His eyes were set close together, two black stones in a head
of sullen granite. The mouth turned down, but not far enough to stop the
top lip looking like it could curl into a malevolent sneer at the next turn of
the giant cube. There was no need for any blurb beneath his face. The
MGM marketing team did not have to tax themselves to think up any
creamy fantasy hook. They did not need to spell out 'Brutal' or 'Violence'.
'*Tyson*' said everything they wanted.

They had to work more positively to peddle the other entertainment on
offer. Why not, they asked, have a pop and a pull at any one of their 3,500
slot machines before taking in a thirty-three-acre Yellow Brick Road tour of
the Wizard of Oz's Secret Adventures? Then you could spend a swell time
in the Grand Spa or Oasis Pool before wishing upon a star at a spectacular
laser show. What about sipping a cocktail at the Flying Monkey Bar? And,
afterwards, why not get lucky and get down to some serious gambling in
any one of the four themed casino areas – namely Emerald City, Hollywood, Monte Carlo and Sports.

Tyson gave the MGM the dark contrast they needed to push such puff. He was the flipside to the dreamy breakaway. Tyson was being traded as Frank Bruno's worst nightmare. The MGM brought you the news as soon as you stepped into the foyer. The entire back wall was given over to a massive screen which showed a loop of Tyson pounding a helpless Bruno seven years earlier. A dramatic voiceover echoed deeper and louder: 'Tyson! Tyson! Tyson!'

But my room was hushed, all sound from the casinos and streets far below lost in the muffled hum of the air-conditioner. Tyson's head came round again. We looked at each other, that enormous metal turret of a face and I. Tyson's unmoving eyes were dead, offering no clue as to where I might find him in the strange days ahead.

I went hunting for him early the next morning. I knew that I had only a few days left before press and television crews from all over the world settled on Vegas. But I felt weariness and doubt as I set out in pursuit of a missing man. Thousands of reporters were hoping to win the lucky dip and catch Tyson alone so that they could stick a tape-recorder under his nose and ask him questions he'd heard so often they had been robbed of all meaning for him: 'How does it feel, Mike, remembering prison?'; 'How does it feel, Mike, knowing you'll earn $30,000,000 in your next fight?'; 'How does it feel, Mike, being called a rapist?'; 'How does it feel, Mike, being an icon again?'

Tyson had had his fill of interviews; and even the meagre few he was coerced into accepting were thick with loathing for the routine. In *Esquire*, Mark Kram was forced to ask Tyson if he was bored.

'I hate interviews,' Tyson answered, 'I really hate them. I don't want to be here.'

'Consider it a conversation,' Kram tried again. 'People want to know what's on your mind. With all these millions, this comfort, they want to know if the passion is there.'

'Don't you know?' Tyson sneered back. 'I'm not supposed to have a mind. I'm a monster.'

Kram watched Tyson furrow his brow and think.

'Look,' the boxer eventually said, 'fighting to me is what theory was to Einstein or words were to Hemingway. Fighting is aggression. Aggression is my nature.' Tyson's eyes, Kram noted, looked away before he confirmed again, 'I don't want to talk about boxing.'

Of course such an ambiguous blend of indifference and emotion served only to heighten our desire to hear more talk from Tyson. As Kram stressed in his exasperated feature, 'Tyson can be extremely articulate, though, about his work, better than anyone ever before. Right now, however, he's obdurate, clumsily evasive. When he doesn't fancy an enquiry, his voice breaks up like a cloud into a mumble.'

Kram turned to a more eccentric line of questioning to get the answers he needed. He asked the fighter about his new pets – Kenya, a seven-month-old white tiger, and Omar, a lion, who was having his nails clipped.

'What's the appeal of tigers?' Kram mused.

'They're solitary,' Tyson said. 'They don't need anyone.'

'Lions?'

'They're great family men.'

'Do you see these things in yourself?'

'Maybe.'

'Can they ever be joined?'

'Maybe never,' Tyson said emptily.

Of his conversion to Islam, Tyson murmured, at first wittily, 'Look, I'm not going to split the Red Sea,' and then more poignantly, 'I'm a very private Muslim. I feel at peace with it. I'd like to go to the mosque, but I don't. Muslims are human beings first and, knowing that, I know what they'll be thinking. The signals will go off in their heads. Here comes the rapist, the thug, to defile their holy place.'

Yet, just as if it seemed that Kram was getting somewhere inside the murky hurt of Tyson's mind, the fighter retreated behind another grey wall – 'Talking isn't my game,' he told Kram.

I understood and even respected Tyson's need to be free from the scrutiny of others. I liked and smiled at his final words to Kram. 'I have a serious thing going on between me and my head; it's just me and my head.' And yet I was no better than the rest. I wanted to be the one who broke through, the one whom Tyson would decide he could trust enough to speak in a way which went beyond circuitous brooding. But, at the same time, I knew how that hope was curdled by my own arrogance. Why should Tyson give up another hour of his life to hear my voice, to respond to my queries?

Still, I forced myself on, thinking instead how smart it would be to complete the circle with another detailed Mighty Mike encounter. Tyson and I together once more, chewing the fat again, spitting out the gristle of his life to uncover the secret man inside the dark iron shell.

Tyson had said, 'I don't want to be perceived as a fighter anymore, just a violent thing. I want to be seen as a man who is ferocious in life, who will not be stopped.'

As dramatic as I found those words, I wanted to be the guy who coaxed Tyson into saying that he didn't really mean it. In my looniest conceit I heard him saying that, having spent such an illuminating afternoon in my irrepressibly thoughtful company, he had decided that life was not so bad after all. Mike and me, boxing nuts and bookish buddies, together. Hey, Mighty, I could say, have you read any stories by Raymond Carver? I think you'd like him, big man.

I stood on the Strip and wondered. Who did Iron Mike like most in

Vegas? I knew Tyson had a surreal admiration for his next-door neighbour, Wayne Newton, describing the Vegas crooner as 'a strong, stable man. I see big courage there. Dignity.' But I could not see a way for me into Wayne's mansion – especially as Tyson's notorious posse of bodyguards would probably already be running a roadblock outside the boxer's desert palace. I decided to go the other way, all the way downtown, where I knew I would find another Vegas character whom Tyson respected. Apart from Wayne Newton, who else but Johnny Tocco had Tyson spoken of with such affection since returning from his jail cell? Tyson had even floated his idea to the eighty-year-old trainer that he would give up his luxuries and bed down in a cot at the back of Tocco's rundown gymnasium.

I hitched a ride on the CAT bus. I liked to use the bus in Vegas. Apart from the fact that I could not afford the taxi fares, the swaying wagon cleared my head. I gave up my wayward imaginings and measured out the difficulties entailed in getting close enough to Tyson to ask him if we might have a gab for old times' sake. Hey, Mighty, remember the last time? What about one more yak just for the hell of it?

But the sheer mass of people pressing in on him was a memo of how many more saps would be arriving in Vegas, bent on sneaking the impossible interview. There were so many of them, of us, gathering together in a ravenous huddle, that Tyson was driven into his hole.

Few of the others, however, with their expense accounts, would ever travel Vegas by bus, and so I relaxed into the chaotic journey, the stop-start jerkiness garnished by the driver shouting out the name of every single casino and hotel we passed. 'Ballys, folks . . . Caesars an' The Mirage, g'luck out there, Imperial Palace on this side o' the street . . . hold tight for Treasure Island . . . Harrahs, don't lose all your welfare cheque in one go, ha-ha . . . here's Circus Circus . . . there's Sahara . . . heading downtown now – Glitter Gulch, Fremont and on to the back o' beyond. We're over the Strip, folks. It's downtown, now, all the way downtown . . .'

All kinds of people travelled the CAT but by the time you reached the far end of the Strip most of the tourists had disappeared. And the deeper downtown you went, the more Vegas changed. The people left on the bus were angular and leathery, their voices blurred and worn. It was as if the dreaming of a sudden fortune, of a way out, had rusted away. They survived downtown on the scraps, riding the buses, knowing that without a car in America you were nothing.

As we left behind the crumbling motels offering rooms for an hour of 'Adult Video Entertainment', you could see the cemetery and the wasteland yet to be developed despite the booming property market. Behind us, the town was the fastest-growing in America, a gambling oasis which sucked in tens of thousands of new home-owners a month. But downtown looked as downbeat as it had ever done, a ramshackle collection of gun and porn shops, of winos on the corner and stray dogs pissing against derelict stores.

There was a library a little further along, closer to the Golden Gloves gym where I had last interviewed Tyson. It also served as a shelter for the drifters and tramps who grew tired of both the sun and the dusty wind. It was an impressive building but it reeked of urine – and I doubted if Iron Mike borrowed his copies of Tolstoy and Voltaire from their creaking shelves.

I got off a few blocks before, on the junction of Charleston and Maine, where I remembered the clearest landmark – the bug exterminator business which advertised its wares by painting pictures of black creepy-crawlies all over its white outside wall. All their gritty promises of rising above the roaches marked an appropriate return to boxing's origins, to one of America's most venerable gymnasiums which occupied a low and slanting space you reached by walking through the oil-streaked backyard of an exhaust repair garage.

Inside, an old man sat on the padded bench, patting his chubby labrador, softly calling her Meg, or maybe Peg, above the thud of two unknown black boxers moving around the big blue ring which occupied the gym's front room. Johnny Tocco greeted me with a weary wave and a quiet 'How ya doin'?'. His rheumy eyes returned to the fighters, following their sparring with the look of a man who had watched the same movements for an allotted seven score year and more.

'Got some Italian TV crew comin' in this afternoon,' he muttered. 'Can you believe it, they wanna ask me about Sonny Liston again. The guy's been dead twenty-five years and, still, they askin' me about him.'

A copy of the *Esquire* interview with Tyson lay untouched on the floor. Kram had described Liston, who had worked for years with Tocco, as presenting 'an image of imminent danger and defiance. He went through life like a big rat in a familiar granary. He and Tyson share the same early jail pedigree, but they divide in the matter of conscience: Liston had none, Tyson seems to have found one.'

Tocco was unimpressed by the words. 'Sonny was Sonny,' he said, 'Mike is Mike.' He gestured to the faded '*Welcome Home Mike!*' banner which hung above the front door to the gym. 'Mike's always been happy here. I like Mike. He's a good kid.'

'Is he doing any work here?' I asked restlessly.

'No, not at the moment,' Tocco sighed. 'He's done most of his training in Ohio. For the next couple a weeks he's gonna be at Golden Gloves. You know the place, you know the Tyson drill. Two till three-thirty most afternoons. If you're lucky you might see him then.'

'Have you spoken to him lately?'

'No. Not for a while. He's keeping to himself. I understand.'

'But Mike called you just before he left prison,' I said.

'Yes.'

'And the stories about him using this gym as his base,' I asked, 'were they true?'

'That's what he said in prison. But it's different outside.'

The fighters had climbed out of the ring and joined us, rubbing their smiley faces with scratchy grey towels. Like most boxers, they were immediately friendly.

'Good to see ya, man!' the first man said.

'You here for the fight?' the second enquired gently.

'Yes,' I answered. 'Who do you like – Tyson?'

'Man,' the first one exclaimed, 'I saw Mike down at Golden Gloves last week. He was busting up some of those sparring partners he got. He looked good. Whaddya think, Johnny?'

They both glanced expectantly at Johnny Tocco, two young black men bursting with health and respect for the ancient white sage.

Johnny kept stroking his dog, occasionally running his gnarled hand down the length of Peg's, or Meg's, back, making the fur stand up in ticklish strands. 'I think Mike's still got some way to go,' the gym-keeper said carefully. 'Mike knows it. It's taking him time to get back to what he once had. There're no shortcuts in boxing. He might be great again. If he keeps his mind clear.'

'If he stays away from the ladies . . .' the older fighter whooped.

I thought of Toney and Tyson swooping through the strip-houses across town, on Industrial Road, and doubted if serenity had yet been reached in the mind of Mighty Mike.

'Hey Johnny,' the younger boxer asked earnestly, 'how long should you hold off before a fight?'

Johnny Tocco looked puzzled. 'Whaddya mean?'

'Doin' it,' the fighter said shyly. 'How long shouldn't you do it?'

'He's talking about sex,' his sparring partner explained to the still bemused Tocco.

'Oh, sex,' the old man murmured. 'Well, they reckon it's best if you don't have sex for at least six weeks before a fight.'

'Johnny!' the second boxer yelped. 'Six weeks!'

'That's what they've always said,' Tocco confirmed.

'They're right,' the first fighter shrugged. 'Man, I learned the hard way.'

'What happened?' I asked.

'I got my dick sucked the night before a fight.'

'Yeah?' his friend said excitedly.

'She was hot. A real looker!'

Johnny Tocco stared down impassively at the labrador, panting gently in the spring heat.

'Jeez, Johnny,' the fighter complained, 'I was foolish. That blowjob! It took my strength away.'

'No shit?' the other boxer said sadly.

'Man, I was winning the fight easy. Then the last round came and I had nothing left. Given it all up the night before. I got knocked out!'

Johnny snorted. 'I can believe it. There are no shortcuts in boxing.'

'You're so right, Johnny,' the more experienced man agreed, 'no shortcuts in this damn business.'

The two fighters went to change in the second room where the heavy bags hung. Johnny walked me round the gym, talking me through the peeling fight posters, tugging at the ring ropes, making sure that there was not too much slack. They were tranquil moments, a shuffling tour round a sweat-stained room of boxing history.

I asked Johnny what he thought about the analogy between Ali and Tyson which Kram had explored. He had written that 'Both men played with the fire of sex. The difference was the media reaction, when they looked at all. With Ali, it was considered cute; with Tyson, it became menace . . . with the coming of Tyson, the ring returned to the dark hearth. When you looked at him, you didn't see neon; you saw the way the ring used to be decades earlier: the single light over the rubbing table, the backed-up toilet and the cold shower . . . [Tyson] brought back the primal rush – men seizing the maleness of other men.'

'Yeah,' Tocco muttered, 'but you know how Mike, at his best, ain't just a killer. Sure he's a great finisher, like Liston. When he got you hurt he's gonna get you. Mike, at his best, has so much more than just power. He got the speed, the movement, the elusive quality. A great defensive fighter – one of the best. But those prison years are gonna tell on him. When Ali was out of boxing he was still able to train, he was still taking punches in the gym. Mike's had to learn how it feels like to be hit again. It ain't a feeling you get back overnight. An' I don't think Tyson's got any of his ol' movement an' timing back yet.'

'Do you think he can ever get that back?' I asked.

'We'll know after Bruno.'

'Does Bruno have a chance?'

'He's got a shot,' Tocco muttered, 'but he's got that chin. An' he's making a big mistake working down at World's Gym.'

'Why?'

'To get to the ring you gotta walk past all these hundreds of ladies in their headbands and pink leotards,' he said despairingly. 'That just ain't the way to prepare for a fight with Mike Tyson. It's madness.'

We stood quietly at ringside, pondering the delusion, imagining the big black boxer picking his way gingerly through the lines of women working out on their stairmasters. Maybe it helped remind him of one area of weakness in Iron Mike. The gym was still and calm and I bent down to pat the ever-smiling labrador. Johnny rubbed his eyes as if he needed a nap. The dog's tail swished lightly on the bare floor.

Our silence was broken by a raucous voice. 'Like a crackhouse whore sucking on a pipe, just like some damn crackhouse whore,' came the chant.

Johnny Tocco nodded impassively. 'That'll be Panama,' he said.

Panama Lewis stepped out of the sunlight and into the shade of the gym, his dreadlocks swinging in time to his carolling crudity. He was big and loud, a man with a reputation more sullied than most, even in boxing's unsavoury line-up of leeches and thieves. Lewis was infamous for having been jailed after he had removed the lining from one of his boxer's gloves so that the fighter's fists killed an opponent. The boxer who did the damage took to the bottle and ended up dead himself in a car crash. But Panama Lewis had done his time and, out again, he had been mentioned often in rumours as to who would train Tyson. Yet in the end he worked with another of King's heavyweights.

They called him 'The White Buffalo'; but he followed the yelling Panama more like an awkward sheep. François Botha, a white Afrikaner, was then the IBF heavyweight champion of the world, having defeated Axel Shultz in Germany a few months before. Botha and Shultz were ridiculed as being the two worst fighters to contest a world heavyweight championship – an opinion which was not challenged by their mediocre display or by the fact that Botha's victory was on the verge of being overturned on a charge that he'd used 'performance-enhancing' drugs.

Early in March 1996, however, Frans Botha was one of four world heavyweight champions – the others being Frank Bruno (WBC), Bruce Seldon (WBA) and Riddick Bowe (WBO). Botha, despite being unbeaten after thirty-four fights, was the worst of the lot. I had met him before, in Belfast in 1994, when Naseem Hamed had danced around Don King and the White Buffalo with glee, as if he thought that he was good enough as a bantamweight to knock out the South African heavy. I had found Botha to be an amiable sort – even if he was bewildered by the rumbustious gang of black Americans with whom King surrounded him.

Yet none were more brazen than Panama Lewis. In Johnny Tocco's gym he picked up his 'Blow 'em down like a crackhouse whore, baby!' holler while he bandaged the hands of his meek champ. Botha whispered, 'Howzit, man,' to me as he moved laboriously to Bob Marley. 'Africa unite, Africa unite,' he mouthed to the old-style reggae as Panama wailed his dirtier dirge on top. They made a bizarre combination. As if he could see no sense in the noise, Johnny retreated to his cubby hole of an office.

'Hey, don't disturb my man,' Panama Lewis bellowed when he saw me watching the White Buffalo sing his Marley songs.

'I'm not doing anything,' I protested.

'Ah, Panama, he's a bro from home,' Botha said tentatively.

'I don't care if he's your crackhouse whore,' Panama repeated his favourite line, 'we workin' now.'

I accepted the subtle hint and moved away. A squat figure, partly hidden by a denim cap and dark glasses, beckoned to me, as if to say I would be safe on his side of the gym. I nodded my thanks and as he inclined his head I saw him in a plainer light. Eddie Mustafa Muhammad, a cool Muslim in shades, friend of Mighty Mike and trainer to James Toney, leaned over and extended his hand. 'How ya' doin', baby?' he grunted.

Before he had embraced Islam, Eddie Mustafa Muhammad had been known more simply as Eddie Gregory, a tough fighter from Brownsville. He converted at the age of twenty-eight and won the WBA light-heavyweight title. As a fighter, Muhammad was most renowned for his tenacity and resilience, having never been knocked out in fifty-six professional fights. Since his retirement he had emerged as an inspirational trainer.

As Panama held up the pads for his Buffalo-Boer to pound with ponderous combinations, Muhammad began to murmur in my ear. 'You can laugh at Botha but he works hard. I'll give him that. He's no Tyson or Toney, but he's a trier. I like that in a man.'

'But heavyweight champion of the world?' I repeated softly.

'Maybe not for long,' Muhammad allowed. 'But I don't want to disrespect no man.'

'I remember you and James Toney having a dig or two at each other,' I whispered.

Muhammad smiled bluntly. 'Before I took over James, we were pretty much enemies. He understood I wouldn't back down. And that's why he respects me. I told him straight: "You're just a young gangster, I'm an old gangster!"'

'He said you tried to intimidate him.'

'I did intimidate him,' Muhammad said in delight. 'I went right up to that big bodyguard of his in Atlantic City and I told him, "I'm gonna knock you out. Then I'll take Toney." I jumped on him at the press conference. I knocked this six-foot seven-inch monster to the ground. I'm a man of conviction. I think I'm the most strong-willed individual that's ever been put on this earth.'

I nodded blankly as Eddie reeled on.

'I am the intimidator. I come from Brownsville. Before Mike Tyson and Riddick Bowe, there was Eddie Mustafa Muhammad. I paved the way for guys like them. They respect that. Same with James Toney.'

'Do you think he fired Bill Miller because he had lost that respect?'

'I was surprised that his relationship with Bill was over. Bill's a good trainer. But maybe James needed a guy who'd talk the same language, a guy who'd scream in his face if that's what's needed. I run the show. If he don't listen to me then I'm outta there. Like him I've done things in my past I ain't proud of. But, the way I look at it, they were forced upon me because of my environment. Look at me as a young man and you can see Toney, you can see Tyson. But I've ended up a worldly person. With Islam I've cast off the bad. I keep a good balance in my life now. But I don't forget the past. Those tribulations help me to help my fighter. I'm an asset to James Toney both in and out of the ring. Y'see, my special skill is that I'm an extension of my fighter. I've been there, I can see what's happening. I've been known to take fighters who everybody else has written off and I've taken them back to prominence. James Toney will be my greatest success yet.'

'What do you think happened against Roy Jones,' I asked.

'He had the wrong people round him; he had all that weight to lose. Before the fight, I thought Toney would beat Jones – but he didn't give more than 40 per cent of himself in the ring. I think Roy is a great fighter. At the moment, because he won that fight, he's pound-for-pound the number one. But, next time, it will be very different. Next time James Toney beats Roy Jones. I truly believe he is the better fighter. I know the quality of the athlete I'm dealing with here. Once we get this weight problem under control there's gonna be no stopping James. He has such skills, he has the mentality – that "I'm the baddest man who ever stepped in the ring" mentality.'

'That's supposed to be Tyson's line,' I said.

'Yeah, but Toney could one day beat Tyson.'

'That's what he kept telling me,' I laughed.

'No question about it, baby! That's how much faith I have in James Toney's ability.'

Eddie Mustafa Muhammad was not the sort of dreamer to encourage dissent and so I turned away from Toney to Tyson. When Iron Mike was in his last months of prison there had hardly been a more regular visitor to the Indiana Youth Center than Muhammad himself.

'When I first went to see Mike in jail, about a year after he'd been inside, they blocked me. Don King thought I was planning to steal Mike away from him. He was so frightened. When Mike heard, he called me in. Y'see, Mike looked up to me when he was still a kid. When he was twelve or thirteen, and then all through his years with Cus, Mike always wanted to meet me. When I went up to Catskills we hit it off right away. We sparred and spoke. I'm fourteen years older than Mike, I'm like an older brother to him. That made Don King even more anxious. But I never went to Indiana to talk about boxing. I went as a Muslim, to see if Mike truly had discovered Islam. He had. Mike is great. Mike is fine. He has Islam – and, with or without Eddie Mustafa Muhammad or Don King, that makes Mike Tyson a bigger man than ever.'

'But what about the speculation that Tyson would ask you to train him?'

'Mike picked other people to run his corner. I respect that. He had to do what made him most comfortable. If those people, his "Team Tyson" people, make him feel good then so be it. Mike and me are friends, we're brothers, from Brownsville through Islam. Nothing can change that. So, still, I niggle inside Don King's big head of hair. Y'see, Don fears me. And he has a right to fear me. I'm a very strong person and I speak my mind. Don King intimidates most other people but he knows he cannot intimidate me. I don't fear Don King. I never have. I fear God, not Don.'

The two strange King employees in front of us played out their ritual in the ring. The sweaty White Buffalo lumbered after his black trainer as the Panama-Man picked up that obscene chant again. But Eddie Mustafa was not listening. He was on a roll. He looked at me with a harsh glint in his eye and shifted so that his mouth moved closer to my tape-recorder.

'I must reiterate this, man. Don King is the most greedy, the most mean, the most treacherous person in the world. That's my opinion. There're guys out there who like Don. But I think Don is the Devil. But, with Islam, Mike Tyson will defeat the Devil. Don knows it too. I think Mike Tyson is on the way to finding himself, I think he's on the path of righteousness, I think he's gonna surprise everyone . . .'

6 March 1996

Five years on I found myself back where I started. The barren patch of ground outside the Golden Gloves gym had not changed. There was still dirt underfoot and a feeling of grime in the air. The blue and yellow corrugated building continued to shimmer in the early-afternoon glare. I settled myself down near the bolted front door and waited – for the baddest man, for Tyson, for Mike.

But there was a small difference. In 1991 I had waited alone, consumed by rumours of a man rushing towards disaster. In 1996, there was someone else ahead of me. He had a snowy bob of hair, a frown on his face and a crammed plastic bag between his sandalled feet. He wore blue dungarees, a white T-shirt and a peaked 'Tyson' baseball cap. In his left hand he carried a pen and a sheaf of photographs. He could not have been more than six years old.

I sat a few feet away from him, said hello and opened a book. I expected a long wait. I started to read. By the time I had reached the end of the first page I had to look up at him. He stood over me, his eyes burning with curiosity.

'You readin' 'bout Mike?' he said in a surprisingly husky voice.

'No,' I stonewalled.

'Why not?' he persisted.

I looked back steadily at him, wondering at his pluck. 'Well, I'm hoping I might get to talk to him instead.'

'Me too,' the boy said gruffly.

'And you're ahead of me in the queue,' I admitted.

'I been waiting an hour.'

'Why?'

'You never know with Mike,' he sighed gravely.

'Have you met him before?'

'Yeah,' the boy muttered, 'loadsa times.'

'How often?'

'Well . . . the other day, he signed lots of these.' He pointed down at the photographs and magazines in his bag.

'Why do you carry them around with you?'

'To show people,' he said as if I was dumber than dumb.

'So you really like Tyson?'

'I love him.'

'Why?'

'He's the best.'

'Have you seen him fight?' I asked.

'I seen him 'gainst McNeeley. My mom's boyfriend took me.'

'Eighty-nine seconds . . .'

'My whole room at home is covered in pictures of Mike. He signed the best last week.'

'So he'll be expecting you then?'

'Maybe,' the boy said with a shy lift of his shoulders.

We were quiet for another ten minutes while I read and he shuffled through his layers of pics and posters. The sun was hot and it made the snow of Ann Arbor from the day before seem like it belonged to another world. Where was the baddest man on this planet? I looked at my watch. It was nearly two-fifteen.

'Don't worry,' the little boy said solemnly.

'I'm not worried,' I said.

'Don't be,' my small friend insisted.

'I'm not,' I replied tetchily.

'He'll come.'

'Okay,' I said. 'That's good. I'm glad.'

'Good,' the three-foot-high expert grunted.

We dug ourselves in for the wait, knowing that we would both sit it out for as long as it took. But I had barely turned another page when the boy stood up abruptly.

'Here he comes,' he said.

'Are you sure?' I asked when I saw the green Range Rover through a cloud of dust. It veered off the road and into the surrounding wasteland. I had anticipated another black Lamborghini or a red Ferrari.

'Maybe,' the Tyson fan murmured with less certainty.

We squinted through the haze as the Range Rover spun quickly across the sand towards us.

I saw him first as the big car banked round. 'Yes,' I breathed, 'it's Tyson.'

'Is it?' the boy gulped.

'Look . . .' I pointed at the stream of green Range Rovers zigzagging across the entrance to the lane leading to 'Lieutenant Hal Miller's Golden Gloves'. Tyson was already turning into a parking spot as the four cars tailed each other in tight convoy.

'Shit,' the tiny poster-man warbled. 'He's here.'

As Tyson turned off the ignition the boy's hands began to shake. The unsigned pictures fluttered in his trembling grip.

The other Range Rovers were still racing to catch him as Tyson stepped out of his car. He wore a loose-fitting black Brooklyn Dodgers T-shirt and a white cap which he pulled down over his eyes as he made the short walk towards the door of the gym.

'Hi Mike,' I said.

He looked up, saw us, hesitated, and then turned our way.

With a few strides he was in front of us. Before he could say anything the boy offered a photograph of Tyson glowering at the camera. The fighter accepted the twitching glossy and slowly put out his other hand. The boy's head was bowed. Tyson had to say, softly, 'The pen?'

The little guy seemed paralysed. 'He needs your pen – to sign your photo,' I said in my best translator's voice.

He managed to open his hand so that Tyson could reach down and lift the pen from his palm. The felt tip squeaked as Tyson scrawled his name. The boy discovered a routine. He accepted the signed photo with his left hand and used his right to feed another to Mighty Mike.

Tyson autographed it and, before he accepted the next, looked at me for the first time. He nodded.

'How are you?' I said with a start.

'I'm cool,' Tyson said as I heard the doors of the following Range Rovers slam. I did not have much time left before my pitch.

'It's been a while since I last saw you here,' I murmured.

'Yeah,' Tyson grunted as he took another shot from the silent and shaking boy.

'How're things going?'

'Okay,' Tyson said quietly as he looked down quizzically at the sheaves of coloured stills. 'You got a lot of these.'

The boy stoically ignored him and handed him another image. Tyson looked at me and lifted his brow. He nearly smiled but, suddenly, a black hand stretched past his right shoulder. Three of Tyson's bodyguards had arrived and the biggest guy, towering over Tyson, put his flat hand against my chest. He held it there for a moment and then, very gently, pushed me back, telling me with his eyes that I should take a few steps away from Iron Mike.

Tyson swivelled round. 'No,' he said quietly.

A baseball bat swung softly in the hand of another man looking over at us from a distance. He had just got out of the last Range Rover and he used the bat as an exercise prop while stretching and swivelling his back in the glinting light. I think he could see the irony in the world's 'Baddest Man' being protected from me and my wee pal.

Tyson took another photo. 'You were saying?'

'I just wondered how you were,' I mumbled.

'Yeah,' Tyson remembered. 'Things are good.' He looked up at me as he completed another signature.

'I heard you've become a father again,' I said, knowing that Tyson's girlfriend, Monica Turner, had just given birth to a baby girl.

He smiled this time. 'She's really beautiful, so gorgeous . . .'

'What's her name?'

'Rayna.'

'Sorry?' I stumbled.

'Rayna,' Tyson repeated. 'R-A-Y-N-A. You like it?'

'Yeah,' I enthused.

'She was born on Valentine's Day,' Tyson said proudly.

'Wow!' I gushed. 'Valentine's Day?'

'Romantic, huh?' He took the next photograph. 'Jeez, how many of these you got?'

The boy shrugged as if he could not afford to interrupt his concentration.

'I can only do a couple more,' Tyson said. The gym door had opened and Rory Holloway, Tyson's childhood friend and current co-manager, peered out.

Tyson said nothing and Rory went back in, leaving the door ajar. We could hear the drum and bass at work, making it sound like Jungle had finally reached America.

'I wondered, Mike,' I said hesitantly.

'Yeah?' he waited.

'I wondered if you could spare me some time for an interview.'

He smiled again. 'Me and interviews,' he said.

'Yeah,' I apologised, 'I know you hate them now . . .'

He handed back the pen to the small boy. 'Most of the time.'

I nodded.

'But, listen,' he said, 'we can do it.'

His bodyguards began to edge towards the door and Tyson turned to follow. He glanced down at the boy. 'Okay?'

For the first time, the kid looked at Tyson. He nodded once, an almost severe nod of his head.

'I'll see you,' he said to me. 'Have a word with John . . .'

'Okay, Mike,' I said happily. 'Thanks, Mike.'

I tried to follow him into the gym but his main bodyguard, a good-looking black man called Anthony, stepped into my path. 'Sorry, man, we aren't letting the press in. It's a private session.'

'I'm not with the press,' I said.

'It don't matter. I got my orders from the camp. Strictly Team Tyson.'

The boy and I shuffled away. We walked past the length of the tin building and out into the wasteland. He was still trembling as he sifted through his photographs, choosing his favourite autographs. But his voice was firm. 'You did good,' he said.

I squinted down at him. 'You think so?'

'Yeah,' he muttered.

'It wasn't easy.'

'He liked me,' the boy said seriously.

'I think he did,' I agreed. 'He signed everything you gave him.'

'Nearly everything,' the boy corrected me. 'I still got three . . . no, four left for him to do.'

'Are you gonna wait for him to come out,' I asked.

'Nah, I got to get back to school,' he said. 'Would you get him to sign them when you talk to him?'

'Well, I'm not sure if I'm definitely talking to him yet,' I said evasively.

'I think you will,' he encouraged me. 'Don't worry.'

'I'm not worried,' I repeated.

'Maybe I'll see you tomorrow. I can bring a whole lot more things to give to you so Mike can sign 'em . . .'

'Maybe,' I said cagily. 'We don't want Tyson to think we're cooking up a business which steals his merchandising.'

'He knows,' the kid said dismissively.

'What?'

'He knows they're for me. He knows they're too good to sell. See ya tomorrow.' He ran across the empty land, the plastic bag swaying in stuttering loops. He stopped to make sure that all his new signatures were safe. Then he turned to wave at me. 'Hey,' he shouted, 'who's John?'

'John Horne,' I answered.

'That his trainer?' the boy hollered.

'No,' I said. 'He's the manager.'

'Who's the trainer then?'

'Jay Bright.'

'Who's he?

The bodyguards were watching us. I kept quiet.

'Who're those guys?' the kid said more boldly.

I turned away from him and walked in the opposite direction.

'Bye-bye,' he cried.

'Bye,' I said, as I headed for the library, thinking I might yet find an inspirational first question for Mighty Mike.

I was back ninety minutes later. 'You just missed him,' one of the remaining bodyguards said.

'Short workout?' I queried.

'Yeah,' he replied sharply. 'Short and brutal.' His thumb jerked over at the crew of big sparring-partners limping out of the gym.

Jesse Ferguson, 'The Boogie-Man', was no longer part of the camp. But I knew two of the older boxers by sight. Jose Ribalta, a tall and mournful Cuban, and Nate Tubbs, a journeyman heavyweight, leaned against the tin exterior.

'Man,' Tubbs said, 'I'm tellin' ya. He's hittin' harder than ever.'

'See?' the Tyson bouncer asked. 'Even six of them couldn't take any more.'

A thin and elegant black man slipped out of the building. John Horne cocked his head at us and spun his keys. I was on him by the time he opened the door to his car.

'John,' I said breathlessly, 'can I have a moment?'

'Yes,' he said coolly.

I introduced myself.

'Oh yeah,' he grinned slyly. 'I heard about you.'

'Could we talk?'

He considered the question carefully as I plugged in my most ingratiating number.

'I've read all the bad publicity you and the rest of Team Tyson have been getting and I wanted, John, to hear your side for a change.'

'Mmm-hmmm,' he responded.

'I haven't seen too many interviews with you,' I persevered, 'and I thought it was time we heard your voice for a change.'

'Okay,' he suddenly smiled. 'There's a public workout at the MGM on Friday. I'll meet you there.'

'Great stuff,' I slobbered.

'We'll talk first,' Horne said, 'then I'll get you Mike.'

'Wonderful,' I winked. 'Thanks John.'

Horne slipped comfortably down into his driving seat. 'No problem, man. See you Friday.'

'Friday,' I confirmed. I was on a Team Tyson roll. Jay Bright walked past me towards his own car. 'Jay,' I called, 'how you doin'?'

'Hi,' Jay said cheerfully.

After Tyson and Horne, Bright was a pushover. 'Jay,' I smiled, 'could I be cheeky?'

'Well,' Bright answered with a camp arch of his brow, 'that depends.'

'Are you going back to the Strip?'

'Yeah, I'm on my way to the MGM.'

'I was hoping you could spare me a few minutes so that we could talk about how you think Mike's doing . . .'

'Now?' Bright said doubtfully.

'Well, if I could sneak a ride back with you we could talk on the way.'

'Where's your car?'

'I don't have one,' I confessed.

'Wow!' Bright said in bemusement. 'You don't have a car?'

'No, not in Vegas.'

'So how did you get down here?'

'I took the bus.'

'You took the bus?' Bright laughed.

'The CAT bus,' I said defensively.

'A brave man,' he smiled. 'I am impressed. Hop in. Let's talk . . .'

Jay Bright was regarded by most boxing connoisseurs as the personification of a bad joke. He was an overweight and bearded white guy in his early thirties who, according to the sceptics, used to make quiche with Camille Ewald while Mike Tyson and the other boys boxed in Cus D'Amato's home in the Catskills. Jay, they said, knew little about boxing. To them he was just Tyson's latest bucket-carrier. He was merely another 'yes-man' who wore a white towel around his chunky neck to differentiate him from the other Team Tyson sweeties lining up to kiss the pouting posterior of the boxer they also called Mighty Mike.

Cus had taken Jay in when he was an unhappy and plainly fat teenager. Bright remained a walking-talking D'Amato doll who would transcribe the 'Testimony According to Cus' more promptly than any bible-puncher could reach for his hottest hellfire quote. The boxing critics, especially the inner-circle from New York, had much fun in ridiculing 'the dullness of Bright', a man they could never imagine having the necessary steel to stand up to Iron Mike even if, as they doubted, he could spot the holes in a rusted reputation.

In his previous fight, his second since his release from Indiana, Tyson had looked terrible. Although he'd knocked out Buster Mathis in the third round, in December, he had missed his portly opponent so many times that it appeared as if he had lost all sense of the timing which had once been as natural to him as breathing. Tyson's claims that his repeated fresh-air swings were purposeful, that he was merely trying to 'lullaby' Mathis with the whistling of his windy misses, were greeted with scorn. If Tyson had a decent trainer, the boxing writers sneered, he would have been made to confront the full extent of his woeful decline. They said a cunning old craftsman like George Benton or Angelo Dundee would force him to relearn the basics he had neglected so wantonly – ever since the first Bruno fight in 1989 which marked the début of Jay Bright as a junior under Tyson's former trainer, Richie Giachetti. The boxing commentators would have been happiest if Tyson had hooked up again with the abrasive Kevin Rooney who had coached him during his great early years when he unified the various heavyweight titles. Rooney himself, knowing both Tyson and Bright better than most, laughed bitterly when asked to assess the qualities which Jay brought to the corner. 'None,' Rooney snorted. 'He's got nothing – unless you count quiche-making as a useful quality in boxing.'

Teddy Atlas, another renowned trainer who had once lived with D'Amato and Tyson, was equally mocking of Bright. 'It's like wearing plastic thongs under an Armani suit. It's ridiculous – a multi-million-dollar fighter surrounded by a menagerie of frauds.'

As we drove through Las Vegas, with the sun sliding in gently through the open windows, Jay Bright spoke methodically about Tyson's improvement under his tutelage. The words were articulate but I thought more of the hurt which lay beneath them.

'Mike is very sharp,' Bright repeated as we side-stepped downtown and took the highway back towards the Strip. 'For the first two fights, against McNeeley and Mathis, we were just working on the big things, the most crude basics of boxing. After three and a half years away he had forgotten what being punched felt like. We also had to get him used to throwing punches again. Now we've been able to pay attention to some of the finer details. Timing. Combinations. Movement. The small things which make the difference between a good fighter and a great fighter. Those things are coming back. I didn't want Mike to think that these things would be there automatically. Cus taught us that human physiology and human nature is such that frustration builds if expectations are not met. So we're taking it slowly – like Cus would have wanted. Cus always told us that boxing is something you learn, or in Mike's current case, re-learn, through repetition. The more he repeats the training, the more he repeats the process of fighting, the more fluid and automatic it will become. We're just following the template of Cus D'Amato.'

It sounded as if Jay Bright carried the ghost of Cus inside his head; but I was more interested in the man beyond Cus, in the Jay who had to hear himself being vilified. He did not look like another Panama Lewis. I could not imagine Jay Bright yelling 'crackhouse whores' back at his critics. He looked a more sensitive soul.

But Jay did not miss a beat. 'I don't get hurt because Cus taught me to be a professional. He taught me not to allow anything to distract me. He told us, me and Mike, about the kind of envy and greed which manifests itself in boxing. I have not forgotten his voice, his words. They still guide me, like they guide Mike.'

'So even when Kevin Rooney rips you to shreds, you don't feel anything?'

'Look,' he said as he stroked his silvery beard, 'a lot of these people have their own agendas. There are trainers and writers out there who wish they were as close to Mike as I am. They covet my position – either for themselves or for their allies. We're talking about boxing. The schemes and the plots are endless. They will do their best to destroy me but they can only do so on the basis of speculation. They have no concept of the improvement I monitor in Mike Tyson. They have no idea of how I'm training him at the moment. When we won't allow them to see him in the gym, naturally we're going to take heat. I'm smiling through the heat.'

'And what about those who might say you're too nice a guy, a "yes-man" in their words, to tell Mike he looks shit?'

'A lot of people, unfortunately, think a boxing corner should be reminiscent of a bad Hollywood movie. Y'know, they expect the trainer to be slapping his guy in the face, the blood flying, shouting, "I'm gonna cut you if you don't shape up, Muggsy!" I'm sorry, it just isn't like that. If you watch film of Cus in the corner with Floyd Patterson he was calm and collected. Cus taught me that the trainer is there for inspiration and instruction. I will be forceful if I think it's necessary but I won't just do it for the sake of drama. Y'see, Mike and me are together because of the Cus D'Amato link – but also because of the Jay Bright link.'

There was a long pause as Jay gathered breath. I could feel his passion.

'It's not like I'm some nobody out of Cus's past who has just come back from Nicaragua. I've known Mike since he was thirteen. Me and Mike were raised by Cus. We have the same roots. We've been friends for a long time. But once we're inside that gym the friendship stays on the outside. If I was just a boot-licker like they say, I wouldn't be helping Mike. You have to give him the honest, concrete truth. If he looks horrible he must be told he looks horrible. If he looks a million dollars he must be told that truth. Mike trusts me. He's receptive to the fact that I'm not going to lie to him, that I'm not going to say something saccharine just to make it sound good to his ears.

'So I tell Mike his biggest problem in the ring. He wants to live up to his image as a destroyer too much. He craves that mystique that Mike Tyson will go out and vaporise every opponent who crosses his path. He sometimes likes to think that a punch from him can annihilate a man. When you go out with that in mind you don't throw combinations. You go looking for the one big bomb. And the opponent has time to spot it because it is so pronounced a punch. But Mike has so much more than just power – he has speed, elusiveness, co-ordination and ferocity. But, most of all, he has such a strong mind – it's that determined mind which is his greatest asset.'

We had reached the bowels of the MGM Grand garage. The gloom of the underground made me voice another of my doubts. 'But Jay,' I said, 'from the outside, his mind seems clouded . . .'

'Why do you say that?'

'He was in a good mood this afternoon,' I admitted.

'Sure he was – he trained well.'

'But there's darkness around him. He sounds like the most troubled man in boxing.'

We circled the carpark as Jay Bright thought of an appropriate answer.

'Mike is my friend,' he eventually said.

'I know – but he doesn't talk often of friendship, of happiness.'

'Mike, basically, is a very private man. A very, very private individual. An extremely private person. And you know, when he was still young, like me, he lost his best friend. He lost Cus D'Amato. We talk about Cus a lot. A lot. I miss him every day. So does Mike. I still live in Cus's house. Me and Camille. She's ninety-one years old. She's happy me and Mike are together. But, still, we miss Cus. He was our mentor, our teacher, our best friend and we lost him. Maybe we're still recovering. Maybe Mike's still grieving . . .'

There were many loud and ostentatious members of the Tyson entourage. But when it came to bombast there was only one leader. His name was Steve Fitch or, as he preferred to be hailed, 'The Crocodile'. A short and beefy black man dressed in combat fatigues, a bandanna and sunglasses, Crocodile liked to walk around the MGM Grand and shout.

'Guerilla warfare!' he would holler excitedly. 'Eight days to wake-up! It's time for guerilla warfare!' It was a chant of which he never tired. Occasionally, for the sake of starting a new cycle, Crocodile would break in with a harshly melodic rendition of 'London Bridge is burning down, burning down . . .' as if Bruno was the bridge and Tyson the great fire of 1996.

Tyson looked askance at his cheerleader as his hands were bandaged in the MGM's white media tent. He did not seem to be in the mood for guerilla warfare, let alone the constant pop of flashbulbs as a pack of photographers crowded in on him. 'Here Mike!' they bellowed. Tyson looked elsewhere instead. 'This way Mike!' they pleaded as Tyson, rather, stared that way.

In the end they decided to zoom in on Crocodile's wide open mouth yelling out his prophecy. Tyson didn't care – as long as they left him alone.

Eventually he had to do what they wanted. He climbed into the makeshift ring and allowed them to pull on his gloves and headgear. Mike Tyson, the bonneted baby again, seemingly oblivious to the squeaky cries of his toy Crocodile.

'Guerilla warfare!' echoed around the tent. A hundred reporters watched Tyson trundle through the motions like a man wading in a vat of treacle. He held and shambled and held again as Jose Ribalta clutched onto him.

I leaned against a metal barrier alongside John Horne as, over the ropes, Jay Bright called mildly, 'Snap it, Mike, go with your instincts.'

Knowing how bad Tyson looked, Horne leaned down and whispered in my ear. 'You know how Mike hates doing these sessions. It don't mean nothing. He just doesn't want to be here. He can't think why he should spar for the benefit of the press.'

Ten minutes later Bright called a merciful halt. As Tyson rushed away to his waiting Range Rover without a word being said, the new trainer addressed the cynical banks of watching pressmen. 'He had an off-day. We all have them . . .'

'Shit,' John Horne muttered, unhappy at such public acknowledgement of Tyson's mediocre performance. I knew then that Jay Bright would have some excuses to make when next he was behind a closed door with the Team Tyson management. 'Let's get out of here,' Horne said to me. 'I'll meet you round the back.'

Horne wore an expensive yellow short-sleeve pullover to match the canary colour of his gleaming Ferrari.

'Yeah,' he smiled, when I commented on his colour co-ordination as, a few minutes later, the Ferrari purred into a slot just outside Don King's trailer in the MGM's private carpark. 'They go well together,' he said with the casual tone of a man who might have bought the car just to duplicate the shade of his jersey. 'Could I get you a drink, a Coke or something?' Horne asked. He was being far friendlier than I had expected. He was portrayed most often as the 'venomous' and 'viper-tongued' Horne. But, with me, he was cautious but cordial. He looked like a man who was open to being questioned.

I had long been interested in John Horne. He had first appeared in reports of Tyson's life soon after the boxer's first co-manager, Jim Jacobs, died in 1989. Tyson was particularly vulnerable, having lost D'Amato and Jacobs while caught up in battle with Robin Givens. The traditional version of Horne's emergence rested on the belief that he was a stooge, one of Don King's 'boys' who had been planted to steal Tyson away from Bill Cayton. He had known Mike in upstate New York and, being young and black, he was seen as being the exact opposite of the patriarchal Cayton. In all the Iron Mike biographies and Tyson features, Horne was painted as a crude homeboy on King's payroll, the guy who did the early spadework for big Don to move in later and sow his 'it's all a white conspiracy to destroy young black boys' denunciation of Cayton and HBO.

I had never been able to square the depictions of Horne as being merely a dupe of Don whenever I saw the intelligence in his lean and handsome face. Horne exuded an instinctive sharpness at odds with media sketches of him as just another fool in the expanded Tyson asylum of gangbangers, homies and assorted crazies. There was an aloof arrogance about him, a cutting vitriol in most of his dealings with the white media. And yet he had a certain sophistication, élan even, which suggested that there was something beyond the coarse caricatures of him as a snake-like hustler.

'My enemies,' Horne smiled as he took off his shades, 'always have to throw in their petty jibes that I'm just Don King's boy. They do this to satisfy themselves. Don never had a real relationship with Mike until I came along. But they prefer to cast doubt on me, to see me as a pawn in some big bad plan. I tell you, man, in this society, when you are a young black man you have to work twice as hard to become successful. And when you do reach the top they hate it if you do not seek out their approval. They hate it if, as a young black man, you keep to yourself and your own people who were with you from the start. They hate it if you do not covert their chatshows or their magazine covers. The flipside to you struggling in the ghetto, the image of you sitting at the wheel of something big and powerful, is not one which sits comfortably with their agenda. And yet I truly believe that as soon as a black person starts looking for acceptance from white America he will never be at peace with himself – because they will never give that acceptance to him.

'The whole situation with Mike Tyson is a perfect illustration. Their Mike Tyson story is not about truth. It's all about Mike Tyson conforming to their preconceived notions. They expect him to act in a certain way, they expect him to do certain things. And they will print it whether it's right or wrong. If he does not follow the path they have laid out, he'd better watch out. They're gonna get him.'

Horne leaned in towards me. He was pleased to be talking, to see how closely I was listening.

'Mike Tyson is one of a tiny handful of young black men who have found a way out. Look at the trouble he has encountered. Look at the troubles of rappers like Tupac Shakur and Snoop Doggy Dog. Let me tell you what happens. You'll understand this, being attuned to South Africa. This society, America, creates all these illegitimate black kids who know that, as they grow up, maybe one in a hundred thousand of them will have the opportunity to make something out of their lives. Now, white America's kids will buy the records made by Tupac and Snoop, they'll pay to watch Mike Tyson fight. But there is no enduring love or concern for young black people because there should be a million Tupac Shakurs, a million Snoop Doggy Dogs. They just need the chance. Without that, what hope can they live on?

'But the people in power in this country do not support the likes of Tupac or Snoop – despite their popularity. They castigate them for being negative, for focusing on the violence and prejudice of this society, for telling stories about ghetto life. But before they became famous they were just ignored. They were just part of the voiceless black underclass. It's okay for millions of black kids to live this dangerous ghetto life, to be limited, to be jailed, to be murdered. Yet as soon as they start writing about it, as soon as they start rapping about it, making a living out of it, creating something out of their pain and suffering, then they are damned. Where's the fairness in that?'

'Do you think Tupac and Snoop, and Mike for that matter, glamorise violence?'

'No. They show it how it is. That does not mean they condone ghetto-life. Let me give you an example. Before Mike Tyson became a fighter and found something he could excel at, something which could offer him an exit, he was in juvenile homes for mugging and stealing and everything else. Yet as soon as Mike found something to focus on, as soon as Mike found someone who would care about him, as soon as Mike saw a way to make a living, he stopped the old life. There's not been a day since when Mike Tyson has mugged anyone or stolen anything. If he was a natural-born thief he would keep at it. He has not. But people who are born that way, whether black or white, always find a way to keep on stealing at a higher level.'

'Many have accused Don King of stealing from fighters like Mike,' I interjected.

'I dispute that. I love Don King. I love him for his values and for what he has created. Don King is the best promoter in the world. He is more involved in his promotions than anyone else. He engenders more atmosphere. Even without Mike Tyson he has proved that he's the best at selling boxing. He creates more fights and generates more money for more fighters than anyone. Mike knows that; that's why we work with Don.'

'How did you and Mike start working together?' I wondered.

'We knew each other as young men. I was from Albany and Mike was in Catskills with Cus. But we went in different directions. Mike was into boxing. I love entertainment. I headed out west, to LA. I started doing stand-up comedy and some movie work. I was in *Harlem Nights* and *Coming to America*. Eddie Murphy is a good friend of mine. Now round about this time Mike was more and more in Vegas. He was in the midst of his marital troubles and strife with Cayton. He did not have anyone to trust. But he knew me in California. So he started coming over. I could tell he really liked being with me. He talked persistently about his troubles. He confided in me. We were friends but he knew I was very business-orientated. Slowly, it evolved. I was doing a lot of Mike's business even before I officially came on board. But Don and I took over when we got him out of his contract with Cayton.

'Now the situation obviously changed when Mike went to jail. There was a lot of jive as to who Mike was gonna work with on the outside. But we were cool. By April '94, almost a year before Mike was released, he asked me and Rory to become his co-managers. He's known Rory from his youngest days and so Rory is a rock for him to lean on. We're a team – it's a family affair.'

I knew that Horne was more likely to make the key financial and promotional decisions in liaison with King.

'Well,' he nodded artfully, 'I've always seen myself as a leader, as a positive thinker. There's no glamour for me in being a gangbanger. I can be sitting in a room and all my friends can be smoking this or that. It doesn't faze me. I have my own path to follow. If anything, I'll just say, "How can you do that?" It goes back to my parents. I was fortunate to have very loving parents. Sadly, a lot of black Americans don't have that support. Look at Mike's hardship. I was so lucky to have both my parents, Nettie and Odell. They're still together after forty-six years, having raised a large family. I was the seventh child of nine. But they gave me the love and the confidence I needed to do well. I still feel their influence in decisions I take for the benefit of Team Tyson.'

'How much say did you have in the decision to keep Tyson off the interview treadmill?'

'I must say that I'm the one who had the most input into that policy. It helped that Mike's not mad about being interviewed, but I felt it was the right tack. The bulk of the American media, especially the writers from New York, have their own warped perspective on Mike Tyson. They're so biased and hateful. I knew they would twist anything he said. So I was determined that they should be given no access to him. Then, just as he came out of prison, I saw how crazy the situation had become. People were desperate to get a chunk of him. I knew that Mike could not meet their demands. What was most important was Mike being given the chance to restore some order in his life. He had to look after himself both as a human being and as a fighter. He had to regain focus. I knew that all the interviews would just harp on about jail. He had to concentrate instead on his future, on the things he truly loves which, you know, are his family and boxing.

'Now, a week tomorrow, on Saturday, 16 March, he has the opportunity to rebuild his identity as he believes in it. When he beats Frank Bruno he will, for the first time in six years, be able to call himself the WBC heavyweight champion of the world. That will be part one in his return to greatness. I know he will then go on to reclaim the WBA and IBF titles. He will again be the undisputed champion. That will bring him fulfilment. Y'see, I know exactly who and what Mike Tyson is – more than the media. He's an exceptional man. Once he got himself together – mentally, physically and professionally – the world media would be even more hungry for him. The demand would be even greater.'

'His silence, in other words, enhances his allure?' I said, tempted to call him Greta Garbo in drag.

'Exactly!' John Horne enthused. 'Supply and demand. But, beyond that, his boxing is what is important. What brings all this attention on Mike Tyson, besides the hoopla, is his fighting in the ring. He's simply a ferocious fighter. That is the source of his fame. He's fighting for the heavyweight championship of the world again. That's what people love. It's not what the media think. People want to see him fight rather than hear him talk about gossip. The gossip is fine sometimes, it's natural to be curious about a man like Mike Tyson – but, listen, we're talking about a man's life here. His life is no joke. He's deadly serious.'

'And what about your life, John,' I said, 'say in five years time, once you've made all that money with Mike?'

'I love being able to make people laugh,' he said earnestly. 'I'd love to be a stand-up comic again.'

'Are you a funny guy?'

John Horne laughed out loud and hammered his knee in delight. 'Yeah, man, I think I'm a funny guy. I've heard I've been pretty good as a stand-up!'

I thought about asking Horne if he had any Tyson jokes to tell but I was still angling for my next Mighty Mike interview. I laughed along and asked him about the movies instead.

'Oh yeah!' he exclaimed. 'Even at this point I would love to be producing films. Did I tell you about Eddie Murphy? Right! You should meet Eddie. He knows Mike. But I figure the movies will still be there when we're through with boxing.'

'What about Mike, though?' I said. 'Where do you think he sees himself five years down the line?'

John Horne shifted in his chair. He knew what I was thinking. While it looked like he was a happy man with his future inked out in glossy detail, Mike Tyson's own horizon was smudged.

'Mike is the kind of guy . . .' Horne said as he eyed my tape-recorder carefully. He began again, considering the best words to use. 'It's very difficult for Mike to talk about his life five years from now. I'll be honest with you. There are days when Mike just does not believe he is still going to be here five years from now. He's not sure how much time is left for him. He does not know what life might throw at him next.'

'Does Mike feel doomed?'

'No, not necessarily. Perhaps it's better if I say that, rather than making any long-term plans, Mike takes one day at a time. But I don't want you to misunderstand me. Mike Tyson loves life. He loves being alive so much that he does not want to be disappointed. Mike just feels it more than you or I might. Mike, I think, lives a little closer to the shadows than the rest of us. Maybe he's more honest than any of us in the end, knowing as he does that nothing is forever.'

'But, in the meantime, he knows he'll get paid $30,000,000 for fighting again next Saturday. It must be confusing, having all this wealth and fame after prison.'

'Mike is a very giving person. He just doesn't like to tell the whole world how much he uses his money to help other people. I would like to publicise his charity work more but Mike does not want the fuss.'

'But the overwhelming bulk of that thirty million will be shared by Mike, Don and yourself,' I suggested.

Horne had moved onto a higher plane. He replied in bizarre fashion. 'To God,' he said, 'no one is more important than anyone else. It is just the way that society is constructed on an economical basis. But I truly believe that most people with economic power have been put there by God because, generally, they are the ones with the capability of spreading that wealth.'

I must have stared in surprise at Horne's theory for he added, 'Well, I know some slip through the net and refuse to help others – but myself and everybody else I've been around lately are people who are committed to having a positive impact on other people's lives. Most of the people I grew up with and all my family are good people, very good people, but I honestly believe that I am the one most equipped to take wealth and share it around. I can help them the most. Do you understand?'

'Er, I think so,' I stumbled, before flashing my most winning grin. 'Do you think you might be able to help me too, John?'

John Horne leaned back in his chair and smiled broadly. 'Yeah, I just might. I checked up on you . . .'

'You did?'

'Sure. I've looked into your dealings with Mike and some other fighters. We're happy. Mike's happy to talk to you. I'm happy he talks to you. So, yeah, you're the one guy we're gonna go with in Vegas this time. Mike ain't talking to anyone else. We've decided to go with you. I'm gonna get you and Mike together. You got a deal with us, man.'

We agreed to meet four days later, on the Tuesday before Tyson stepped into the ring to challenge Bruno. Horne and Rory Holloway were due then to meet the media in the MGM press tent and, once that onerous chore had been completed, we would drive out to see Tyson. Despite finding a way into Tyson's hermetic camp I was still edgy about the outcome. It would not be a done deal until I had Mighty Mike across the table from me, knowing that he had no way out until he agreed to read out and discuss his latest book list.

I was intrigued, too, by the prospect of talking to Holloway – the less refined partner of the managerial duo. Holloway did not have either the candy or viperous tongue of Horne but he had known Tyson longer than almost anyone else. If there were still secrets to be discovered about Tyson there was as good a chance as any that Holloway would be in on them.

A few days before I met Horne, Holloway had spoken to the British press pack outside Golden Gloves. After ridiculing Bruno's prospects, Holloway said, softly, 'People make the mistake of thinking Mike no longer has the fire inside him. They are wrong. Mike is much more humble and far less vocal but he is still vicious deep inside . . . he's been knocking out two sparring partners a day. We came here with fourteen and we've only got three left. They've been leaving camp in the middle of the night without their pay-cheques. Some of 'em have been hit so hard they think that Tyson has a personal vendetta against them.'

If Jay Bright could unravel a little of the mysterious hold Cus D'Amato exerted on Tyson, and if Horne uncovered a measure of his fighter's fatalism, I felt sure Holloway would be able to tell me more about the disturbing intensity of Iron Mike. There was a chill to those words – 'he is still vicious deep inside' – which suggested that Holloway had seen something in the post-prison Tyson which went beyond rhetoric.

But, along with two hundred others, I waited hopelessly for Horne and Holloway that Tuesday morning – with nothing to entertain us beyond the increasingly frenzied pitching of Don King conducting five-minute live interview bolts with radio and television stations around America. With a seemingly impossible gusto and zing, King sat in the centre of the ring and sold his promotion to listeners in New York and Los Angeles and to viewers in Detroit and Miami. His torrential stream of consciousness was overwhelming.

'Frank Bruno has changed tremendously,' he gushed. 'Bruno is no longer the reticent young man. He is still a very distinguished, classy guy, a quintessential Englishman of royal stature. But now the fellow is becoming somewhat loquacious. He dares to say with Churchill's fortitude – remember we will fight them on the beaches, we will fight them in the breeches, we will fight them in the trenches – that he will knock Mike Tyson into my lap.

'Now Tyson used to be the guy who would say "I'm gonna knock your nose back into your brain, I got bad intentions!". But now Mike Tyson is a family man. He just had a little girl, y'know, Rayna by name, a beauty by nature. So Mike has quietened down. So what we have here at the MGM Grand is the startling sight of two fighters turning each other round. One's become more loquacious, the other less loquacious. An', man, I just love it. I think the contrast makes for a helluva fight, one which you just cannot afford to miss! So call your pay-per-view cable operator NOW! DO IT, BABIES! SIGN UP!'

King then stepped up his polemic as he examined each boxer's particular allure. 'Frank Bruno is the Scarlet Pimpernel. You seek him there, you seek him here, you seek him everywhere but no one can find that darned Scarlet Pimpernel. But he will show up on Saturday night. Y'see, Frank is not only practising boxing, he is also practising the magic of Siegfried & Roy, selling the illusion that he can knock Tyson right into my lap. But, hey, this is Las Vegas, fantasy-land, and we're all travelling the Yellow Brick Road. Bruno is the champion. He is so popular in Britain, man, that when he beat Oliver McCall to win the title they had a procession through London-town on a day they called VB Day, "VB" meaning "Victory for Bruno"! There was a crescendo at Trafalgar Square before 100,000 merry Englishmen. Yessireee, even the pigeons were paying homage to him, floating around, making a crown of pigeon-glory round his head. Those pigeons gave Frank Bruno British pride, they had him walking in clouds. You can see it. This is a confident man, an extraordinary man. Frank Bruno is just ripped – you should see this guy's body, baby!

'And yet, and yet . . .' Don paused to briefly mop his fevered brow, 'Frank Bruno does not have that boy Winston in his corner. So we will have to send him back with a lot of politeness, love, understanding and fraternity because Mike Tyson is determined to regain his title which he rightfully describes as belonging to him. Tyson will demonstrate his savage talents and show the world he is truly the baddest man on the planet. He will become the world's first billionaire athlete. The smackeroonies will just keep rolling in for him. This is a man who will make more in a night than Michael Jordan gets paid in a year. That is the hard cash scale of this man mountain. But Mike Tyson has become a much more mature human being. He's found God and I think he's gonna be a tremendous asset to society. He's a gem. I love the man. But Tyson in the ring is gonna be evil and hostile. Bruno will have to give way to such a malevolent force. Iron Mike will not yield. He is fulfilling a prophecy laid down in holy writ. I met an old Chinese Martial Arts guru and he says, "Ah-So, Ah-So! Mr Tyson! He has double-joint power! He is guru of boxing! Ah-So! Ah-So!" Double-joint fisticuffs will be declared on Bruno. It's gonna be war! It's gonna be sensational! You cannot be left snoozing like Rip van Winkle. Call your operator NOW! HURRY! HURRY!'

King had a right to be happy. Not only had he regained control of boxing and the heavyweight division, but he had stayed out of jail. Four months before, in mid-November, he'd been on the verge of being found guilty of fraudulently claiming $350,000 from Lloyds of London – a charge which had hung over his shocked head of hair for more than two years. If convicted, King knew that he could face up to forty-five years in a federal prison and be fined $2.25 million on nine counts of insurance wire fraud. Desperate Don insisted on his innocence but the evidence was piled high against him.

Yet, in the end, as if to prove that he could still work miracles, King escaped when Judge Lawrence McKenna lamely declared a mis-trial after describing jurors as 'hopelessly trapped' in their efforts to reach a decision. The normal procedure would have seen the judge order the jury back in again to debate the verdict further. They had apparently spent little more than five hours in serious discussion of the six-week long trial.

'We thought he would send us back in with more information,' said Michelle Lieber, one of the jurors. Yet McKenna was compromised by the fact that he'd already dismissed all four alternate jurors even though he knew that one of the black women sitting in judgement of King had a firm commitment to fly to South Africa on 17 November whether a decision had been reached or not. On that exact day, as they announced their deadlock, with only a slight majority voting that King should be found guilty, McKenna said, 'I'm very reluctant to permit an eleven-member jury as this is a very close case. I don't want to do this any more than you do – but I have to declare a mis-trial.'

Both the FBI and Lloyds professed outrage at Dashing Don's getaway and vowed to seek 'a prompt retrial'. But Don King smiled hugely. He was still free to bark 'Only in America!'.

In Las Vegas, King, in a manner of speaking, thanked his 'lucky stars and stripes and the family that is America!'. He turned briefly away from 'those contesting gladiators, Mr Bruno and Mr Tyson', to reveal his renewed humility. 'My liberty prevails because of my fellow Americans. The day I allow my ego to possess my humanity to such an extent that I say, "It is all I and not we," then my star will cascade to earth precipitously and there will be no more Don King. But, fear not, viewers, that shall not happen. I am a promoter of the people, by the people and for the people. My whole thing is people! My magic lies in my people ties!'

My own ties to Team Tyson, however, seemed to have lost their lustre. John Horne and Rory Holloway refused to leave their guerilla warfare bunker to meet the press that day. Like Tyson himself, they had gone into hiding, finding renewed power in seclusion. The Mighty Mike interview seemed to be slipping away, lost in his desire to be alone. Surrounded by the roar of Dangerous Don, I could not blame him.

The night before the fight. My room was quiet. I pulled back the curtain on Las Vegas. Mike Tyson still rotated on the MGM's monstrous metal cube. He gave me that same death-head stare, his clouded eyes revealing nothing.

By then I knew that, like everyone else, I would have to wait a while longer for Tyson. He'd appeared with Horne and Holloway at an obligatory press conference on the Wednesday at the same MGM theatre staging Michael Crawford in EFX's virtual reality extravaganza. Yet Tyson had no time for fantasy. He was even more loath to part with words.

I had snuck a way into the front-row seat – which still left me twenty feet away from the two-tiered table seating forty-eight fight participants. Tyson kept his head down, looking at no one, while Horne nodded and smiled at me. I smiled back, resigned at last to the enforced silence between us. He lifted his right shoulder in a gesture of apology and held an imaginary phone to his ear. Perhaps we would yet talk – later.

After enduring seventy-five minutes of rumbustious blather from King, Tyson was coerced into taking a turn at the mic. While Rory Holloway appeared alongside him in burgundy morning-dress and trilby and John Horne dazzled in a white suit, Tyson had chosen a starker look. His black leather jacket and jeans were topped by a brown baseball cap which read 'Live Hard'. Tyson was at his most forbidding and monosyllabic in his sixteen-second delivery.

'I'm just happy to be here,' he said dourly. 'I'm in great shape. I'm fit. I'm ferocious and I'm looking forward to a good fight and to being victorious and champion of the world. That's all I have to say. I'm ready to get it on.'

Jay Larkin, the executive director of Showtime, was bemused. 'I've seen more levity at a funeral,' he said on the podium. 'If I was making this kind of money I'd be grinning from ear to ear.'

Tyson made no effort to link his ears with a smile. His scowl deepened. He did not need to be told that he should feel happy. He nodded faintly when he was hailed from the floor by a young black woman who praised him for the $50,000 donation he had made that day to the Martin Luther King Youth Center in Las Vegas. When asked to comment on his contribution, Tyson resisted. 'These are just projects I involve myself in,' he said blankly. 'It doesn't make me a nice guy . . . everything is more of a burden now, more responsibilities. I don't know if I should use the word "burden". But I'm just not a happy type of guy . . . I try to do my best but I always fall short of the mark.'

He had only a few more questions to endure for it seemed as if even the media realised the futility of forcing Tyson to speak. I remembered some of his earlier words. 'I'm very excited,' he had murmured of baby Rayna. 'Her mother is beautiful, but [Rayna] is so beautiful and gorgeous that she makes her mother look like a yard dog.' Tyson brooded down on us as if he knew he could still fight like a yard dog himself.

Surprisingly, he spoke again. 'I'm competitive, that's the way I am. I'm ferocious that way. It's just been bred into me. I've been conditioned to fight since I was twelve years old. It's all I know.'

After the obligatory stare-down with Bruno, Tyson was gone. He was ushered away by Horne, Holloway, the Crocodile and rest of the coterie, bar Jay Bright who was still in trouble for criticising Tyson in public. A flurry of journalists and TV crews tried to break through the security and clamber on stage. I was relieved to know that my own hustling was over. Tyson pulled free from the rest to walk ahead, alone again. My urgency to meet with him had always been built on an eroding pretence. I could no longer sustain the belief that an hour in his company would solve either the mournful contradictions of his character or the enigmas of my fascination with him.

There were times when Tyson had become more than a person to me. His violence in the ring and his discontent on the outside had tapped into something darker in my own life. With Alison I was happier than I had ever been; and yet Tyson reminded me of sadness and pain in the past, of all I had left and lost in South Africa, of the moments which, much as I parried the thought, I knew would return again in new form. They would come again, for different reasons than before, but still they would come. There would have to be some sorrow and loss in the years ahead.

Tyson, meanwhile, lived and fought with the fury of knowing that 'nothing is forever', as if it was hard for him to find any lasting joy in the present. Even his gorgeous daughter made her beautiful mother look like a yard dog.

I felt sorry not only for Monica Turner, Tyson's mysterious girlfriend, but for the fighter himself. There were distressing streaks of hurt in so much of what Tyson said. No wonder he preferred to shut his mouth.

But Tyson, as an icon, as some more personal symbol for me, was not solely a barometer of heartache. As the illuminated steel head spun slowly on its emerald MGM dais, I could picture his face softening above the little boy as he scribbled his name over a boxing image. Outside the Golden Gloves gym he had been patient and gentle with the tiny collector, looking up at me with that brief smile he sometimes used. It was then that Tyson rekindled my memories of Soweto, when I had come face to face, heart to heart, with the self-proclaimed township hardcases, the militant boys, the 'comrades' who had been through detention and would do so again before apartheid was over. They were the guys I used to shiver to meet, wondering what they would make of a soft white teacher, no older than them, from the rolling suburbs.

But, ultimately, they were exceptionally good to me, opening up and telling me jokes and stories to which I could respond – despite a relationship built on the ironies of our difference. They stopped being 'comrades', clandestine soldiers, and became friends instead. They offered proof to me, in the early '80s, that as troubled a country as it was, South Africa could still be a place like no other, a fantastic amalgam of colour and emotion, of tumult and hope. We were buddies, and it almost broke my heart to leave them. Who in England would talk to me about boxing like they had done, who would be as activated by the emergence of the young Tyson as those township believers, those Soweto schemers, those Diepkloof dreamers?

Well, I did find other people in London. I found Alison. Yet I could not forget the eloquent bruiser who, instead of handing in essays about *Tess of the D'Urbevilles*, took it upon himself to write me poems about Muhammad Ali. I still have those boxing poems of his, of Gibson Khumalo's, with their hand-written words drifting off the page in praise of 'Bra Ali's' dancing feet. And I recall almost weeping when, a few years later, he wrote to me in London. Gibson was not long out of prison. After his 'problems', Gibson said, he was 'relatively well'. He was nearly fine again. He was going to be okay. He felt good enough to pick up a newspaper. He had even managed to read an article. It was a piece about Mike Tyson, ruling the ring in 1988, and the words had made Gibson think of the schooling he had never finished, of the poems he had once written in class.

'Hey, bra,' he wrote to me, 'I thought of you when I read again. This Tyson. Do you like him too? I'm sure. I find him most interesting. Boy! I composed a poem. After so long, can you believe? This is what I write today:

Iron Mike
Iron Mike
Fists forged
Full of fire
And fury
With skin as dark as mine

From a heart as black as mine
As savage as mine
As sad as mine
From here to there
New York to Soweto
It's a hell of a way
Will he ever know my name?
Will he ever know my name?
I think not
I think not
Iron Mike
Iron Mike.

PS: Please correct any spelling.'

My Soweto days had gone forever but Tyson helped me to remember. The fiercest men were not always the hardest. 'Comrades' and boxers, fighters and soldier-boys, Toney and Tyson, my friends from home, sometimes they blurred into one and the same, into people I knew. Even Tyson. At last, no longer begging my way towards an interview, I could think of him not just as the Baddest Man or Iron Mike or Mighty Mike. He was another man. A man on his own, alone with thoughts and feelings. But, still, not a head or an icon; just a man.

I worked through much of that night, transcribing my tapes of James Toney, Eddie Mustafa Muhammad, Jay Bright, John Horne and Don King – men who all laid claim to some corner of Tyson's heart even if they secretly knew that, in the end, he preferred to be on his own. As I listened and wrote down their words I would sometimes look out at the shimmering neon below and then back to Tyson's turning head. It was John Horne's voice which struck me the most as it resounded through the tiny headphones.

'Mike is the kind of guy . . .' he started and stopped and started again. 'Mike, I think, lives a little closer to the shadows than the rest of us. Maybe he's more honest than any of us in the end, knowing, as he does, that nothing is forever . . .'

15 March 1996

There was a less poetic strain to the songs sung about Mike Tyson by Frank Bruno's supporters – although the bemused Americans seemed to find them quaint. 'Ain't this swell?' and 'They got some rhythm, all right' were a couple of comments I overheard late on Saturday afternoon as I struggled through the crowds of British fight fans and American visitors to Vegas. It made for a startling collision of cultures as, outside the MGM's Mexican Coyote Café, boozy banks of Union Jack-draped lads pumped out their raucous terrace chants to beaming white Nevada families and glitzy African-American lovers out for a night with Mighty Mike. Perhaps because they could not fully decipher the Essex lilt embedded into the words, the Americans loved the sound of men singing together. After a dozen years on the North Bank, hearing Arsenal ditties, my ear was more attuned to the message. At first there was the pleasantly familiar adaptation of Saturday afternoon crooning: '*There's only one Frankie Bruno, Only one Frankie Bruno, Walking Along, Singing a Song, Walking Along in a Winter Wonderland.*'

But, as the beer began to lend an edge of gravel to the voices, another British football melody was given a whirl and a slight change of text: '*Tyson is a rapist, Tyson is a rapist, La la la, La la la, Tyson is a rapist, Tyson is a rapist, La la la, La la la!*'

'What are they saying now?' one black woman dressed in a spangly dress turned to ask her heavily jewelled Mr T lookalike.

'Beats me, baby,' he muttered, 'but it sounds kinda pretty.'

There had been less of a misunderstanding two nights previously, on the Thursday evening, when Tyson and Bruno stepped on the scales. While some of the British fans did not quite get the street-slangy joke embossed into Tyson's 'Phat Farm' jacket, they clearly decoded the sign given to them by his cheerleader. The Crocodile yelled 'Guerilla warfare, two days to wake-up time, guerilla warfare!' and then, pointing to Frank Bruno's wife, Laura, drew a finger across his throat. 'Hey baby,' he shouted to Laura, 'your man is gonna get hurt by my man!'

Standing with her two daughters and a whole gang of friends from Brentwood a few feet in front of me, Laura reacted with fury. 'Fuck off!' she screamed at Crocodile. 'You can fuck right off!'

Her indignation was picked up by the English boys in the balcony. 'You fat bastard, you fat bastard,' they harmonised as Laura turned to give them the thumbs-up, her face glowing with excitement.

They resumed their chronic paean to masturbation when Tyson stripped down to his gleaming white underpants to weigh-in at 220 pounds. A sea of fists jerked in the air at Tyson, the barracking Brits feeling safe to mock and heckle at a distance. Bruno was the one who would do their fighting. He cut an imposing and confident figure as his 247 pounds of chiselled muscle were clenched for the sake of both the scales and the cameras. He held up a single finger and pulled his face into a grimacing mask of defiance. He did not look like a man who might fear Mike Tyson. He was the heavyweight champion of the world.

Tyson let slip a smirk as he glanced up at the title-holder. Frank Bruno had owned the WBC belt for six months. But Tyson knew. Nothing lasts forever.

There had been so much uncertainty around Tyson, and so little to laud against McNeeley and Mathis, that his return to the ring was questioned by many. A solid body of boxing opinion predicted that he would be tested by Bruno. I felt my own doubt drain away as the two fighters took their time-worn walk to the ring.

Tyson looked oddly serene in his eagerness to climb through the ropes. His movements were fluid, his face calm. He did not have any need to sneer or gesture for he had reached his spiritual home, the 'dark hearth' of which Mark Kram had written. He wore a black towel over his head.

Bruno, in contrast, was dressed in a red, white and blue satin dressing-gown which I imagined Laura had helped choose for him. His own face was smeared in thick patterns of Vaseline. But not even those whitened stains could hide the misgiving which tumbled through him. The long wait must have been unbearable, for it seemed as if all kinds of terrible visions had been let loose in his mind. He looked confused and apprehensive. He was about to fight Mike Tyson. It was hard to imagine the full extent of feeling which had taken hold of him, making him mark the sign of the cross every few steps. His constant genuflecting was a more moving emblem of a certain rout than the repeated hand across the throat slash favoured inside the ring by the dubious Crocodile.

Ringside was electric. Don King's hair stood to attention in tribute both to the American anthem and the sheer charge of the crowd. There must have been at least forty people between the ropes before, eventually, they were cut down to three after the referee's shriek: 'This is for the championship of the world. Any questions, Mr Bruno? Mr Tyson? Let's Get It On!' Mills Lane stood between the two boxers, alone at last in their opposing corners. His arm dropped as the bell sounded. The noise from sixteen thousand people was frightening, but exhilarating.

Tyson was quick and elusive, like the Mike of old, from his chilling youth. He moved inside and hit Bruno with one, two, three hard punches. Bruno forgot his ramrod jab and grabbed Tyson by the head, trying to delay the certain damage by holding him in a vice-like grip. Tyson broke away. Bruno missed again. Tyson hammered home a combination of blows. Bruno snatched his neck and tried to grapple. When he did manage to land a left hook to the body, Mighty Mike simply walked through the heavy punch to detonate a right against Bruno's swelling head. Tyson's malice was controlled and even graceful for a heavyweight. Bruno was fretful and cumbersome, fouling Tyson incessantly in a failed attempt to disrupt the accelerating tempo of his attack.

By the end of the first, there was a deep red groove above Bruno's left eye. Even his most resolute followers were not blind. They could tell. Although they unleashed their 'Broooo-no, Broooo-no, Broooo-no!' cry, it sounded like the lowing of cattle being led to the slaughterhouse. The second round was an equally bitter experience for Bruno. Even his persistent holding was interrupted – first by Tyson who used the weight of a meaty forearm to push him back and then by Lane who deducted a point.

But there was never going to be any need to resort to the scorecards and, in the next, fifty seconds into the third, Tyson ended the fight with characteristic brutality. He was, as Rory Holloway had promised, 'still vicious deep inside'. Bruno turned southpaw, leading with his right hand. Tyson ducked under the clumsy guard to bang a right to the body and a left to the chin. As Bruno said later, Tyson was on him 'like a harbour shark', throwing punches so fast and furious, so icily accurate, that they left the bigger man sprawling against the ropes. Hooks and uppercuts fired from Tyson, shooting up the powerful expanse of his body to hit Bruno with sickening impact. Tyson had discovered himself in boxing once more. He was the champion of the world again.

Mills Lane sank down to lift the guard from Bruno's mouth before his arms encircled him in a conciliatory hug. Tyson turned away with his arms spread wide as if to say 'see, I told you'. He fell onto his knees and kissed the sky-blue canvas. He was alone for maybe two seconds before they climbed into the ring to lift him high.

Crocodile was screaming, the back of his jacket rippling with the words printed out in deference to Tyson: 'Liked By Few, Hated By Most, Feared By All!'

Even in his triumphant moments of pitiless violence, those words did not reveal the full story of Mike Tyson – either as a boxer or a man. I looked away from the howling entourage and followed Tyson with my eyes. He walked alone, pushing his way through the ring, heading for Frank Bruno slumped on his stool. Laura held her husband but she made room for Tyson to stretch out and embrace Bruno. I could see him talking to Bruno, whispering compassion into his ear, trying to break the stricken champion's fall. He had words then. He wanted to speak. Tyson stayed low, cradling Bruno, rising only to stroke him on the head with his open glove. He looked lost in his own world, Tyson, gently stroking the head of a man he had just beaten. They would call him 'The Baddest Man' again; but, then, he was just a man, trying to comfort another.

THE BEACON

T HE END WAS NEAR. OSCAR DE LA HOYA AND JULIO CESAR Chavez shared the weary look of men who knew that it was almost over. Their smiles were worn and their voices faded. In their tiredness they twitched involuntarily. De La Hoya was full of nervy grins and misty eye-rolling, while the boxer he called 'my idol', Chavez, continually flexed his neck as if a slow orbit of the head might loosen the body below. Caesars Palace was their last stop on tour.

They'd travelled to twenty-three American cities in twelve days to plug a fight Bob Arum and Don King both tagged 'Ultimate Glory'. The two smartest promoters in boxing had announced a brief truce; for they knew how much money could be made from a fight between their respective boxers. De La Hoya would challenge Chavez for his WBC super-light-weight crown on 7 June at Caesars – in a 'Fight of the Decade' promotion led by Arum, 'in association with Don King Productions'.

Bob Arum was happy. He gazed down at the two boxers who had found their familiar seats on either side of his mock Roman Emperor's dais. The Mexican band struck up a jaunty beat. Gleaming images of Chavez and De La Hoya pounding a variety of opponents lit up the screens above our heads. Two hundred boxing writers munched on, devouring the mounds of Mexican delicacies, lamb, salmon and pasta which, according to the Caesars' PR team, were complemented by 'crunchy green vegetables and salads, warm baguettes and cheeses, and a dozen tempting desserts'. We had already swapped our free bottles of Corona for crystal goblets of red wine.

The Bordeaux was a colour co-ordinated match for the bloody exploits on film. De La Hoya and Chavez carved through their meaty rivals, hooks and uppercuts cleaving away, forcing men to the ropes or dropping them to the canvas. Behind us, the Caesars chef sliced on, lifting sumptuous slices of rare lamb from the bone. We knew we could eat as much as we liked. The food and the videoed punches would keep coming. We were at a feast, at a promotional festival of boxing. We were amongst friends and icons.

Julio and Oscar. Chavez and De La Hoya. The revered Mexican butcher and the glamorous East LA hunk. Chavez had fought ninety-nine times before, losing only once. Fight #100 would be against De La Hoya, who had won all his twenty-one fights, nineteen of them by knockout. Chavez had lifted world titles at three different weights, a distinction De La Hoya was hoping to equal by moving up from lightweight to challenge him.

The Mexican had never bothered to improve his English despite King's attempts to market him in America. He remained more articulate in the language of violence. In contrast, Oscar was the smooth, shaving-gel model who spoke fluent Spanish and English, a looker and a puncher, a mover and a thinker, the sensitive cutie whom the hardcore audience doubted. Chavez had *conches* (balls); De La Hoya had fancies. Chavez wanted to fight; De La Hoya preferred to study architecture. Julio boxed and drank beer; Oscar had a corporate identity and played golf.

The deeper truths about each man, however, were more shadowed. Chavez was a fighter struggling against time. His best years as a boxer were gone. But the memories lingered. 'His punches drain the blood from your heart,' one of his more poetic foes said. 'It's like slow torture,' recalled another, 'knowing he'll get you in the end.' The Hispanic myth said that Chavez, even the ageing Chavez, never backed off, he never stopped punching. 'Never' was a word used more than any other by his choir of followers. They were right, too, to stress that some of the best fighters Chavez had beaten – Edwin Rosario and Meldrick Taylor – had never been the same after losing to him. For his first eighty-seven victims, a night with the young Julio Cesar had been a terrible ordeal. But it could never last.

In his eighty-eighth fight, in September 1993, Chavez finally met someone better than him. Pernell 'Sweet Pea' Whitaker, the WBC welterweight holder, was simply too elusive and accurate a puncher for the thirty-one-year-old Mexican. Chavez's legs and fists slowed noticeably on a night when Bert Sugar of *Boxing Illustrated* said that 'Pernell Whitaker did for boxing what Degas did for ballerinas, what Van Gogh did for sunflowers, what Warhol did for soup cans. He laid layer after layer of his masterpiece on the canvas in the San Antonio Alamodome . . .'; and was stunned when only one judge awarded him the fight, the two others deciding that it had been a 115–115 majority draw.

Three fights later, in January 1994, Chavez was knocked down by Frankie Randall in Las Vegas. Having already had two points deducted for punching below the belt, the Mexican could not be saved again. Randall won a split-decision. The Chavez mystique, and the dream of remaining undefeated in a hundred fights, had splintered. A perfect 87–0 had deteriorated to 89–1–1, and there were further rumours that Chavez's entourage had padded his early record by 'inventing' a fight.

Although lucky to win a rematch against Randall, Chavez had eyes only for his century of fights. With some difficulty, he ploughed on for two more years until he'd reached the 97–1–1 mark. He promised that he would be 'in the best shape of my life' when he met De La Hoya. Chavez was too proud a fighter to give in to another, especially not a *Chicano*, an American-born Mexican, like De La Hoya. They had sparred together four years before, when Chavez was at his most magnificent and De La Hoya on the verge of winning his Olympic gold. Oscar had stood up to Julio even then. But in the professional ring De La Hoya was considered to be a babe in comparison to Chavez. The veteran had to win. Everything that was good and certain in his life depended on him beating De La Hoya.

On the podium, the two boxers looked away from the pictures of them-selves fighting. But they did so more out of fatigue than squeamishness. De La Hoya studied the empty plate in front of him while Chavez's scurrying eyes searched the audience for his young sons. The age difference between the fighters was made obvious in that moment. It was one of the factors which made the fight an irresistible match for Arum.

'This is a classic confrontation of experience versus youth,' he gushed. 'The old warrior takes on the young gladiator. Julio Cesar Chavez has the blood of Aztec warriors flowing through his veins. But Oscar De La Hoya was named 1995's Fighter of the Year by virtually every boxing publication around the world. When Julio's experience and resilience meets Oscar's speed and strength, something will have to give. It is the biggest fight, outside the heavyweight division, in the history of boxing. Speaking personally, I cannot wait to see this bout.'

The boxers appeared less enthusiastic, even though Chavez was guaran-teed nine million dollars and De La Hoya a digit less at $8,900,000. But the money seemed a long way off as they watched us lap up the hype and the nosh with the same relish that twenty-two different collections of writers and camera crews had shown in locations as far apart as Dallas and Detroit, New York and Los Angeles.

As Arum warbled onstage, I looked at my 'Ultimate Glory' publicity pack and learned that, 'despite his legendary status, Chavez is a humble person, whose values are grounded in God and family. He and his wife Amalia Carrasco have three sons, Julio Jr, Omar and Christian.' There was no mention of their threatened divorce – an open secret in the rest of boxing.

Oscar, meanwhile, the PR notes told me, 'is refreshingly humble and dedicated to the memory of his mother's ideals – she died of breast cancer just prior to his Gold Medal run . . . he remains close to his family, living with his father, brother Joel Jr and sister Ceci, in Montobello, Calif., not far from his East LA roots. Outside the ring, one of De La Hoya's favourite activities is delivering stay-in-school, no-drug and crime-free messages to kids, especially to those living in disadvantaged areas. His magnetic per-sonality, broad smile and unruffled style appeals to the general public. De La Hoya simply melts cynics with his warm personality.'

It was precisely that sort of buff which undermined De La Hoya in the eyes of the East LA homeboys. Latino boxers were meant to be cold-hearted killers rather than 'warm personalities'. Even the tiniest boxing fans on the West Coast adhered to the cliché. Chavez was the hero, De La Hoya the pretender.

Oscar's girlfriend, Veronica Peralta, a schoolteacher in Santa Fe Springs, near Los Angeles, had been taunted repeatedly by her students. Whenever they saw her, the kids would chant, 'Chavez, Chavez, Chavez,' as if they could tell that the venerable Julio Cesar would hurt her gorgeous boy. 'It's difficult,' Veronica sighed, 'because I am their teacher, I have to try stay unbiased . . .'

I was glad that Oscar had found a woman to love. He'd given Veronica 'a locket' and 'a promise ring' as a sign of his enduring commitment. Yet it still did not sound as if she and Oscar had found a cure for the lament he had made to me at the Bonaventure exactly two years before. Then, he had longed for normality, defined by him as the ability to go out and have a dance with your girl.

'We're always home,' Veronica said in confirmation of their non-dancing lives. 'I cook for him and we rent movies at Blockbuster that we hardly ever return. We never go out in public. And I know he won't complain about it, but I will. I worry about our safety. These jerks say to him, "Come over here and I'll show you what a real man is about." These guys just can't stand his pretty face . . .'

De La Hoya's pretty face looked drawn as he listened to Arum's promotional shtick. He'd heard the words over and over. Even the six cruel weeks of training which awaited him in the mountains of Big Bear would feel like a reprieve. I was more interested in that streak of gravity than in his proclaimed desire to help those less fortunate than him. It was as if he did not want us to think that he had lost his conscience, even as his fame and riches grew in tandem with his brutality.

His image as a fighter had become more grizzled in 1995. After his victories over Molina and Ruelas, he'd crushed another tough East LA rival, Genaro Hernandez, in September. Hernandez had been the WBA's unbeaten junior-lightweight champion but he surrendered at the end of the sixth. Despite the bloodied mess De La Hoya had made of his face, Hernandez was condemned for 'giving up'. But there were few further complaints from those in the plush seats when it was revealed that a right uppercut had broken Hernandez's nose in twenty-two different places.

De La Hoya had won over Las Vegas and New York. On 15 December he was invited to relaunch boxing at Madison Square Garden. His two-round demolition of 'Jesse' James Leija was acclaimed by a packed arena. It was the brooding style as much as the destructive content of De La Hoya's performance which delighted New Yorkers.

Oscar seemed snared between the vicious talents of his body and the dreamier hopes of his mind. He yearned to be someone more than a fighter. But he was more circumspect than Eubank or Tyson in stating his intellectual ambitions. He knew that the idea of a boxer becoming an architect was a risible lark. Yet his desire to design buildings towered above his earthier business in the ring.

In pursuit of a more layered identity, De La Hoya had also shaken free of his father. In the same way that Roy Jones Snr no longer influenced his son's boxing career, Joel De La Hoya had been forced to step back. He did not hover over Oscar anymore. The boxer relied on Arum, a Monterry Park businessman called Mike Hernandez and his attorney Leigh Steinberg for advice. Steinberg, who also represented all-American heroes like the quarterback Steve Young, had set up deals for Oscar with Anheuser-Busch, Budweiser, Chevrolet, Colgate and John Henry.

'I'm the one in control,' Oscar said frequently. Contrary to the publicity material, he no longer lived at home. He had found a hillside condo for himself in Whittier, overlooking East LA. But, besieged by groupies, De La Hoya hoped to move again to the even more pristine neighbourhoods of South Pasedena or Newport Beach. 'I would like a nice home,' he told Rob Buchanan in *Details*, 'very spacious, with a lot of land, where nobody can get in.'

Onstage at Caesars, as if in deference to that lonely fighter's look, his hair was cropped close to his pretty business-head. Arum contented himself with a quick pat before promising us that De La Hoya and Chavez would be available for interviews at separate ends of the ballroom.

After five years I had learnt a little about the niceties of the boxing circuit. You got in first, asked your questions, and got out. I skipped ahead of three Hispanic camera crews, elbowing my way past the goateed soundmen and the presenters faffing around with their clipboards and microphones. I was first in the queue.

'Oscar,' I said before anyone else got a chance.

'Hi,' Oscar grinned.

'How are you?'

'A little tired, but great . . .'

I noticed that some of the journalists around us had started taking notes of our scintillating exchange. The cameras rolled and husky Hispanic voices translated Oscar's words. My time was short.

But Oscar moved in early. 'I saw a tape of Naseem Hamed the other day.'

'Who?' a woman whispered to her cameraman. He shrugged in confusion.

'What did you think?' I wondered.

'He seems a pretty good fighter – a very entertaining guy,' Oscar said. 'The fight only lasted a couple of rounds but I liked what I saw. I think he'd do really well over here . . .'

'Even with those leopard-skin shorts?'

Oscar laughed. 'Especially with the trunks – and all those somersaults!'

'Who they talking about?' the worried woman whispered again.

'Some British fighter,' another Vegas voice muttered.

In an effort to quieten the others, I shuffled Oscar onto more familiar territory. 'How strange have these last twelve days been?' I asked.

'Like Bob Arum said, it's been a unique experience.'

'But being next to Chavez, day in, day out . . .'

Oscar nodded. 'I'm used to seeing my opponent once or twice before a fight – not every day. As much as I admire Julio Cesar Chavez, I'm happy we don't have to fly to another city again.'

'You've always understood,' I said, 'why he is loved more than you in the Latino fight communities.'

There was silence as we waited for Oscar to respond. Feeling the glare of the television lights and hearing the reel of cassettes, he added a sheen to his answer.

'Chavez has achieved so much that it is natural that we should look up to him. He's a great fighter.'

'But he's an old fighter,' I parried.

'I don't think he's the same fighter he was four years ago.'

'So you might have an easy night on June 7?'

Oscar smiled. 'This is his hundredth fight, maybe his last ever. You cannot underestimate Chavez. He thinks he can win.'

'Do you like Chavez?'

Oscar paused before he answered. 'He's my hero.'

'Do you have any qualms about hurting your idol?'

'You cut off your natural feelings. I see myself stopping him in the fourth or fifth round.'

'And after you win?'

Oscar looked down at his hands, seemingly lost in thought. 'I might take some time out from boxing after this fight. Architecture is still the dream . . .'

If we'd been alone I might have offered up Alison's suggestion that she and the dreamboat eventually open up an architecture practice of their own. I was not quite sure if 'The De La Hoya & McRae Partnership' had an authentic ring, but it would have been different – with offices in East LA and South London for the sake of further distinction. But, with so many others breathing down on us, I returned to boxing.

'You seem to have discovered yourself as a fighter during the last year.'

'Definitely,' Oscar bubbled. 'I want to fight the best fighters now. I don't want to be boxing as an old man. After thirty, fighters roll down the hill. Right now I'm improving with every fight. I can feel the confidence flowing. And, wow, it's a nice feeling . . .'

'I remember "wow" and "nice" being your two favourite words a couple of years ago.'

'Oh,' Oscar exclaimed, 'I was so *young* then!'

'You still are,' I laughed.

Oscar suddenly looked serious. 'My body is young but, you know, it feels like this head of mine has grown old.'

'Is that a good thing?' I asked.

'In the ring, sure. I've been through too much to crack now.'

'But . . . ?'

'But, sometimes, it would nice to be carefree.'

'At least you don't have to worry about paying the bills any more,' someone else chipped in.

'Yes, the money's good now.' Oscar looked at the pack closing in on him, waiting impatiently for their turn. He slipped in a supporting rider. 'But I've sacrificed a lot.'

The Hispanic broadcasters, encouraged that I would finally step aside to give them their chance, had begun to chorus, 'Oscar, Oscar!' He let slip a chuckling sigh and opened his palms to me.

'Well, good luck, Oscar,' I said.

He stretched out his hand and said, with an earnest style of American charisma, 'Thank you!' Then, more spontaneously, he winked, 'It's been good talking again . . .'

I shook him by the hand, the right which was nearly as good as his left, believing in that moment that Oscar De La Hoya could become America's first Hispanic president if he so chose. Even at twenty-three he had the fame and the wealth, the looks and the patter, the crossover image and language, the publicist's promise of a 'warm personality' and 'magnetic appeal' which seemed more suited to the political arena than a boxing ring. I could not see either Mike Tyson or James Toney running for the Oval Office – Toney's ticket to the White House would have to be built on a 'Free Burger King and Pizza Hut Vouchers for Everyone' programme. But Oscar, with his charm and talk of role-models and helping the underprivileged, was a presidential sort of guy. The idea of a Latino boxing legend as America's main honcho in 2024 appealed to me.

My place was taken by the breathless reporter behind me. 'Oscar De La 'Oya,' she exclaimed, 'do you have a message for our listeners?'

Oscar smoothly switched up a gear. 'I hope I can inspire people when I face Julio Cesar Chavez. It is an honour to be fighting such a legend . . .'

The Mexican icon was also surrounded by reporters. I watched him from a distance as Oscar paddled through his river of questions with casual assurance. He had heard every one before. After forty-five minutes, I wandered over to Chavez. There were only a couple of Mexican TV teams left for him to meet. As they fiddled with their lights and recorders I slipped between them.

Chavez gave me an end-of-term beam when we were introduced. The skin covering his square rock of a face was tight and shiny. His translator stepped forward. 'Julio is ready . . .'

I wondered if I should tell him I was one of De La Hoya's keenest followers. 'I've been an admirer of yours for many years . . .' I said instead.

The translator began to speak softly into Chavez's ear, his Spanish words sounding more resonant than mine. The fighter looked back impassively at me. The praise was not new.

'But,' I hesitated, 'do you sometimes think it would've been easier if you'd stopped fighting three years ago?'

Chavez shook his head. 'No,' the translator explained, 'never.'

'De La Hoya's just told me,' I ventured, 'that fighters should stop when they reach thirty.'

Chavez and the interpreter conferred for a moment. 'De La Hoya is a nice kid,' the translator eventually said, echoing Chavez. 'But I will teach him a lesson about boxing, about life . . .'

'Do you like Oscar?'

Chavez nodded again but his look was serious as he spoke. 'Oscar's a good guy,' his sidekick told me, 'but his smile won't stop me punching him.'

'Do you feel the end, for you, is very close?'

'Yes,' Chavez agreed, 'the end is coming.'

'Does that sadden you?'

'Everything must end. We all die.'

'Will this be your last fight?' I suggested.

'Maybe,' Chavez smirked, 'I have a few more. I'd like one hundred victories.'

'And then?'

His translator repeated the lines as if reciting an old poem. 'I watch the sun set on my land, a beer in my hand, my children around me. It will not be so bad.'

'But you'll miss boxing?'

'It's not over yet. Next week I begin training for a very hard fight.'

'You'd agree that De La Hoya's become a great fighter?'

Chavez bristled, understanding me even before he heard the Spanish version. His black eyes locked with mine as the answer came back at me in tight bursts of translation. 'Oscar's a good boxer. But my punches will destroy him.'

The Mexican TV journalists had begun talking over me, calling out to Chavez, telling him that they were ready to film. 'I'm sorry,' said the translator.

Yet Chavez had a few more words. He pointed across the ballroom to Oscar, to the young man who hailed him as his idol. 'See,' Chavez said in English, a chill breezing through his broken words. 'I beat him bad . . .'

I wanted to see James Toney fighting in Vegas again, slouching through a ballroom with stony intent, Sherry at his side, holding up Jasmine for the cameras, telling us to watch out, that it was 'Lights Out' time.

I latched onto Bob Arum. I wanted to know if he had retained his faith in Toney. 'Bob,' I said apologetically, 'it's me again . . .'

'Yeah,' Arum croaked.

'I just wanted to ask you a quick couple of questions.'

'Okay,' Arum breathed. He gathered himself for one last sale. 'Wasn't that great? Oscar and Julio were tremendous! June 7 is gonna be a helluva night . . .'

'I wanted to talk about James Toney.'

'Toney?' Arum asked in bewilderment.

'He's still one of your fighters?'

'Sure,' Arum said as he watched the stragglers leave the hall.

'I've been thinking about all your blockbuster promotions. Toney against Barkley. Toney and De La Hoya opening the Olympic in '94. Toney–Jones . . .'

'Yeah, yeah,' Arum mumbled, his mind pushing forward to the closed-circuit receipts he could still build up in the three months left before De La Hoya–Chavez. He had done so much in twelve days; just imagine what he could do in twelve weeks.

'Do you think Toney can get back to this level again?' I persisted.

'Why not?'

'He told me last week that he wants to fight Roy Jones again.'

'Yeah?' Arum said blankly.

'Could you make that fight?'

'I can make any fight I like.'

'Do you think Toney could beat Jones?' I had finally snared his attention.

'Yeah,' Arum said forcibly. 'I thought he could beat him last time. But I didn't know then how much of a weight problem he had. If he takes off the pounds, I think he could match Roy Jones. But I'll tell you something about James Toney.' Arum moved in closer, lowering his voice in the process. 'Look, I like the guy but he's got an eating disorder!'

'He's getting on top of it, Bob!' I said defensively.

'Let's hope so,' Arum murmured as he shook my hand and tried to move on.

'If he keeps working hard,' I asked, holding on like a frantic politician, 'you'd put on a rematch against Jones?'

Arum looked at me closely as if searching for my angle. 'What's it to you?' his shrewd stare seemed to say.

Jones could hurt Toney badly and yet, as if I was his ambitious manager, I wanted him to have another shot. If he could somehow beat Jones he might be able to leave boxing with his broken heart restored.

'A fit Toney against a still untested Jones,' Arum mused. 'I can see us putting on that fight. But Toney's gotta show me he's serious again. Anyway, we got a bigger fight first . . .'

'Of course,' I nodded. 'De La Hoya–Chavez. What's your prediction?'

Arum's eyes flicked down to my recorder. 'The tape's off now, Bob,' I said with a click of the button.

'Oscar,' Arum murmured, 'Oscar, Oscar . . .'

While unsurprised by the way in which Arum had transferred the bulk of his promotional support from Toney to De La Hoya, I was unsettled by the accompanying emphasis. James Toney had an 'eating disorder'. The frustration in Arum's voice was obvious. He was a relentlessly tough hustler. Why should he worry about Toney's waistline when he had De La Hoya's smile? He did not waste time with fighters who let him down.

Yet I did not consider Arum to be a callous man. As a lawyer and a millionaire, he had a grounding in hard practicality rather than vague sentiment. Perhaps he thought Toney needed to be shocked into shape.

My instinct was to call Sherry Toney to get her to trash the Arum diagnosis; but I knew she was embroiled in a different kind of struggle. It was a struggle, streaked with issues of class and race, which had fermented for years. Sherry had enough to bear without taking on Bob Arum as well. She had Jackie Kallen in her sights.

The first call from Sherry came the day after I'd left her and James in Ann Arbor. My head swirled from that brief encounter with Tyson. The MGM telephone's orange light blinked steadily. I had one message.

'How's Vegas?' Sherry's disembodied voice asked. 'Listen, I been thinkin' about some of the things we spoke about on that drive we took. There's more. Give me a call. Oh yeah, this is Sherry Toney, in case you're wonderin' . . .'

Her voice slowed and deepened when I phoned her back. 'I don't care if James never makes another dime in the ring,' she said. 'The truth is more important than money. I been sitting on the sidelines watching Jackie Kallen beat up my son in the media. But there's another side to this story. Are you up for it?'

Sherry did not have to wait for my answer. She had a plan. She would write a detailed account of everything that had happened both before and after the Jones fight. 'I'll give it to you straight, fact upon fact,' she promised. 'But I'll write to you from the heart, I want you to feel what it's been like.'

A week later, Sherry called her seven-page summary 'Out Loud and Actin' Up'. She sent it to the MGM by Federal Express. There were no cookies this time to sweeten the pain. I found her words both sharp and poignant. She turned an abrasive deconstruction of a parting between a fighter and his manager into a plain address to Jackie Kallen.

'Jackie,' she concluded, 'this is for the record. For six years I took a back seat to you, but you got credit for everything! You had it all – the best of the best; suites, food, fights and airline tickets. And I never said one word about it so long as James was happy . . .

'And make no mistake about it – James ain't no angel, and sometimes he is hard – but I have always made him do right and respect you. I came out from the bottom of my heart because I thought you were a true friend of mine! But I wised up . . .

'As I make my closing remarks, Jackie, you can go from here to East of Eden and you will never find another James "Lights Out" Toney as long as you live.'

I knew Sherry had another idea and so I waited.

'Maybe . . .' she began shyly when she next called.

'What?'

'Maybe we can try to get the whole thing published. Listen, Don, do you think you might be able to help me?'

On Friday, 5 April, Sherry and I were pleased to see her name and article in *Boxing News* under a 'Toney's Mother Lifts Lid on an Explosive Story' headline. An editorial insert suggested that 'The aftermath of James Toney's loss to Roy Jones in 1994 was one of the most bizarre in boxing history, with the beaten fighter reported to have wrecked his mother's house and gone after his manager, Jackie Kallen, with a gun. Here, for the first time, the ex-champ's mother Sherry tells their side of the story. Ms Kallen, a *Boxing News* reader, is welcome to respond.'

While disappointed that her most provocative satirical humour was cut from the printed article, Sherry and James loved the accompanying photograph of them standing together. Her generosity also made me feel that, for once, I had helped a fighter and his family in some small way. I knew that Jackie Kallen would not agree but I was glad to have given Sherry a space for her own words.

'Yeah,' Sherry agreed on the phone from Ann Arbor, 'it's a start. But, next time, I want us to go to a magazine that ain't gonna edit out a single word of my political satire. I think we should keep working on this. Why don't you see if you can get the article printed in the States, even closer to home? I ain't gonna rest till we get the whole truth out. Whaddya say?'

We had moved into something darkly personal. I must have hesitated because Sherry chuckled and said, 'Come on. We ain't even finished round one yet . . .'

Two nights later, on Sunday, 7 April, Mike Tyson re-acquainted himself with trouble. A year had passed since he left Indiana but, on the Chicago South Side, he proved again that he had not lost his eerie touch.

The Clique was a nightclub which James Toney might have called 'funky'; in the white American and British press, however, it was described as 'a sleazy pick-up joint in one of Chicago's seamier districts'.

After midnight it was a familiar scenario. Tyson was the subject of much ogling from the excited dancers. Then, with bleak predictability, he brushed against a young black woman who was ready to tell a court of law exactly what she thought of him.

We heard the shocking accusation first. On Tuesday, 9 April, newsdesks across the world published sketchy details of an alleged 'sexual assault' by Tyson against an unnamed twenty-five-year-old beautician from Gary, Indiana. It was reported that she had received hospital treatment after being 'attacked' by Tyson at the club. Both Tyson and the woman were being interviewed by the Chicago police. He would be jailed if he had violated any of the conditions relating to his three-year probation.

The doom-laden clippings provided a terse echo from five years before. In 1991, three weeks after I had interviewed Tyson at the Golden Gloves gym, he was accused of raping Desiree Washington. In 1996, a month after the little autograph-hunter and I had swapped pleasantries with Mighty Mike outside the same building, the sexual allegation was nearly as serious.

I thought of Tyson saying a few months before, 'Sometimes I'm in a situation where my girlfriend says, "I love you, I love you," and it just doesn't affect me. And I say, "Well, thank you, I love you too," but it's not really in my heart.' There seemed to be too much tangled chaos in his heart for light or love to ever last.

The following day, on Wednesday, 10 April, it was revealed that the woman's name was Ladonna August. She claimed that she had been ushered into a private room to meet Tyson and that, after he had spoken to her for five minutes, he lunged towards her as she said goodbye. She accused him of biting her cheek.

Tyson's 'spiritual adviser', Muhammad Sideeq, claimed that 'I cannot give credence to this. I'm just hoping this is one of those rip-off queens.'

Oliver McCall, meanwhile, was quoted as saying that weeks earlier Tyson had confided his fear of being 'set-up and preyed upon'. McCall stressed that 'Mike has got to look out for the vultures with dollar signs in their eyes. There are a lot of chancers out there who want to take him for all they can. He must be careful not to get into situations where they can cry rape where none exists . . .'

But Tyson's link with Toney was picked up by the British broadsheets. Toney's assertion to me that he and Tyson had spent a night in Vegas 'hitting the strip-clubs' was accepted as further proof that Mighty Mike, egged on by his scrambled crew of fight pals, was on his way down to a prison cell, via the gutter.

Ladonna August's lawyer, Jerry Lee Peteet, suggested that 'She feels like she has opened Pandora's Box and knows she can't close it. Some people are looking at her in disgust and disbelief. She regrets making the complaint but is still going ahead with it. Her story has not wavered.'

The support of those around her, however, was less solid. Her best friend,

Tammy Batty, who was with her at the club, emphasised that 'I certainly saw no bite mark on her. Something might have happened, but not a lot.' There were less ambivalent descriptions from her other supposed friends who pointed to her mercenary streak after the murder of her husband, Jeffrey Mills, only seven weeks previously. He had been stabbed to death in a drugs deal in Gary. A 'pal', as *The Sun* labelled her, said that 'Ladonna had hardly dried her tears before she was out on the town.' It was depressing stuff.

The Clique's owner, Moody Andrews, derided Ladonna as a 'regular customer who would often cruise the club looking for wealthy men'. According to Andrews, 'Mike was mixing with other athletes, shaking their hands. A lot of groups were trying to get close to him. He did nothing but drink water from 1 a.m. to 2 a.m. Mike was never alone with her or anyone else. He had two security guards that he didn't hire – two off-duty policemen that we hired – to watch over him.'

Brandi Phillips, one of the club's co-managers, also scorched August's edition of events. 'Nothing happened,' she said on television news programmes across America and Britain. '[Tyson] was chilling out, acting really cool. He didn't seem the sort of guy who was going to start molesting anyone. A lot of people approached him and he wasn't fazed at all. He did nothing to anyone . . .'

Tyson's own denials were resolute. A hush settled over the case for the next few days, as Tyson was ordered home to Ohio to await a final decision.

On Friday, 12 April, after five fraught days, a source for the Chicago police stressed that 'the charge will be dismissed. The allegations are very flaky.'

While the accusation made headline news across the world, its subsequent quashing was tucked away on the inside pages. Tyson had years to go before, if ever, he could free himself from his past. The gloomy melodrama of his life, meanwhile, would grind on.

'What do I have to do?' Tyson snapped. 'Live in a capsule to be happy?'

A fortnight later, in an effort to save Tyson from himself, the American courts sealed his liberty more tightly. Under the terms of his parole he was ordered to stay out of all bars, strip-clubs and 'other establishments that serve alcohol or feature erotic entertainment'. George Walker, a chief probation officer, explained that 'the purpose of these new restrictions is to keep Tyson out of potential trouble situations'.

Yet Tyson had looked strangely happy when he fought Frank Bruno. He could console himself in the ring; for boxing remained his salvation as much as his curse.

'If I go to prison,' Sherry Toney wrote, 'don't forget why and, yeah, send me some presents . . .'

I could hear the laugh behind her faxed words. She was unlikely to follow the jailhouse path of Mighty Mike but, still, the feud had intensified. Sherry had taken to the Internet. A certain Edward H. Edwards had given her 'Out Loud and Actin' Up' a twist on his boxing web-site.

Jackie had already warned Sherry's lawyer of the likely legal ramifications. Mrs Toney was delighted. 'She said she'll sue me,' Sherry scrawled in her note to me, 'so I said, "Go right ahead. I'm waiting." I'll fax you a copy of the letter I've just sent to her . . .'

The tone of Sherry's reply to Jackie was as graphic as it was formal. 'Mrs Kallen,' she began, 'in response to your memo to Mr Gil Gugni, my word-for-word exposé about you has nothing to do with your gym – nor James's present career. However, in March, Don McRae contacted me. He was doing an article on James Toney up and coming. While he was at it, I was asked to set the record straight regarding the blow-up after the Roy Jones fight. I did!

'A year and a half has passed since that incident. I haven't said a word, even though you continued to make cynical, caustic remarks about James in magazines and newspapers – like a turncoat – and your latest dramatic play: you as Princess Leia and James as Darth Vader. What I have done is set the record straight and cut him from your apron strings – permanently.'

We had sunk a long and painful way from the days when 'The James & Jackie Show' served as an exuberant antidote to boxing's ills. I had not forgotten the romance of their early years, how the black kid and the Jewish mother had swept through the putrefying fight-game. They were such startling opposites but, together, they breathed rare hope into boxing. They came at us straight down the line, sparkling past the traditional connivance and machismo of everyone around them. She took on the cigar-dragging czars in their tight offices while he dazzled in the ring, the yellow Star of David on his black trunks showing up shiny in tribute to her.

My snowy visit to Ann Arbor had opened up an embittered outbreak of enmity. But Sherry was exhilarated. I think I understood why. My first writing about James and Jackie had been at the height of their fame. On a grey afternoon in Tulsa, Sherry had looked out silently across the flatlands of Oklahoma while Jackie and I discussed her son, exploring his black rage. Then, in Los Angeles, Alison and I saw her sitting alone, writing fervently, while the Kallen clan basked in James's violent success. And, later, after he'd lost his unbeaten allure she had to listen to all those jibes. How he needed a fat-farm to curb his eating disorder, how her hard bully had turned to blubbery beef.

James initially went along with it, stoking that bravado with all his mean gun and drug stories, making us laugh, too, with his consistent praise for the equal pleasures of Burger King and Pizza Hut – 'They're tied for number one,' he insisted when asked to nominate his favourite cuisine.

But, for Sherry, the joke had soured, just as the gangbanging hype had always been a curdled truth. There was nothing, she stressed to Jackie Kallen, which could be said to hurt them again.

'The boxing world knows all about James. Between the hamburgers and the motherfuckas – what else is new? As for me, anything you have, use it! Quite frankly, I don't give a damn.'

I had become aware of just how much she did care. 'Between the hamburgers and the motherfuckas', her son existed.

Toney had found himself again. The pounds slid away at last. They fell from him every time he went to the gym.

'James is doing well,' Sherry confirmed in another fax to me, finally believing that their fate had turned. 'He's down to 177 pounds! He will be fighting as a light-heavyweight again on USA network television on Tuesday, 14 May. He is the main event. He's on his way back – for real.'

A couple of Saturday evenings before the fight they phoned me in London. 'Here's James,' Sherry growled into the phone. 'Say hello to him!'

As always, James Toney on the phone was a quiet and low voice.

'Hello,' he said first.

'Hi, how're things?' I asked.

'Beautiful,' he murmured.

'Where's all this weight of yours going?' I wondered.

'They gotta mop it off the floor,' he grunted.

'Sounds like you're working hard . . .'

'Harder than I ever done before. I'm gonna show 'em, man . . .'

Ten days later, at the Foxwoods Casino in Ledyard, Connecticut, Toney stopped Earl Butler in the fourth of a scheduled twelve-round fight. He weighed 175 pounds – twenty-five less than he had done in his previous fight on 1 March, a few days before we met in Ann Arbor. His performance in the ring was his finest in almost two years, since his deadly KO of Tim Littles in Los Angeles in March 1994. Toney's counter-punching was as blistering as it was unerring. He showed his old speed and accuracy as he startled the veteran. In the third he eased back onto the ropes before uncorking a left hook which knocked Butler off his feet. The stunned journeyman staggered up, the 'Sweetness' message on his belt appearing more as a tribute to the Lights Out punch than Toney's tooth.

The bell saved the Butler; but early in the next round Toney backed him into a corner with fast combinations. 'Sweetness' melted under the heat. It seemed as if a burning Toney might scald him badly until the referee finally jumped between them. Round four had ended after forty-six seconds.

Randy Gordon, the former boxing commissioner for New York, was amongst the returning Toney disciples. 'Before he began his decline,' Gordon enthused to *Boxing Monthly*'s Graham Houston, 'I thought Toney was pound-for-pound the best in boxing. But he ate himself out of the fight with Jones – he beat himself more than Jones beat him, and I think the world of Roy Jones.

'It took him a while just to wake up. He watched tapes of his [last] fight with Richard Mason and didn't like the way he looked. His mother, Sherry, had a lot to do with it. She saw him in his underwear one day and told him: "You look like you're pregnant." I don't know what chord that struck, but he became as dedicated as he's ever been in his life. He came here at Foxwoods a week before the fight at about 176 pounds, trained double sessions a day including very hard basketball games. You could just see the whole re-dedication that he's got, and he says he's not going to stop here, he wants to completely tone himself up.

'And I just think he's the one guy to beat Jones on this planet, because if Toney really wants any fight there's nobody out there that can beat him – and that includes Roy Jones . . . you saw the best of Roy Jones against James Toney, but you didn't see the best of James Toney. Against Earl Butler, I saw the timing back, the speed, the defensive skills – I don't think he's lost anything. I think he's the finest fighter in the world.'

We flew to America for the last time. We were almost at the end of our strange journey through the old fight-game. Boxing had been a part of Alison and I as long as we had known each other. In between everything else that had happened, there had always been another fighter for me to meet, another fight for us to watch. Now, we had just one left, De La Hoya and Chavez, one for the road back home to our more ordinary lives.

To all the non-believers who knew me, those who would raise a questioning eye whenever they even heard the word 'boxing', I would sometimes do my little sham-dance. 'Can't wait till it's all over,' I'd lie. 'I never want to think about another fighter as long as I live. I've had enough of boxing.'

Alison was more honest. 'You're not just going to give it up . . .' she said.

We would still watch the best fights on television. We might even visit Las Vegas again one day, for the sake of this book's sweetest times. We'd still phone up James and Sherry to shout 'good luck!' down the phone. And we would keep on following Toney, Tyson, De La Hoya, Jones and Hamed, wondering what they might do next.

I had taken so much from them and all the other fighters I'd ever met. Boxers stripped down great shuddering moments of fear and bravery, heartbreak and joy. They served them up to us, revealing their humanity with the starkest intensity. They were ruthless, they were compassionate. They were like no one else. That difference both sustained and scarred them. I never envied them. Sometimes, I even feared for them. But, mostly, I liked them.

They found the most profound truths about themselves between the ropes. In that cramped and perilous zone, under the black lights, they expressed themselves in a language which stretched beyond mere words. They wrote their own large life stories in dark and gaudy colours.

Tyson's, inevitably, was the wildest. Even he had given up trying to predict what would happen next. All that remained certain was his brutal progress between the ropes. He knew, if he put his mind to it, that he could beat any man alive – from Lennox Lewis to Riddick Bowe. But what about his life beyond the ring? Mark Kram had written that '[Tyson] could end up as a rare-book collector, a prophet with a long beard in the back of a limousine, or rolling on the grass with his children while the steaks sizzle, his violence long at bay and his inherent humanity in full restoration.'

It was a pretty image and yet, whenever I tried to make it last inside my head, it curled and faded at the edges, leaving Tyson in shadow, waiting for trouble.

Beyond Tyson there were lighter patterns outside the ring. I began to ask people in boxing about Michael Watson. The answers were encouraging, if brief. The most significant pointers turned back towards the gym. I heard that Michael might be found some lunchtimes in the east end of London, in Canning Town, at the Peacock Gym. Occasionally, around noon, he would be wheeled through the door.

The day we left for America, I wrote to Michael Watson. I sent my letter to him at the Peacock, knowing that to be the one place where he would be sure to find it. Maybe after I got back, I said, maybe after I finished this book, we might meet again. I left it at that. It was enough to know that he'd still be around; that, both despite and because of boxing, he was recovering.

Yet most boxers remain victims. I think, deep down, they know that they're fated to lose. They are not 'losers' in terms of their character but, rather, in the more overpowering sense of destiny being stacked against them. It does not matter how many millions they might make or how many world titles they might win. In the end, almost always, no matter how hard they train or abstain, boxing gets them. They get beaten, they get hurt, they get shafted, they get forgotten. Fighters are manipulated and exploited. They're punched in the head and hit in the pocket. Michael Watson, for all his extraordinary courage, had been destroyed as a boxer. He had virtually given up his life in the ring. And yet he went on, with humbling fortitude.

Chris Eubank, in contrast, sometimes humbled himself without even realising it. Most of my friends just laughed at him. I remembered how Eubank had clawed his way back against Watson and Benn. I could not fully mock a man who had tried to so hard to do the seemingly impossible. Chris Eubank had exploited boxing, he had defied the modesty of his talent to mince his way to ten million pounds.

But, still, Eubank appeared lost in his head as if he thought it a cube consisting of coloured squares. Eubank's problem remained that he imagined himself as a Rubik-like figure, puzzling the rest of us with his dated tests of logic. When he was not talking about becoming the first black James Bond, he was spending tens of thousands on trinkets which were meant to enhance his social standing. He was said to have bought an outrageously expensive 'Lord of Brighton' title and to have waged a bidding war to buy customised number plates with snappy titles like 'CHR11S'. Eubank was also enchanted to appear on television whether as an unlikely presenter of *Top of the Pops* or as a garbled cultural guru alongside Tony Parsons on Channel 4. But Eubank seemed unsure as to whether or not 'Mrs Merton' was a real person when he was a guest on Caroline Quentin's spoof chat-show. He was more comfortable appearing as an occasional 'Surprise Celebrity' on woeful early Saturday evening TV shows. But they did not quite conform to his higher calling.

He explained some of his more noble academic pursuits to Harry Mullan in *Boxing News* in early May. 'I have been to schools and colleges, to universities and prisons, telling kids how to be successful in whatever they want to do. I went to Trinity College in Dublin before Christmas, I've been to Cambridge three times, to London University, to the LSE, and to Durham Prison . . . I tell them that being hard means being able to walk away from violence, from drugs, from drink. Giving in to temptation is easy, but walking away is hard. There's nothing hard about shouting "wanker" at me or scratching my car because it's expensive and I earned it through hard work. If you do that then you're the wanker, not me.'

As usual with Eubank, it was meant to be heady stuff. At least it kept him out of the ring although, despite his constant denials, he sounded as if he was on the edge of a return. 'If the press give me a platform from which to get my point across to the youngsters,' he advised Mullan, 'if they would for once portray me as a positive role model, I'll come back to boxing . . .'

He was on his way back, despite his belief that 'the price is too high and too hard to pay, living the spartan life and obeying the rules and regulations of training'. While his new acting career failed to spark, he mixed in a couple of 'maybes' ito his temporary boxing exile.

Most of all, he craved the chance to strut his nostrils again to 'Simply the Best'. 'I miss the glory and the acclaim,' he admitted to Mullan. 'But I'm not an idiot. Glory is fine, but it only gets you hurt.

'If I'm a good role model for youngsters, which I believe I am, then use me as such. If the press want to use me positively and give me a platform, I'll come back. But their agenda denies that possibility.'

Their agenda skewered towards Naseem Hamed. The Prince had conquered Eubank's previous territory. He had become as interesting to the tabloids as he was to the British boxing press. *The Sun* chartered some of his worst excesses – the most notorious being the claim that he had threatened an airline assistant.

'That was totally blown out of all proportion,' Hamed told Glyn Leach of *Boxing Monthly*. 'She was just being so funny. We were just rapping some tune that had "shotgun" in it, having a laugh. Then she made out that I threatened her with one, but not at all. A load of rubbish. As if I'm gonna carry a shotgun . . .'

I could not see Hamed either as Sheffield's answer to James Toney. He did not need to collect guns when he had such a fast mouth on him. 'It's totally silly,' the Prince scolded, 'but one of those things you have to put up with when you're famous. Like girls selling their stories when they don't even know you, probably never ever seen you before.'

But the boy who had once made us sigh despairingly with his 'women – they're so devious it's not true!' spiel had since found love himself. The *News of the World* announced breathlessly on 14 April that 'Naz Hits Hotspot in Bid to Win a Bride!' They were thrilled with their Exclusive Pictures. 'Boxing sensation Prince Naseem Hamed,' they thundered, 'knuckles up to his knockout lover Eleasha Elphingstone on a Caribbean paradise isle. But his smile hides the fact that he is fighting the biggest ring battle of his life – and she is in the other corner! Unbeaten WBO featherweight champ Naz has the title belt but he desperately wants his belter titled – MRS NAZ! He was KO'd when his twenty-three-year-old live-in princess recently replied to his marriage proposal with a bone-crushing "No!" But millionaire Naz – though reeling from the blow – refused to throw in the towel. He treated his No 1 contender to a two-week dream holiday at Sandals luxury resort on St Lucia. And the gloves really came off when Naz made a typical forecast – by booking a honeymoon suite!'

We liked the look of Eleasha. She seemed an intelligent young woman from Wakefield in West Yorkshire who apparently had never even heard of Naseem Hamed when the little charmer first started his chat-up line with a 'Don't you know who I am?' corker. We could only hope that she might help ground the excitable Prince. It had not calmed Hamed that, on the night Tyson dispatched Bruno, he had needed only thirty-five seconds to knock out Said Lawal, a hapless Nigerian, with a blurring trio of punches. Beforehand, Hamed had been lowered towards the ring on a platform ablaze with fireworks in an entrance which transcended even Eubank's.

Hamed was careful to distance himself from Eubank. Although he had been embarrassed on *Fantasy Football* to a point where he'd eyeballed the chuckling Baddiel and Skinner, Hamed insisted that he had a finer grasp of irony than Eubank. 'I've learned,' he suggested to Leach. 'I get so many offers of chatshows and that, but if the presenters are a bit dodgy, now I just refuse. I've seen what Mrs Merton did to Chris Eubank and that was just a total disaster. I feel so sorry for Chris because he was just being shown up on national TV and he couldn't do anything about it whatsoever. And seeing Chris on *Top of the Pops* . . . he was just an absolute . . . an absolute . . . what is the word? What is the word I can use for that man? He looked so stupid. He should have known better. He made a total balls-up of it. The producer has been after me to present *Top of the Pops* for ages, but I don't want to know.'

The Prince, naturally, was more pop star than presenter. He had already made the Top 40 himself with a mild toe-tapper which entailed the man himself barking out the 'Prince is in the House' title over a limping house beat. For a couple of months I always knew when Alison had arrived home because she'd stick her head round the door and intone, *à la* the tiny bounder, '*Prince* is in the House, *Prince* is in the House!'

Hamed told Glyn Leach, 'I'm gonna stay out there and become a legend, earn millions, maybe one day a billion, and own my own island in the sun. It's gotta be done, and I'm the man to do it!'

On 8 June a young Puerto Rican boxer called Daniel Alicea punched out a different perspective at the Newcastle Arena. It was Hamed's first appearance on live American television. Frank Warren had found him a headline slot on Showtime. Hamed was certain. His fight with Alicea would merely mark his next step to greatness. He was the Prince, soon to become King.

We watched the fight on Showtime with similar expectations, sneering only at his royal arrival. The Prince was carried to the ring on a giant silky-sheeted bed. He lolled around while looking out at the 9,000-strong crowd of Geordies roaring 'Na-seem, Na-seem!' The princely bed was supported by long wooden poles held aloft muscley shoulders by six Nubian slaves. Their feet walked softly on the path of rose petals scattered in front of them by two lovely but barely dressed Lolitas. It was great, if you like wrestling or *Gladiators*.

Alicea, however, was a lean and rangy boxer of purer ambition. He was ready to knock Hamed off his feet. We might not have believed it; but he did. He threw searching punches with a fluidity and purpose missing from any other opponent Hamed had met before. The Prince, of course, dropped his hands low. He stuck his chin out as if the Puerto Rican, so far from home, might need a map to find his target. Alicea ignored the taunts. Instead he boxed cleverly behind his high guard and elastic reach. With less than thirty seconds of the opening round left, the unthinkable happened. The Prince absorbed two cracking rights before a skimming third punch knocked him down. For only a second Alicea stood ominously over Hamed. But the Prince was up as soon as the count began. He waited for the referee to reach eight and then waved Alicea in again as if relieved to be fighting again. He circled away from the challenger, keeping him at a safe distance until the bell. Yet another boxing myth had ended. Naseem Hamed returned ruefully to his corner, briefly aware of his own fallibility.

His earlier bed-show was forgotten as, in round two, he held his gloves closer to his chin. He gestured to his jaw again as if he might welcome another taste of Alicea's power. The jabs kept coming but Hamed slipped under the hardest. Alicea had only been in the professional ring fifteen times before. He was not a foxy master like Azumah Nelson or a stringent finisher like Marco Antonio Barrera, the latest fantastic Mexican successor to Chavez. He was still part of a lesser class.

Hamed decided it was time to widen the gap. He crashed a devastating right into the side of the Puerto Rican's head. At first Alicea seemed to shrink slowly inside himself, as if he had been punctured by a small hole in the skull. He drifted down like a sinking balloon emptying itself of air. When he managed to rise again he spread his arms wide and rested them on top of the ropes as if he might deceive us into thinking that he was merely resting. He tried to blow himself back into shape as the referee counted.

But the party was over. Alicea clung on for one more dance but Hamed pulled away. They swapped punches on the ropes as if exchanging goodbyes – Hamed fiercely, Alicea sadly. To end it, Hamed found yet another furious triptych. Two left uppercuts interspersed with a straight right splattered Alicea against the canvas. Flat on his back, he lifted his head just high enough to see Hamed's celebratory somersault.

'Yeah, I went down, as you do,' Hamed said later. 'I'm only human. I never thought I would go down, but that's boxing. He's a terrific fighter. He's strong, ambitious and I wish him the best in life. I got floored, tested the canvas out for him, and got back up . . . [my] power's just awesome, I promise. It comes from God. I've been blessed with a gift. I can't see any way that God will ever let me lose.

'Embarrassed? Never. I boxed a very good kid, he was strong, he'd never been beat, he didn't know that feeling until tonight. You press that button, you get knocked down, you get back up. Even Mike Tyson got knocked down. Now who would have believed that? But if you're strong, you've got the heart there, and you believe in Allah, you're cool.'

The Prince was twenty-two years old and still a believer in his own immortality. He remained young, unbeaten and brilliant – as he doubtless will be for years to come. But, on a hot Saturday night in June 1996, he learnt a truth that he imagines he can keep secret for a while longer. One day, maybe many years away, he will also lose. His icons, Muhammad Ali and 'Mighty' Mike Tyson, already knew. The older you get, the less legendary you feel. One day Naseem Hamed will understand. Until then, he may as well keep dreaming he's different.

7 June 1996

It was still light in New York as, just before ten, we left the bar. Friday night and the streets were heaving. But it was an urbane kind of heave. We were on the Upper West Side. Bob Arum and his people had, as usual, taken care of us. His man in New York had mapped out our evening.

'You should watch it uptown,' he said. 'First off, to get you in the mood, take your lovely wife out for a meal. Beautiful restaurant. Great meal. Good bottle of wine. On to a bar. Have a beer. Watch the game. Game 2 of the World Series. Jordan on fire. Have another beer. What could be better? I'll have a couple of tickets waiting for you a few blocks down Broadway at The Beacon. Three thousand fight fanatics. 'Cept for you two every one of 'em will probably be Hispanic. Noise like you never heard before. "Cha-vez, Cha-vez, Me-hee-co, Me-hee-co!" Oscar in the other corner. Electrifying. Just like the old days.'

I had asked him if we could watch the fight on screen at Madison Square Garden. Twenty-five years before, at the Garden, Ali had lost to Frazier on one of boxing's most memorable nights. I was still living in Germiston then, across the road from Cassius, ten years old and pining for Ali. A quarter of a century on, I thought there could hardly be a more touching end to this book. Alison and I in the Garden. I would think of Cassius dancing above the drains outside my own garden in the South African suburbs of the 1960s and '70s. I'd remember him talking about Ali. I would picture the first time I saw a boxer. In downtown Germiston, Ali in black and white, on screen at The Rialto, screaming, 'I'm pretty! I'm a bad man! I shook up the world! I am The Greatest!', inventing the litany of chants which I'd heard so many times since from virtually every fighter I had ever met.

'Look,' my man said, 'for Chavez and De La Hoya, The Beacon's gonna be the better bet. You wanna see this fight with the hardcore Hispanic fans. Word is they're all heading for The Beacon . . .'

I listened doubtfully, still yearning for my nostalgic trip to the Garden.

'I'll come clean with you,' he finally admitted. 'I ain't been given any openings at the Garden. I got The Beacon. It's a hot venue. Listen, follow my plan and you'll have a great time.'

He was right. We ate and drank and murmured pleasurably as we did later when, in a dark and packed bar, Michael Jordan whirled above our heads on the wall-to-wall screens. Jordan looked serene, unlike America's other black Mike, the bad Mike. Jordan had basketball, Tyson had boxing. I could imagine Roy Jones watching Jordan driving down court with the ball attached to his huge hand like a spinning orange yo-yo and understand why he wished he had been born a basketball player rather than a boxer. If both sports were about power and movement, basketball was still defined most by grace, boxing by violence.

Outside, that approaching savagery cleared the streets. The Manhattan set crossed over to avoid the stream of young Hispanic men surging the same way as us. It was a warm summer night, but many of them had pulled hoods over their heads. I was disturbed more by the odd hush which had filled Broadway as we aimed for the corner with Seventy-Fourth. The Latino boys concentrated on the fight ahead, the occasional lone echo of 'Cha-vez, Cha-vez' sounding ghostly in our shuffling quiet. Alison reached out and held my hand.

We were meant to be at a party in a small and pretty town called Cold Spring, an hour outside of New York, on the banks of the Hudson. We were meant to be celebrating the wedding of two of our best friends the next day. I knew we would make it in the morning, that we would see them marry on a memorable and sun-filled Saturday; but, on the night before, we were lost in boxing.

Bob Arum had returned to the closed-circuit coverage which he and King had favoured in the 1970s and early '80s, during the more glorious reign of fighters from Ali to Sugar Ray Leonard. But Arum had not discarded pay-per-view for nostalgic reasons. He and King, in their unlikely alliance, claimed that too many fight fans had worked out a P-P-V scam. The smartest hustlers amongst them would slip in a fake card to activate their free screening. Arum was determined not to drop money to them again. If millions across America and Mexico wanted to watch the fight live then they would have to pay their $35 at a cinema or theatre box-office.

The Beacon was one of thousands of American outlets but it was amongst the very biggest. The noise rolled down like booming breakers as we climbed to the balcony. As our pal had promised, the building rocked to a cacophonous 'Cha-vez, Cha-vez! Me-hee-co, Me-hee-co!' chant. But New York, more than his own home town of LA, had also taken to De La Hoya. 'Os-car! Os-car!' broke over the top of the Chavez waves. There were probably three hundred women to the three thousand men spilling out into the aisles and stairwells. All of them, young and pretty Hispanic women excited to be out on such a night, were on Oscar's side. Some of their boy-friends, especially the more sharply dressed guys, were with De La Hoya as well.

Our seats were bang in the middle of the Chavez connoisseurs. Men in their thirties and forties talked passionately in Spanish, the husky growl of 'Chavez' and 'De La 'Oya' suggesting that they only had words for the fight less than an hour away. They watched the prelim bouts with diligent endeavour, bellowing with pride when the camera cut away to Chavez in his dressing-room. There was instant applause when Tyson arrived to shake hands with the Mexican. They knew how much Mike revered Latino fighters. But, as Don King filled the screen, the Beacon boos hummed against the humid walls. The promoter was rumoured to have placed a $600,000 bet on Julio to beat Oscar. Chavez smiled tightly as King put an arm around him. He had been one of King's fighters for too long. His fans knew he was trying to break his contract with the Don.

Their anger towards King turned into an ambivalent hissing as we moved into De La Hoya's room. Oscar threw fast and nervy combinations in the air. At the weigh-in a day earlier he had been described as jittery and skittish. 'I feel very anxious,' he'd said. 'I want to get this over with. It's the first time I felt this way.'

The sweat poured off De La Hoya. Earlier that afternoon the tempera-ture in Las Vegas had scorched up to 119 degrees. It had been so hot on the Strip that a Swedish television crew had fried two eggs on the burning pavement. It was still searing as De La Hoya accepted a gown to cover himself.

At midnight in New York our building almost erupted. Feet crashed down against the floor in staccato rhythm. De La Hoya, the challenger, moved first towards the ring. The hood covered his face in shadow.

He'd once said to me that 'the worst is the walk. It's a feeling you never get used to. Your heart is thumping, your head is bursting. I want to run away, like a small boy. But I don't. This is what they pay me to do.'

He walked slowly, with a grave step, down the long fight gangway. There were none of the baubles or lasers, the dancing girls or huge beds favoured by the Prince. De La Hoya raised his arms when he stepped through the ropes; but he let them fall just as quickly. He readied himself for another wait.

I had not forgotten how De La Hoya had recently compared boxing to golf. 'I love golf,' he said. 'I don't even like boxing. To tell you the truth, I hate boxing. If I'm not doing it, I don't want nothing to do with it . . .' In that moment it was easy to believe him. How much better and more natural it would have seemed to him to saunter up the eighteenth fairway on a summer evening, a club swinging gently in his hand, the sun sinking behind him, the course looking lush and green in the dappled light. A chip and a putt and he would be home. He swallowed hard and blinked, enduring the fact again that he was not a golfer.

The camera panned across the tumultuous rows of celebrities. Mike Tyson and Sugar Ray Leonard were muted, understanding the moment better than the rest of us. Beyond them, the stars' smiles glittered. Jack Nicholson, Bruce Willis, Don Johnson, Racquel Welch, Rod Stewart, Billy Crystal and Tracy Ullman. Magic Johnson and Charles Barkley were further along, glad to be basketball giants rather than lightweight fighters.

In contrast to his young rival, Chavez grinned as he walked. He was even more content when he joined the singing of another interminable version of the Mexican anthem. While Chavez sang lustily, De La Hoya kept his head low. He suffered in those moments. The waiting dragged on.

'The Star Spangled Banner' was next. Oscar's tongue snuck across his lips. His eyes were fixed in an empty stare. It was as if some unbearable force pressed down on him. When they hit the 'home of the brave', he at last found himself able to shake his shoulders in a gesture which was less patriotic than it was traumatic. They had inched a little closer.

Michael Buffer picked up the microphone. In awed anticipation The Beacon took a collective breath, long enough for us to hear his blaring voice. It was the fight of the year and big Buff knew it. He would have loved to be in his favourite tux but his throaty larynx might have melted. He had opted for casual sportswear. But a white short-sleeved shirt and beige slacks were not enough to cool him. He looked sticky and frazzled.

'And now, ladies and gentlemen,' he cried out to ringside and beyond, 'from the site where legends are made, Caesars Palace of Las Vegas, Nevada! This is the moment we have all been waiting for!' We paused again, like a demented chorus, allowing him to slip into the phrase which suckered us like little else in boxing: 'LUUUHHHHH-ETS GIT READY TO RRRRRRUM-BULLLLLLLLL!'

By the time he'd hit the 'git', The Beacon had joined him in unhinged rapture. His 'ready to rumble' was echoed by seemingly every other voice beyond our own. Alison and I looked at each other in helpless recognition. Our silence meant nothing. We wanted the fight, as badly as anyone shrieking behind or below us.

Buffer hit another orgasmic peak when he introduced 'The Golden Boy'. 'Oscar De La 'Oyaaa-aaaaahhhhhhhh . . . !' he groaned blissfully. Bob Arum grinned hugely while De La Hoya, summoned so sexually, had already done the obvious and slipped out of his silky gown. His stomach was ridged with muscle, his upper body springy with power. Yet he could not bring himself to leer or to posture. He was too deep inside himself to show anything. He had Chavez in front of him. Nothing else mattered.

Chavez himself was exultant. He jumped frenetically as he was introduced, lifting his legs almost level with his chin as Buffer ripped into the 'Julioooooo Cesarrrr . . .' The 'Cha-aaaaa-vezzzzzz' was sucked into The Beacon's booming tunnel of sound, the noise clattering and echoing around us.

I felt fluttery with excitement. Alison's grip was firmer. Her hand dug into my arm, holding on tightly as the two boxers came together. They stood a few feet apart. Joe Cortez, the referee, said a few words in both Spanish and English but we had given up trying to listen. The din was everything. They returned to the corners knowing that only moments remained.

The bell must have rung. De La Hoya stepped out, his head down and his fists held high like the horns on a bull. Chavez was no matador but he trod carefully in those opening seconds. The Beacon exhaled in expectation as we finally heard a snatch of commentary. Chavez, the mic-man told us, had his first professional fight when Oscar was only seven years old, sixteen years before.

De La Hoya was not only ten years younger than Chavez. He was four inches taller, his reach five inches longer. He was quicker and stronger. The Mexican took a step forward and attempted to land a blow to the body. De La Hoya pushed him back with a hurtful left. Chavez circled out of range. De La Hoya kept working off his jab, an austere reminder of the force in his left hand. But he had a right too. He landed with both. After a cautious minute he followed another stiff jab with a scraping right which careered off Chavez's head.

The pictures being beamed across America were grainy, but the coarse quality of the Beacon print could not hide the immediate impact of that blow. I think I noticed the cut first because I saw Chavez's left hand dab frantically at the eye. As soon as he lifted his glove I saw the blood. It looked almost brown on screen.

'He's cut,' I told Alison.'

'What?' she mouthed back.

'A cut,' I shouted in her ear, 'it's a terrible cut.' We heard the groans as the tempo quickened. De La Hoya dug in another slick combination, his feet planted on the canvas to lend substance to his blurring hand-speed. Chavez swung a hook which De La Hoya calmly avoided. He tracked the champion and found him again with another straight left and a right cross.

Chavez turned towards the camera. The Beacon wailed. The entire left side of his face was covered in blood. It pumped from his eye like a dirty river bursting through a blasted dam wall. Chavez pawed at the gouge again as if he might fathom its depth. De La Hoya followed him with icy composure. Lesser fighters would have bombed in, seeing victory in the flaring red slash. But De La Hoya had his plan. He refused to rush.

The blood poured on. Bob Arum had said three months earlier that Chavez had the blood of ancient Aztec warriors seeping through his veins. But it seemed as if Chavez had slipped on a gruesome mask from something less grand, from some Friday-night horror story. With less than a minute left in the opening round, Joe Cortez ushered Chavez over to one of the three ringside doctors.

The Beacon sounded on the verge of gagging. The 'Cha-vez, Cha-vez' chant had choked in the throats of his most ardent supporters. A baleful muttering rose up from the seats downstairs as we watched the doctor wipe away some of the blood to reveal a gaping gash across Chavez's left eye. If it had been any other fight they would have stopped it then. But, in his hundredth bout, against Oscar De La Hoya, defending his WBC super-lightweight championship belt, Chavez was given a chance to search for a miracle. The stream of blood was rubbed away into ribbon-like streaks. They sent him back into the brawl.

He survived the rest of the round. But the red had spread around the circle of his eye. It was an exaggerated copy of one of Chris Eubank's largest monocles. Chavez blinked in confusion. It was meant to be his finest night in the ring.

They cleaned the cut and spread a clogging salve over its length and breadth, the cornerman using his squat fingers to dip inside the fleshy slit. Chavez stared vacantly across the ring at De La Hoya, hearing his trainer's Spanish lie that 'it's nothing, it's nothing'. He would have to knock out De La Hoya, and soon. The producer cut away to slow-motion footage of De La Hoya spearing in his jab and that jolting right. The Beacon whimpered a horrified '*oooohhhhh!*' as we saw again the punch open up that crimson trench.

De La Hoya had settled into a slicing rhythm. He was able to both box and fight, standing back to counterpunch in two-handed flurries or switching to the inside. The influence of a Mexican 'professor' in his team, the tiny Don Jesus Rivero, showed as he unbalanced Chavez. He used his left hand to hold on to the champion's shoulder. Whenever Chavez swayed in doubt, De La Hoya would leap in with the right. It was a masterful display of tactical acumen and brute force.

At the end of the second a dejected Chavez walked towards an empty part of the ring, away from the others. 'Julio,' Joe Cortez's lips could be seen to call. He guided Chavez back to the temporary sanctity of his corner.

They could not stop the bleeding of their own man or the patient brilliance of Oscar. The third offered up more of the same. De La Hoya seemed to connect with every punch while weaving away from Chavez's futile counters. He banged in two lightning lefts to the wounded eye and then went thunderously below with a hook to the stomach. He wrestled with Chavez as if hoping for a change of pace. Cortez barked out a warning which De La Hoya acknowledged with a theatrical bow of his head. It was almost embarrassing to watch. Even when Chavez did sink a left into De La Hoya's flank, the younger man responded with a cold replica.

Chavez made a last charge at the start of the fourth. He went after De La Hoya with his famous desire. He opened up and Oscar retreated to the ropes. Chavez whacked home his best shots of the night. De La Hoya was unflappable. He used his jab to blunt the surge. And then, with harsh precision, he decided to end it. His combinations were vicious. A right uppercut and left hook broke Chavez's nose. The blood fanned across his face.

Alison could no longer watch. Joe Cortez had also seen enough. He led Chavez towards Flip Homansky, the bushy-moustached boxing doctor, who reached for a white towel. He watched it change colours from pink to ruby red while pressing it against the smashed nose and torn eye. Homansky eyed Cortez gloomily. It was over. The old boxer hung his head and shovelled the white gumshield out of his mouth, knowing that he had been rescued from even more humiliation and hurt.

Oscar De La Hoya climbed the ropes. He beamed in ecstasy. He listened to the cheering. He cocked a jokey Charles Atlas pose, bunching his muscles for a laugh. Only boxing, because it is so callous and grim, could bring this relief. He felt such elation because he had survived so much. The isolation, the sacrifice, the fear, the fight – suddenly everything seemed to make sense to him. He had crushed the great Chavez. The Mexican's blood stained a scarlet half-moon onto his right shoulder, as if in reminder of the dangers he had survived.

His entourage paraded him round the ring on their own shoulders. Oscar opened his arms wide, sometimes throwing his head back to praise the sky above. It seemed ironic that he should be the one, the guy who even said he hated boxing, who should end up riding round Caesars as the fight-game's last hero. De La Hoya grinned on as if, finally, he had accepted his destiny.

As soon as he was prised to the ground his publicist grabbed his arm. Dena DuBoef, Bob Arum's step-daughter and Oscar's relentless PR guide, pushed the hair from her eyes and spoke urgently into his bent ear. Amid the clamour he listened to her and nodded. Less than a minute after he'd attacked Chavez he had to talk politely on camera.

Oscar was like no one else in boxing. He was Dena's dream. 'That was very tough for me because Julio Cesar Chavez has been a great champion and will always be my idol. But my job is to win fights. Julio Cesar Chavez is a true warrior but when I cut his eye and broke his nose with a left hook – I think I felt it break – I knew I had him.'

The Chavez devotees walked quickly to the exits. We wondered again at boxing's brutality – the only supposed sport where such a bloody end could seem almost anti-climactic. The fight had been so one-sided that it had hardly begun to fulfil the three-month build-up. It had come three years too late for Chavez – and Oscar was wise enough to acknowledge it. 'Now I'm going back to the gym,' he promised. 'I still need work. I still need one or two years to become a really good fighter.' He laughed again as if he knew, after tonight, that he was already there, that he could only become greater.

Chavez, however, disputed the truth. They had managed to scrape most of the blood from his face when the interviewer reached him. 'Nothing,' Chavez said despondently. 'De La Hoya has nothing. I never felt his punches. I just couldn't see because of the blood.'

In an effort to convince themselves of their own enduring splendour, boxers are taught to lie. But, when it ends, most are able to confront the truth. Chavez insisted instead that he had 'a lot of fight left inside'. He claimed that he been cut in sparring a few weeks before, that the wound had only partly healed before being nicked again the day before by his three-year-old son. A hard-hitting toddler, probably. Chavez wanted a rematch. A couple more victories and then Oscar, again, for his hundredth victory.

Bob Arum had heard it all before. He smiled magnanimously. His 'Golden Boy' had already won. He could afford to humour the fallen champion. 'For me,' he said as Chavez nodded limply at his side, 'it will always be a great honour to promote Julio Cesar Chavez. He and I have become good friends and he's a terrific fighter. Who knows? One, two fights and he can have a rematch . . .'

When De La Hoya was told later that Chavez had derided his power he showed a rare lick of anger. 'Well, that goes to show you the kind of person he is. I think I deserve a little bit of credit. For somebody to say that his opponent doesn't hit hard, that he's a no-good fighter, it hurts my feelings. But if Chavez believes that, that's his opinion. But why have I got the belt – why I am the champ? Julio Cesar said there'd be no excuses. He said whoever wins takes the ultimate glory. And now here he is making excuses . . .'

But he smiled again when Arum took the mic to talk of future 'super-fights' for Oscar. There was no such thing as 'Ultimate Glory'. There was always the next fight, and the one after that. Each one bigger than the one before. Miguel Angel Gonzales. Kostya Tszyu. Pernell Whitaker. And, somewhere, in the depths of 1997, another of Don King's fighters, the explosive and unbeaten young Puerto Rican IBF welterweight champion, Felix Trinidad.

'I want to fight the best fighters in the world at an early age and then retire from boxing while I'm still young,' Oscar gleamed.

His trainer since the golden amateur days, Roberto Alcazar, could see the trap. 'Chavez was supposed to be his toughest test. And it turned out to be the easiest fight he ever had . . . so it's going to be hard for Oscar to stop as long as keeps winning. If he wins, the promoters will just make him a better offer. You can't say no . . .'

Bob Arum agreed. 'I think Oscar demonstrated tonight,' he mused, 'that not only is he a great fighter but he may become one of the greatest fighters of all time. Oscar De La Hoya can be bigger than anyone else in boxing – Mike Tyson, Sugar Ray Leonard. Oscar can be bigger than everyone – except Ali . . .'

Chavez would have to cope with the defeat on his own, knowing that even with a staggering record of 97–2–1 he would not hear Bob Arum compare him to Muhammad Ali. That would be Oscar's privilege and burden in boxing.

The Beacon was almost deserted. As we reached the theatre door, thankful for the early-morning cool, it seemed fitting that the last voice on screen should belong to another Hispanic boxer, Gabriel Ruelas. On the night, a year before, when his brother Rafael had been stopped by Oscar, Gabriel's fists had ended the life of Jimmy Garcia. He still struggled with that death but Gabriel Ruelas could not hide his admiration, as a fighter, for De La Hoya or his concern for Chavez. 'Julio Cesar,' he said as the credits began to roll, 'has been a great fighter . . . but I think he should quit while he's still ahead. He should just let Oscar take the torch now . . .'

Alison took my arm and we stepped back out into the city. It was 1 a.m. All around us, New York glistened and shimmered. The buildings seemed to float above our heads. We searched for the tallest, hoping that, despite his performance that night, Oscar would not forget their beauty. He would not be a boxer forever.

We turned away from the brooding boys still hanging outside The Beacon. We needed to get back to our own lives. We needed a beer. We were thirsty. We were parched.

A month later, in the middle of July, on a cloudless Wednesday morning, I rode the underground. Just before twelve, after the tube had passed through Victoria, Monument, Tower Hill, Whitechapel and Mile End, we broke through the tunnel and swayed out into the sunshine again. Bow Road, then Bromley-by-Bow. The east end sparkled in the bright light, the derelict warehouses and colossal steel gas cylinders looking more beautiful than bleak.

I got off at West Ham. The platform and the ticket-office were both empty. I strolled down the grimy walkway to the street outside. It was exactly noon but there were no bells to be heard. West Ham was still and quiet. I saw a girl leaning against a wall a block away. The studs in her nose and belly-button glinted as I walked towards the bus-stop. She stared down at the varnish on the nails of her right hand, ignoring me, looking bored.

I asked her if I could catch a bus into Canning Town.

She smothered a yawn. 'Where in Canning Town?'

'Caxton Street North,' I said. 'The Peacock Gym?'

'Yeah, 'course,' she said with sudden interest. 'I know it. You seein' a boxer or somethin'?'

I nodded.

She narrowed her eyes as if she might guess which fighter. 'Not Nigel Benn?' she murmured.

I shook my head. Benn had just lost his second straight fight. Four months earlier, after he had been defeated by Sugar Boy Malinga, his retirement speech had not long left his bleeding lips when he changed his mind. On the first Saturday in July, he fought Steve Collins in Manchester. In the fourth round, Benn's ankle gave way, twisting awkwardly as he fell. He tottered up on one good leg but soon turned away as Collins tore into him. It was a sign of good sense rather than surrender.

Benn took the mic and poured out his heart once more. He told his fiancée Caroline and his father, and the rest of us as well, that this time he meant it. He had just had his last fight. We had no need to worry about him. A quarter of an hour later plans were already being laid for an autumn rematch.

'I don't think he's ever gonna give up,' the riveted girl sighed.

'He'll have to,' I said, 'eventually.'

She looked thoughtful. 'I suppose . . . '

I glanced at my watch.

'You might as well walk there,' she said. 'You'll get there quicker.' She told me the way. I thanked her and started my trudge. 'Oi,' she called out. I turned round. A hand, each finger covered in rings, shielded her eyes against the glare. 'You never told me,' she said. 'Who are you seeing?'

I said his name. It sometimes seemed as if he had been forgotten. He was different to the others. Eubank. Benn. Bruno. And now the Prince. Everyone knew them. But he had always been on the less visible flipside. He was at one with all those other struggling boxers who were more representative of the fight-game in this country. Like most of them he had been a pro rather than a star, even when he outboxed Benn and Eubank. But almost five years had passed since his last fight.

She surprised me. Her twinkling hand dropped to her mouth. She opened her eyes wide. 'Michael Watson!' she repeated. 'Jesus . . . ' She pushed herself away from the wall and moved towards me. 'How is he?' she asked.

'I heard he's getting better,' I said.

She cracked a smile which opened up her face. 'That's good. I always liked him . . .'

'Me too.'

'Say hello,' she said, 'say hi to him for me . . .'

I told her I would but, as we said our awkward goodbyes, I suddenly realised how nervous I felt. What could I say to Michael Watson? What could I ever ask him?

I passed the Canning Town roundabout and Gosling Biscuits, as the girl had promised. I remembered the sound in her voice when she said, 'I always liked him.' Her ardour gave me faith. He was getting stronger. I saw The Peacock.

I stopped at the statue of a boxer with his fists raised in front of his face. I read the inscription:

In Loving Memory of Bradley Stone
Little Gem
1970–1994

A Brave Young Man
Who Died
In Pursuit of His Dream

I shivered and then stepped into the gym, looking for Michael.

'Hello, Don!' Jimmy Tibbs yelled from the centre of the ring. He squirted an arc of water into the mouth of his twenty-three-year-old prospect, Wayne Alexander, a winking light-middleweight from Croydon.

'Whew,' Jimmy laughed, 'it's steamin' in here! Look at me, looks like I been in the shower already!' The back of his grey T-shirt was ringed with damp patches, highlighting its message: 'The Older I Get The Better I Was.'

Jimmy Tibbs used to be a fighter. He had since become the best boxing trainer in Britain. He had worked at various stages with Bruno, McGuigan, Honeyghan, Pyatt, Collins – and Bradley Stone. But he was best known for helping Nigel Benn reinvent himself in the five fights leading towards Gerald McClellan. He'd also been in Michael Watson's corner for his last two bouts – against Chris Eubank.

It was a memory which still scarred him but, almost five years on, he was ready to talk. While his latest contender took to the rope, feet jumping lightly on the gymnasium floor, we spoke about that fateful night. Jimmy Tibbs had just turned fifty but he was still a handsome and charismatic man. He leaned forward, drawing me back towards that fight. I could feel his hurt.

'Against Eubank, Michael was in awesome shape. When I said he must ease off, his idea of rest was this – walkin' and backin' him up and slippin', an' *wham*, left hook, *bam*, right hook, slippin' again. He boxed beautifully.

He was miles ahead. Six or seven rounds up.

'Then the eleventh came. Michael knocks Chris down. Jab, right hand, left hook. No power but Eubank collapses. He's that tired. But Eubank got up. An', straightaway, he slung that right uppercut. It lifts Michael off the floor. He's down. The bell goes. "Ding". I jump into the ring and Michael's up. He walks to the corner with me. I ask him if he's okay. An' he says, "I'm fine, Jim." I sit him in the corner. But I say, "Now listen, do you want to pull out?" An' he says, "No, I'm okay." I ask him again: "You wanna go on?" He says, "Yeah!" So I tell 'im: "You got one round an' you're champion of the world!" I clean him up.

'When the bell went again he stays in the corner. Standin' there. An' I still think he's okay. I think he's being clever, wastin' time. So I'm encouragin' him: "Stay there, Michael, good, stay where you are!" Then Eubank reaches him. The last flurry comes. He doesn't land a punch but the referee could tell that Michael's gone. He steps in. Even then I didn't know. Michael collapses in my arms but I still think it's just exhaustion.

'It was only an hour later, when he finally reached hospital, that the doctors told me. They didn't think he was gonna pull through. So we got down on our knees and we prayed, Michael's family an' me. His mum's a born-again Christian – like me. An' Michael hung on, he hung on even when they said there was no chance.

'The doctors in that hospital were wonderful but they said that, even if he did live, Michael would be a vegetable. He would not be able to do anything. He would not be able to walk or talk again, even feed or clean himself. They said he was ruined. But now Michael can do everything they said he wouldn't. 'Cos Michael's a believer. He came to the Lord.

'I went to see him in hospital one day. He was out of the coma but he's still lying there, all crippled up and damaged. It hurts me to see him, remembering him as he had been. But Michael smiles at me. He says, "I've seen Jesus, Jim." I was quiet, looking at him. Eventually I said, "What did he look like, Michael?" He told me. "Did he speak to you, Mike?" I ask. An' he says, "Yeah." Michael looks at me. He's paralysed but his eyes are shining. I bend lower to hear his voice. "The Lord said, 'Stay humble, Michael, stay humble' . . ." I could have broken down then but I didn't. I knew Michael was going to get better.'

'Have you ever spoken to him about the fight?' I asked.

'Y'know, Don, I never wanted to see it again. But they had the tape on here a few weeks ago. I steeled myself. I sat down and watched it for the first time since the night itself. An' I was sayin', "Cor, I don't believe this. Look what he's doin' to Eubank." An' then I saw the eleventh and the start of the twelfth. An' the doubts started to come.

'When Michael came in the next day I told him I'd seen the fight again. I said, "Listen, Michael, I think I should've stopped you after the eleventh . . ." An' he looked at me straight in the eye and he smiled. He shook his head. "No, Jim. It's not your fault." That's Michael today. You never hear him moan or say "why me?". He has the forgiveness an' the force of Jesus in him. When Michael's completely well again I can see him travelling the world, spreading the gospel . . .'

Jimmy patted me on the shoulder. He sauntered over to instruct another of his new fighters, a young white boy called Paul who had yet to decide whether he should turn pro. 'C'mon, Paulie-boy, lets go to work.'

His assistant, the rotund and smiley Frank Black, joined me at ringside. I asked him if he saw much of Michael Watson. 'Sure,' the old trainer said. 'Michael likes to come into the gym and talk to the fighters. They got so much respect for him. He exercises here, too, trying to get his movement back.'

'How's he doing?' I wondered.

'I wish you'd been here yesterday. He got on his feet. An' then he was walking. It was a wonderful sight. Michael Watson walking again. He walked straight over to me, down the whole length of this gym. "Hello, Frank," he says as usual. You should've seen it . . .'

Frank stopped in mid-sentence. He looked across the gym. 'I don't believe it!' he said. I followed his pointing finger. 'There he is! Do you see him? Can you see Michael walkin'?'

He had passed the statue of Bradley Stone. He walked through the small café which leads into the gymnasium. His step was stiff but methodical. But he did not need a stick or a helping arm. He moved slowly but calmly across the floor, past the first boxing ring and the black bags hanging from the ceiling. If he had looked to his left he would have seen himself walking in the mirror which covered the opposite wall. But his head turned the opposite way to talk to his friend who sauntered alongside him, swinging a bag in time with their steady pace.

'Hello, Michael,' Frank Black shouted. 'We just been talking about you!'

Michael Watson lifted his hand in greeting. 'Go on,' Frank said. 'Go say hello to Michael.'

I walked over and waited for him at the line of exercise bikes. I could hear Jimmy Tibbs working with his boy in the ring. 'That's it,' Jimmy encouraged, his back to Michael and me, 'step in and hit, step in and hit, bang, bang, then slip, slip and slide and then back again, *pah-pah, pah-pah-pah-pah!*' I looked away from Michael and into the ring. The young boxer smacked a right and then a left into Jimmy Tibbs' leather pads. 'Good,' Jimmy crooned, 'that's good. And again, one-two, one-two . . .'

'Hello, Michael,' I said.

He was dressed in a red tracksuit, his head was bare and his eyes were covered by dark glasses. I had forgotten how tall he was as I held out my hand. He was much bigger than he had been when I'd last spoken to him. At first he looked a little alarmed, but then he relaxed. I said my name. He stretched out his hand to take mine. 'I got your letter,' Michael said softly and clearly. 'Thank you . . .'

He spoke with the voice of the man I remembered. He looked like the man I remembered. He was that same man again.

'You look so well, Michael,' I said, 'you look great . . .'

'Thanks,' he smiled.

It was like a weight had been lifted from me. I did not need to ask him how he felt. I didn't need to know what he thought of Chris Eubank. I did not have to ask him whether he still dreamed of boxing. Like him, I felt as if I could let it go, as if I could move on, to the future. The only important question had already been answered. He was improving every day, his health was slowly returning.

A few minutes later, after we had talked a little more, he stepped over to a bike. His friend slipped into the seat alongside. With a kind parting nod in my direction, Michael Watson began to pedal. He gripped the handle-bars. He looked into the empty ring in front of him. A few feet away, just outside the far corner, Jimmy Tibbs towelled down his fighter.

'I enjoyed that, Jim!' the young boxer said.

'That's good,' Jimmy murmured. 'That's the main thing at this stage. There's no rush, son, no rush . . .'

Michael Watson, meanwhile, kept turning his legs, only breaking off to laugh when his friend upped the stakes. 'Thirty-two,' he said breathlessly to Michael, 'thirty-three, thirty-four . . .' His voice quickened in time with Michael Watson's whirring feet. They were racing, they were flying again.

At nine o'clock that evening, as arranged, I called him. James Toney was in Los Angeles, in his Beverly Hills hotel suite, having moved earlier that day from the Hyatt on Sunset Boulevard. I was tempted to ask if they served a better class of burger in Beverly Hills, but he was in such a bright and winning mood that I resisted.

'What's happenin', man?' he exclaimed. 'How you doin'?'

'Pretty good,' I said. 'How's LA?'

'Couldn't be better.'

'What's the time there?' I asked.

'One o'clock. Lunchtime. But you know me these days. I'm stayin' in shape. I ain't gonna eat much.'

'Having a light lunch in Beverly Hills must seem a long way from selling crack in Ann Arbor,' I suggested.

'Sure is,' he chuckled. 'Boxing's brought me all the way. I love it. 'Cos here I am, in LA, getting ready for my next fight. I fight in August and then in October. Six weeks between fights. That's the way I like it. Keepin' busy, workin' hard, trainin' like hell. Damn, it feels good.'

Toney had fought again since his breathtaking demolition of Earl Butler. On 2 July, he'd outpointed a gangly journeyman called Charles Oliver at the

Station Casino in St Charles, Missouri. Sherry Toney had phoned me the day after to complain that the fight should have been stopped after the third round. 'The other guy looked like a gargoyle,' she moaned. 'He was just hangin' on, splatterin' blood all over James's trunks. They were white satin when the fight started and stained bright red by the end. It was real messy. They shoulda called it off.'

While the local press agreed with her, *Boxing News*'s American correspondent was more dubious. 'On 14 May,' he wrote, 'Toney looked superb battering Earl Butler. But once Toney weighs more than twelve stone seven pounds, his hand-speed diminishes greatly and he loses his sharpness.'

Sherry had already drafted a sharp letter of rebuke to the magazine – which *Boxing News* published under a 'Leave My Son Alone!' warning. Toney was equally indignant. 'How could he say that? I was quick enough and sharp enough to beat up this guy with ease. I bust his jaw. I broke his cheekbone. But he was fighting in front of his home crowd. He was gonna do anything he could to see out the ten rounds. That's all he cared about. Survival. But he was the guy who ended up in hospital. I was real happy with my performance.'

But soon after the fight, Toney replaced Eddie Mustafa Muhammad as his trainer. The 'old gangster' was too vocal for young James – he'd since selected the quietly studious Freddie Roach to advise him in the corner. Post-Bill Miller and Eddie Mustafa, Act III of the Toney ring saga was about to unfold.

Yet the perennial question remained. 'What about your weight?' I asked Lights Out, knowing that Toney had stepped through the ropes five pounds heavier than he'd done against Butler.

'My weight was fine. I ain't blowing up like I did before. You can ask my mom – she'll tell you.'

As always, I found it endearing that Toney should refer me to Sherry, that such a tough guy could be open enough to turn to his mom.

Sherry herself had been candid enough to say after returning from Missouri: 'Look, there ain't no two ways about it. James is a hamburger kid. Always has been. Always will be. After a fight he'll take Jasmine to Vegas and they'll eat a burger or two. But he won't go mad. Within a couple of days he's back in the gym. I tell him he can never go more than ten pounds over the limit. Ten pounds is easy. He only had problems when he had to lose twenty-five pounds or even forty – like against Roy Jones. He's learnt his lesson since then. Those days are long gone.'

Roy Jones remained a magnetic name for Toney. 'I got the guy on the brain,' Toney enthused. 'Roy Jones . . . Roy Jones . . . Roy Jones! I'm gonna keep calling for him. I ain't gonna holiday till the day I beat him.'

'Did you see his last fight?' I wondered.

'What fight?' Toney snorted. 'It was a joke!'

The week after Oscar De La Hoya joined him at the very top of boxing's pound-for-pound ratings, Roy Jones fought an unheralded Canadian called Eric Lucas. It was one of boxing's most brazen mismatches and yet Jones only stopped Lucas at the end of the eleventh round. The reasons were complicated. Jones made much of the fact that, by turning out for the Jacksonville Barracudas on the afternoon of the fight, he had become the first athlete to play professional basketball and defend a world boxing title in the course of the same day. But, far from being exhausted by his fourteen minutes on court, Jones looked as if he was more intent on carrying Lucas through as many of the twelve rounds as possible. He produced flashy volleys of punches but rarely sought to knock out his opponent. It was a strategy he had used often during his most recent fights. Jones's intention seemed to be one of overwhelming his opponent with zip and dazzle rather than the sheer concussive force he possessed in both fists.

He confirmed that the violence of the ring had wearied him. 'The Gabriel Ruelas and Jimmy Garcia fight ruined me,' he said. 'I don't want to end up brain dead. I don't want to get hit.'

Against Eric Lucas he was in no such danger; but Jones tried to defend his choice of opponent. 'I'm not trying to denigrate Lucas,' he protested, 'but at least this way, with me playing basketball a few hours before, he has a better chance. Some guys lose the urge when they get to the top. Reaching the top in basketball is a challenge I need.'

Jones also needed a challenge in the ring to sustain his genius and interest in boxing. There were clear signs that his television paymasters, HBO, considered a rematch with the revamped Toney as one of the few options left open to Jones. Whereas De La Hoya had a legion of ambitious young fighters lined up to challenge him on HBO, the station would not allow Jones to cruise for much longer.

'Exactly!' Toney said. 'He's got this big fat deal with HBO and I know how unhappy they are with him. He just won't fight anyone anymore. He's lost the taste for boxing. He's happier playing in some two-bit basketball game. But he ain't gonna be linin' up against Michael Jordan. It's like my mom said, Roy Jones's got as much chance of making it to the NBA as she has of turnin' into Marilyn Monroe. I mean, my mom's got blue eyes and blonde hair like Roy Jones got NBA basketball skills. He's livin' in a land of fantasy. But he's gonna have to fight me. They're putting me back on HBO for the October fight, buildin' up for a showdown with Mr Jones in the spring of '97. That's cool. I can wait till then . . .'

'Have you seen Roy since your fight?' I asked.

Yeah, I seen him,' Toney said darkly.

'Have you spoken to him?'

'I wanted to but he just runs away whenever I come near him.'

I smiled again at his bravado. He was not the man I had seen at his forlorn party at the MGM after losing to Jones. He had his boxer's fire back again.

'I'm gonna whup him, Don,' he said, 'I'm gonna do it!'

'I think you might,' I said encouragingly. I'd given up all pretence of objectivity. I settled into my pom-pom wielding 'Lights Out' cheerleader role with a merry twirl. I had nothing against Roy Jones, apart from every weighty ounce of my affection for Toney. 'You can beat him, James,' I said, sliding into a whooping mix of fandom and gym talk. 'If you put your mind to it, you can take him, you can whup him!'

We both liked the sound of my attempted 'whup'. Toney laughed again. 'You know I can! I know you do! An' when it happens, I want you there, baby, next to me. 'Cos you been in my corner for so long now. You ain't never lost faith in me . . .'

We both paused. It felt strange to talk so intimately to a boxer with as mean a persona as Toney's, especially with a plastic sucker on top of the phone feeding our conversation back into my tape-recorder. But I could not resort to a more conventional interview routine. We had come too far, we had got too close even to attempt the charade. I reminded him instead of how anxious I had been before I'd first met him, when I knew him only as boxing's most ferocious presence, as a fighter who spat out peppery defiance at anyone who came near him. We settled into our contented lull, thinking back over the years, of time together in Tulsa, Los Angeles, Las Vegas and Ann Arbor.

'Yeah, it's been good,' he decided.

'Yeah,' I grunted back, playing the hard man for a change.

'How's your beautiful wife?' he asked.

'She's great,' I answered. 'How's Jasmine.'

'Sweet as pie! I love Jasmine. She's everything to me. Her and my mom.'

'Have you spent much time with her lately?'

'I took Jasmine out to Vegas after the last fight. We had a fine time. When you guys come over again, you and me can hang out with our girls.'

'Alison and Jasmine,' I said, thinking of the double-date picture my thirty-year-old wife would make with the fighter's three-year-old heart-throb.

'Sounds pretty,' Toney said.

We were sounding a little too cute for our own good. 'Have you seen Tyson lately?' I asked, returning to bad-man basics.

'Sure. I hung out with Mike in Vegas.'

'You, Jasmine and Mike?'

'Well, Mike's got his little girl too. But, no, it was jus' me and Mike. We been kickin' it back, chillin'. Havin' a good time. Getting to know each other a whole lot better.'

'How is Mike?'

'He's cool.'

'Is he over that incident in Chicago?' I asked.

'Yeah, 'cos that was bullshit!' Toney stressed. 'Mike is really cool. He's doin' great. He's on a mission – same as me. We're calm, we're happy. We're gonna clean up boxing again. We're gonna do it! When you comin' to see us again?'

'I'm not sure,' I confessed.

'Come to LA. Or Vegas. Jus' jump on a plane!' he urged, sounding like the boxing millionaire he'd become years before.

'It's quite a trip from London,' I said.

'I guess,' Toney agreed reluctantly. 'So, how's London these days?'

I looked out of my office window. The sun sank slowly over the city, dragging a languid light across the new steel and glass building to my left and the Victorian block to my right. At nine-fifteen the sky was still blue at its core, with red and yellow streaking across its darkening borders. 'It's really beautiful right now. It's a gorgeous evening . . .'

'Mmmmhmmm,' Toney mumbled poetically. 'So what you doin' tonight? You writin' again?'

'No, I'm going home soon.'

'Sounds good . . .'

'It'll be a nicer drive than that night I skidded from Detroit to Ann Arbor.'

'Yeah,' he laughed, 'I remember. All that snow. That's why I like LA. The sun keeps shinin'. All year round. No dark days. No snow. No slippin', baby, no slippin'.'

I took the scenic route home. The road was warm and sure beneath the tread of our old car. I drove steadily down the Chelsea Embankment, along the Thames, looking out the open window at the last of the day's light shimmering against the abandoned walls and broken windows of Battersea Power Station. The soft glare flattened across the water, changing colour until it matched the arching pink of the Albert Bridge. Like the Chelsea Bridge behind and the Battersea Bridge ahead, the Albert and the Embankment itself were strangely empty. It was a night made for ambling and drinking rather than driving.

Yet it also felt like a time for wistful and hopeful thinking. My head echoed with the day's voices, boxing voices extending from the east end to Hollywood, from Canning Town to Beverly Hills. I knew it would not last long. Heartache and loss would return again to the fighters I had followed. They were fated to endure more hurt and sorrow because, as boxers, they would never be free of trouble. But then, at least for a while, life was flowing again for all of them.

Sherry Toney, my own personal boxing heroine, had also moved on. 'I got Jackie Kallen out of my system,' she'd told me a few nights before. 'I've had my say. I wanna write instead about me and James, about the days we been through and the championship days still comin'. We've been through the ol' grinder but I guess we made it. It feels like we're out on the other side.'

Meanwhile, Oscar De La Hoya, Roy Jones and Naseem Hamed all believed that they were unbeatable, that they could turn their bewitching hands to anything they liked – whether it be architecture, basketball or world domination. Chris Eubank, the exotic Lord of Brighton, had been acting grandly in television commercials, telling himself that he was the ad-man's answer to 007. He also readied himself for his inevitable million-pound return to boxing. His comeback fight, in October, would be held in Cairo and sold as 'The Style on the Nile'. I thought Egypt would be the perfect backdrop for a man who considered himself more a latter-day Sphinx than a fighter.

His own icon, the man he used to visit so often in Plainfield, Mike Tyson, was more realistic. Casting aside his 'Mighty Mike' tag, he tried instead to find his lost self. He was somewhere in America, away from the ring for a few more months, playing with his baby girl and sparring with his giant white tiger, waiting for whatever would come next. But, according to his and my pal, James Toney, Mike was cool. He was calm, he was on a mission towards serenity – or something.

I thought of Tyson, and of Michael Watson walking through the gym, of James Toney laughing down the phone. And I knew. Even if it could not last, even when darkness returned either in or outside the ring, we would still remember these different times. The road cut away from the river and curved towards more shadowy and secluded streets. I pressed my foot down a little harder, wanting to be home again.